子連れ狼

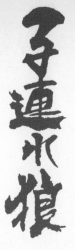

LONE WOLF AND CUB

子連れ狼

story
KAZUO KOIKE

art
GOSEKI KOJIMA

DARK HORSE COMICS

translation
DANA LEWIS

lettering & retouch
DIGITAL CHAMELEON

cover artwork
FRANK MILLER with **LYNN VARLEY**

publisher
MIKE RICHARDSON

editors
DAN HARRIS and **MIKE HANSEN**

assistant editor
TIM ERVIN-GORE

consulting editor
TOREN SMITH for **STUDIO PROTEUS**

book design
DARIN FABRICK

art director
MARK COX

Published by Dark Horse Comics, Inc. in association
with MegaHouse and Koike Shoin Publishing Company.

Dark Horse Comics, Inc.
10956 SE Main Street, Milwaukie, OR 97222
www.darkhorse.com

First edition: August 2000
ISBN: 1-56971-502-5

5 7 9 10 8 6 4

Printed in Canada

To find a comics shop in your area, call the
Comic Shop Locator Service toll-free at 1-888-266-4226

THE
ASSASSIN'S
ROAD

子連れ狼

By **KAZUO KOIKE**
& GOSEKI KOJIMA

V O L U M E
1

A NOTE TO READERS

Lone Wolf and Cub is famous for its carefully researched re-creation of Edo-Period Japan. To preserve the flavor of the work, we have chosen to retain many Edo-Period terms that have no direct equivalents in English. Japanese is written in a mix of Chinese ideograms and a syllabic writing system, resulting in numerous synonyms. In the glossary, you may encounter words with multiple meanings. These are words written with Chinese ideograms that are pronounced the same but carry different meanings. A Japanese reader seeing the different ideograms would know instantly which meaning it is, but these synonyms can cause confusion when Japanese is spelled out in our alphabet. *O-yurushi o* (please forgive us)!

LONE WOLF AND CUB

TABLE OF CONTENTS

the first

Son for Hire, Sword for Hire

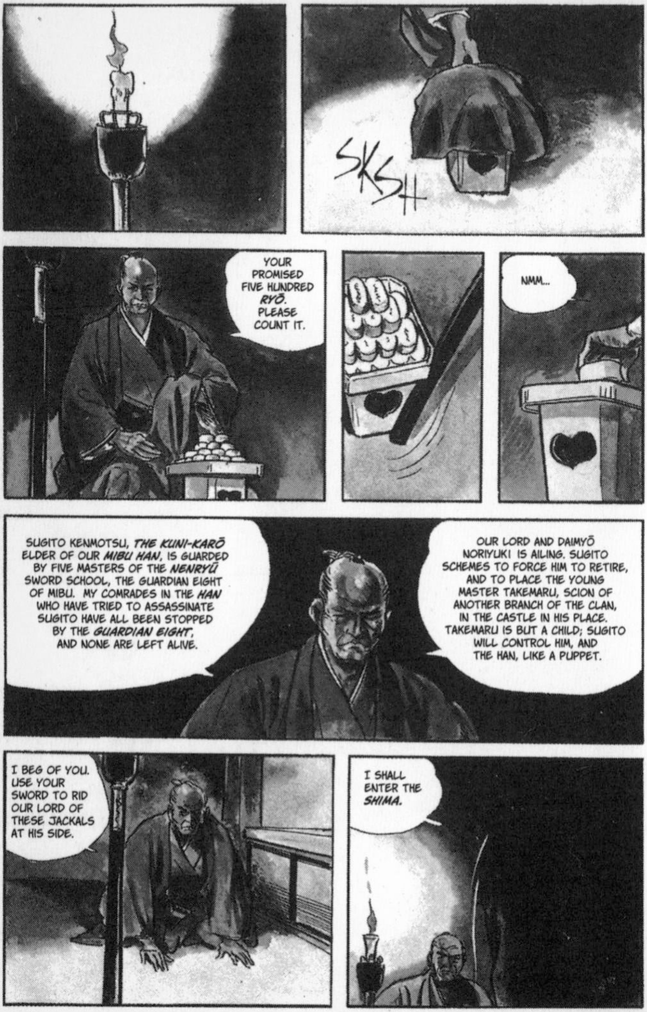
SKSH
YOUR PROMISED FIVE HUNDRED RYŌ. PLEASE COUNT IT.
NMM...
SUGITO KENMOTSU, THE KUNI-KARŌ ELDER OF OUR MIBU HAN, IS GUARDED BY FIVE MASTERS OF THE NENRYŪ SWORD SCHOOL, THE GUARDIAN EIGHT OF MIBU. MY COMRADES IN THE HAN WHO HAVE TRIED TO ASSASSINATE SUGITO HAVE ALL BEEN STOPPED BY THE GUARDIAN EIGHT, AND NONE ARE LEFT ALIVE.
OUR LORD AND DAIMYŌ NORIYUKI IS AILING. SUGITO SCHEMES TO FORCE HIM TO RETIRE, AND TO PLACE THE YOUNG MASTER TAKEMARU, SCION OF ANOTHER BRANCH OF THE CLAN, IN THE CASTLE IN HIS PLACE. TAKEMARU IS BUT A CHILD; SUGITO WILL CONTROL HIM, AND THE HAN, LIKE A PUPPET.
I BEG OF YOU. USE YOUR SWORD TO RID OUR LORD OF THESE JACKALS AT HIS SIDE.
I SHALL ENTER THE SHIMA.

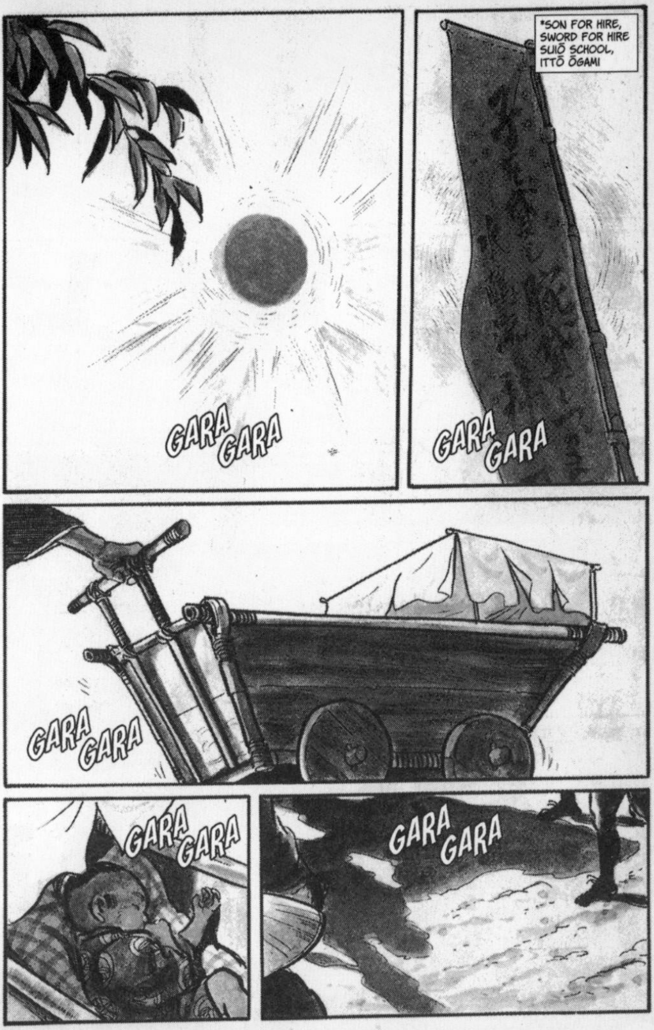
GARA GARA
*SON FOR HIRE, SWORD FOR HIRE SUIŌ SCHOOL, ITTŌ ŌGAMI
GARA GARA
GARA GARA
GARA GARA
GARA GARA

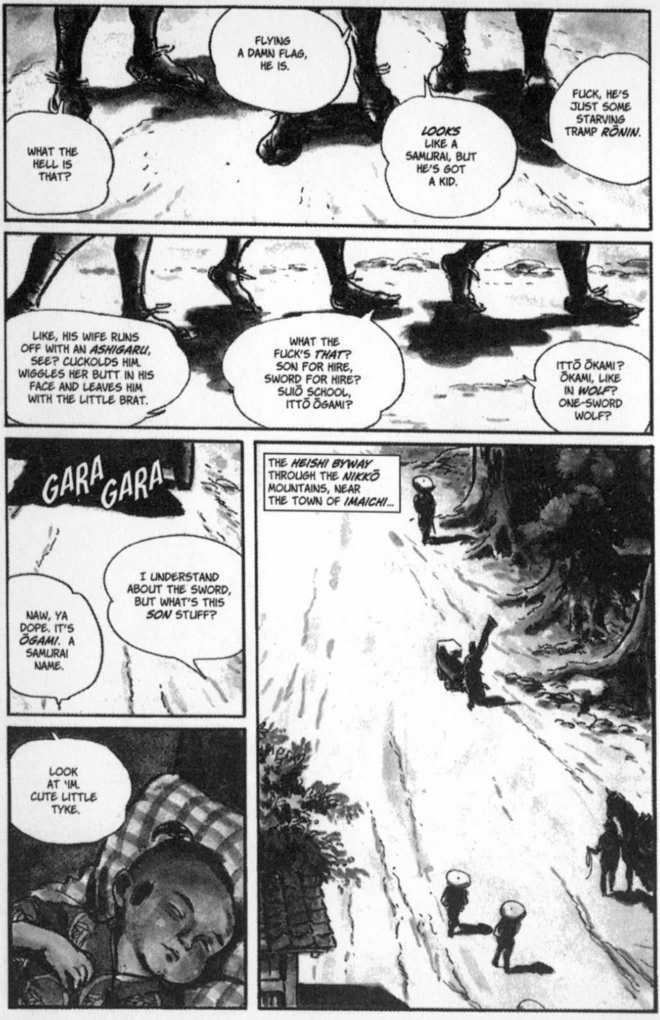
WHAT THE HELL IS THAT?
FLYING A DAMN FLAG, HE IS.
LOOKS LIKE A SAMURAI, BUT HE'S GOT A KID.
FUCK, HE'S JUST SOME STARVING TRAMP *RŌNIN*.
LIKE, HIS WIFE RUNS OFF WITH AN *ASHIGARU*, SEE? CUCKOLDS HIM. WIGGLES HER BUTT IN HIS FACE AND LEAVES HIM WITH THE LITTLE BRAT.
WHAT THE FUCK'S *THAT*? SON FOR HIRE, SWORD FOR HIRE? SUIŌ SCHOOL, ITTŌ ŌGAMI?
ITTŌ ŌKAMI? ŌKAMI, LIKE IN *WOLF*? ONE-SWORD WOLF?
GARA GARA
I UNDERSTAND ABOUT THE SWORD, BUT WHAT'S THIS *SON* STUFF?
NAW, YA DOPE. IT'S *ŌGAMI*. A SAMURAI NAME.
LOOK AT 'IM. CUTE LITTLE TYKE.
THE *HEISHI BYWAY* THROUGH THE *NIKKŌ* MOUNTAINS, NEAR THE TOWN OF *IMAICHI*...

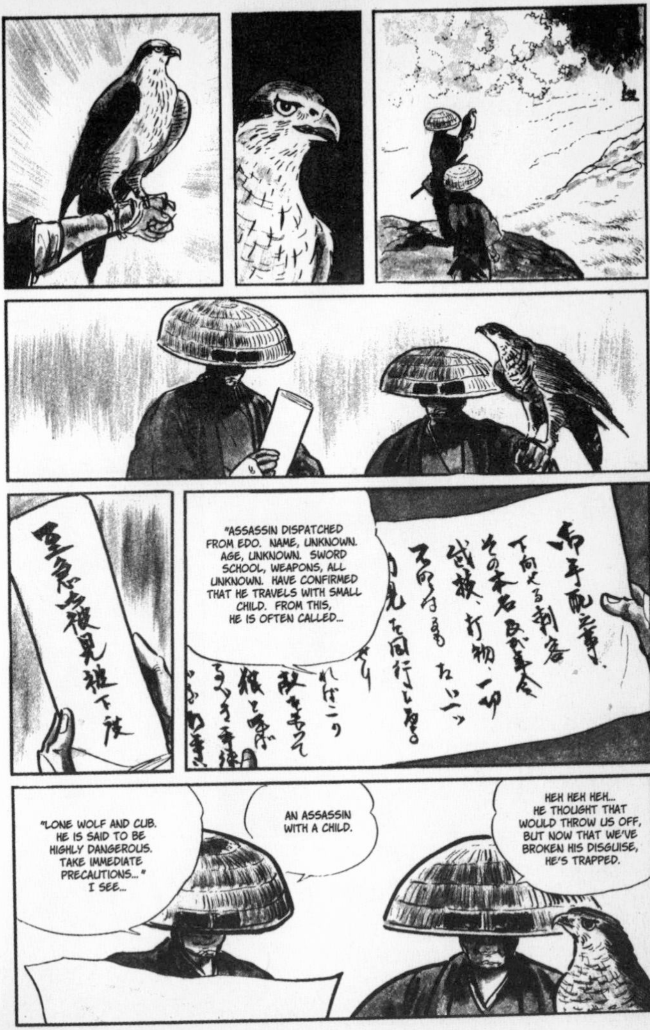
"ASSASSIN DISPATCHED FROM EDO. NAME, UNKNOWN. AGE, UNKNOWN. SWORD SCHOOL, WEAPONS, ALL UNKNOWN. HAVE CONFIRMED THAT HE TRAVELS WITH SMALL CHILD. FROM THIS, HE IS OFTEN CALLED...
"LONE WOLF AND CUB. HE IS SAID TO BE HIGHLY DANGEROUS. TAKE IMMEDIATE PRECAUTIONS..." I SEE...
AN ASSASSIN WITH A CHILD.
HEH HEH HEH... HE THOUGHT THAT WOULD THROW US OFF, BUT NOW THAT WE'VE BROKEN HIS DISGUISE, HE'S TRAPPED.

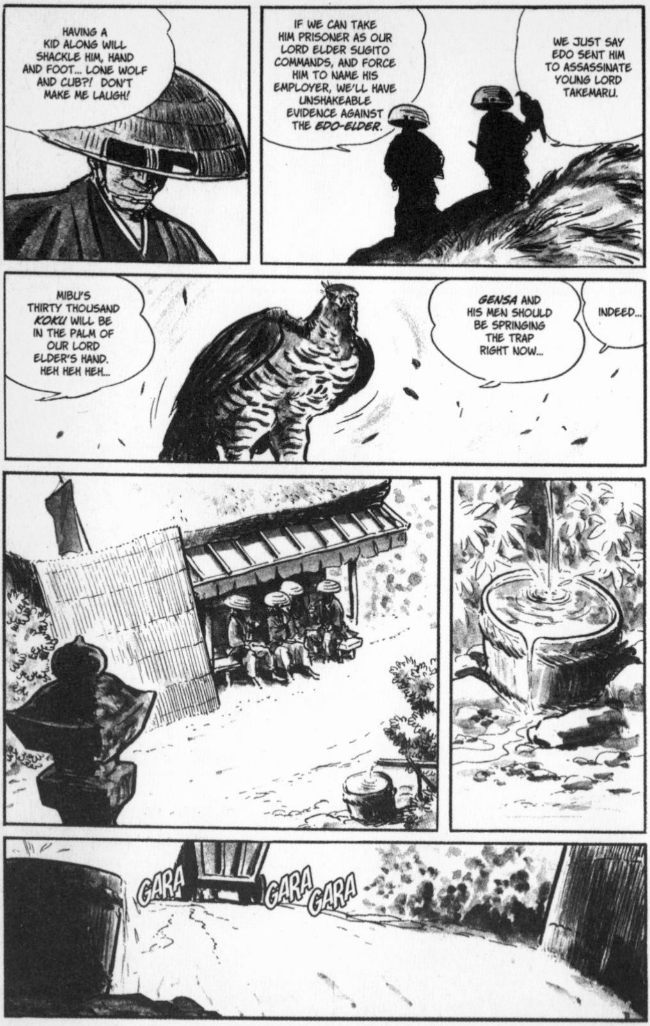
HAVING A KID ALONG WILL SHACKLE HIM, HAND AND FOOT... LONE WOLF AND CUB?! DON'T MAKE ME LAUGH!
IF WE CAN TAKE HIM PRISONER AS OUR LORD ELDER SUGITO COMMANDS, AND FORCE HIM TO NAME HIS EMPLOYER, WE'LL HAVE UNSHAKEABLE EVIDENCE AGAINST THE *EDO-ELDER*.
WE JUST SAY EDO SENT HIM TO ASSASSINATE YOUNG LORD TAKEMARU.
MIBU'S THIRTY THOUSAND *KOKU* WILL BE IN THE PALM OF OUR LORD ELDER'S HAND. HEH HEH HEH...
GENSA AND HIS MEN SHOULD BE SPRINGING THE TRAP RIGHT NOW...
INDEED...
GARA
GARA GARA

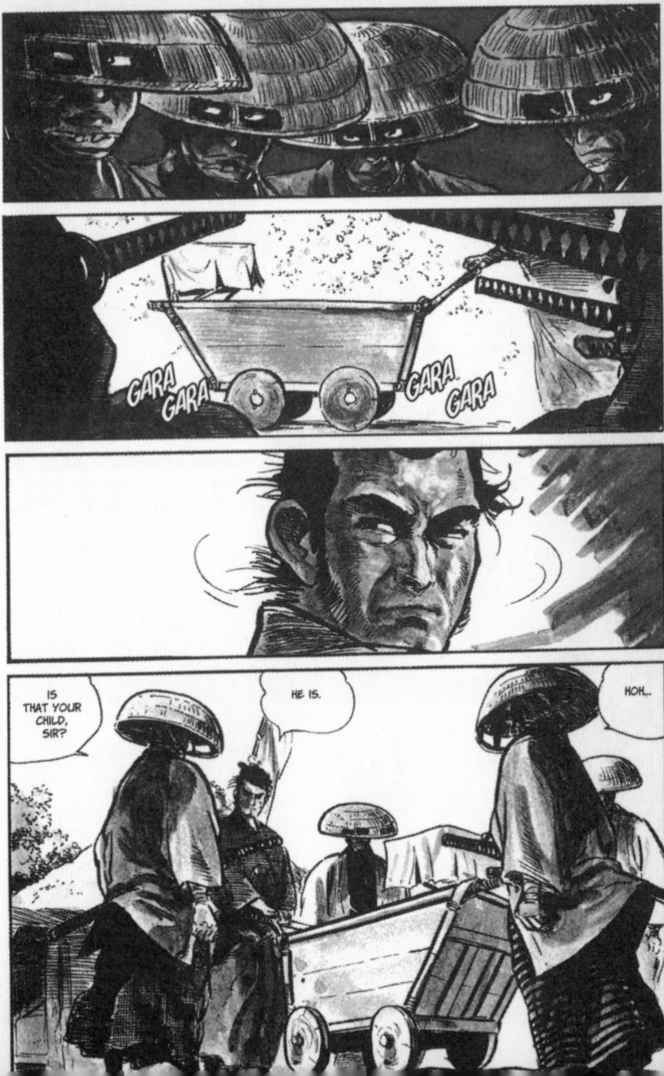
GARA
GARA
GARA
GARA
IS THAT YOUR CHILD, SIR?
HE IS.
HOH...

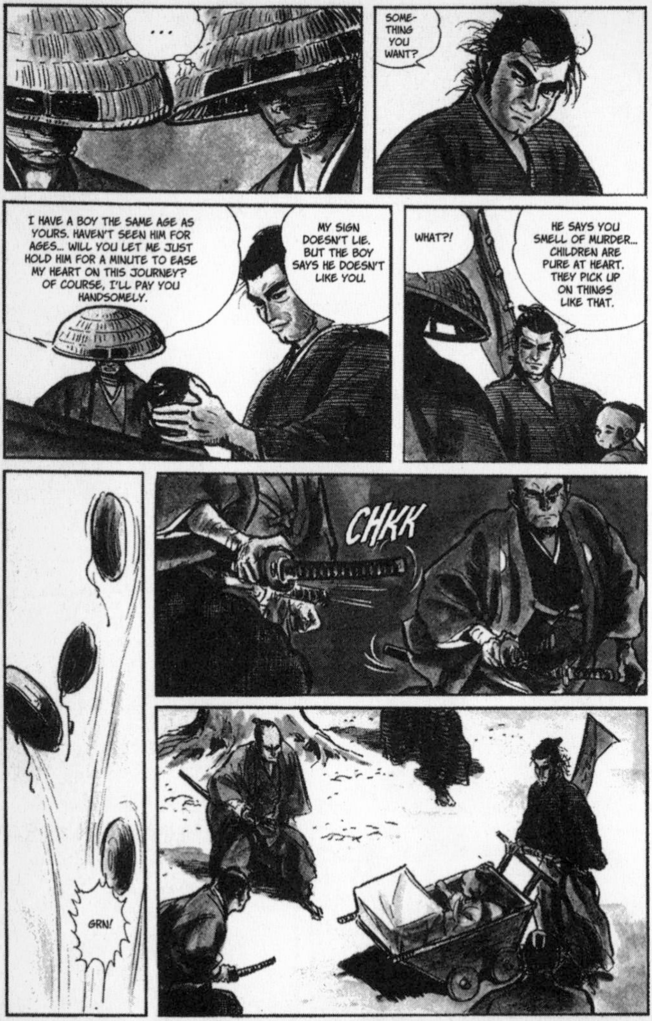
...
SOME-THING YOU WANT?
I HAVE A BOY THE SAME AGE AS YOURS. HAVEN'T SEEN HIM FOR AGES... WILL YOU LET ME JUST HOLD HIM FOR A MINUTE TO EASE MY HEART ON THIS JOURNEY? OF COURSE, I'LL PAY YOU HANDSOMELY.
MY SIGN DOESN'T LIE. BUT THE BOY SAYS HE DOESN'T LIKE YOU.
WHAT?!
HE SAYS YOU SMELL OF MURDER... CHILDREN ARE PURE AT HEART. THEY PICK UP ON THINGS LIKE THAT.
GRN!
CHKK

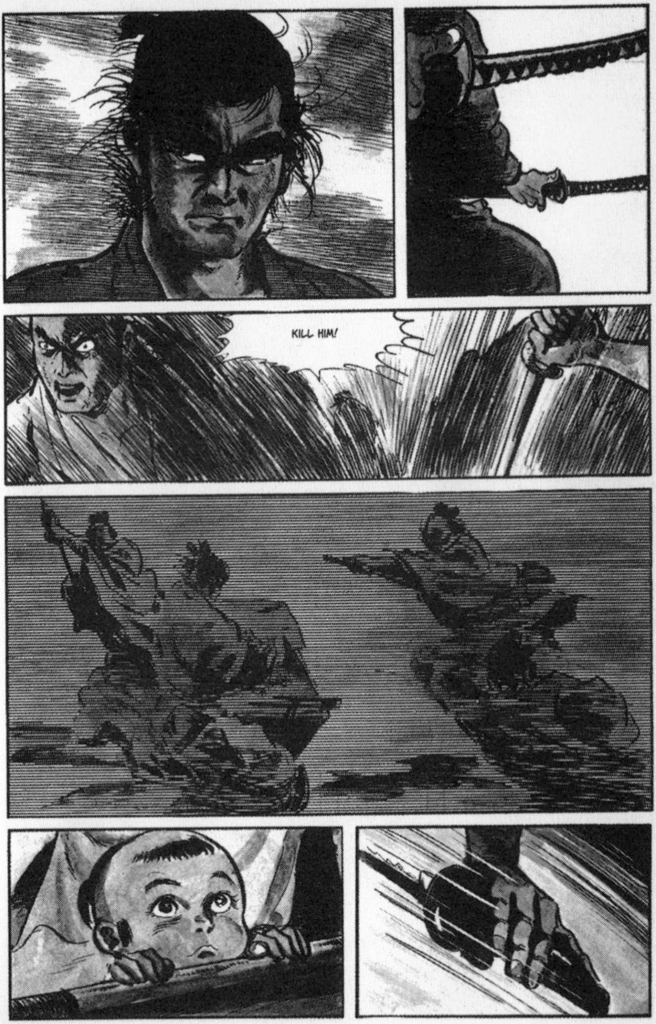
KILL HIM!

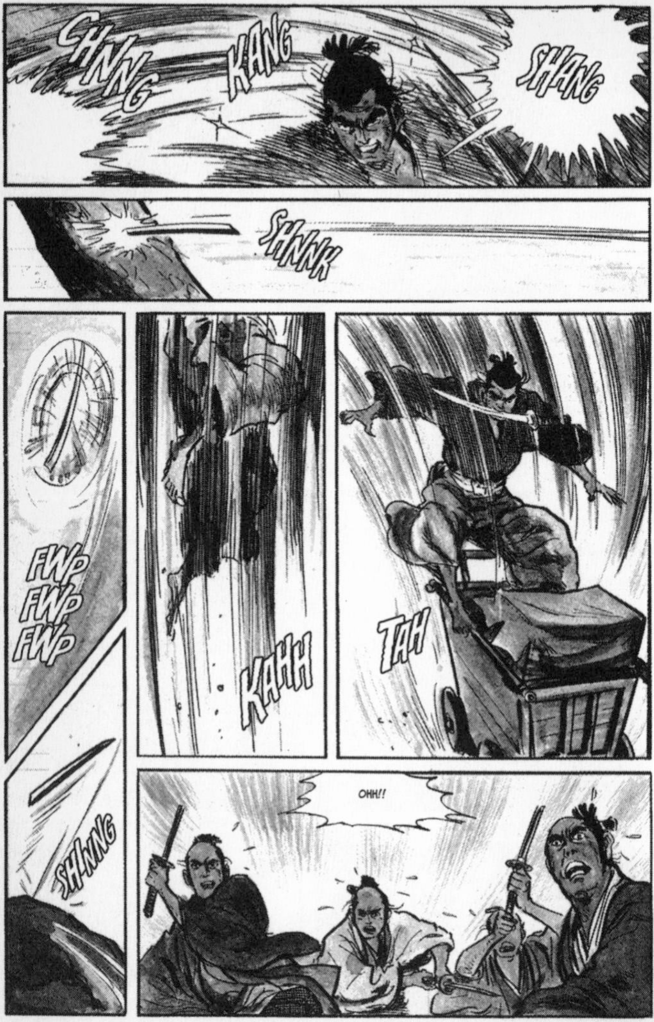
CHNNG
KANG
SHANG
SHNNK
FWP FWP FWP
SHWNG
KAHH
TAH
OHH!!

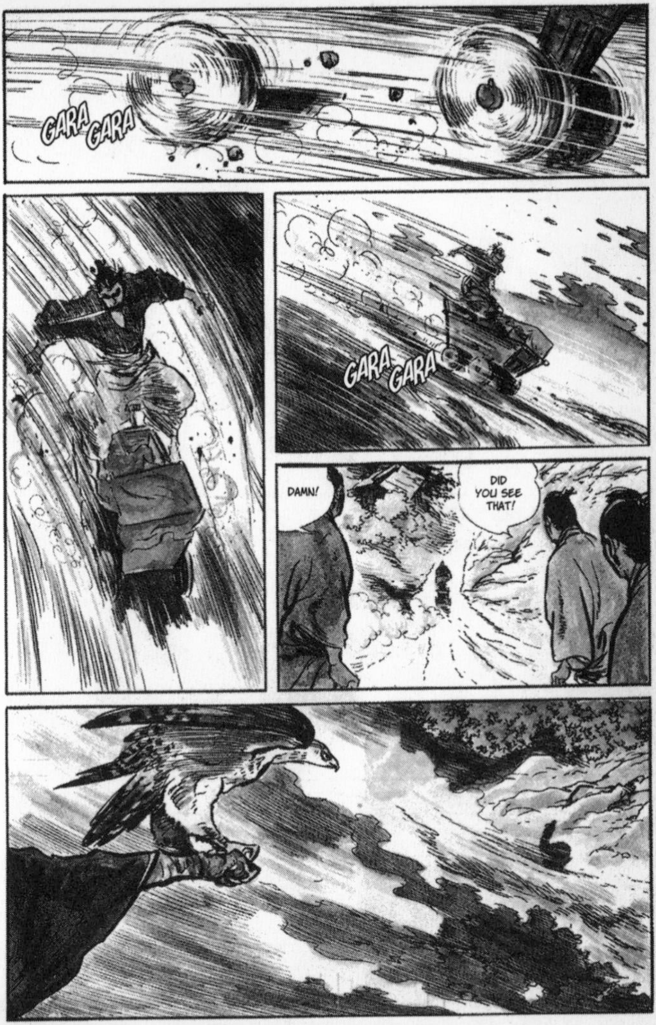
GARA GARA
GARA GARA
DAMN!
DID YOU SEE THAT!

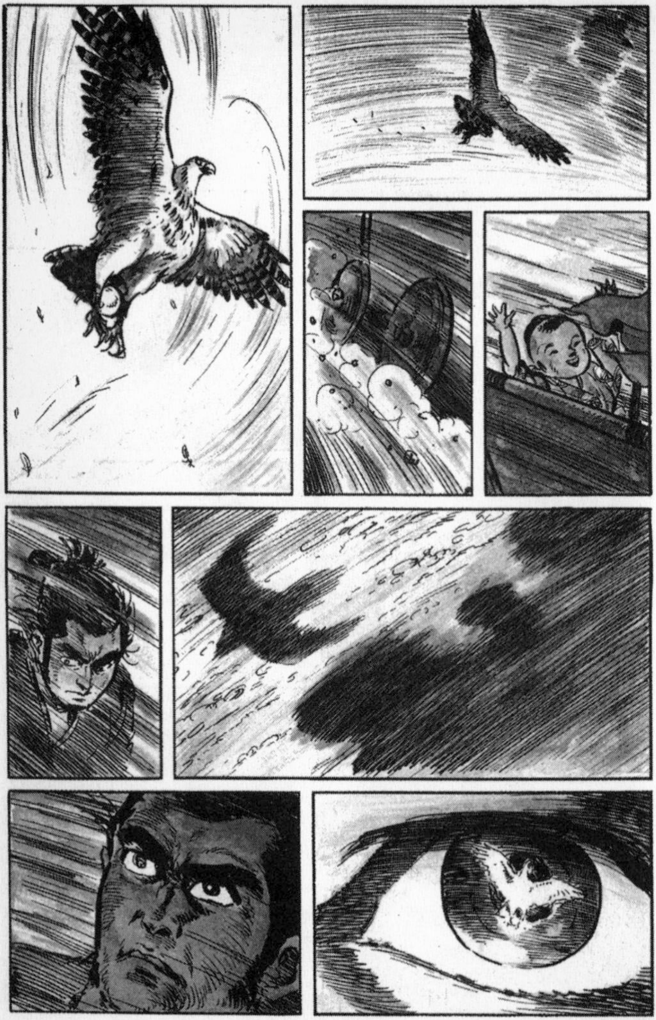

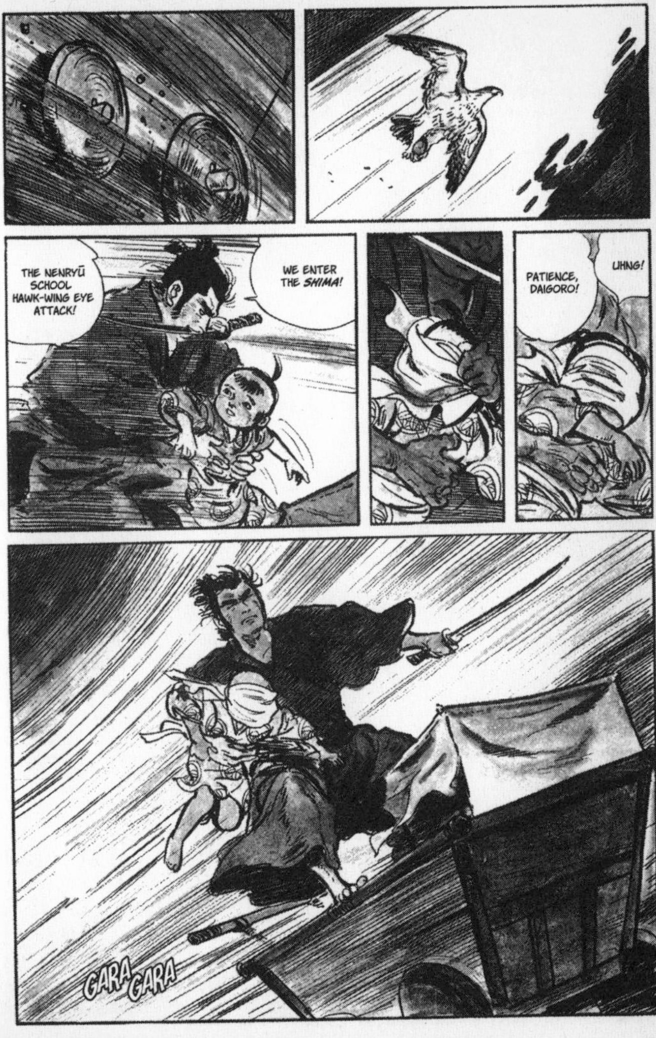
THE NENRYŪ SCHOOL HAWK-WING EYE ATTACK!
WE ENTER THE *SHIMA*!
PATIENCE, DAIGORO!
UHNG!
GARA GARA

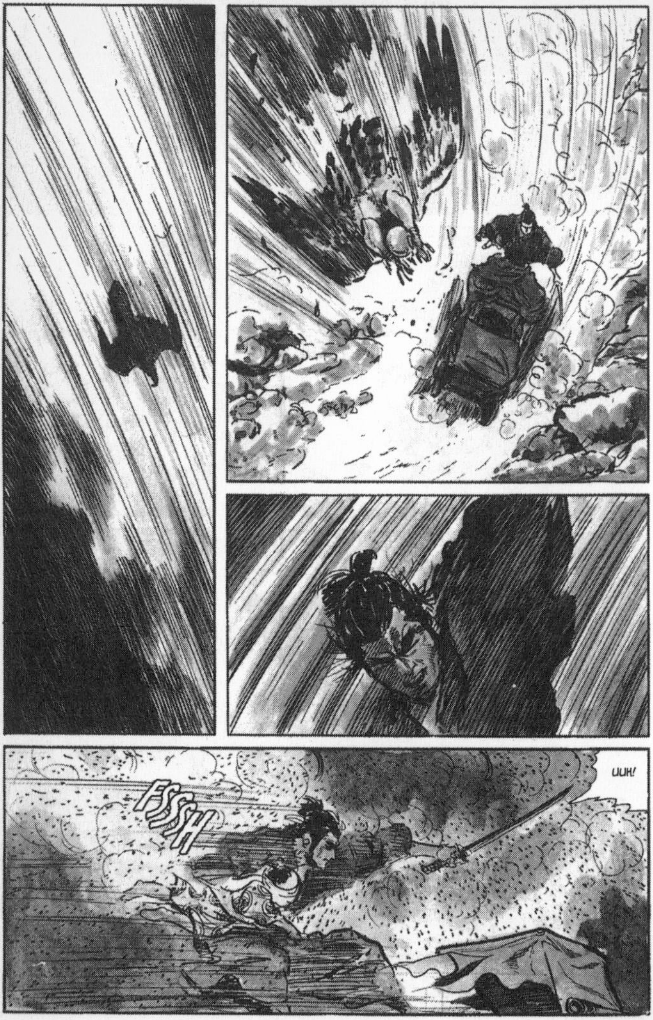
FSSSH
UUK!

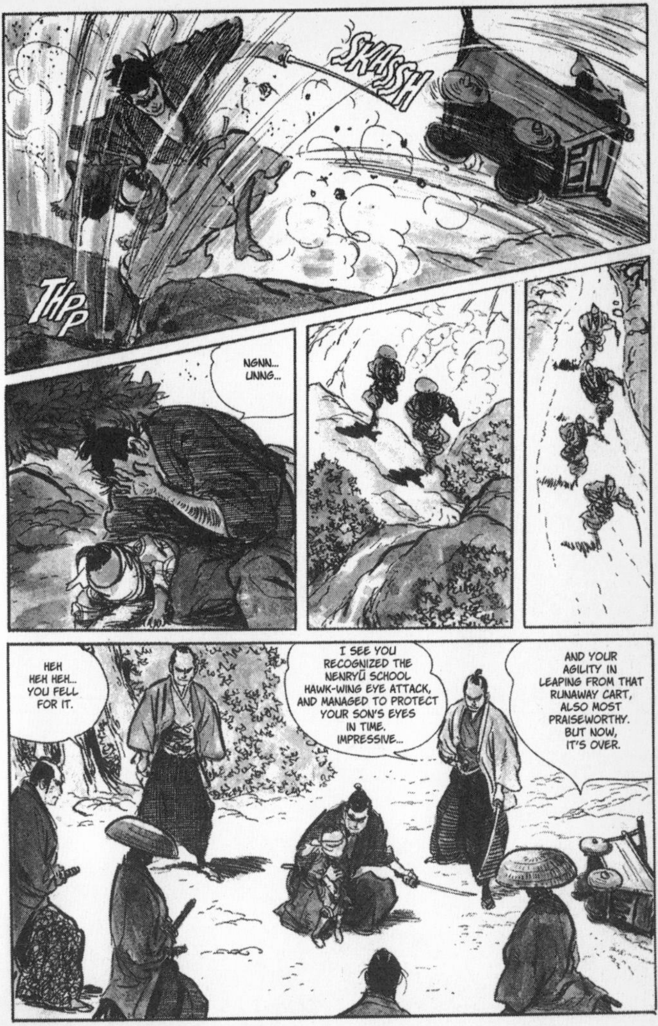
SKASSH
THPP
NGNN... UNNG...
HEH HEH HEH... YOU FELL FOR IT.
I SEE YOU RECOGNIZED THE NENRYŪ SCHOOL HAWK-WING EYE ATTACK, AND MANAGED TO PROTECT YOUR SON'S EYES IN TIME. IMPRESSIVE...
AND YOUR AGILITY IN LEAPING FROM THAT RUNAWAY CART, ALSO MOST PRAISEWORTHY. BUT NOW, IT'S OVER.

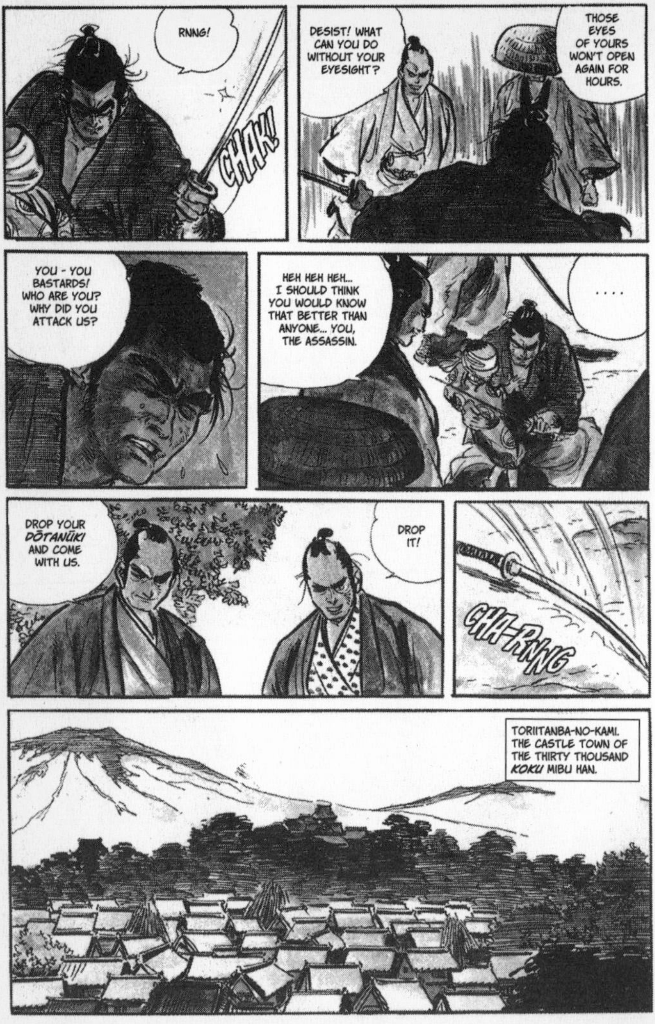
RNNG!
CHAK!
DESIST! WHAT CAN YOU DO WITHOUT YOUR EYESIGHT?
THOSE EYES OF YOURS WON'T OPEN AGAIN FOR HOURS.
YOU - YOU BASTARDS! WHO ARE YOU? WHY DID YOU ATTACK US?
HEH HEH HEH... I SHOULD THINK YOU WOULD KNOW THAT BETTER THAN ANYONE... YOU, THE ASSASSIN.
. . . .
DROP YOUR *DŌTANŪKI* AND COME WITH US.
DROP IT!
CHA-RNNG
TORIITANBA-NO-KAMI. THE CASTLE TOWN OF THE THIRTY THOUSAND *KOKU* MIBU HAN.

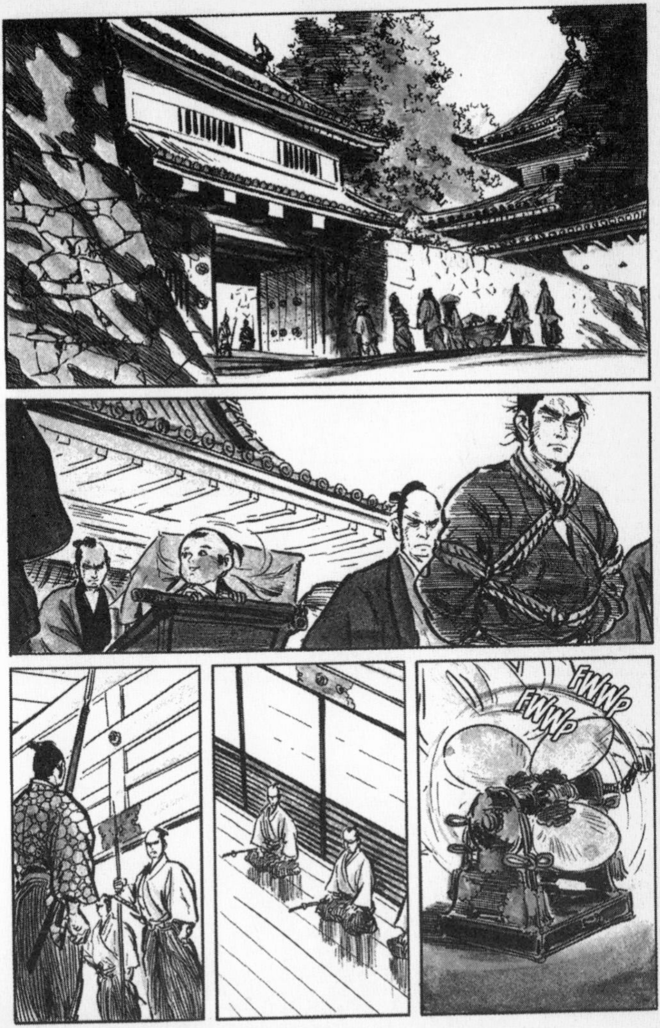
FWWP
FWWP

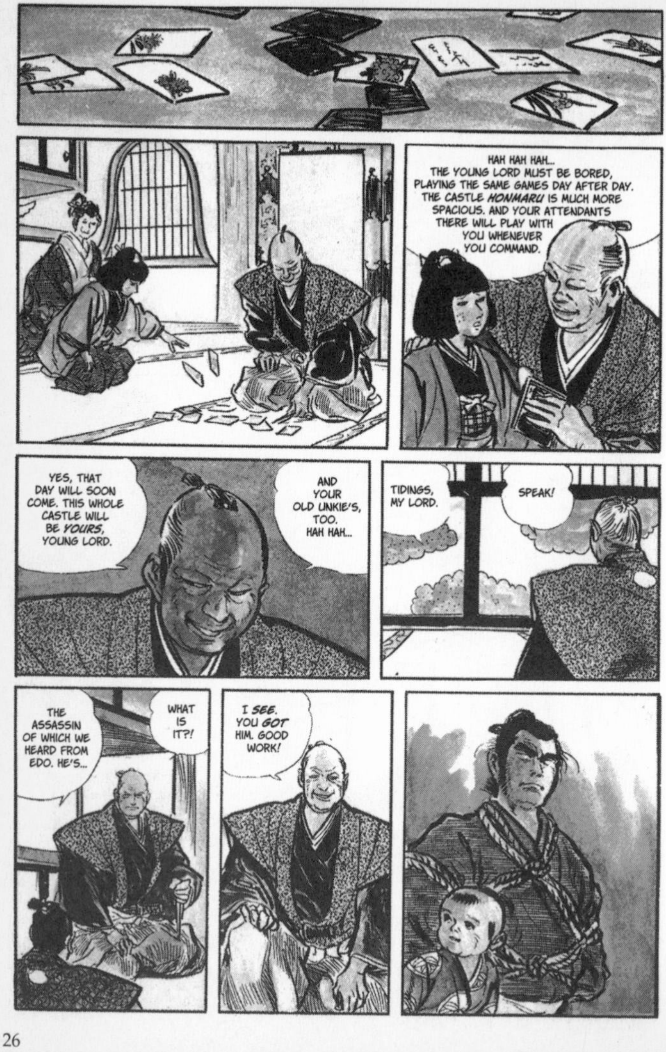
HAH HAH HAH... THE YOUNG LORD MUST BE BORED, PLAYING THE SAME GAMES DAY AFTER DAY. THE CASTLE *HONMARU* IS MUCH MORE SPACIOUS. AND YOUR ATTENDANTS THERE WILL PLAY WITH YOU WHENEVER YOU COMMAND.
YES, THAT DAY WILL SOON COME. THIS WHOLE CASTLE WILL BE *YOURS*, YOUNG LORD.
AND YOUR OLD UNKIE'S, TOO. HAH HAH...
TIDINGS, MY LORD.
SPEAK!
THE ASSASSIN OF WHICH WE HEARD FROM EDO. HE'S...
WHAT IS IT?!
I *SEE*. YOU *GOT* HIM. GOOD WORK!

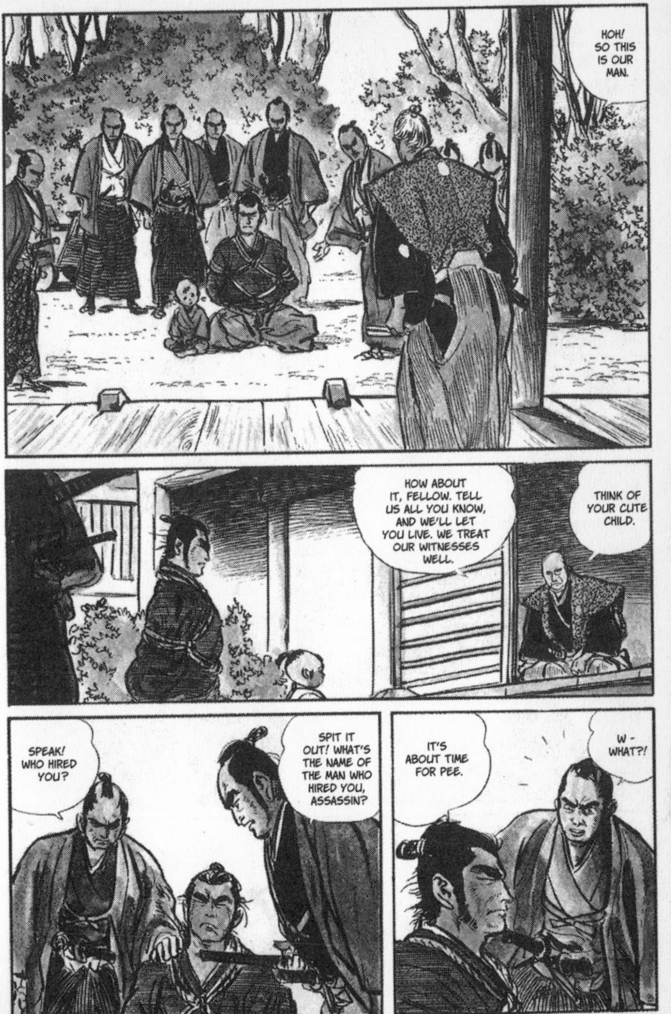
HOH! SO THIS IS OUR MAN.
HOW ABOUT IT, FELLOW. TELL US ALL YOU KNOW, AND WE'LL LET YOU LIVE. WE TREAT OUR WITNESSES WELL.
THINK OF YOUR CUTE CHILD.
SPEAK! WHO HIRED YOU?
SPIT IT OUT! WHAT'S THE NAME OF THE MAN WHO HIRED YOU, ASSASSIN?
IT'S ABOUT TIME FOR PEE.
W - WHAT?!

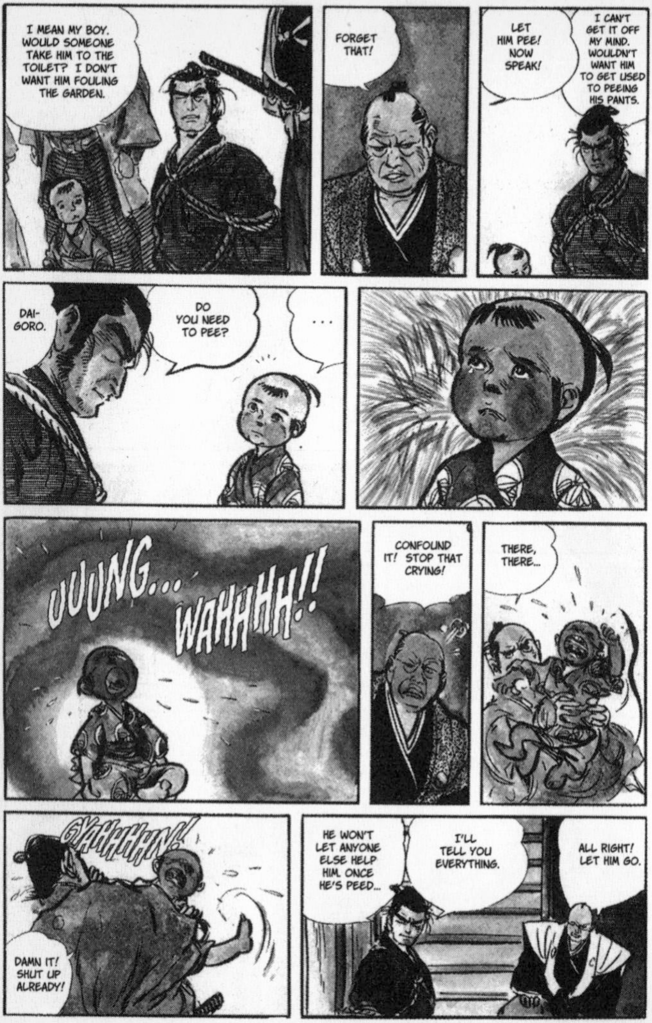
I MEAN MY BOY. WOULD SOMEONE TAKE HIM TO THE TOILET? I DON'T WANT HIM FOULING THE GARDEN.
FORGET THAT!
LET HIM PEE! NOW SPEAK!
I CAN'T GET IT OFF MY MIND. WOULDN'T WANT HIM TO GET USED TO PEEING HIS PANTS.
DAI-GORO.
DO YOU NEED TO PEE?
. . .
UUUNG... WAHHHH!!
CONFOUND IT! STOP THAT CRYING!
THERE, THERE...
GYAHHHHN!
DAMN IT! SHUT UP ALREADY!
HE WON'T LET ANYONE ELSE HELP HIM ONCE HE'S PEED...
I'LL TELL YOU EVERYTHING.
ALL RIGHT! LET HIM GO.

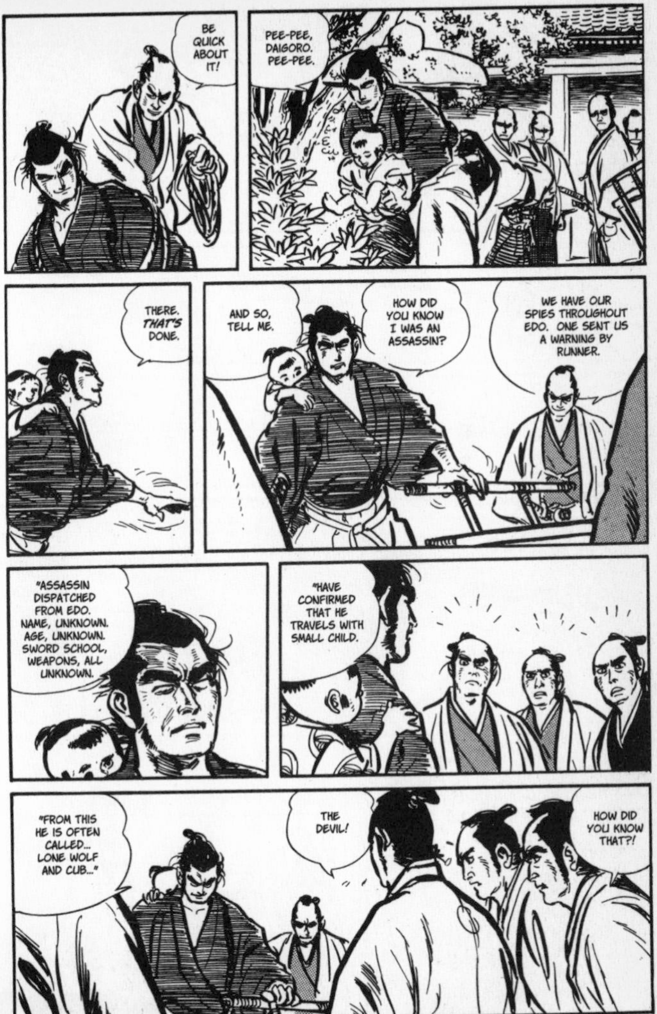
BE QUICK ABOUT IT!
PEE-PEE, DAIGORO. PEE-PEE.
THERE. *THAT'S* DONE.
AND SO, TELL ME.
HOW DID YOU KNOW I WAS AN ASSASSIN?
WE HAVE OUR SPIES THROUGHOUT EDO. ONE SENT US A WARNING BY RUNNER.
"ASSASSIN DISPATCHED FROM EDO. NAME, UNKNOWN. AGE, UNKNOWN. SWORD SCHOOL, WEAPONS, ALL UNKNOWN.
"HAVE CONFIRMED THAT HE TRAVELS WITH SMALL CHILD.
"FROM THIS HE IS OFTEN CALLED... LONE WOLF AND CUB..."
THE DEVIL!
HOW DID YOU KNOW THAT?!

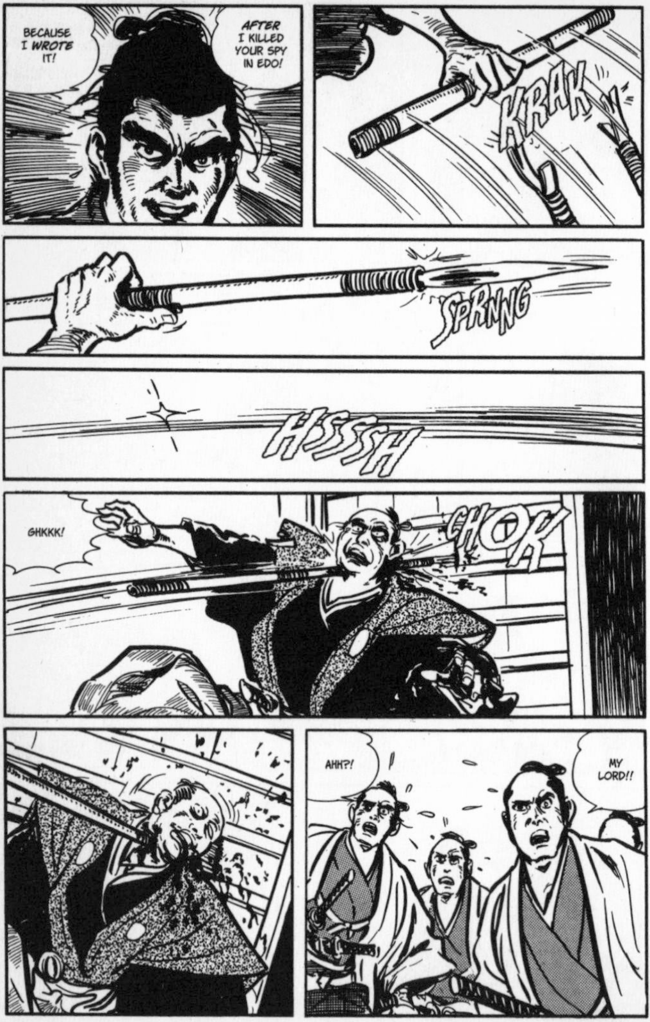
BECAUSE I WROTE IT!
AFTER I KILLED YOUR SPY IN EDO!
KRAK
SPRNNG
HSSSH
GHKKK!
CHOK
AHH?!
MY LORD!!

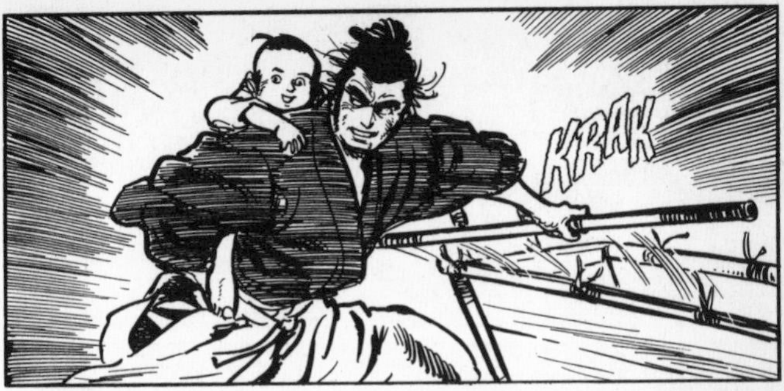
KRAK

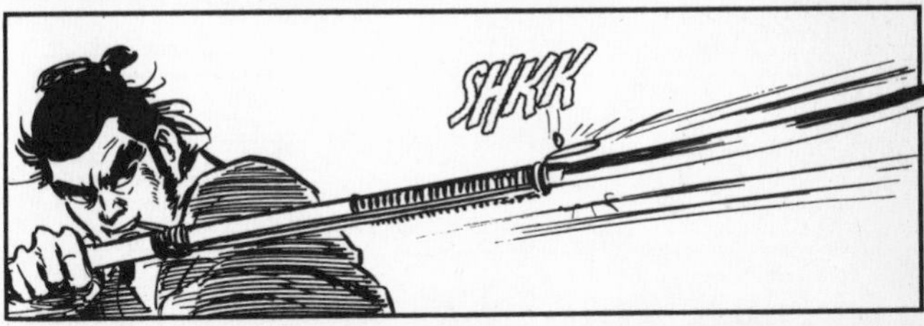
SHKK

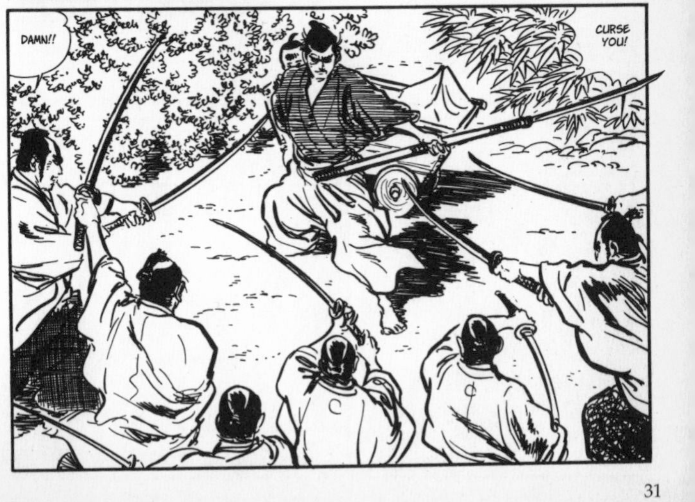
DAMN!!
CURSE YOU!

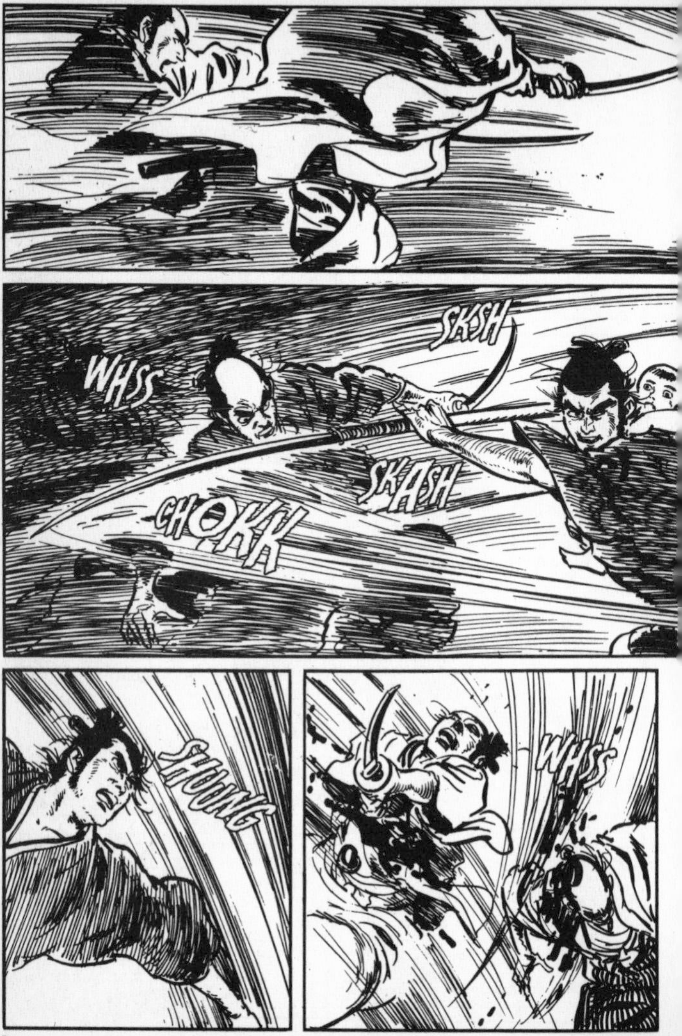
WHSS
SKSH
SKASH
CHOKK
SHUNG
WHSS

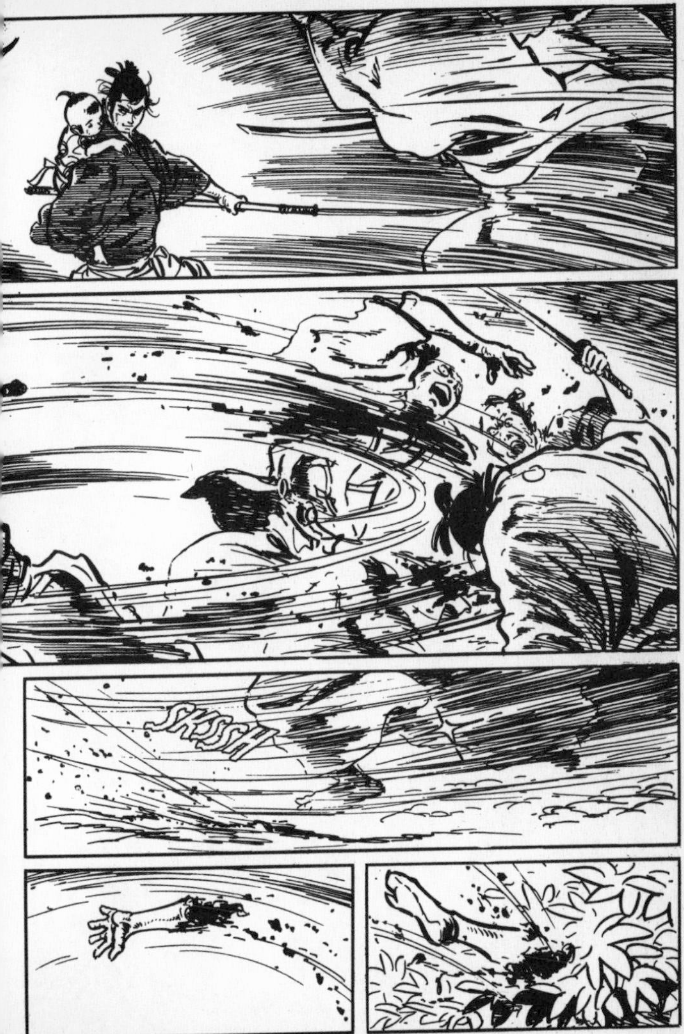
SKSSSH

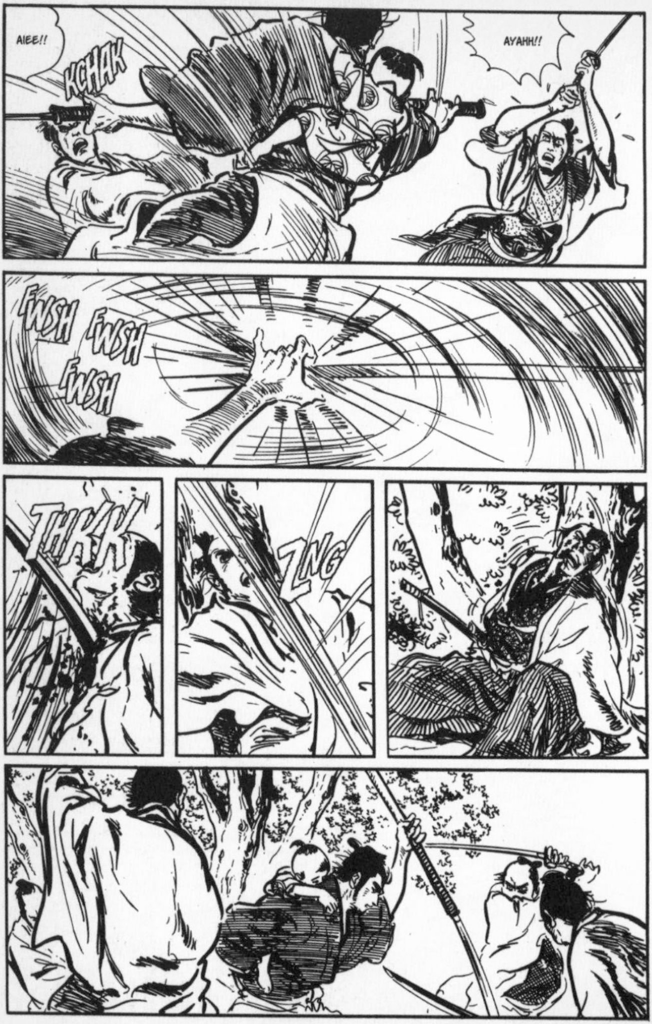

AIEE!!
KCHAK
AYAHH!!
FWSH
FWSH
FWSH
THKK
ZNG

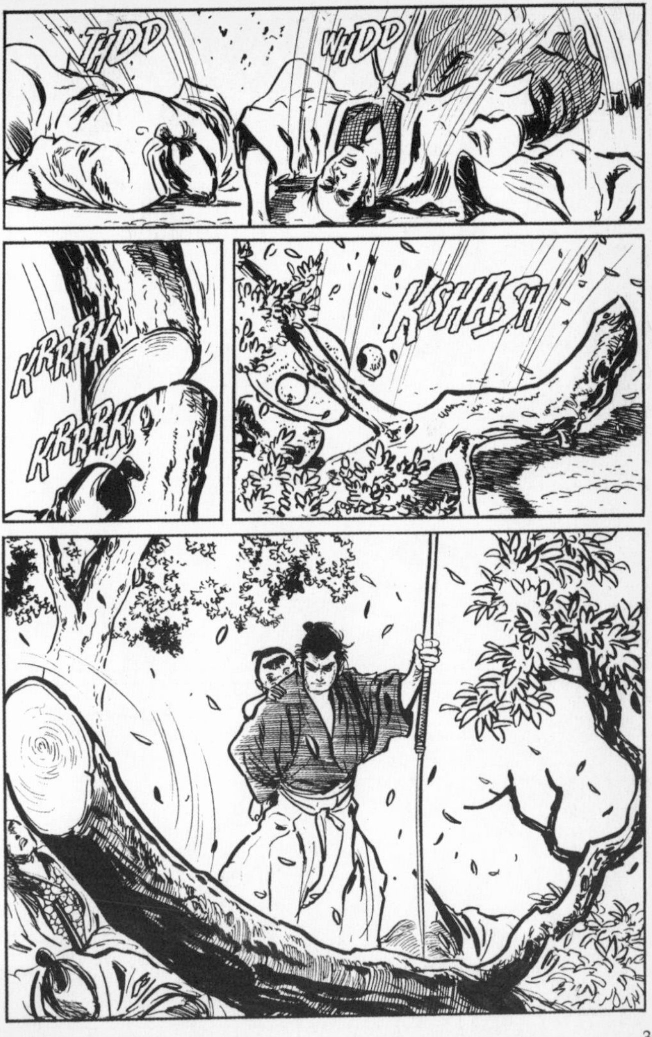
THDD
WHDD
KRRRK
KRRRK
KSHASH

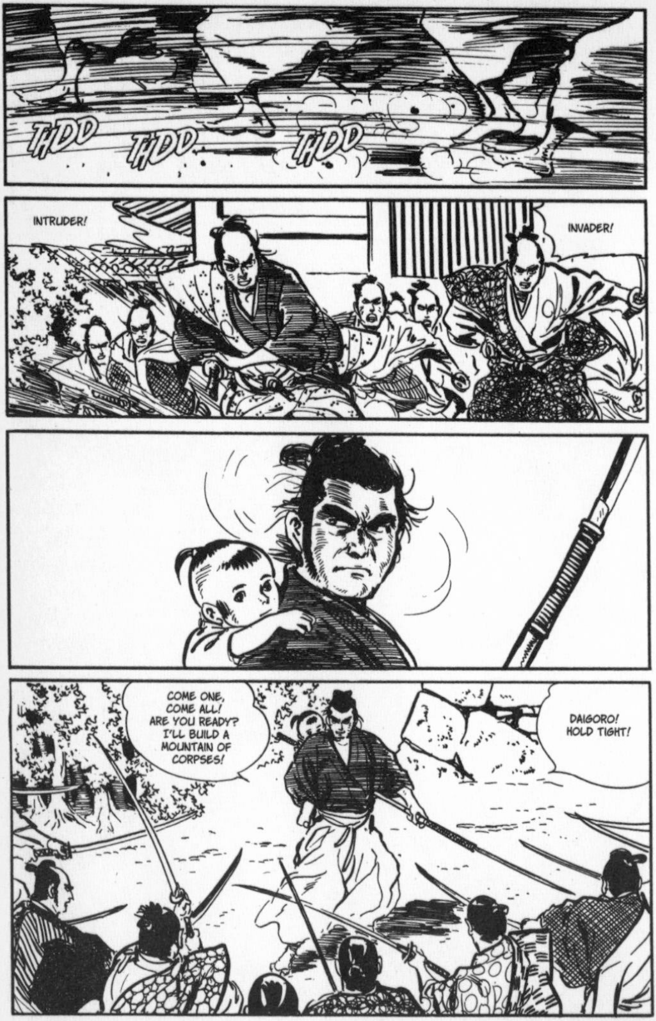
THDD
THDD
THDD
INTRUDER!
INVADER!
COME ONE, COME ALL! ARE YOU READY? I'LL BUILD A MOUNTAIN OF CORPSES!
DAIGORO! HOLD TIGHT!

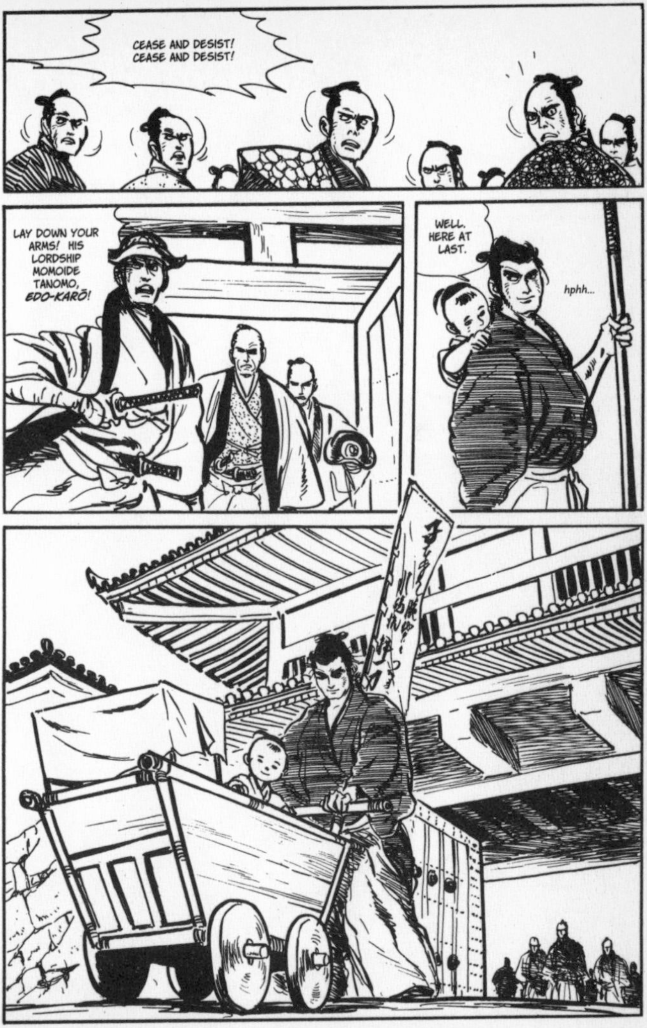
CEASE AND DESIST! CEASE AND DESIST!
LAY DOWN YOUR ARMS! HIS LORDSHIP MOMOIDE TANOMO, *EDO-KARŌ*!
WELL. HERE AT LAST.
hphh...

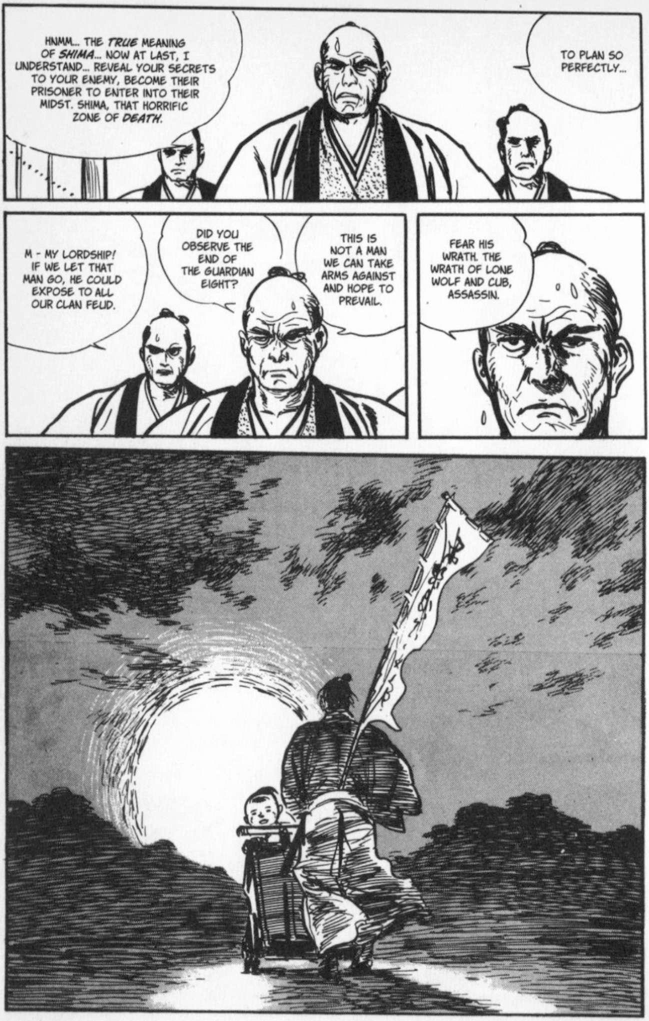
HNMM... THE TRUE MEANING OF SHIMA... NOW AT LAST, I UNDERSTAND... REVEAL YOUR SECRETS TO YOUR ENEMY, BECOME THEIR PRISONER TO ENTER INTO THEIR MIDST. SHIMA, THAT HORRIFIC ZONE OF DEATH.
TO PLAN SO PERFECTLY...
M - MY LORDSHIP! IF WE LET THAT MAN GO, HE COULD EXPOSE TO ALL OUR CLAN FEUD.
DID YOU OBSERVE THE END OF THE GUARDIAN EIGHT?
THIS IS NOT A MAN WE CAN TAKE ARMS AGAINST AND HOPE TO PREVAIL.
FEAR HIS WRATH. THE WRATH OF LONE WOLF AND CUB, ASSASSIN.

the second

A Father Knows His Child's Heart, as Only a Child Can Know His Father's

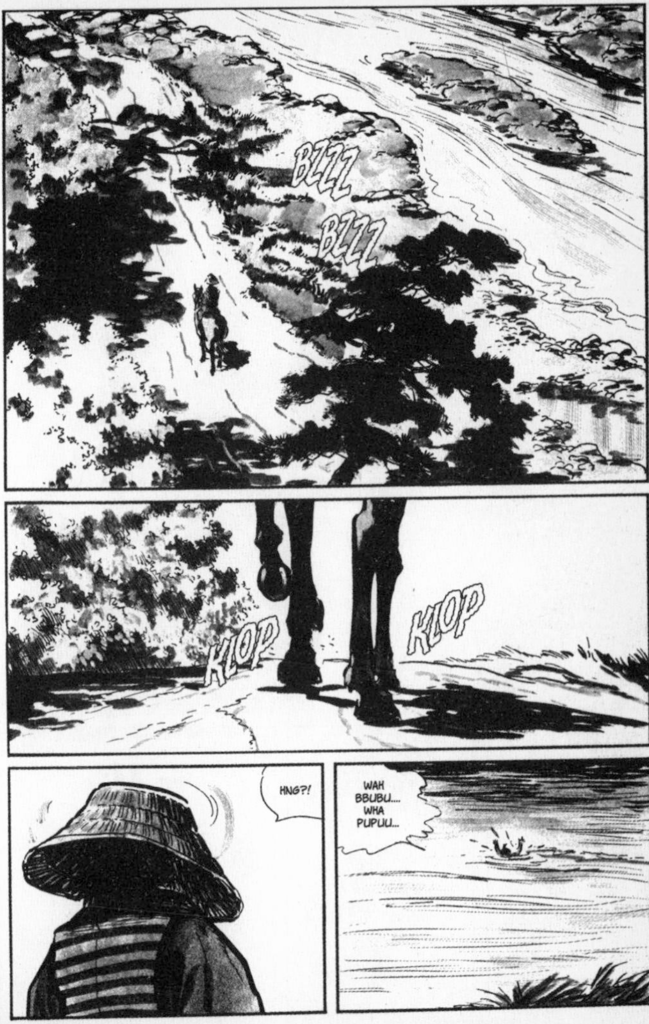
BZZZ
BZZZ
KLOP
KLOP
HNG?!
WAH BBUBU.... WHA PUPUU...

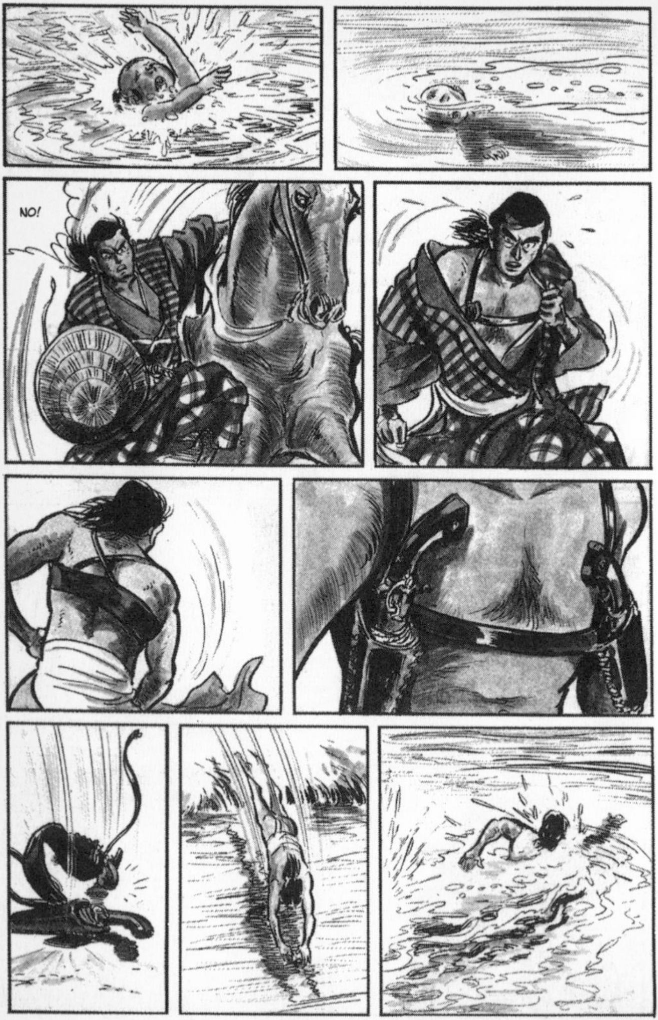
NO!

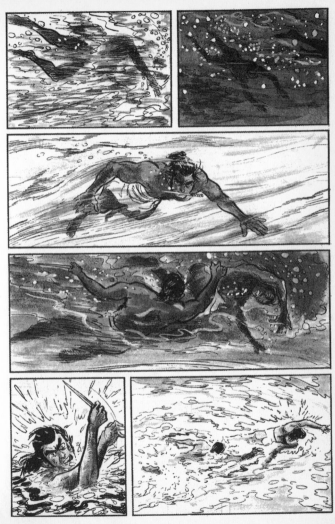

43

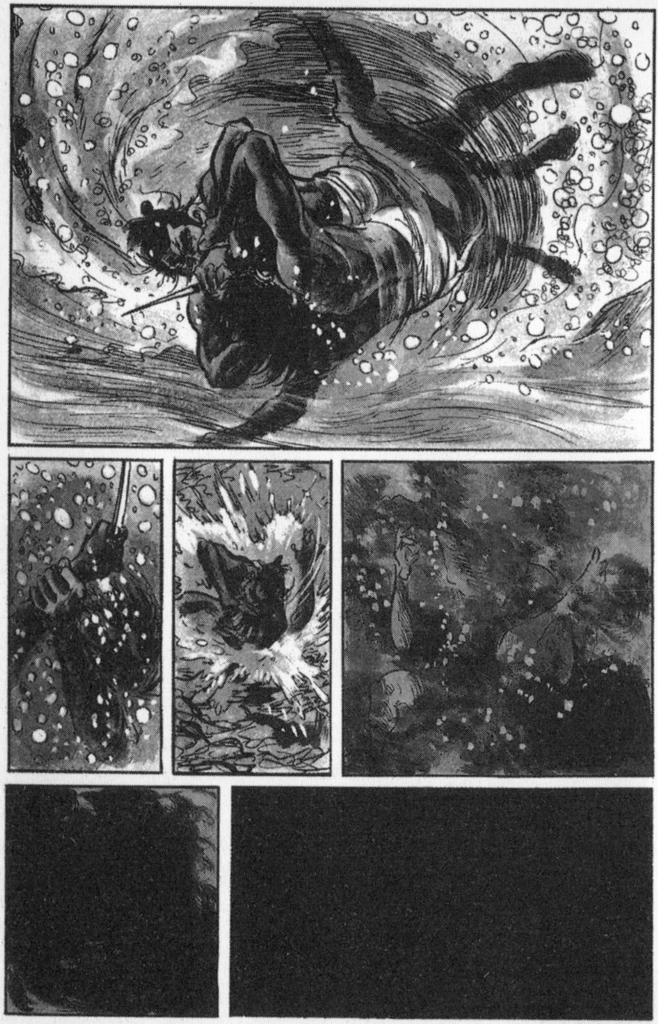

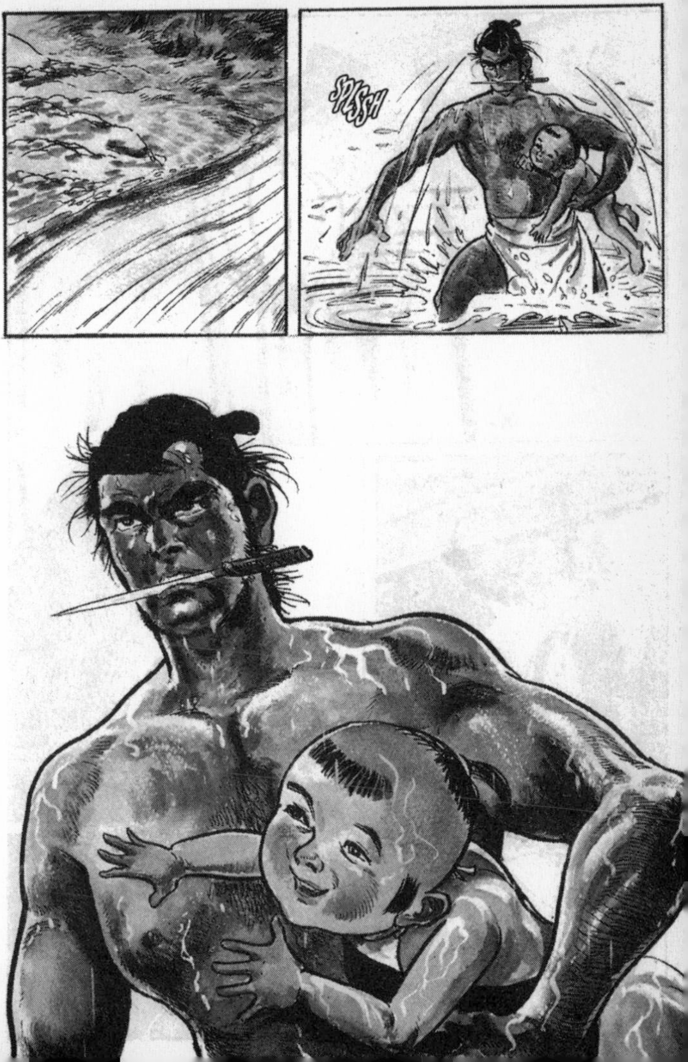
SPLSSH

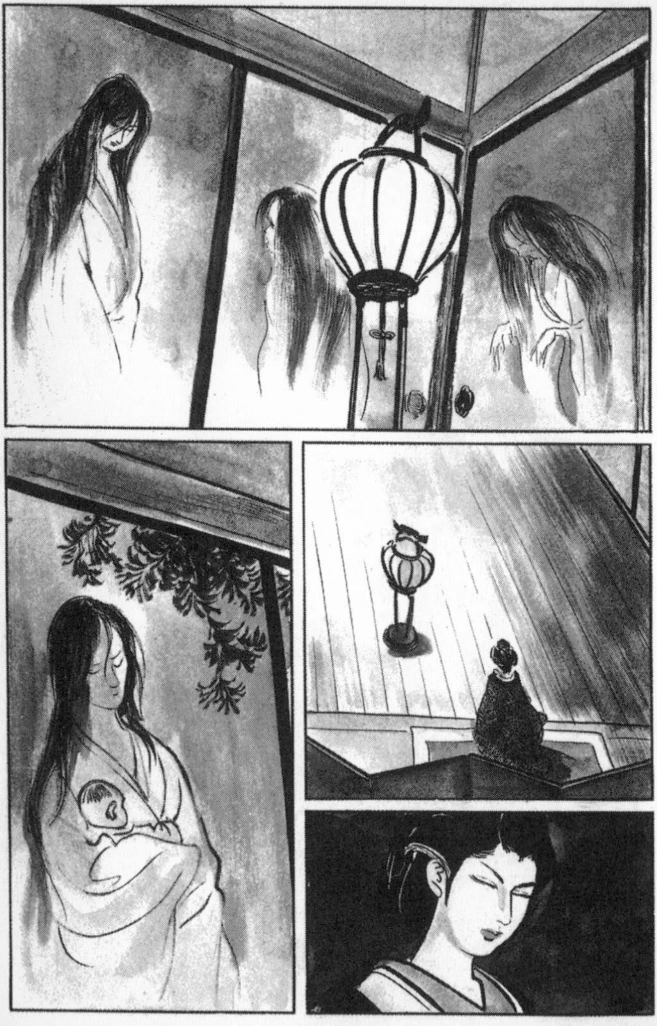

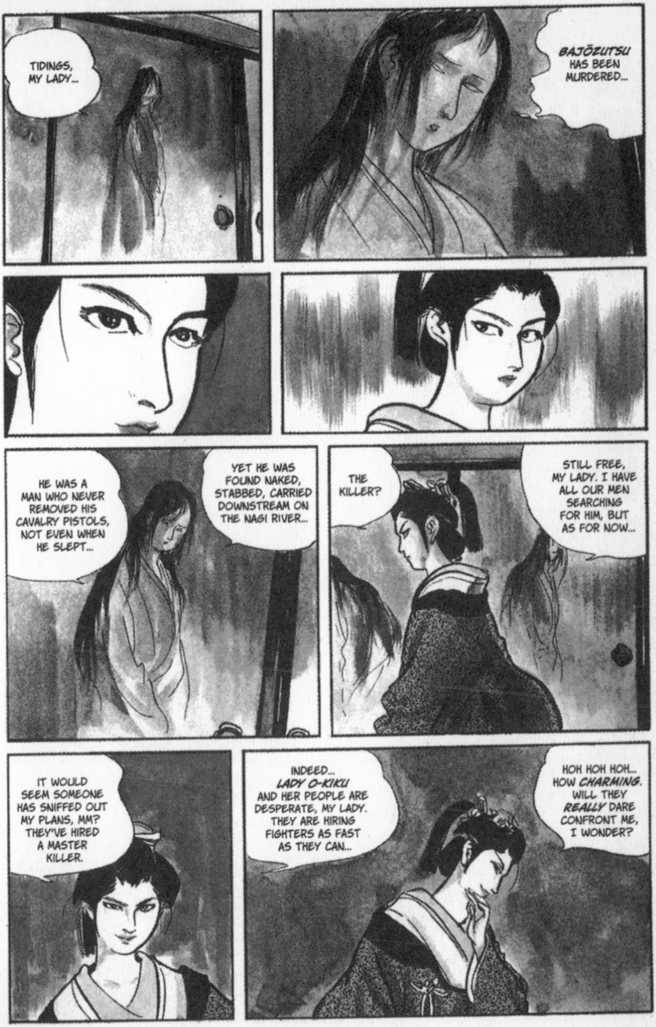
TIDINGS, MY LADY...
BAJŌZUTSU HAS BEEN MURDERED...
HE WAS A MAN WHO NEVER REMOVED HIS CAVALRY PISTOLS, NOT EVEN WHEN HE SLEPT...
YET HE WAS FOUND NAKED, STABBED, CARRIED DOWNSTREAM ON THE NAGI RIVER...
THE KILLER?
STILL FREE, MY LADY. I HAVE ALL OUR MEN SEARCHING FOR HIM, BUT AS FOR NOW...
IT WOULD SEEM SOMEONE HAS SNIFFED OUT MY PLANS, MM? THEY'VE HIRED A MASTER KILLER.
INDEED... *LADY O-KIKU* AND HER PEOPLE ARE DESPERATE, MY LADY. THEY ARE HIRING FIGHTERS AS FAST AS THEY CAN...
HOH HOH HOH... HOW *CHARMING*. WILL THEY *REALLY* DARE CONFRONT ME, I WONDER?

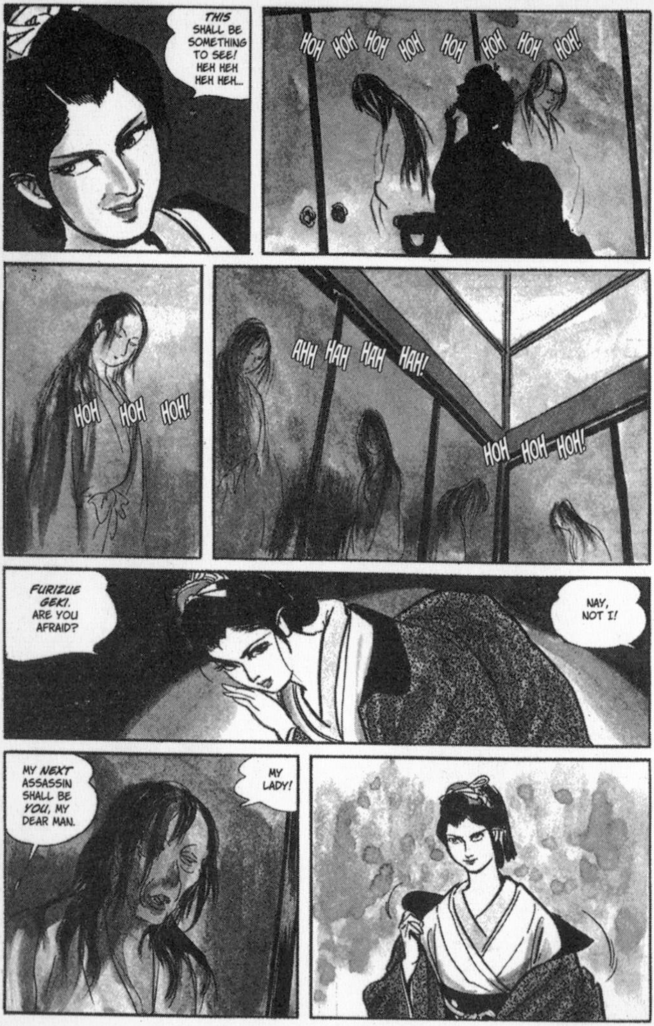
THIS SHALL BE SOMETHING TO SEE! HEH HEH HEH HEH...
HOH HOH HOH HOH HOH HOH HOH HOH!
HOH HOH HOH!
AHH HAH HAH HAH!
HOH HOH HOH!
FURIZUE GEKI. ARE YOU AFRAID?
NAY, NOT I!
MY NEXT ASSASSIN SHALL BE YOU, MY DEAR MAN.
MY LADY!

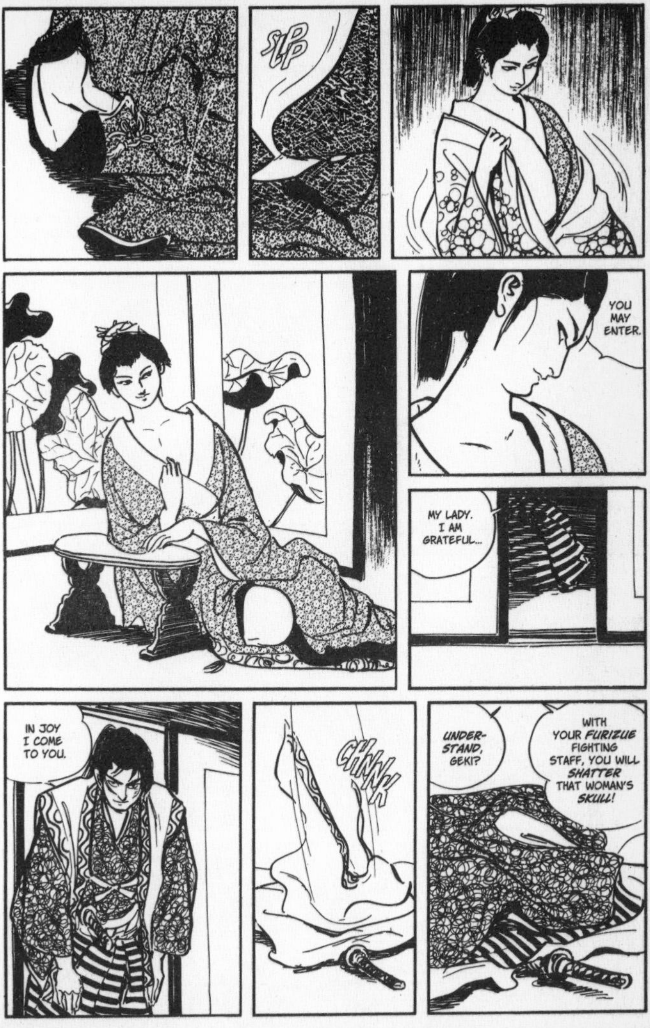
SLPP
YOU MAY ENTER.
MY LADY. I AM GRATEFUL...
IN JOY I COME TO YOU.
CHNNK
UNDER-STAND, GEKI?
WITH YOUR *FURIZUE* FIGHTING STAFF, YOU WILL *SHATTER* THAT WOMAN'S *SKULL*!

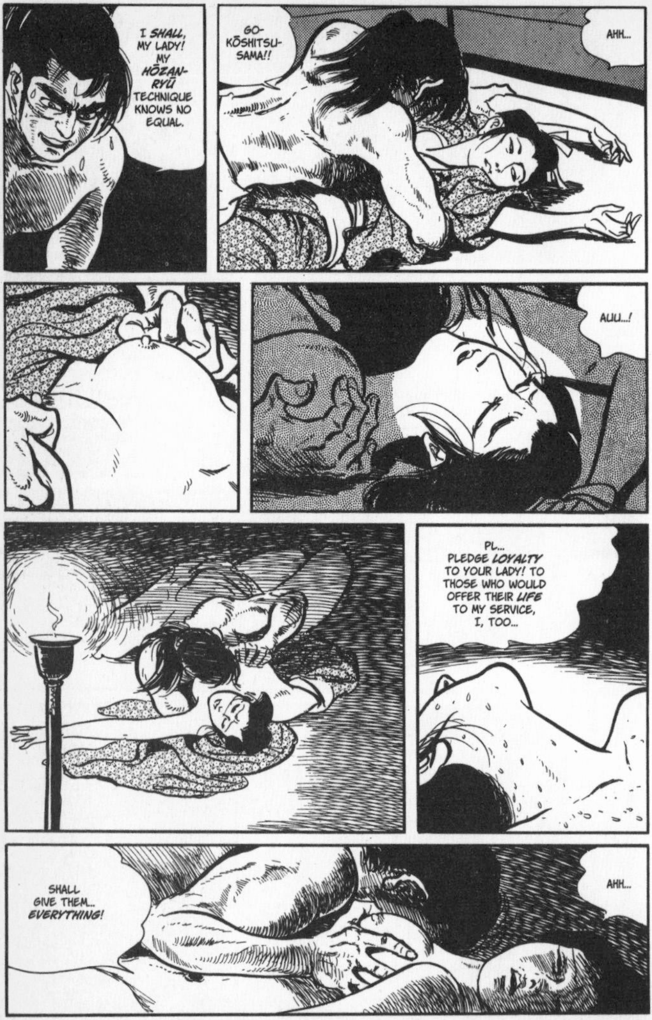
I SHALL, MY LADY! MY HŌZAN-RYŪ TECHNIQUE KNOWS NO EQUAL.
GO-KŌSHITSU-SAMA!!
AHH...
AUU...!
PL... PLEDGE LOYALTY TO YOUR LADY! TO THOSE WHO WOULD OFFER THEIR LIFE TO MY SERVICE, I, TOO...
SHALL GIVE THEM... EVERYTHING!
AHH...

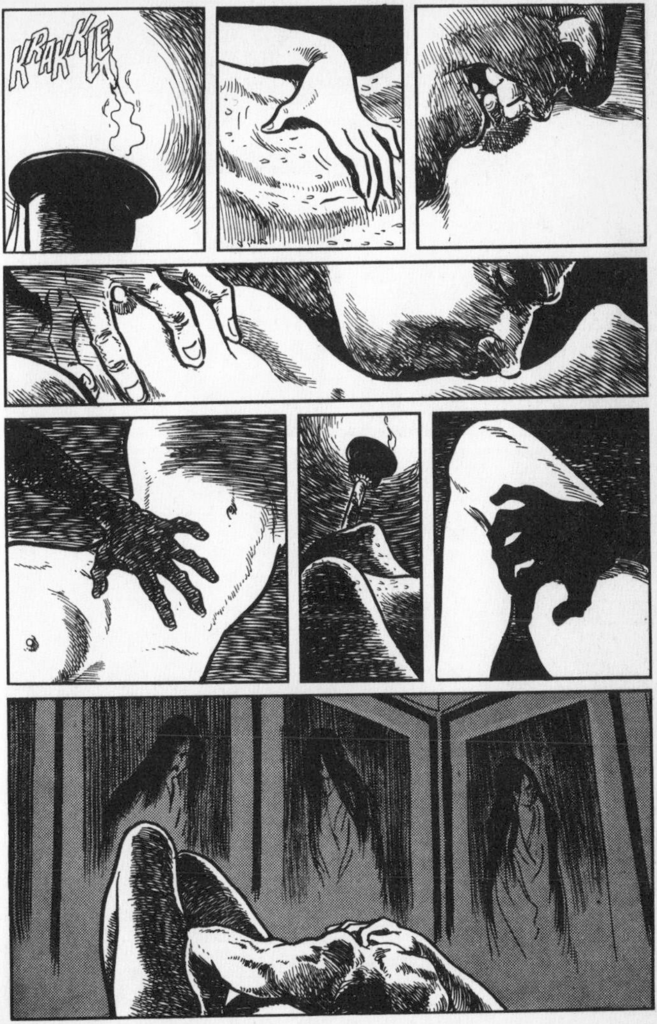
KRAKKLE

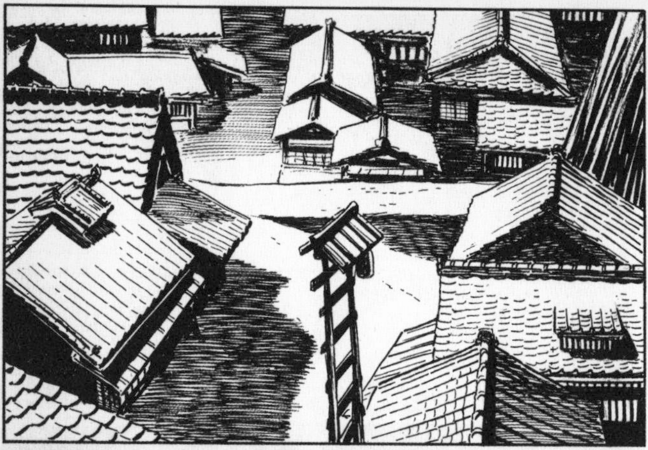

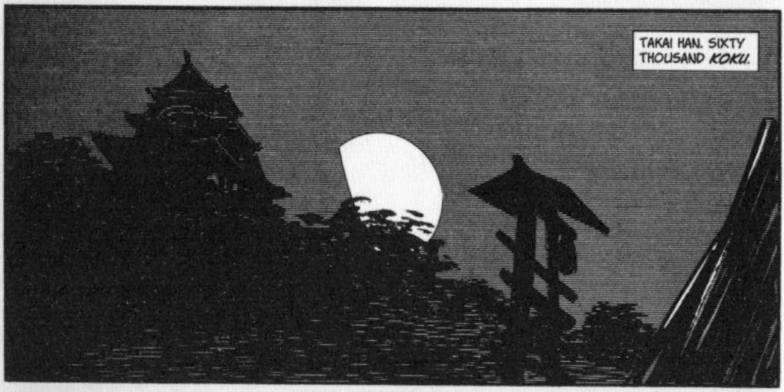
TAKAI HAN. SIXTY THOUSAND KOKU.

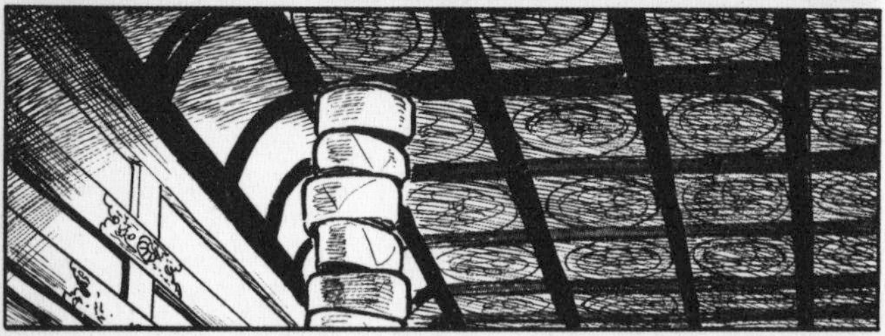

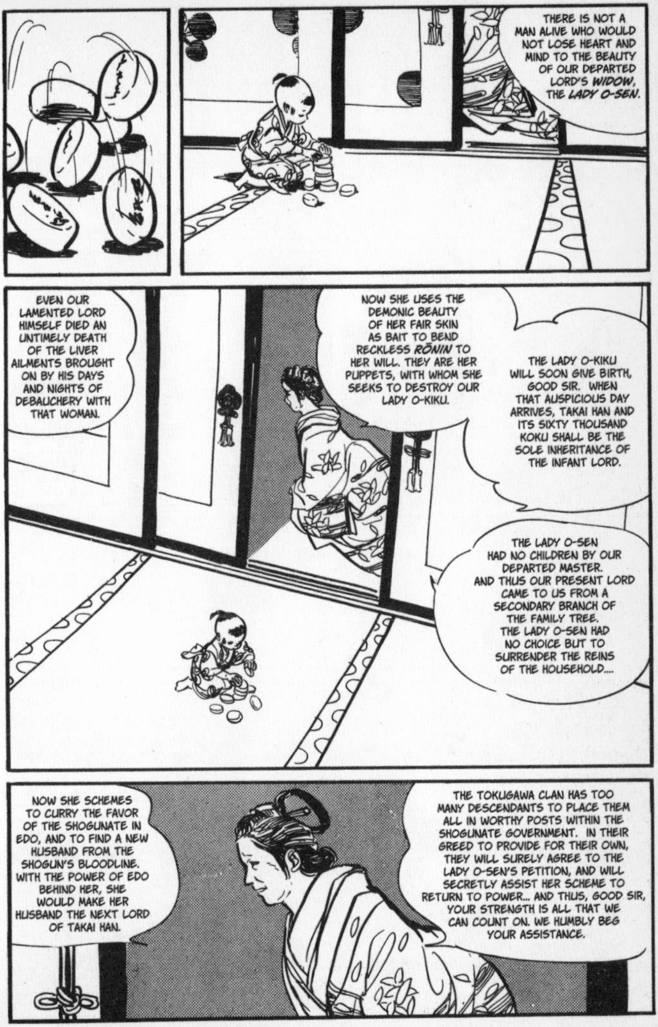
THERE IS NOT A MAN ALIVE WHO WOULD NOT LOSE HEART AND MIND TO THE BEAUTY OF OUR DEPARTED LORD'S *WIDOW*, THE *LADY O-SEN*.
EVEN OUR LAMENTED LORD HIMSELF DIED AN UNTIMELY DEATH OF THE LIVER AILMENTS BROUGHT ON BY HIS DAYS AND NIGHTS OF DEBAUCHERY WITH THAT WOMAN.
NOW SHE USES THE DEMONIC BEAUTY OF HER FAIR SKIN AS BAIT TO BEND RECKLESS *RŌNIN* TO HER WILL. THEY ARE HER PUPPETS, WITH WHOM SHE SEEKS TO DESTROY OUR LADY O-KIKU.
THE LADY O-KIKU WILL SOON GIVE BIRTH, GOOD SIR. WHEN THAT AUSPICIOUS DAY ARRIVES, TAKAI HAN AND ITS SIXTY THOUSAND KOKU SHALL BE THE SOLE INHERITANCE OF THE INFANT LORD.
THE LADY O-SEN HAD NO CHILDREN BY OUR DEPARTED MASTER. AND THUS OUR PRESENT LORD CAME TO US FROM A SECONDARY BRANCH OF THE FAMILY TREE. THE LADY O-SEN HAD NO CHOICE BUT TO SURRENDER THE REINS OF THE HOUSEHOLD....
NOW SHE SCHEMES TO CURRY THE FAVOR OF THE SHOGUNATE IN EDO, AND TO FIND A NEW HUSBAND FROM THE SHOGUN'S BLOODLINE. WITH THE POWER OF EDO BEHIND HER, SHE WOULD MAKE HER HUSBAND THE NEXT LORD OF TAKAI HAN.
THE TOKUGAWA CLAN HAS TOO MANY DESCENDANTS TO PLACE THEM ALL IN WORTHY POSTS WITHIN THE SHOGUNATE GOVERNMENT. IN THEIR GREED TO PROVIDE FOR THEIR OWN, THEY WILL SURELY AGREE TO THE LADY O-SEN'S PETITION, AND WILL SECRETLY ASSIST HER SCHEME TO RETURN TO POWER... AND THUS, GOOD SIR, YOUR STRENGTH IS ALL THAT WE CAN COUNT ON. WE HUMBLY BEG YOUR ASSISTANCE.

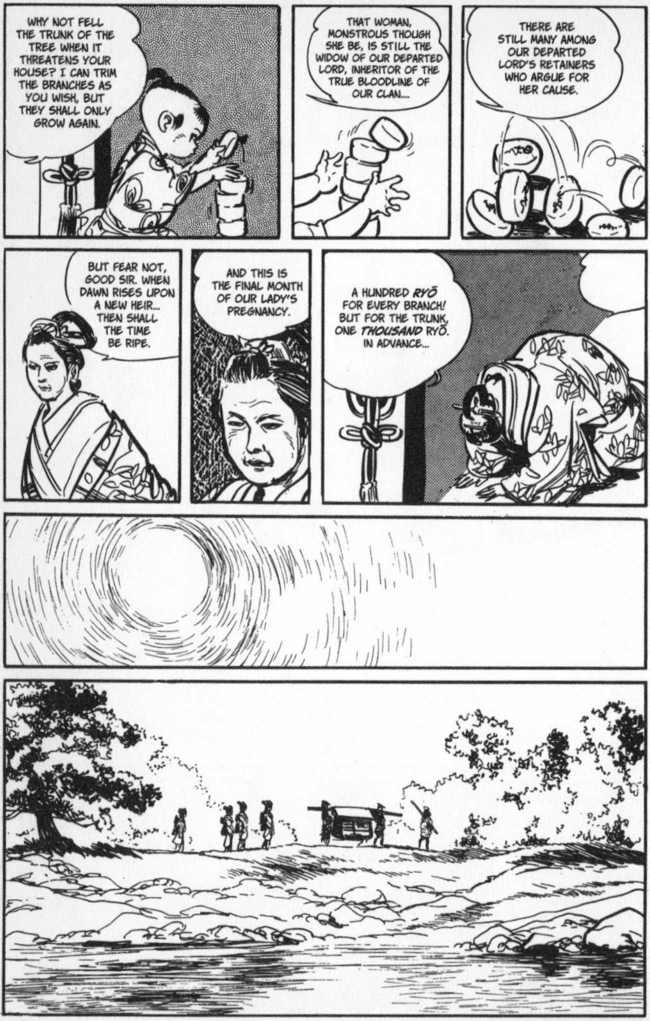
WHY NOT FELL THE TRUNK OF THE TREE WHEN IT THREATENS YOUR HOUSE? I CAN TRIM THE BRANCHES AS YOU WISH, BUT THEY SHALL ONLY GROW AGAIN.
THAT WOMAN, MONSTROUS THOUGH SHE BE, IS STILL THE WIDOW OF OUR DEPARTED LORD, INHERITOR OF THE TRUE BLOODLINE OF OUR CLAN....
THERE ARE STILL MANY AMONG OUR DEPARTED LORD'S RETAINERS WHO ARGUE FOR HER CAUSE.
BUT FEAR NOT, GOOD SIR. WHEN DAWN RISES UPON A NEW HEIR... THEN SHALL THE TIME BE RIPE.
AND THIS IS THE FINAL MONTH OF OUR LADY'S PREGNANCY.
A HUNDRED *RYŌ* FOR EVERY BRANCH! BUT FOR THE TRUNK, ONE *THOUSAND* RYŌ. IN ADVANCE...

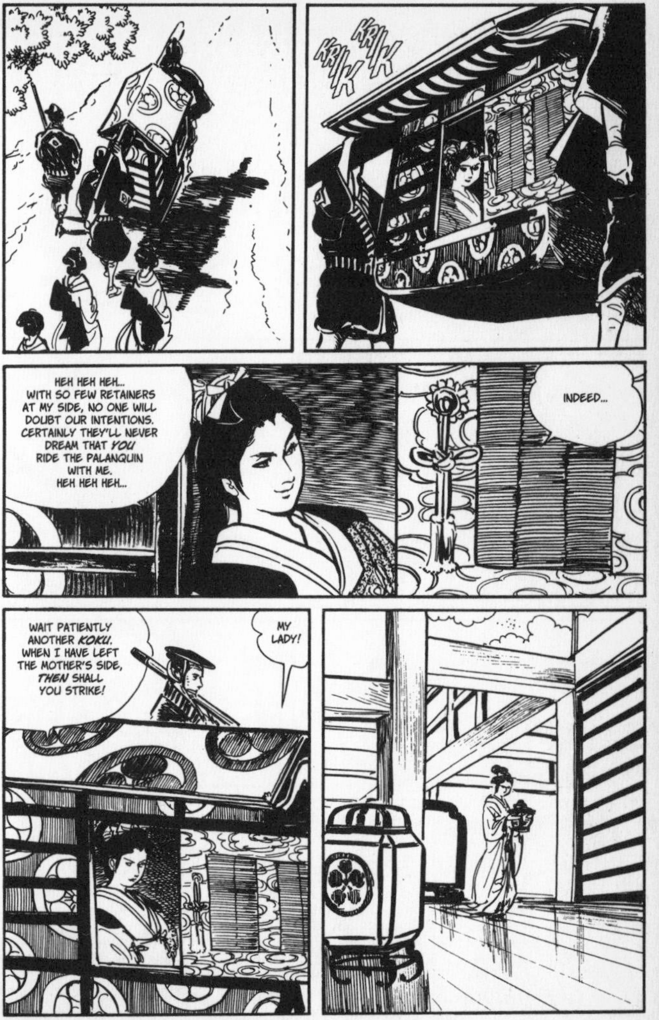
KRIK KRIK
HEH HEH HEH... WITH SO FEW RETAINERS AT MY SIDE, NO ONE WILL DOUBT OUR INTENTIONS. CERTAINLY THEY'LL NEVER DREAM THAT *YOU* RIDE THE PALANQUIN WITH ME. HEH HEH HEH...
INDEED...
WAIT PATIENTLY ANOTHER *KOKU*. WHEN I HAVE LEFT THE MOTHER'S SIDE, *THEN* SHALL YOU STRIKE!
MY LADY!

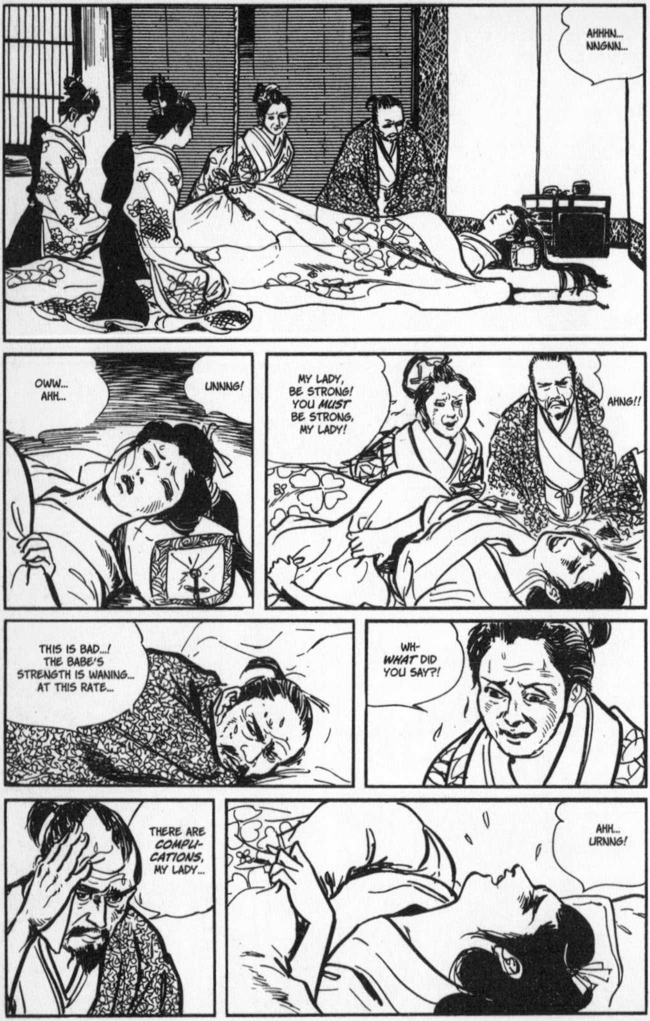
AHHHN... NNGNN...
OWW... AHH...
UNNNG!
MY LADY, BE STRONG! YOU *MUST* BE STRONG, MY LADY!
AHNG!!
THIS IS BAD...! THE BABE'S STRENGTH IS WANING... AT THIS RATE...
WH-*WHAT* DID YOU SAY?!
THERE ARE *COMPLICATIONS*, MY LADY...
AHH... URNNG!

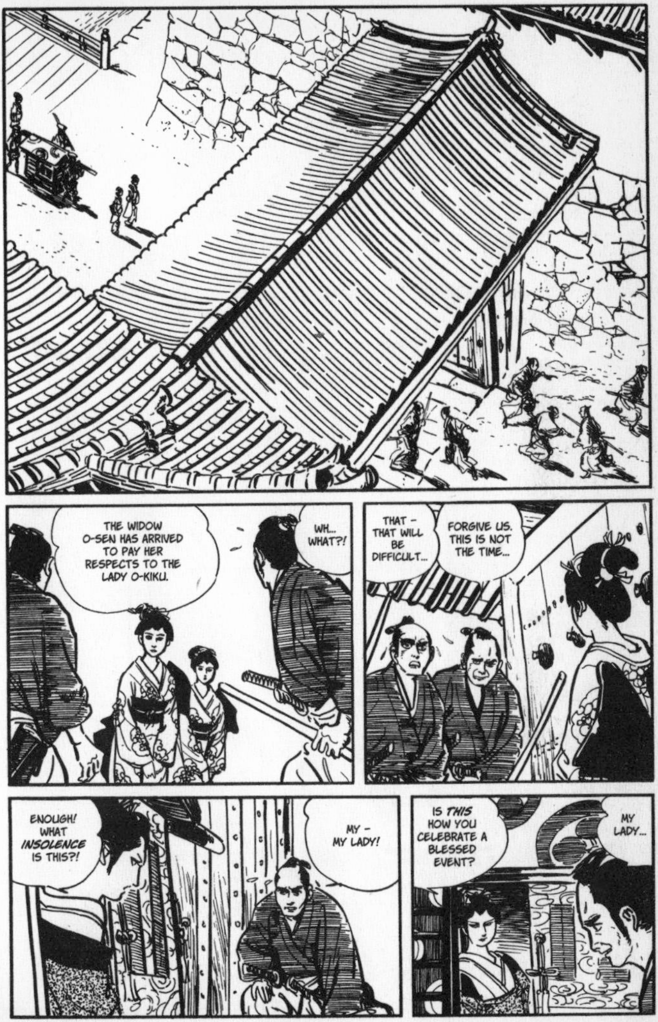
THE WIDOW O-SEN HAS ARRIVED TO PAY HER RESPECTS TO THE LADY O-KIKU.
WH... WHAT?!
THAT - THAT WILL BE DIFFICULT...
FORGIVE US. THIS IS NOT THE TIME...
ENOUGH! WHAT *INSOLENCE* IS THIS?!
MY - MY LADY!
IS *THIS* HOW YOU CELEBRATE A BLESSED EVENT?
MY LADY...

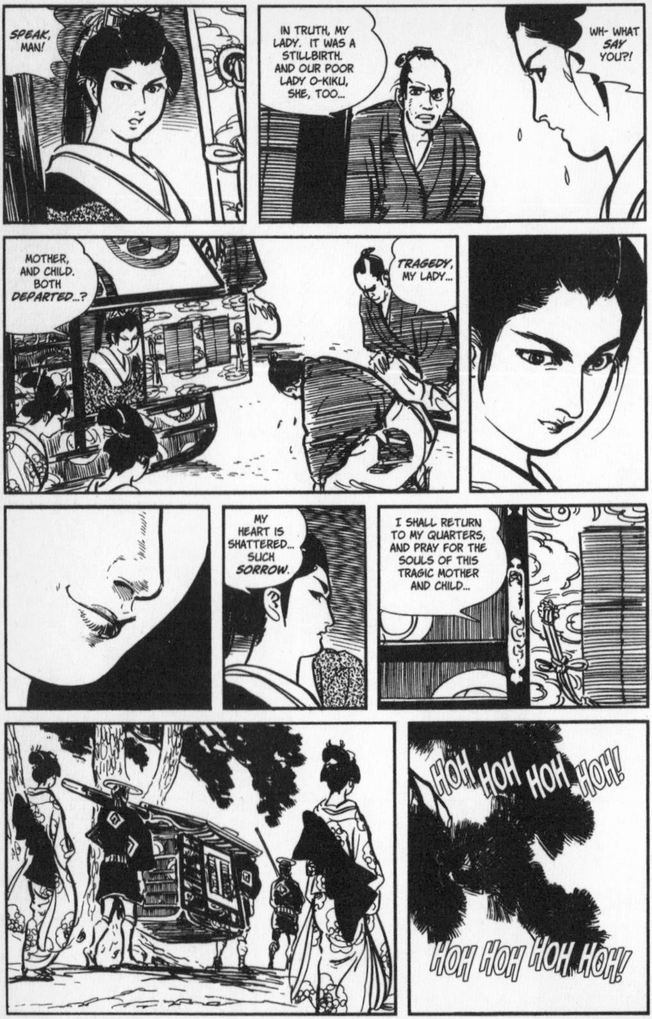
SPEAK, MAN!
IN TRUTH, MY LADY. IT WAS A STILLBIRTH. AND OUR POOR LADY O-KIKU, SHE, TOO...
WH- WHAT SAY YOU?!
MOTHER, AND CHILD. BOTH DEPARTED...?
TRAGEDY, MY LADY...
MY HEART IS SHATTERED... SUCH SORROW.
I SHALL RETURN TO MY QUARTERS, AND PRAY FOR THE SOULS OF THIS TRAGIC MOTHER AND CHILD...
HOH HOH HOH HOH!
HOH HOH HOH HOH!

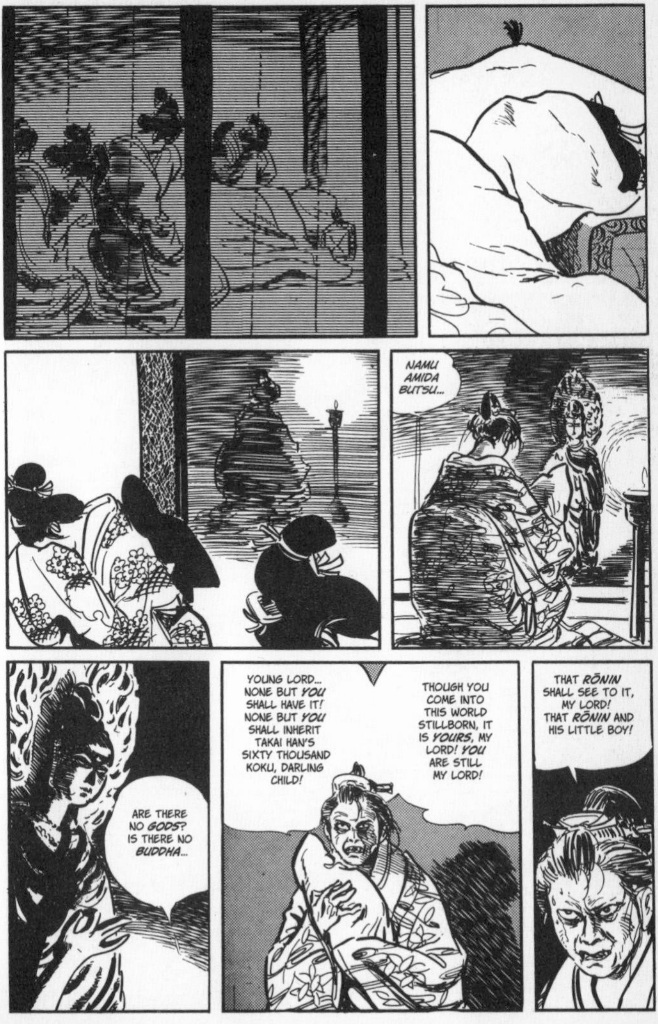
NAMU AMIDA BUTSU...
ARE THERE NO GODS? IS THERE NO BUDDHA...
YOUNG LORD... NONE BUT YOU SHALL HAVE IT! NONE BUT YOU SHALL INHERIT TAKAI HAN'S SIXTY THOUSAND KOKU, DARLING CHILD!
THOUGH YOU COME INTO THIS WORLD STILLBORN, IT IS YOURS, MY LORD! YOU ARE STILL MY LORD!
THAT RŌNIN SHALL SEE TO IT, MY LORD! THAT RŌNIN AND HIS LITTLE BOY!

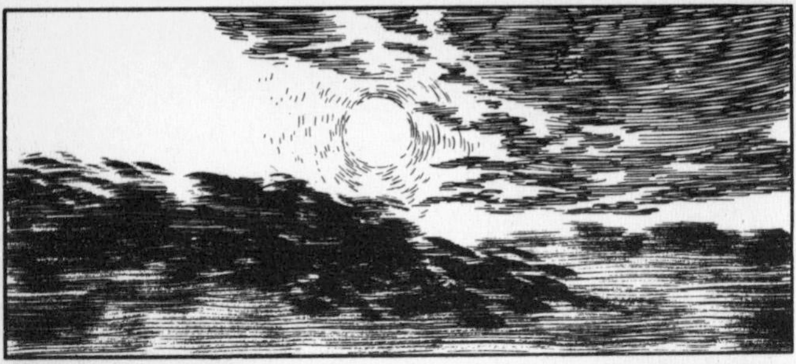

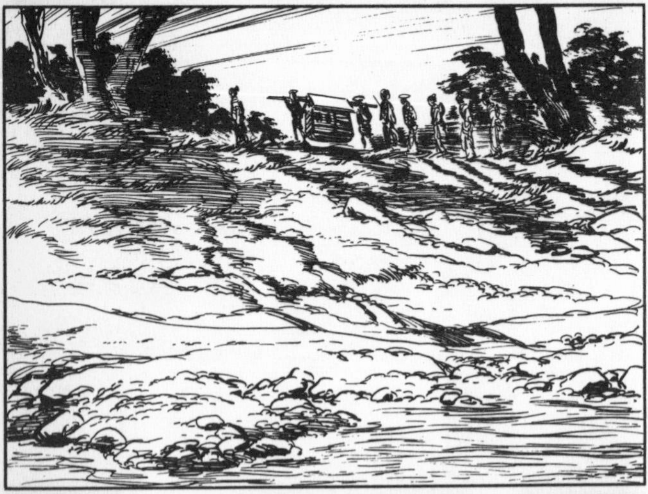

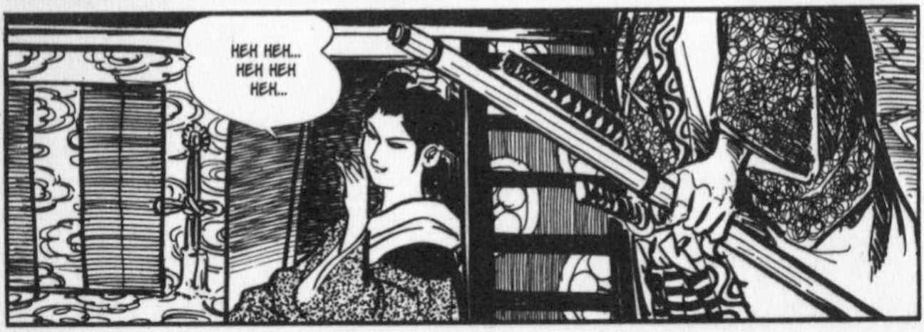
HEH HEH... HEH HEH HEH...

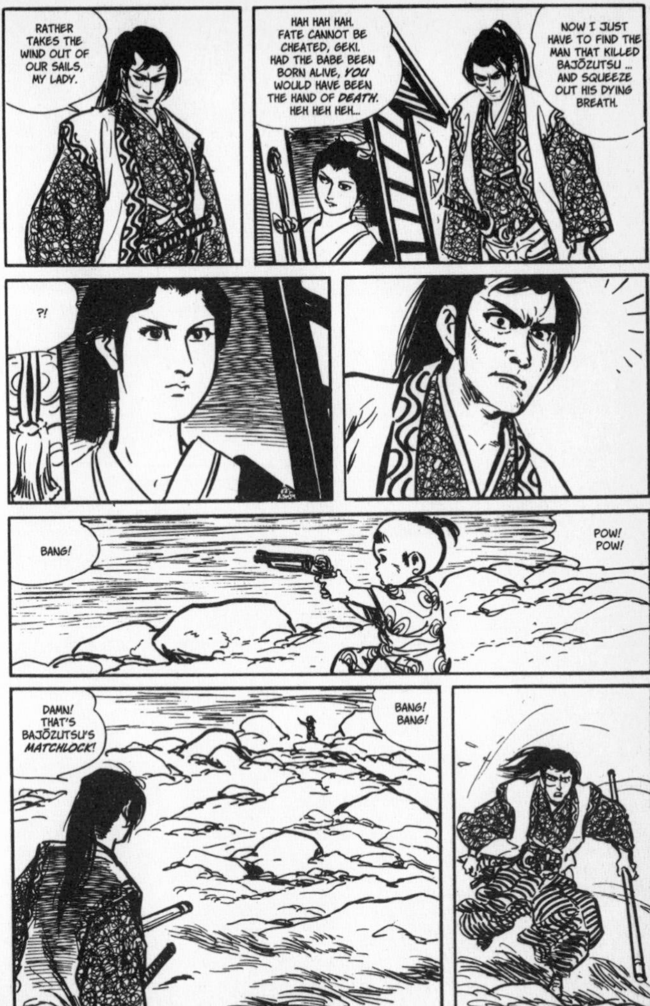
RATHER TAKES THE WIND OUT OF OUR SAILS, MY LADY.
HAH HAH HAH. FATE CANNOT BE CHEATED, GEKI. HAD THE BABE BEEN BORN ALIVE, *YOU* WOULD HAVE BEEN THE HAND OF *DEATH*. HEH HEH HEH...
NOW I JUST HAVE TO FIND THE MAN THAT KILLED BAJŌZUTSU ... AND SQUEEZE OUT HIS DYING BREATH.
?!
BANG!
POW! POW!
DAMN! THAT'S BAJŌZUTSU'S *MATCHLOCK!*
BANG! BANG!

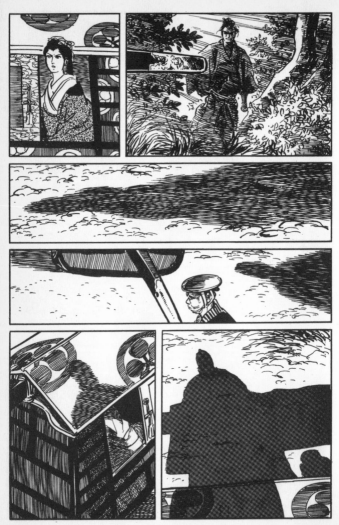

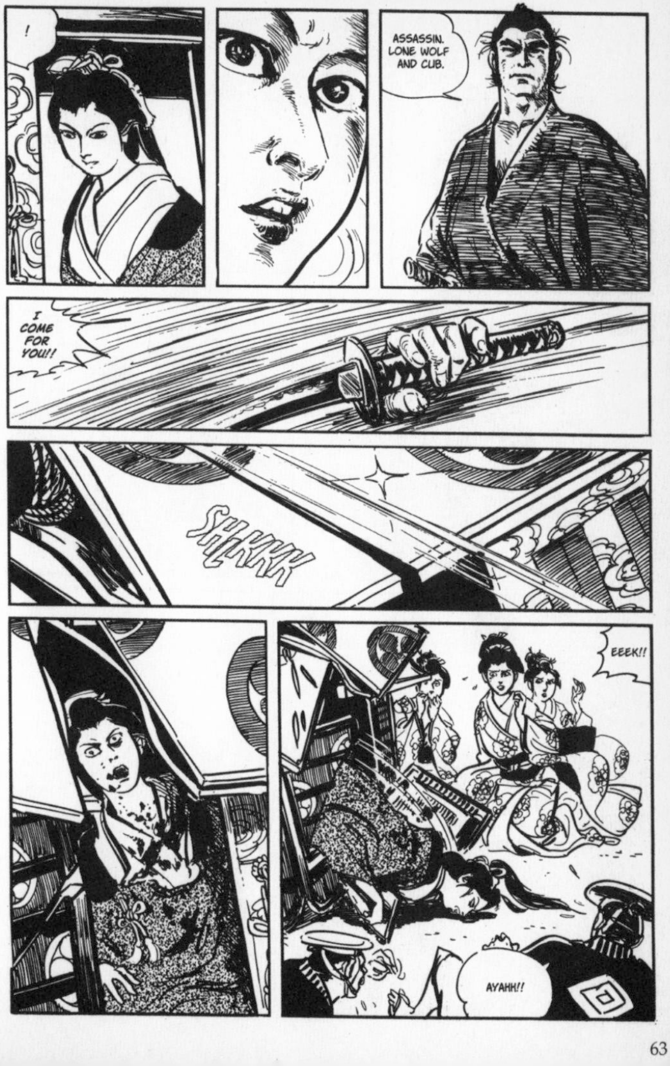
!
ASSASSIN. LONE WOLF AND CUB.
I COME FOR YOU!!
SHKKK
EEEK!!
AYAHH!!

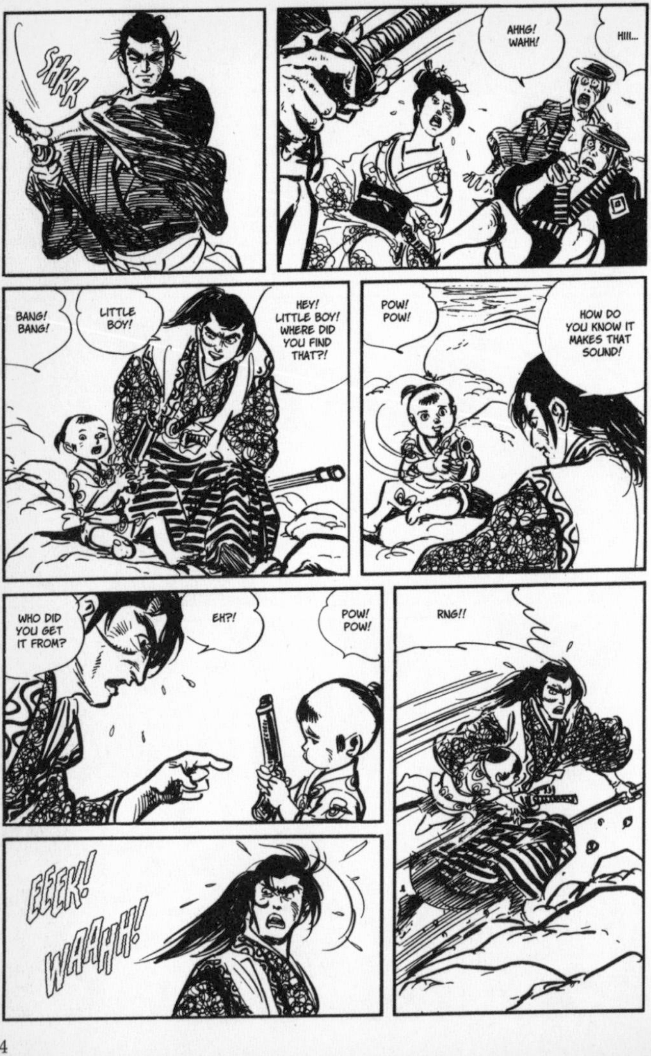
SHKK
AHHG! WAHH!
HIII...
BANG! BANG!
LITTLE BOY!
HEY! LITTLE BOY! WHERE DID YOU FIND THAT?!
POW! POW!
HOW DO YOU KNOW IT MAKES THAT SOUND!
WHO DID YOU GET IT FROM?
EH?!
POW! POW!
RNG!!
EEEK!
WAAHH!

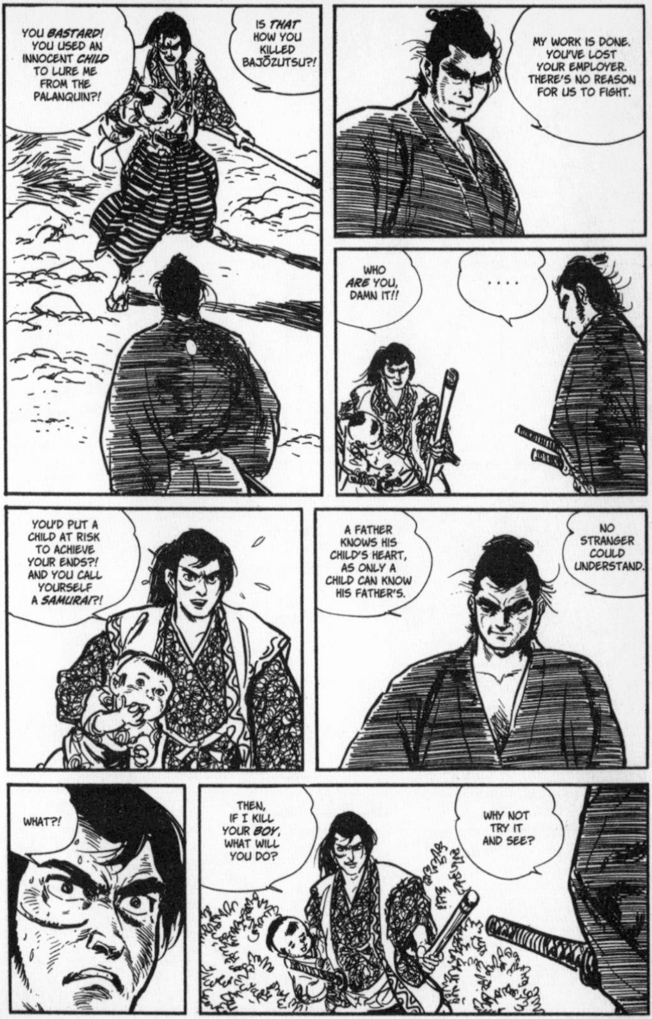
YOU *BASTARD!* YOU USED AN INNOCENT *CHILD* TO LURE ME FROM THE PALANQUIN?!
IS *THAT* HOW YOU KILLED BAJŌZUTSU?!
MY WORK IS DONE. YOU'VE LOST YOUR EMPLOYER. THERE'S NO REASON FOR US TO FIGHT.
WHO *ARE* YOU, DAMN IT!!
. . . .
YOU'D PUT A CHILD AT RISK TO ACHIEVE YOUR ENDS?! AND YOU CALL YOURSELF A *SAMURAI*?!
A FATHER KNOWS HIS CHILD'S HEART, AS ONLY A CHILD CAN KNOW HIS FATHER'S.
NO STRANGER COULD UNDERSTAND.
WHAT?!
THEN, IF I KILL YOUR *BOY*, WHAT WILL YOU DO?
WHY NOT TRY IT AND SEE?

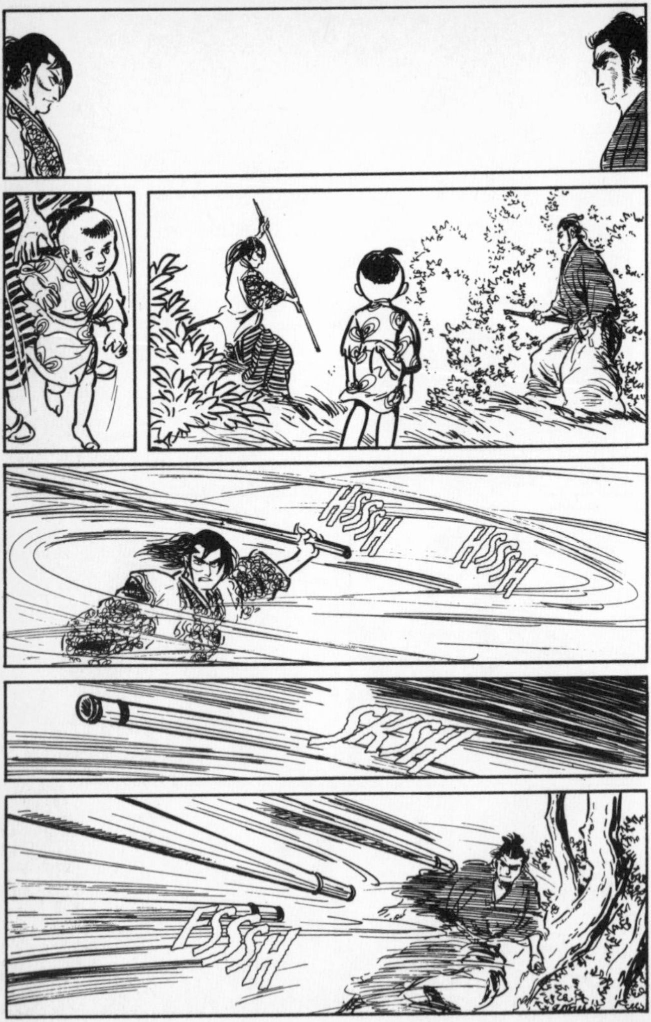
HSSH
HSSH
SKSH
FSSH

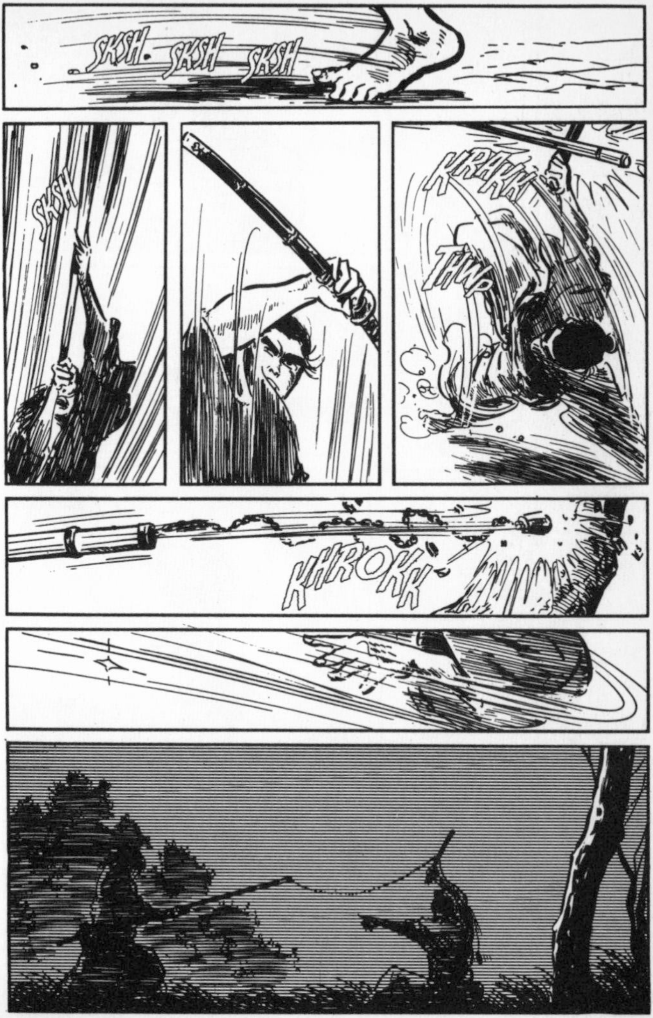
SKSH SKSH SKSH
SKSH
KRAKK
THWP
KHROKK

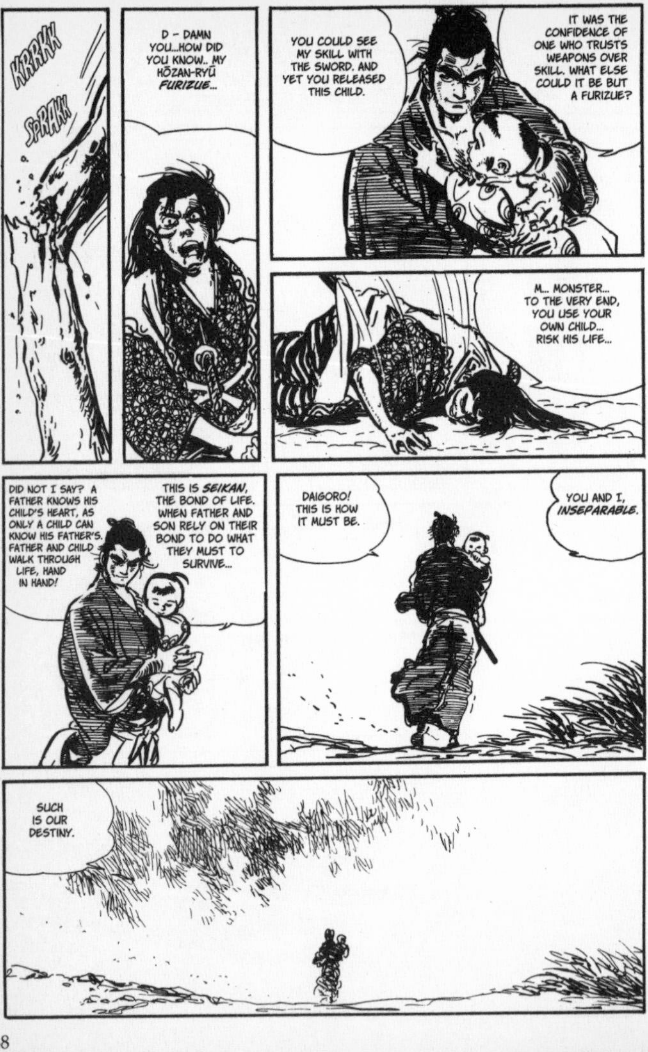
KRRKK
SPRAKK
D - DAMN YOU...HOW DID YOU KNOW.. MY HŌZAN-RYŪ *FURIZUE*...
YOU COULD SEE MY SKILL WITH THE SWORD. AND YET YOU RELEASED THIS CHILD.
IT WAS THE CONFIDENCE OF ONE WHO TRUSTS WEAPONS OVER SKILL. WHAT ELSE COULD IT BE BUT A FURIZUE?
M... MONSTER... TO THE VERY END, YOU USE YOUR OWN CHILD... RISK HIS LIFE...
DID NOT I SAY? A FATHER KNOWS HIS CHILD'S HEART, AS ONLY A CHILD CAN KNOW HIS FATHER'S. FATHER AND CHILD WALK THROUGH LIFE, HAND IN HAND!
THIS IS *SEIKAN*, THE BOND OF LIFE. WHEN FATHER AND SON RELY ON THEIR BOND TO DO WHAT THEY MUST TO SURVIVE...
DAIGORO! THIS IS HOW IT MUST BE.
YOU AND I, *INSEPARABLE*.
SUCH IS OUR DESTINY.

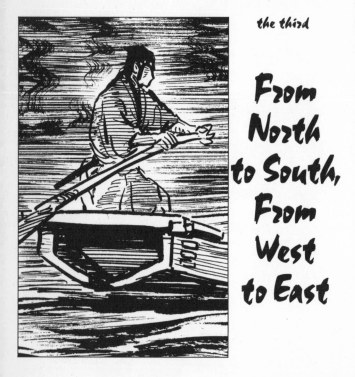

From North to South, From West to East

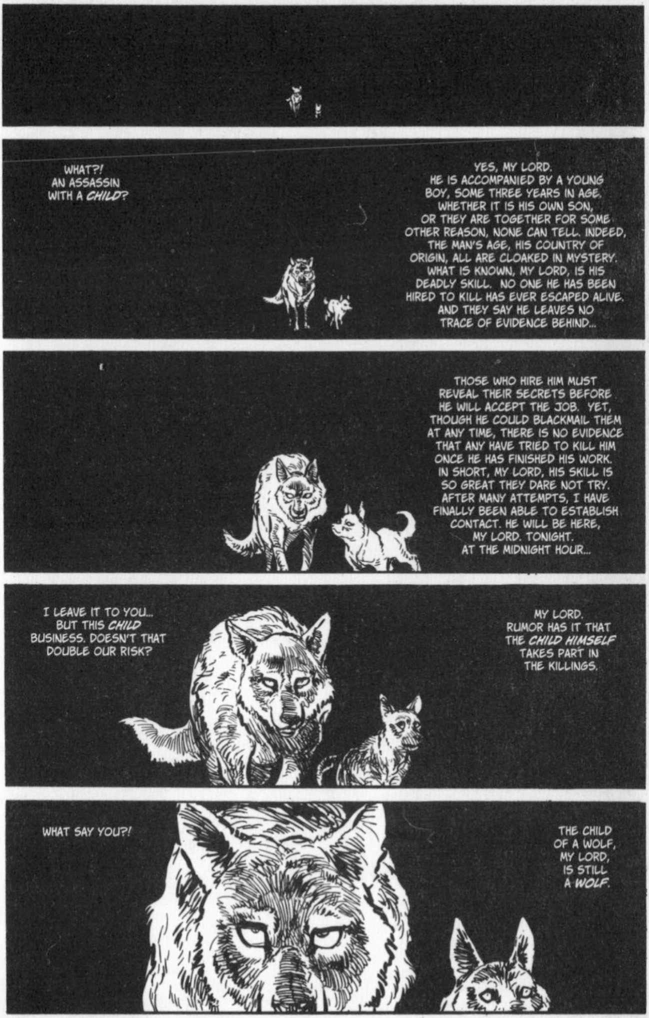
WHAT?! AN ASSASSIN WITH A CHILD?
YES, MY LORD. HE IS ACCOMPANIED BY A YOUNG BOY, SOME THREE YEARS IN AGE. WHETHER IT IS HIS OWN SON, OR THEY ARE TOGETHER FOR SOME OTHER REASON, NONE CAN TELL. INDEED, THE MAN'S AGE, HIS COUNTRY OF ORIGIN, ALL ARE CLOAKED IN MYSTERY. WHAT IS KNOWN, MY LORD, IS HIS DEADLY SKILL. NO ONE HE HAS BEEN HIRED TO KILL HAS EVER ESCAPED ALIVE. AND THEY SAY HE LEAVES NO TRACE OF EVIDENCE BEHIND...
THOSE WHO HIRE HIM MUST REVEAL THEIR SECRETS BEFORE HE WILL ACCEPT THE JOB. YET, THOUGH HE COULD BLACKMAIL THEM AT ANY TIME, THERE IS NO EVIDENCE THAT ANY HAVE TRIED TO KILL HIM ONCE HE HAS FINISHED HIS WORK. IN SHORT, MY LORD, HIS SKILL IS SO GREAT THEY DARE NOT TRY. AFTER MANY ATTEMPTS, I HAVE FINALLY BEEN ABLE TO ESTABLISH CONTACT. HE WILL BE HERE, MY LORD. TONIGHT. AT THE MIDNIGHT HOUR...
I LEAVE IT TO YOU... BUT THIS CHILD BUSINESS. DOESN'T THAT DOUBLE OUR RISK?
MY LORD. RUMOR HAS IT THAT THE CHILD HIMSELF TAKES PART IN THE KILLINGS.
WHAT SAY YOU?!
THE CHILD OF A WOLF, MY LORD, IS STILL A WOLF.

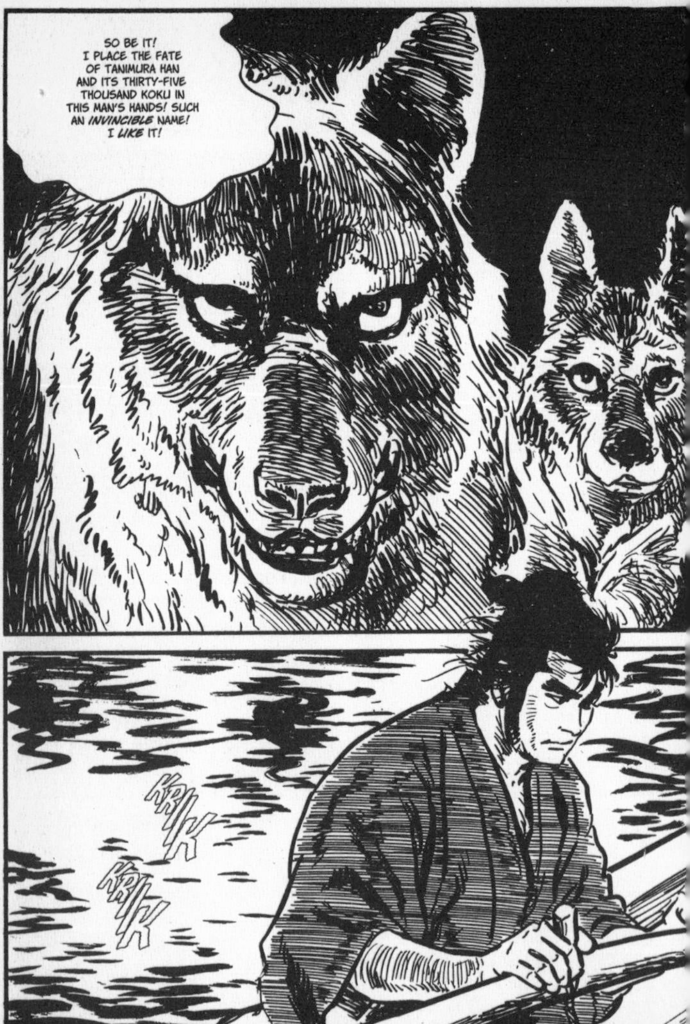
SO BE IT! I PLACE THE FATE OF TANIMURA HAN AND ITS THIRTY-FIVE THOUSAND KOKU IN THIS MAN'S HANDS! SUCH AN *INVINCIBLE* NAME! I *LIKE* IT!
KRIK
KRIK

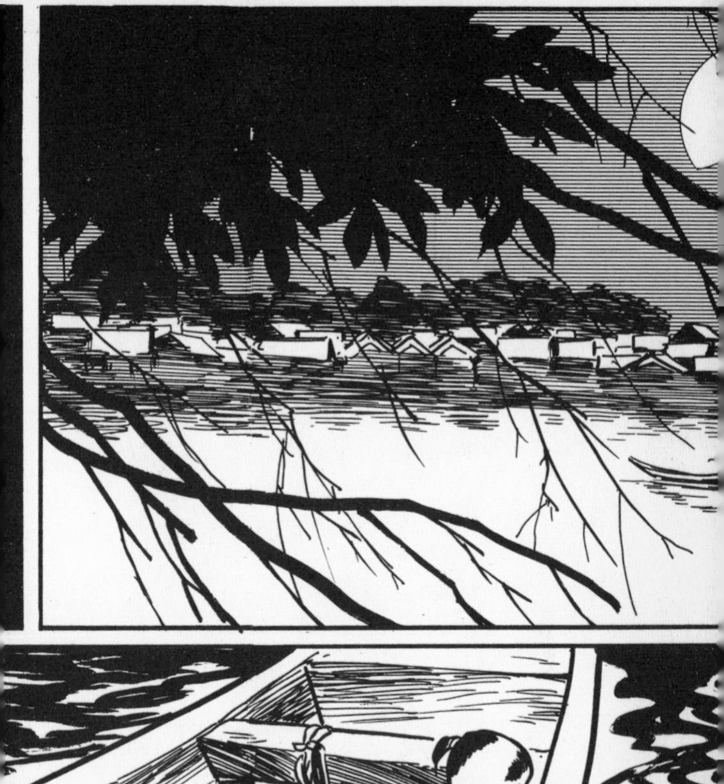
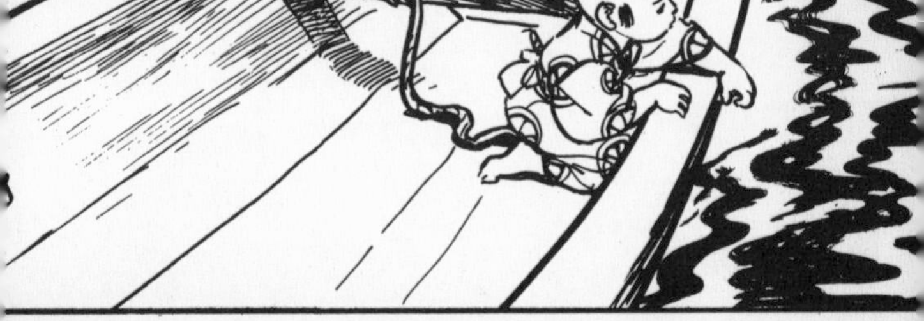

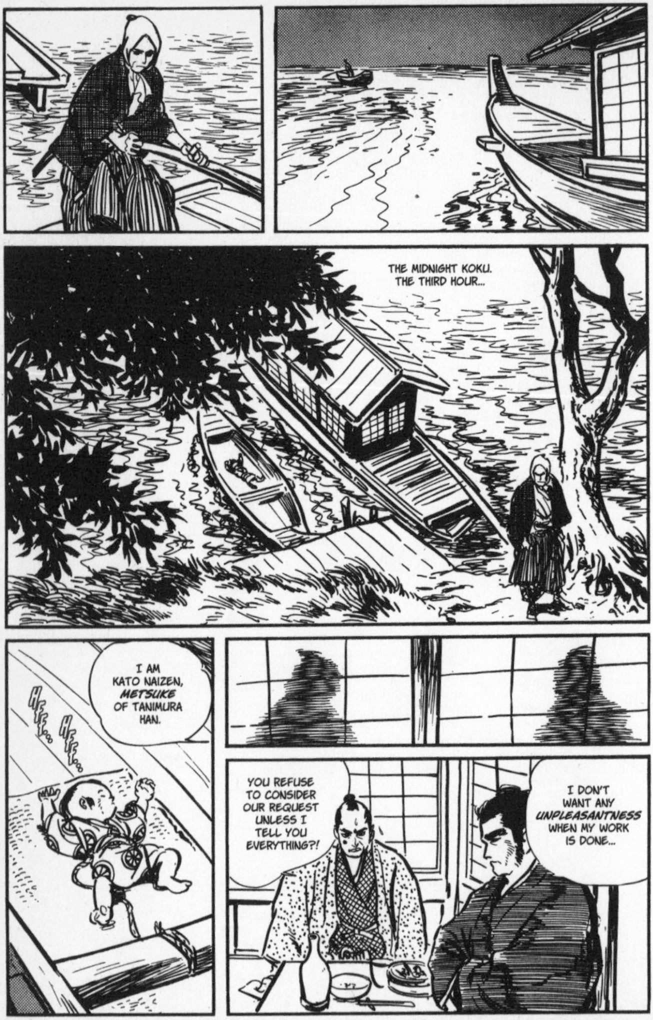
THE MIDNIGHT KOKU. THE THIRD HOUR...
I AM KATO NAIZEN, *METSUKE* OF TANIMURA HAN.
HFF... HFF...
YOU REFUSE TO CONSIDER OUR REQUEST UNLESS I TELL YOU EVERYTHING?!
I DON'T WANT ANY *UNPLEASANTNESS* WHEN MY WORK IS DONE...

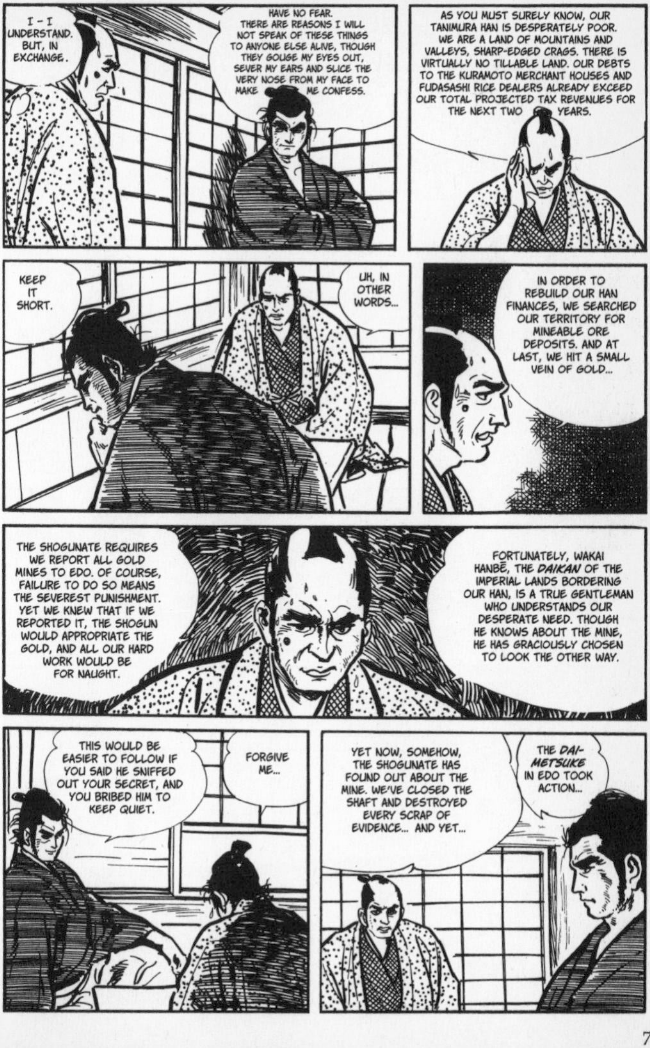
I - I UNDERSTAND. BUT, IN EXCHANGE.
HAVE NO FEAR. THERE ARE REASONS I WILL NOT SPEAK OF THESE THINGS TO ANYONE ELSE ALIVE, THOUGH THEY GOUGE MY EYES OUT, SEVER MY EARS AND SLICE THE VERY NOSE FROM MY FACE TO MAKE ME CONFESS.
AS YOU MUST SURELY KNOW, OUR TANIMURA HAN IS DESPERATELY POOR. WE ARE A LAND OF MOUNTAINS AND VALLEYS, SHARP-EDGED CRAGS. THERE IS VIRTUALLY NO TILLABLE LAND. OUR DEBTS TO THE KURAMOTO MERCHANT HOUSES AND FUDASASHI RICE DEALERS ALREADY EXCEED OUR TOTAL PROJECTED TAX REVENUES FOR THE NEXT TWO YEARS.
KEEP IT SHORT.
UH, IN OTHER WORDS...
IN ORDER TO REBUILD OUR HAN FINANCES, WE SEARCHED OUR TERRITORY FOR MINEABLE ORE DEPOSITS. AND AT LAST, WE HIT A SMALL VEIN OF GOLD...
THE SHOGUNATE REQUIRES WE REPORT ALL GOLD MINES TO EDO. OF COURSE, FAILURE TO DO SO MEANS THE SEVEREST PUNISHMENT. YET WE KNEW THAT IF WE REPORTED IT, THE SHOGUN WOULD APPROPRIATE THE GOLD, AND ALL OUR HARD WORK WOULD BE FOR NAUGHT.
FORTUNATELY, WAKAI HANBĒ, THE *DAIKAN* OF THE IMPERIAL LANDS BORDERING OUR HAN, IS A TRUE GENTLEMAN WHO UNDERSTANDS OUR DESPERATE NEED. THOUGH HE KNOWS ABOUT THE MINE, HE HAS GRACIOUSLY CHOSEN TO LOOK THE OTHER WAY.
THIS WOULD BE EASIER TO FOLLOW IF YOU SAID HE SNIFFED OUT YOUR SECRET, AND YOU BRIBED HIM TO KEEP QUIET.
FORGIVE ME...
YET NOW, SOMEHOW, THE SHOGUNATE HAS FOUND OUT ABOUT THE MINE. WE'VE CLOSED THE SHAFT AND DESTROYED EVERY SCRAP OF EVIDENCE... AND YET...
THE *DAI-METSUKE* IN EDO TOOK ACTION...

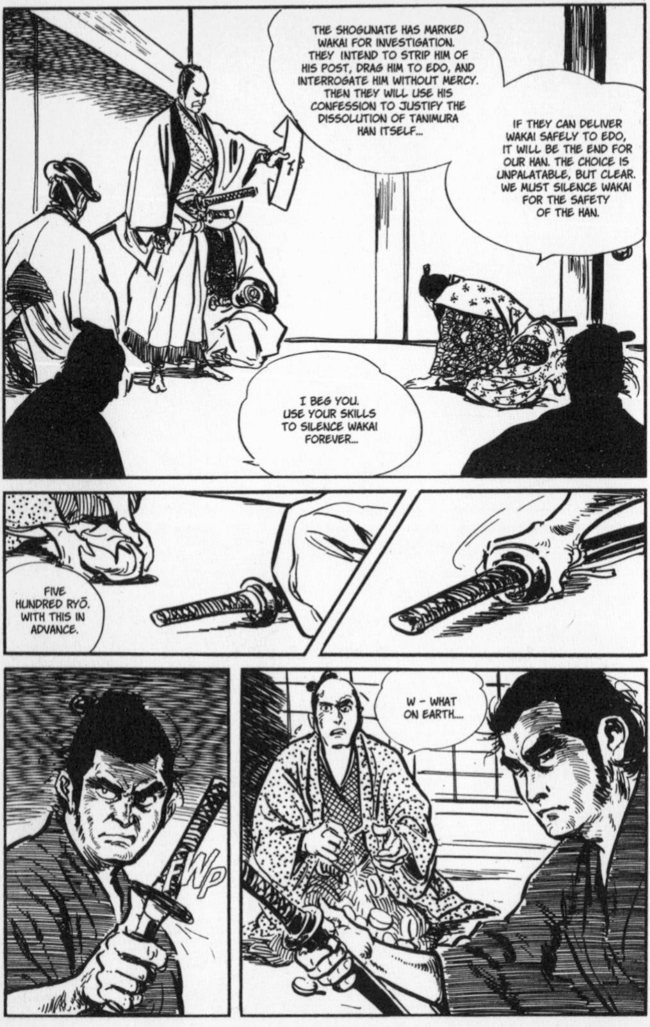

THE SHOGUNATE HAS MARKED WAKAI FOR INVESTIGATION. THEY INTEND TO STRIP HIM OF HIS POST, DRAG HIM TO EDO, AND INTERROGATE HIM WITHOUT MERCY. THEN THEY WILL USE HIS CONFESSION TO JUSTIFY THE DISSOLUTION OF TANIMURA HAN ITSELF...
IF THEY CAN DELIVER WAKAI SAFELY TO EDO, IT WILL BE THE END FOR OUR HAN. THE CHOICE IS UNPALATABLE, BUT CLEAR. WE MUST SILENCE WAKAI FOR THE SAFETY OF THE HAN.
I BEG YOU. USE YOUR SKILLS TO SILENCE WAKAI FOREVER...
FIVE HUNDRED RYŌ. WITH THIS IN ADVANCE.
FWP
W - WHAT ON EARTH...

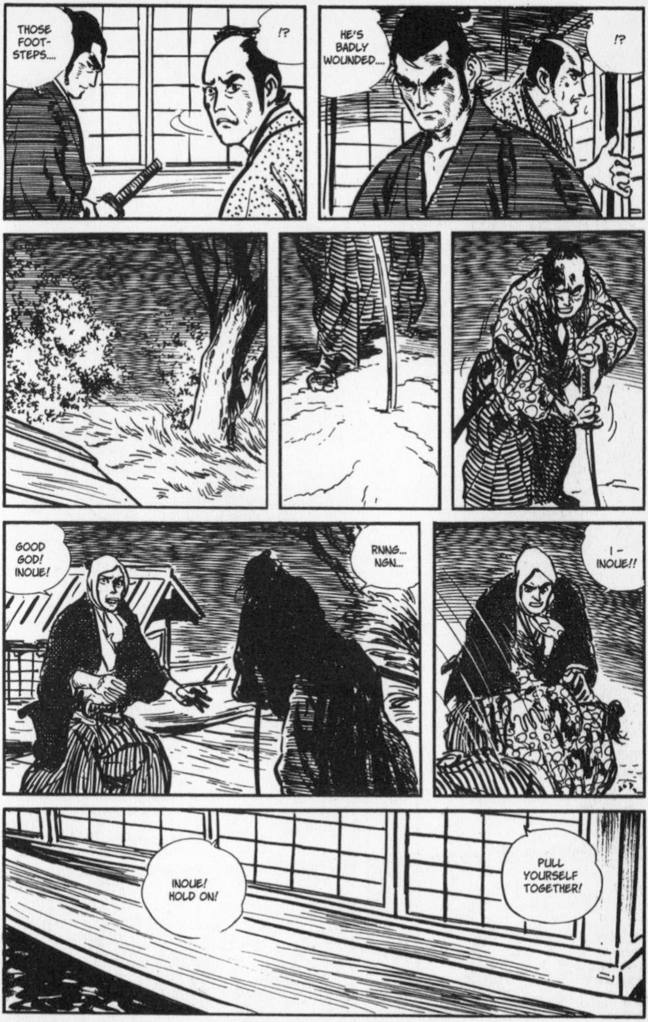
THOSE FOOT-STEPS....
!?
HE'S BADLY WOUNDED....
!?
GOOD GOD! INOUE!
RNNG... NGN...
I- INOUE!!
INOUE! HOLD ON!
PULL YOURSELF TOGETHER!

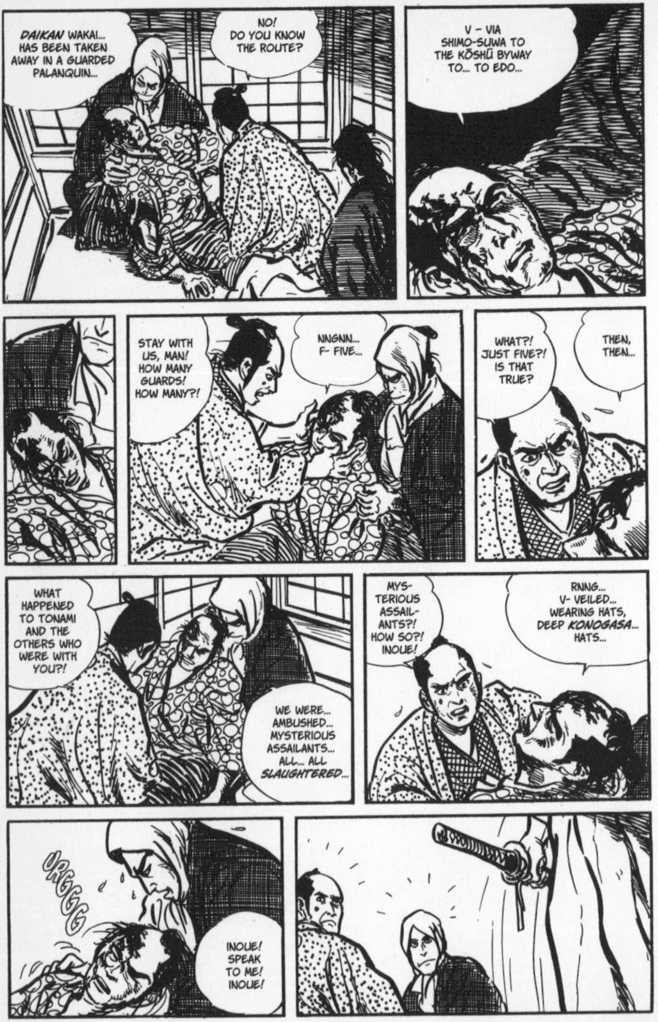

DAIKAN WAKAI... HAS BEEN TAKEN AWAY IN A GUARDED PALANQUIN...
NO! DO YOU KNOW THE ROUTE?
V – VIA SHIMO-SUWA TO THE KŌSHŪ BYWAY TO... TO EDO...
STAY WITH US, MAN! HOW MANY GUARDS! HOW MANY?!
NNGNN... F- FIVE...
WHAT?! JUST FIVE?! IS THAT TRUE?
THEN, THEN...
WHAT HAPPENED TO TONAMI AND THE OTHERS WHO WERE WITH YOU?!
WE WERE... AMBUSHED... MYSTERIOUS ASSAILANTS... ALL... ALL *SLAUGHTERED*...
MYS-TERIOUS ASSAIL-ANTS?! HOW SO?! INOUE!
RNNG... V- VEILED... WEARING HATS, DEEP *KONOGASA*... HATS...
URGGG
INOUE! SPEAK TO ME! INOUE!

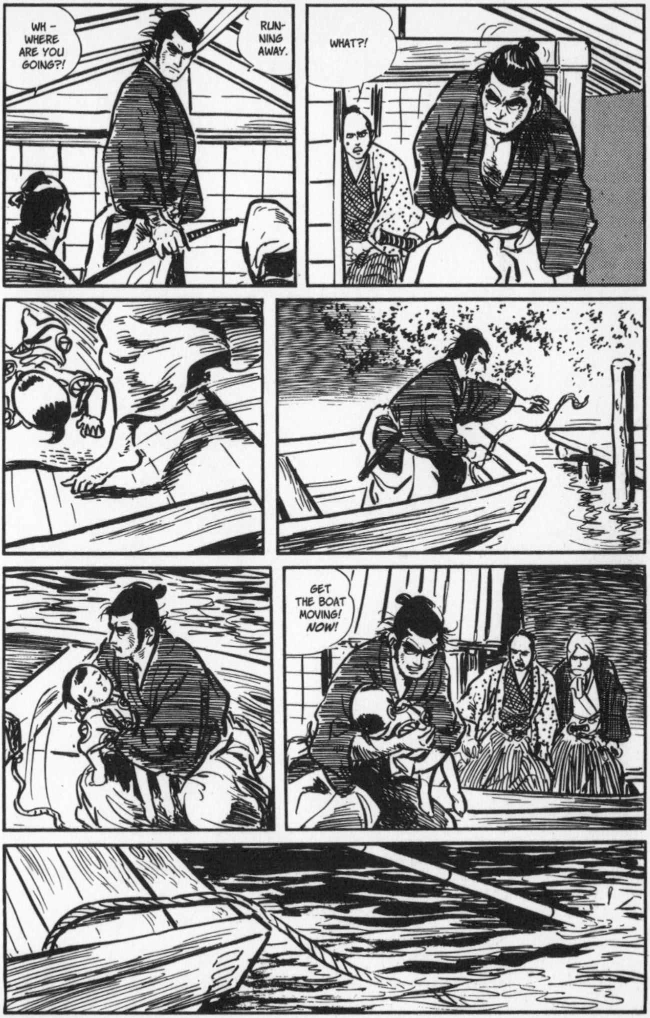
WH - WHERE ARE YOU GOING?!
RUN-NING AWAY.
WHAT?!
GET THE BOAT MOVING! *NOW!*

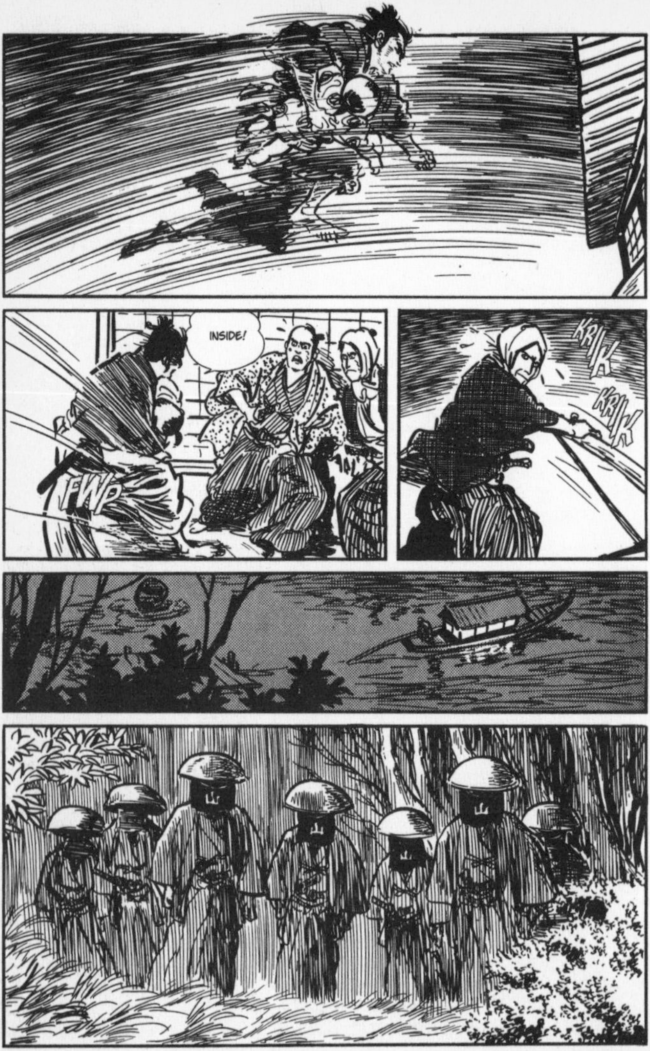
INSIDE!
FWP
KRIK
KRIK

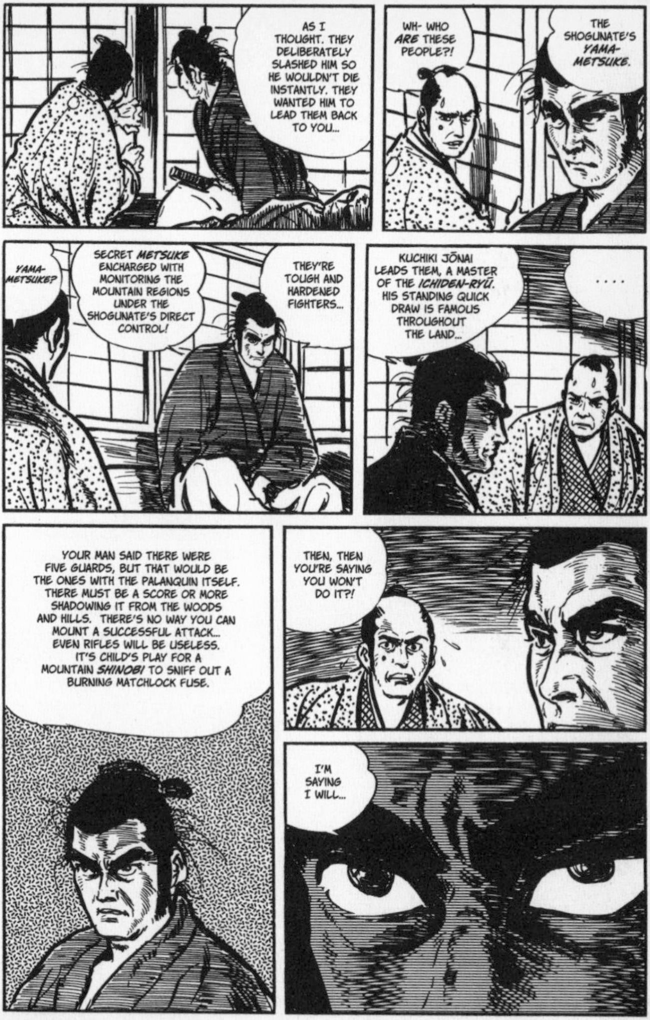
AS I THOUGHT. THEY DELIBERATELY SLASHED HIM SO HE WOULDN'T DIE INSTANTLY. THEY WANTED HIM TO LEAD THEM BACK TO YOU...
WH- WHO *ARE* THESE PEOPLE?!
THE SHOGUNATE'S *YAMA-METSUKE.*
YAMA-METSUKE?
SECRET *METSUKE* ENCHARGED WITH MONITORING THE MOUNTAIN REGIONS UNDER THE SHOGUNATE'S DIRECT CONTROL!
THEY'RE TOUGH AND HARDENED FIGHTERS...
KUCHIKI JŌNAI LEADS THEM, A MASTER OF THE *ICHIDEN-RYŪ.* HIS STANDING QUICK DRAW IS FAMOUS THROUGHOUT THE LAND...
. . . .
YOUR MAN SAID THERE WERE FIVE GUARDS, BUT THAT WOULD BE THE ONES WITH THE PALANQUIN ITSELF. THERE MUST BE A SCORE OR MORE SHADOWING IT FROM THE WOODS AND HILLS. THERE'S NO WAY YOU CAN MOUNT A SUCCESSFUL ATTACK... EVEN RIFLES WILL BE USELESS. IT'S CHILD'S PLAY FOR A MOUNTAIN *SHINOBI* TO SNIFF OUT A BURNING MATCHLOCK FUSE.
THEN, THEN YOU'RE SAYING YOU WON'T DO IT?!
I'M SAYING I WILL...

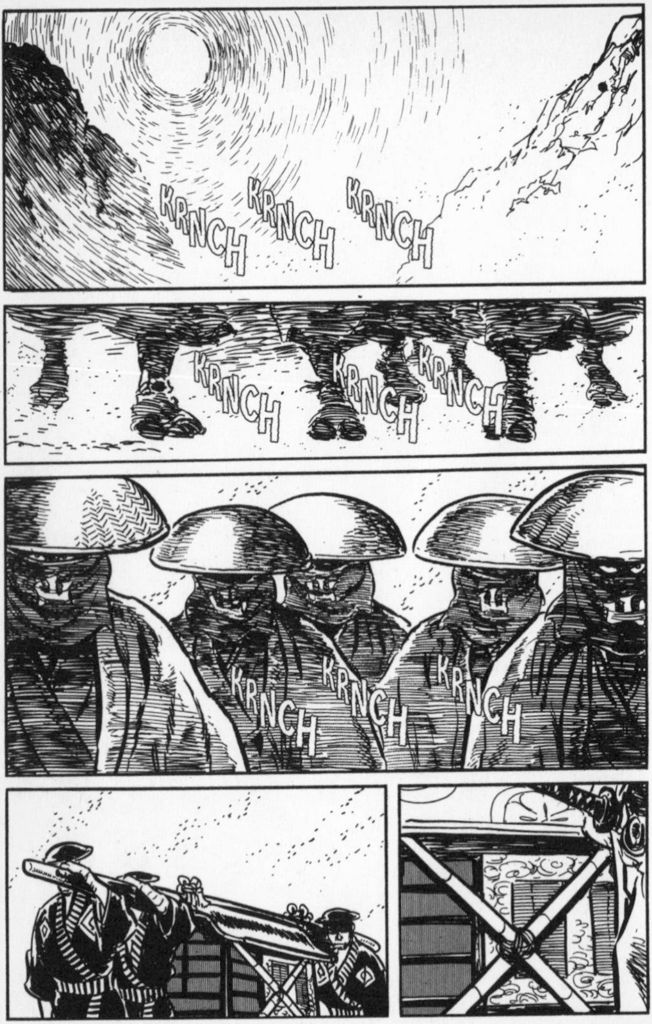
KRNCH
KRNCH
KRNCH
KRNCH
KRNCH
KRNCH
KRNCH
KRNCH
KRNCH

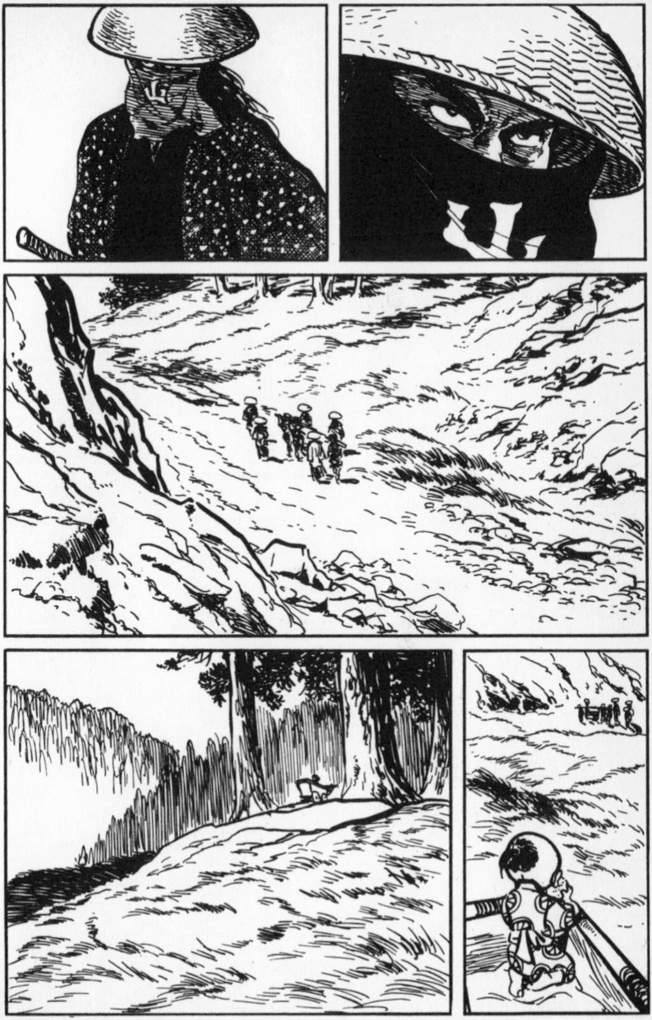

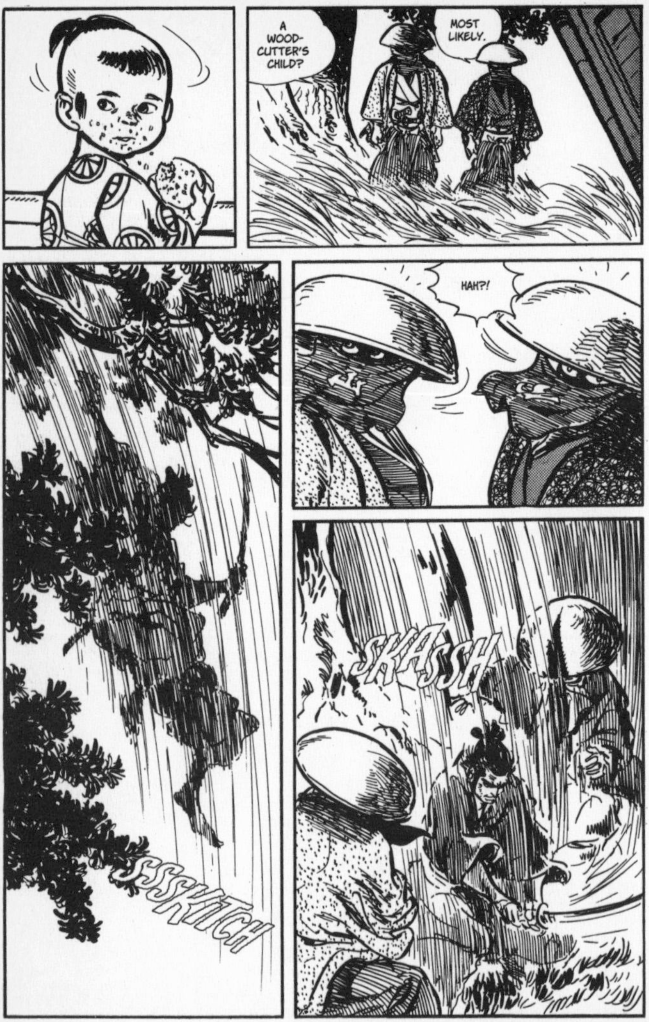

A WOOD-CUTTER'S CHILD?
MOST LIKELY.
SSSKTCH
HAH?!
SKASH

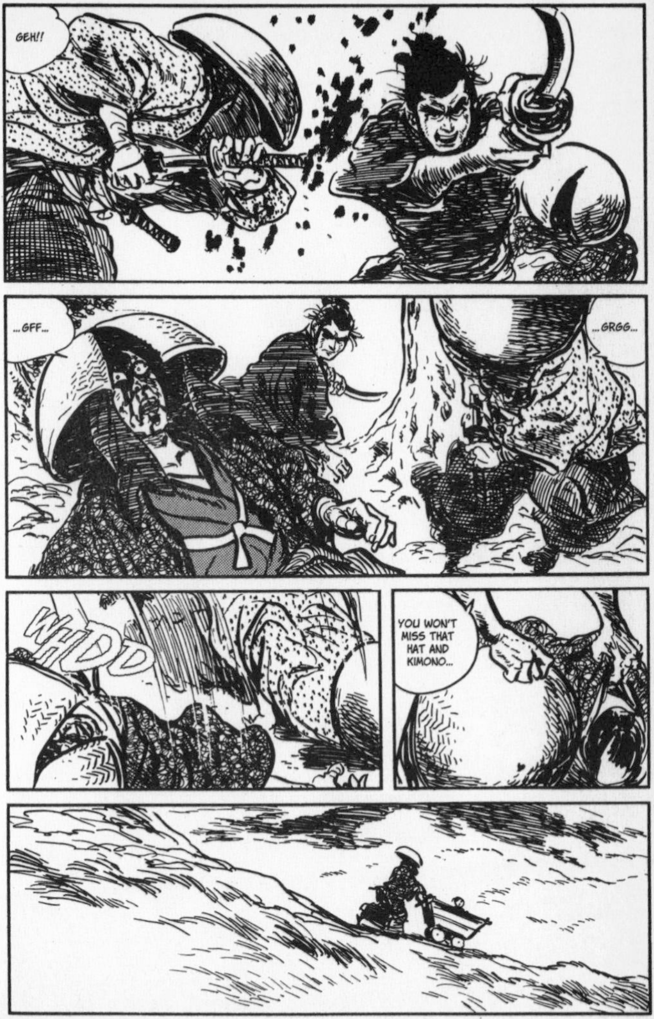
GEH!!
...GFF...
...GRGG...
WHDD
YOU WON'T MISS THAT HAT AND KIMONO...

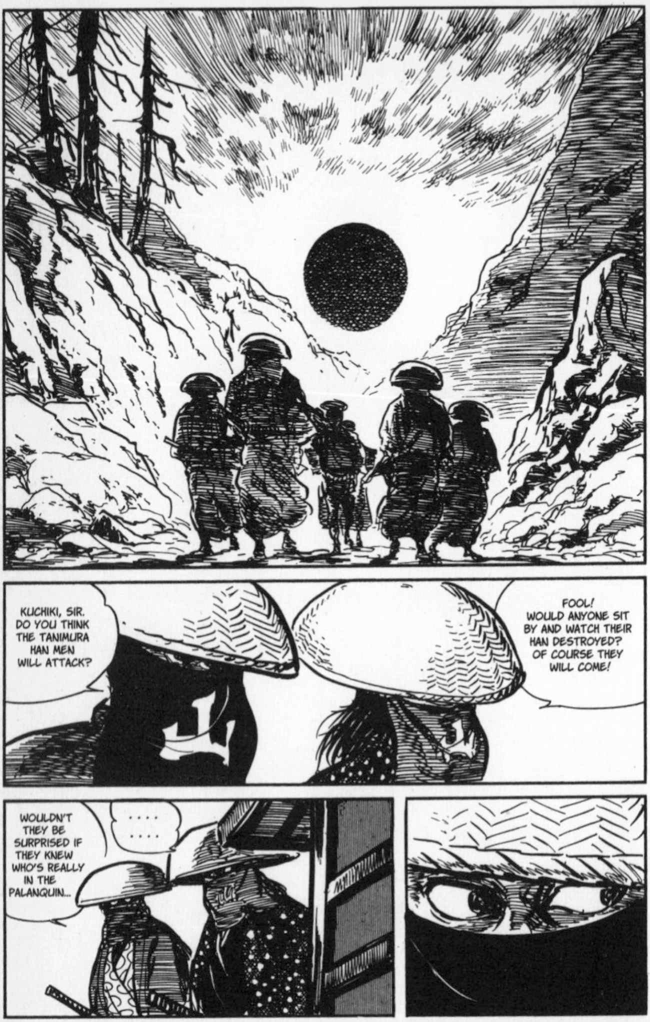
KUCHIKI, SIR. DO YOU THINK THE TANIMURA HAN MEN WILL ATTACK?
FOOL! WOULD ANYONE SIT BY AND WATCH THEIR HAN DESTROYED? OF COURSE THEY WILL COME!
WOULDN'T THEY BE SURPRISED IF THEY KNEW WHO'S REALLY IN THE PALANQUIN...
....
....

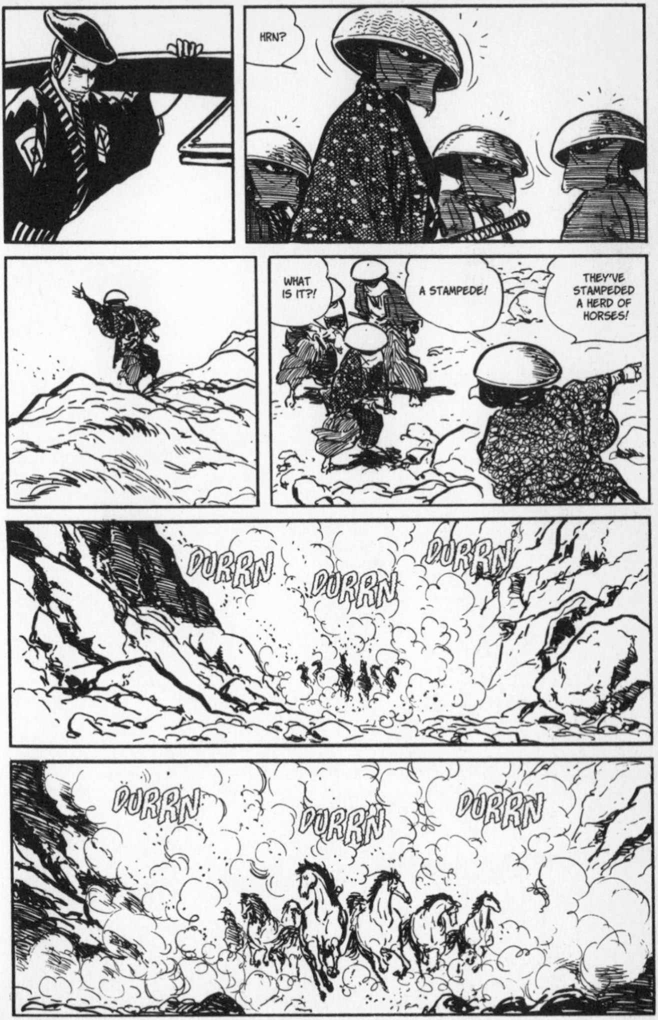
HRN?
WHAT IS IT?!
A STAMPEDE!
THEY'VE STAMPEDED A HERD OF HORSES!
DURRN
DURRN
DURRN
DURRN
DURRN
DURRN

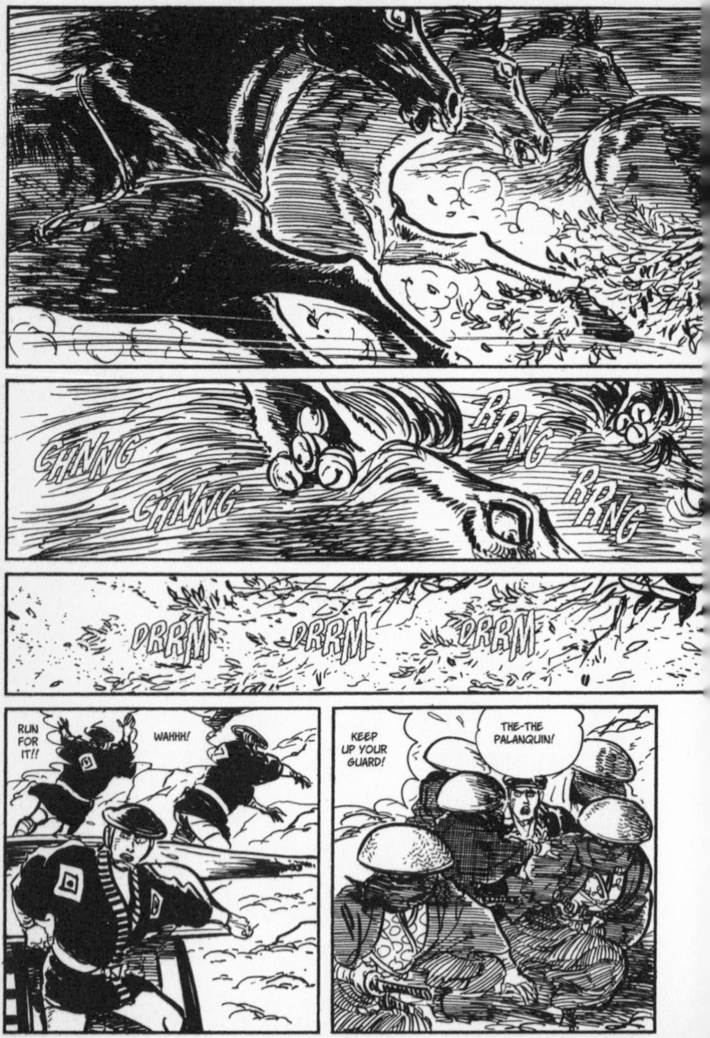

CHNNG
CHNNG
RRNG
RRNG
DRRM
DRRM
DRRM
RUN FOR IT!!
WAHHH!
KEEP UP YOUR GUARD!
THE-THE PALANQUIN!

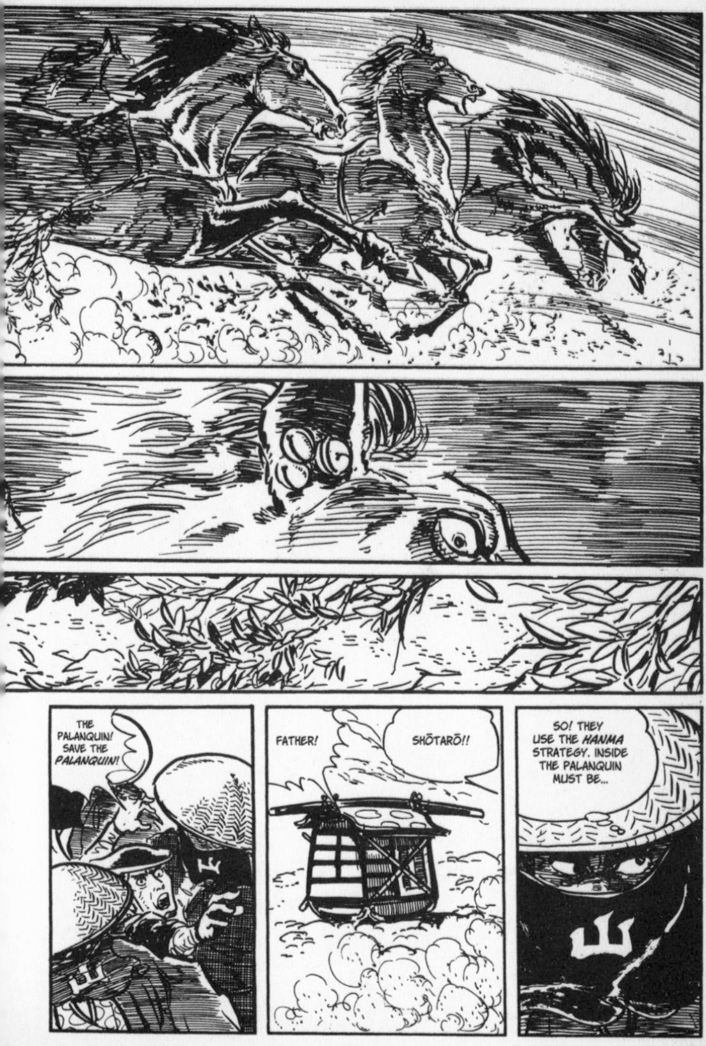
THE PALANQUIN! SAVE THE *PALANQUIN!*
FATHER!
SHŌTARŌ!!
SO! THEY USE THE *HANMA* STRATEGY. INSIDE THE PALANQUIN MUST BE...

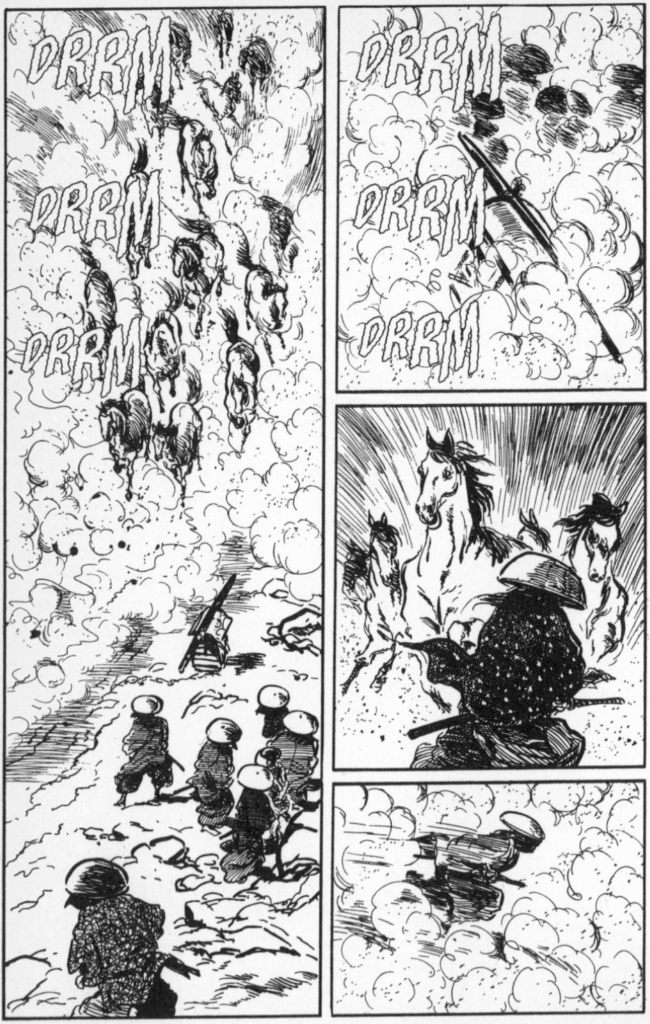
DRRM
DRRM
DRRM
DRRM
DRRM
DRRM

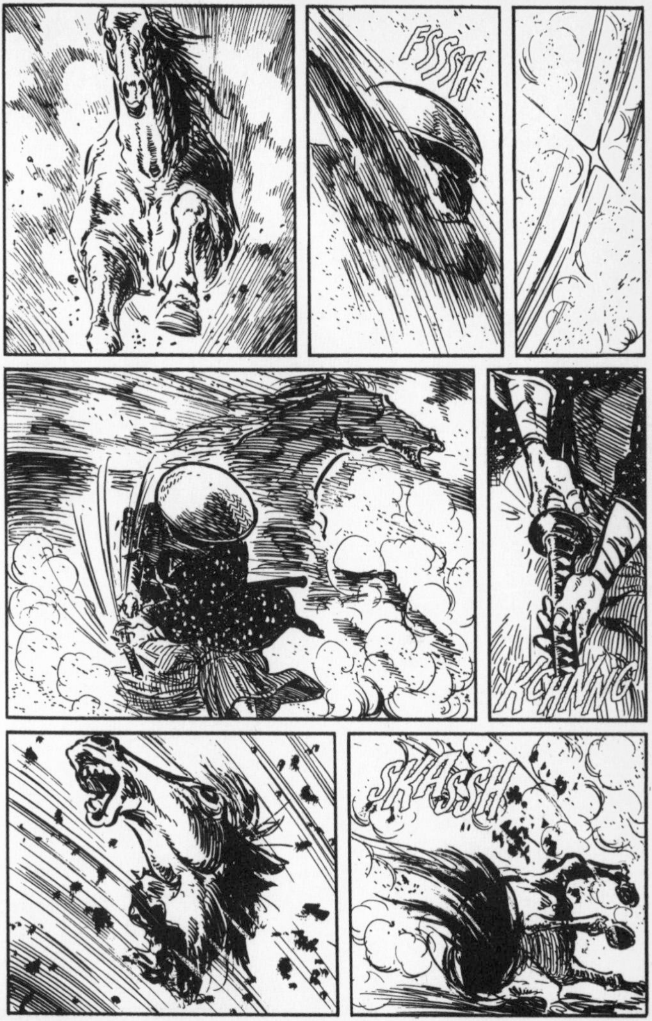
FSSSH
KCHNNG
SKASSH

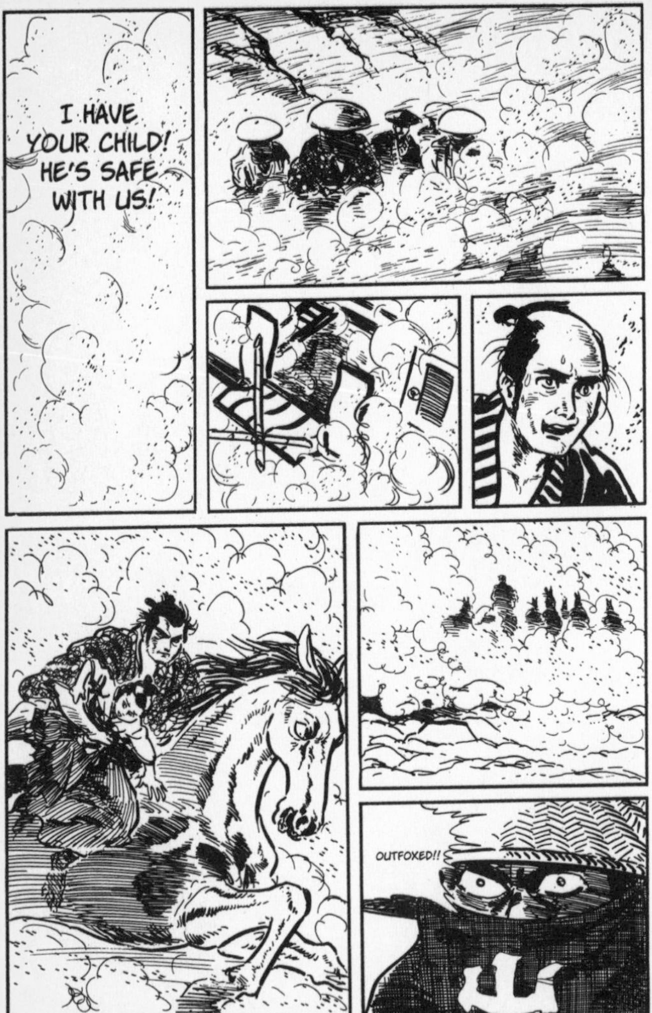
I HAVE YOUR CHILD! HE'S SAFE WITH US!
OUTFOXED!!

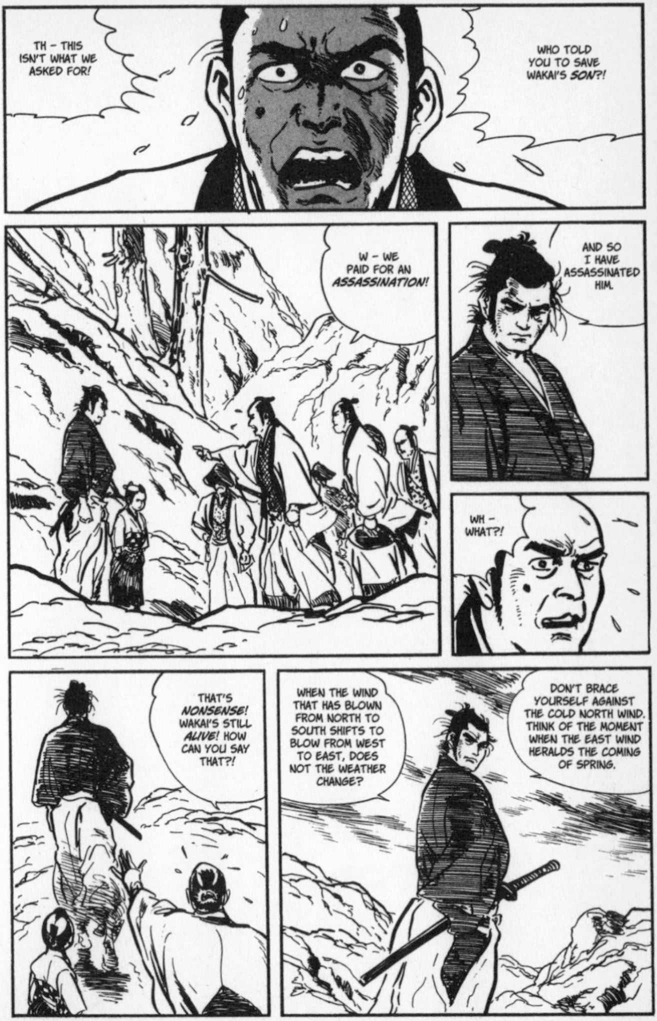
TH - THIS ISN'T WHAT WE ASKED FOR!
WHO TOLD YOU TO SAVE WAKAI'S *SON*?!
W - WE PAID FOR AN *ASSASSINATION*!
AND SO I HAVE ASSASSINATED HIM.
WH - WHAT?!
THAT'S *NONSENSE*! WAKAI'S STILL *ALIVE*! HOW CAN YOU SAY THAT?!
WHEN THE WIND THAT HAS BLOWN FROM NORTH TO SOUTH SHIFTS TO BLOW FROM WEST TO EAST, DOES NOT THE WEATHER CHANGE?
DON'T BRACE YOURSELF AGAINST THE COLD NORTH WIND. THINK OF THE MOMENT WHEN THE EAST WIND HERALDS THE COMING OF SPRING.

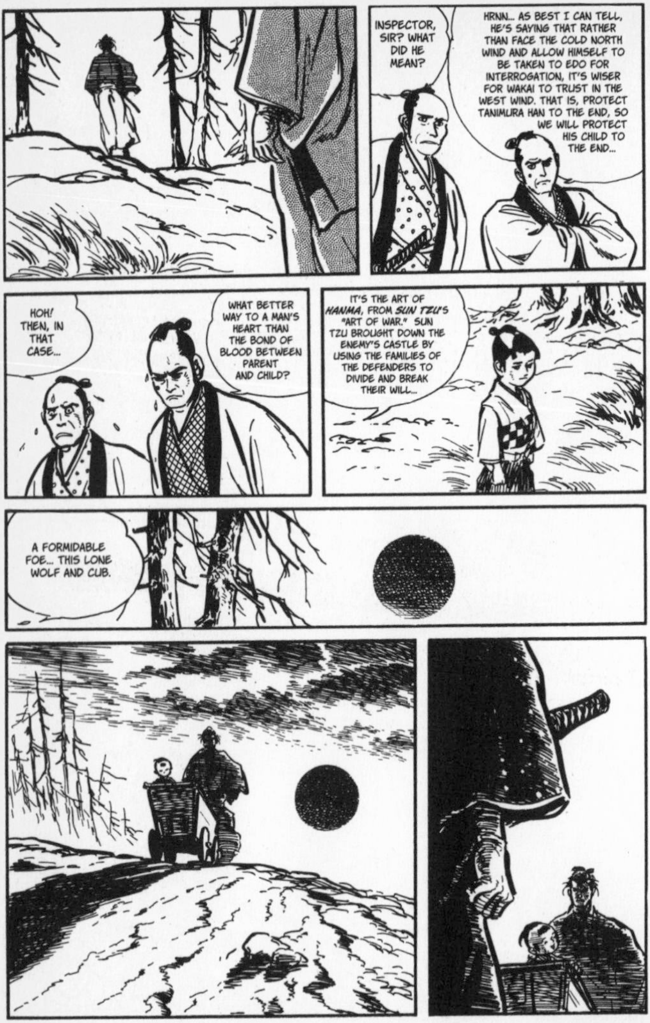
INSPECTOR, SIR? WHAT DID HE MEAN?
HRNN... AS BEST I CAN TELL, HE'S SAYING THAT RATHER THAN FACE THE COLD NORTH WIND AND ALLOW HIMSELF TO BE TAKEN TO EDO FOR INTERROGATION, IT'S WISER FOR WAKAI TO TRUST IN THE WEST WIND. THAT IS, PROTECT TANIMURA HAN TO THE END, SO WE WILL PROTECT HIS CHILD TO THE END...
HOH! THEN, IN THAT CASE...
WHAT BETTER WAY TO A MAN'S HEART THAN THE BOND OF BLOOD BETWEEN PARENT AND CHILD?
IT'S THE ART OF *HANMA*, FROM *SUN TZU*'S "ART OF WAR." SUN TZU BROUGHT DOWN THE ENEMY'S CASTLE BY USING THE FAMILIES OF THE DEFENDERS TO DIVIDE AND BREAK THEIR WILL...
A FORMIDABLE FOE... THIS LONE WOLF AND CUB.

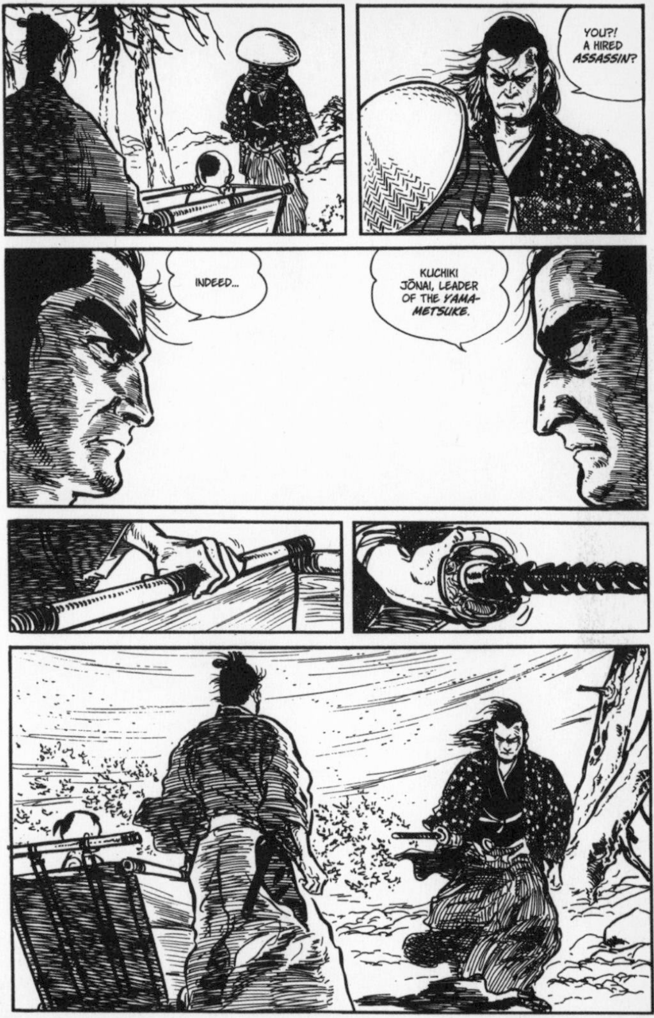
YOU?! A HIRED ASSASSIN?
INDEED...
KUCHIKI JŌNAI, LEADER OF THE YAMA-METSUKE.

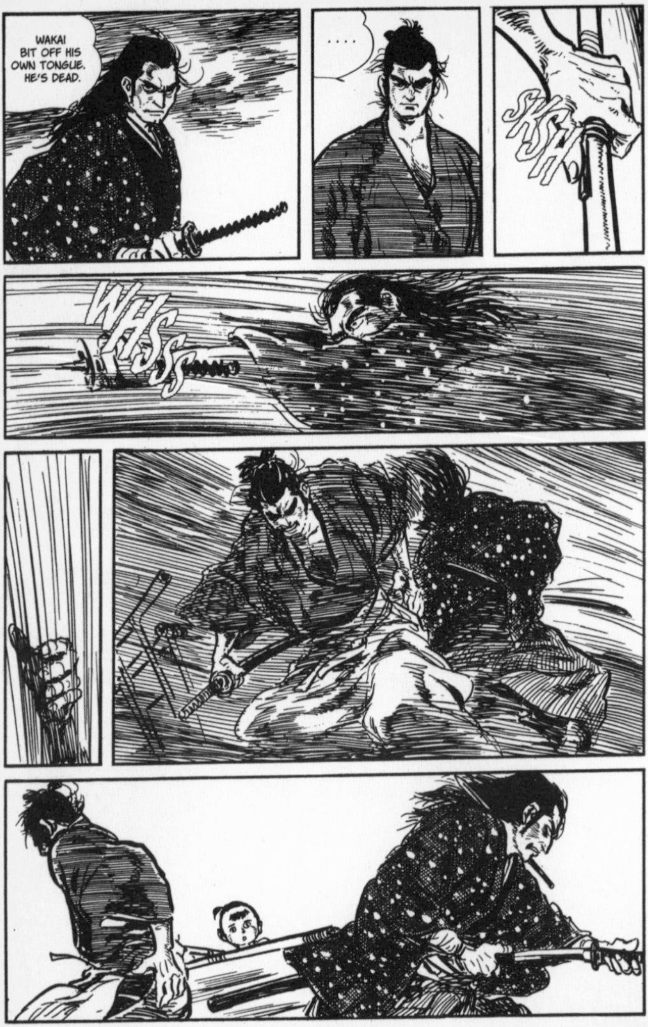
WAKAI BIT OFF HIS OWN TONGUE. HE'S DEAD.
....
SKSH
WHSSS

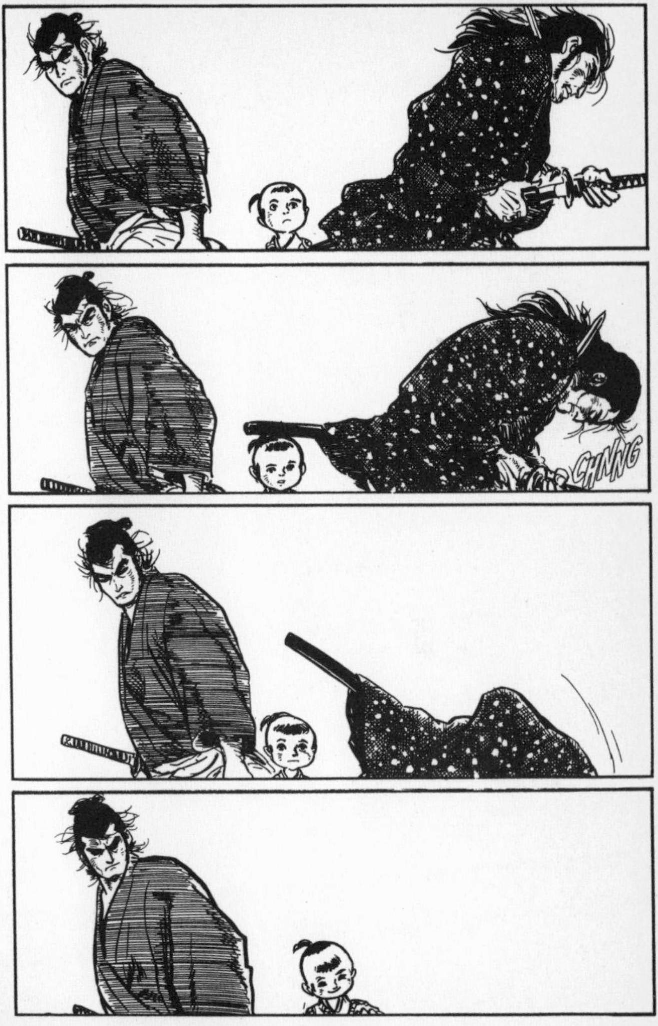
CHNNG

the fourth

Baby Cart on the River Styx

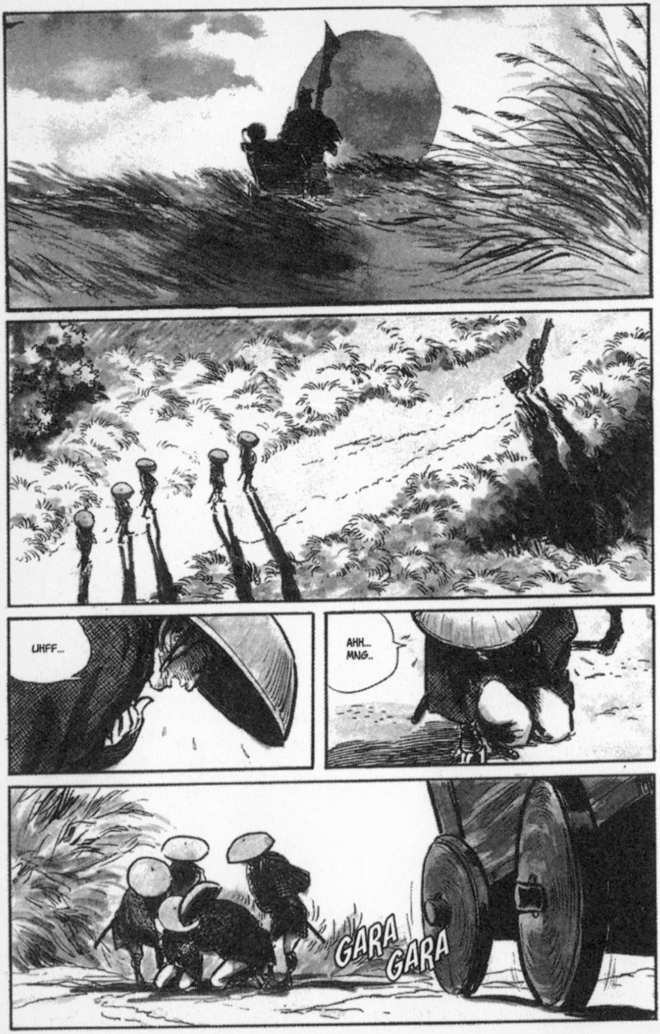
UHFF...
AHH... MNG..
GARA GARA

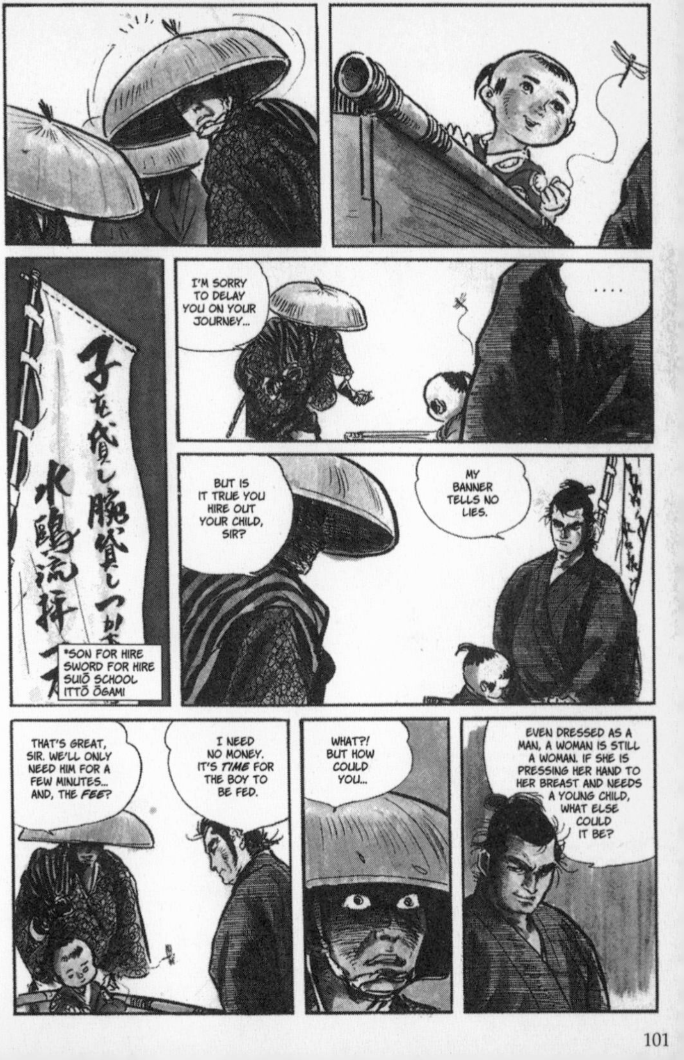

I'M SORRY TO DELAY YOU ON YOUR JOURNEY...
....
*SON FOR HIRE SWORD FOR HIRE SUIŌ SCHOOL ITTŌ ŌGAMI
BUT IS IT TRUE YOU HIRE OUT YOUR CHILD, SIR?
MY BANNER TELLS NO LIES.
THAT'S GREAT, SIR. WE'LL ONLY NEED HIM FOR A FEW MINUTES... AND, THE *FEE*?
I NEED NO MONEY. IT'S *TIME* FOR THE BOY TO BE FED.
WHAT?! BUT HOW COULD YOU...
EVEN DRESSED AS A MAN, A WOMAN IS STILL A WOMAN. IF SHE IS PRESSING HER HAND TO HER BREAST AND NEEDS A YOUNG CHILD, WHAT ELSE COULD IT BE?

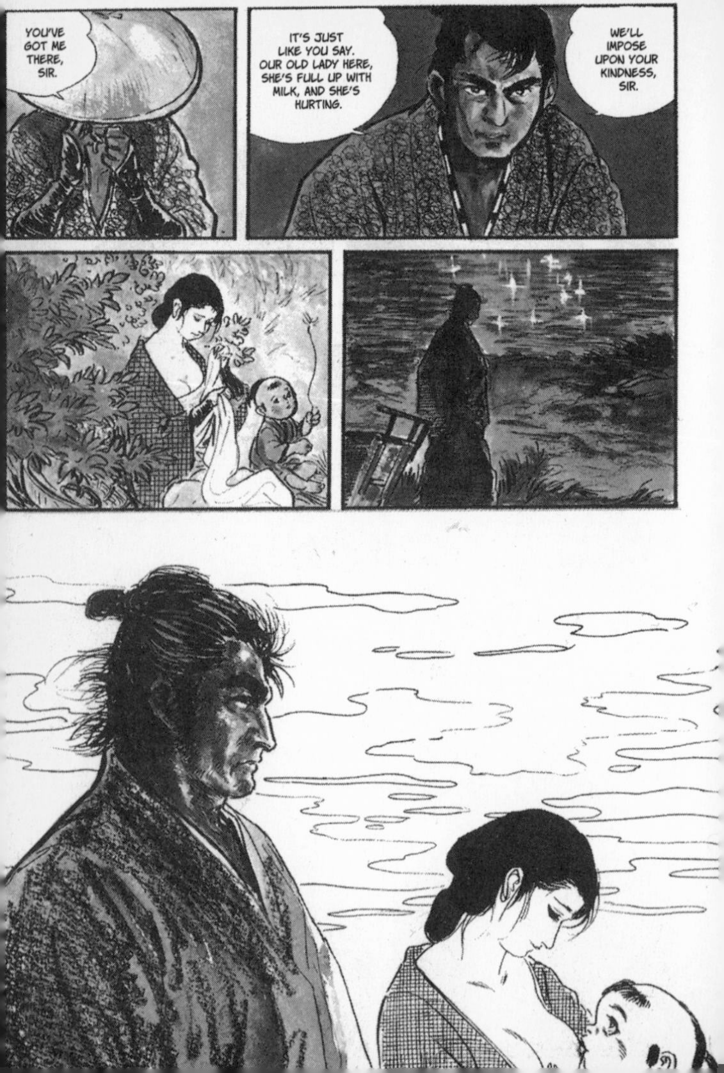
YOU'VE GOT ME THERE, SIR.
IT'S JUST LIKE YOU SAY. OUR OLD LADY HERE, SHE'S FULL UP WITH MILK, AND SHE'S HURTING.
WE'LL IMPOSE UPON YOUR KINDNESS, SIR.

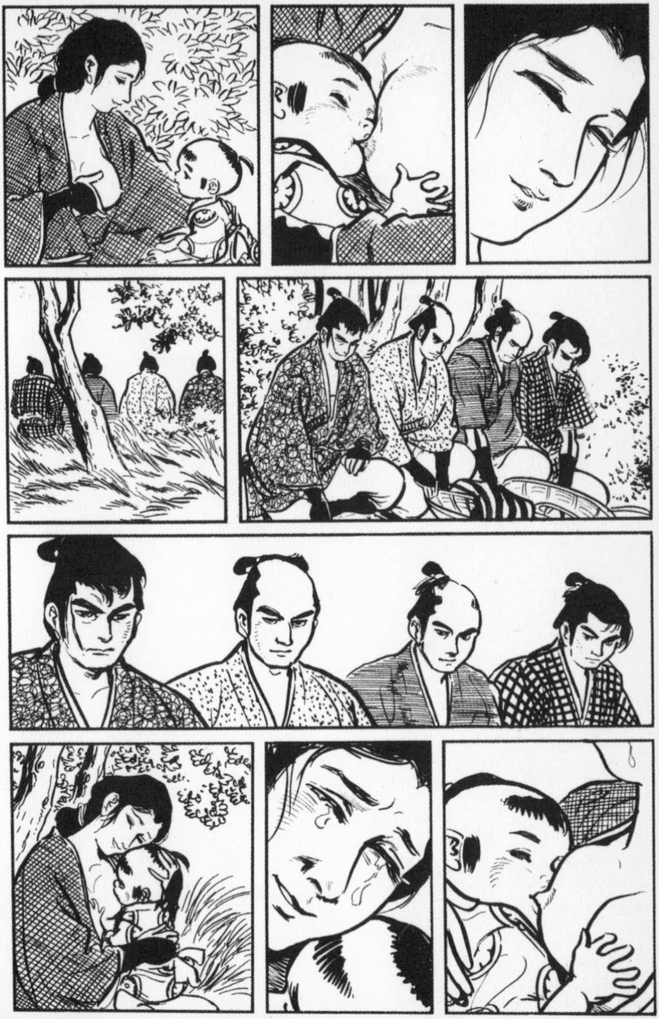

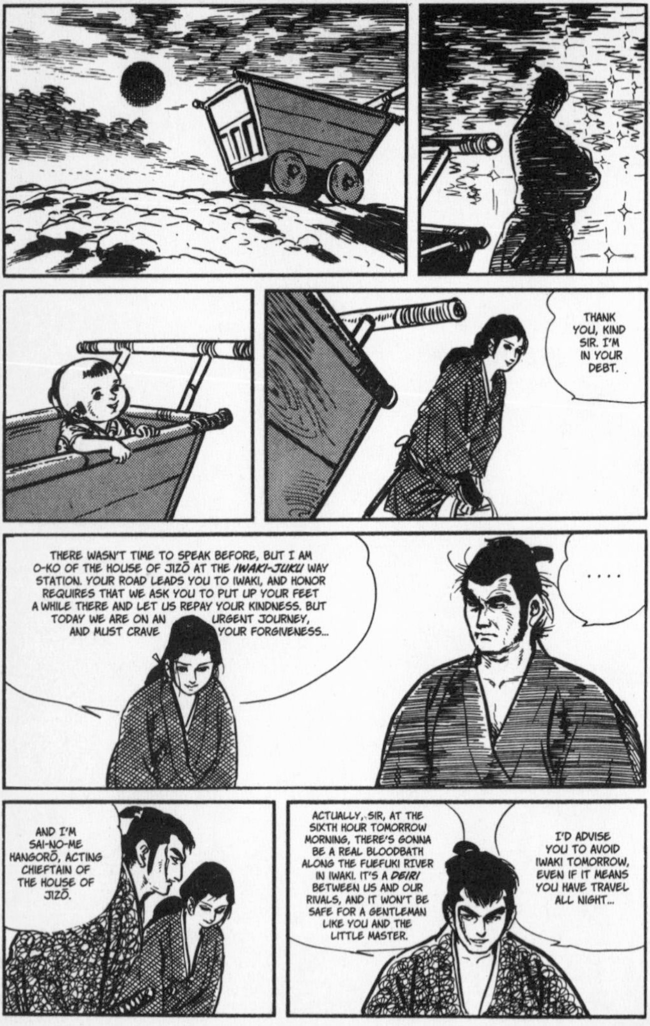
THANK YOU, KIND SIR. I'M IN YOUR DEBT.
THERE WASN'T TIME TO SPEAK BEFORE, BUT I AM O-KO OF THE HOUSE OF JIZŌ AT THE *IWAKI-JUKU* WAY STATION. YOUR ROAD LEADS YOU TO IWAKI, AND HONOR REQUIRES THAT WE ASK YOU TO PUT UP YOUR FEET A WHILE THERE AND LET US REPAY YOUR KINDNESS. BUT TODAY WE ARE ON AN URGENT JOURNEY, AND MUST CRAVE YOUR FORGIVENESS...
. . . .
AND I'M SAI-NO-ME HANGORŌ, ACTING CHIEFTAIN OF THE HOUSE OF JIZŌ.
ACTUALLY, SIR, AT THE SIXTH HOUR TOMORROW MORNING, THERE'S GONNA BE A REAL BLOODBATH ALONG THE FUEFUKI RIVER IN IWAKI. IT'S A *DEIRI* BETWEEN US AND OUR RIVALS, AND IT WON'T BE SAFE FOR A GENTLEMAN LIKE YOU AND THE LITTLE MASTER.
I'D ADVISE YOU TO AVOID IWAKI TOMORROW, EVEN IF IT MEANS YOU HAVE TRAVEL ALL NIGHT...

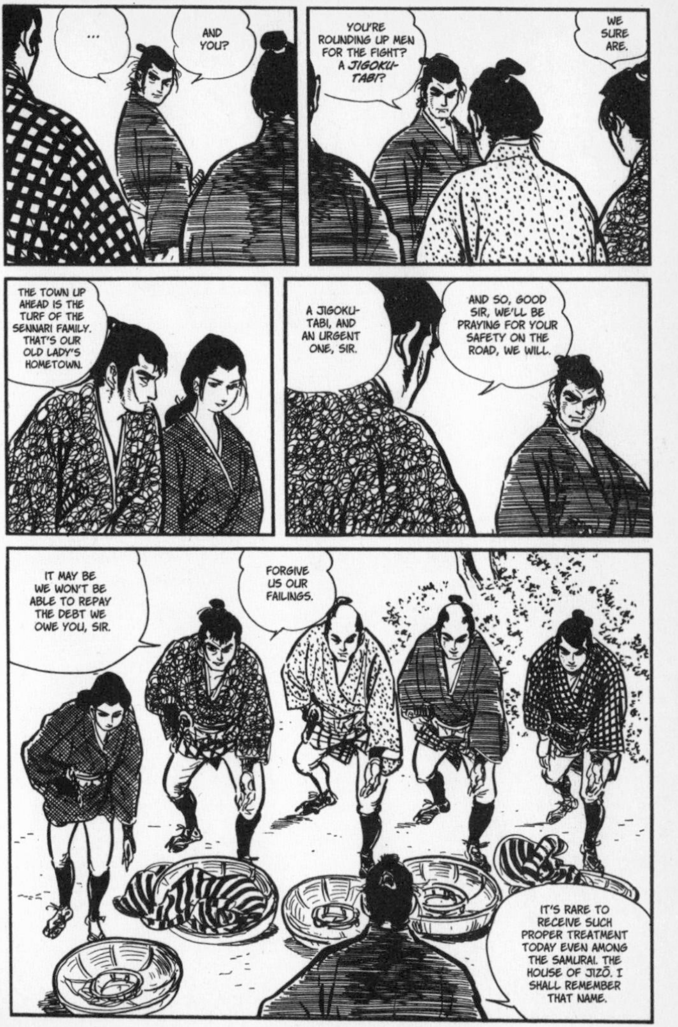
...
AND YOU?
YOU'RE ROUNDING UP MEN FOR THE FIGHT? A *JIGOKU-TABI*?
WE SURE ARE.
THE TOWN UP AHEAD IS THE TURF OF THE SENNARI FAMILY. THAT'S OUR OLD LADY'S HOMETOWN.
A JIGOKU-TABI, AND AN URGENT ONE, SIR.
AND SO, GOOD SIR, WE'LL BE PRAYING FOR YOUR SAFETY ON THE ROAD, WE WILL.
IT MAY BE WE WON'T BE ABLE TO REPAY THE DEBT WE OWE YOU, SIR.
FORGIVE US OUR FAILINGS.
IT'S RARE TO RECEIVE SUCH PROPER TREATMENT TODAY EVEN AMONG THE SAMURAI. THE HOUSE OF JIZŌ. I SHALL REMEMBER THAT NAME.

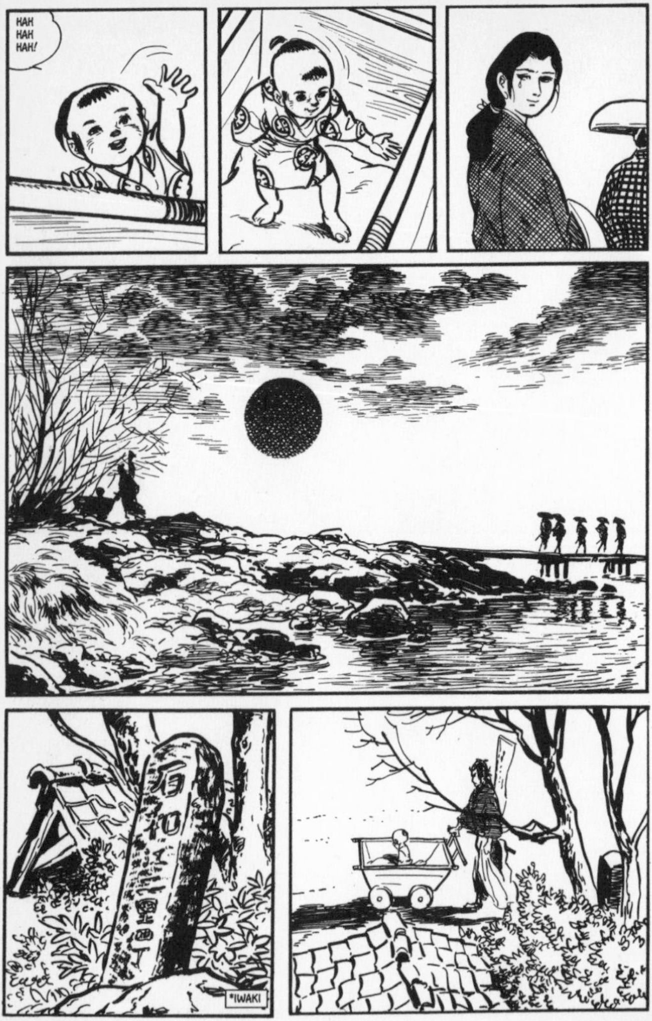
HAH HAH HAH!
*IWAKI

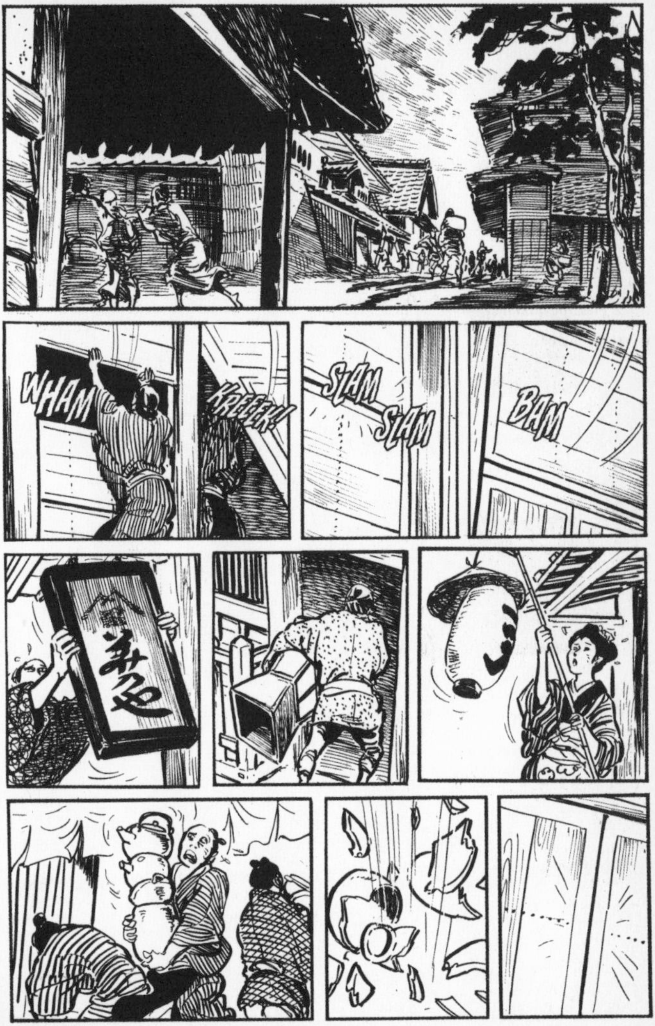
WHAM
KREEEK!
SLAM
SLAM
BAM

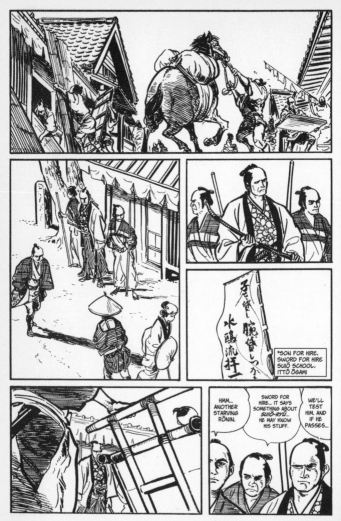

*SON FOR HIRE, SWORD FOR HIRE SUIŌ SCHOOL, ITTŌ ŌGAMI

HMM... ANOTHER STARVING RŌNIN.

SWORD FOR HIRE... IT SAYS SOMETHING ABOUT *SUIŌ-RYŪ*... HE MAY KNOW HIS STUFF.

WE'LL TEST HIM AND IF HE PASSES...

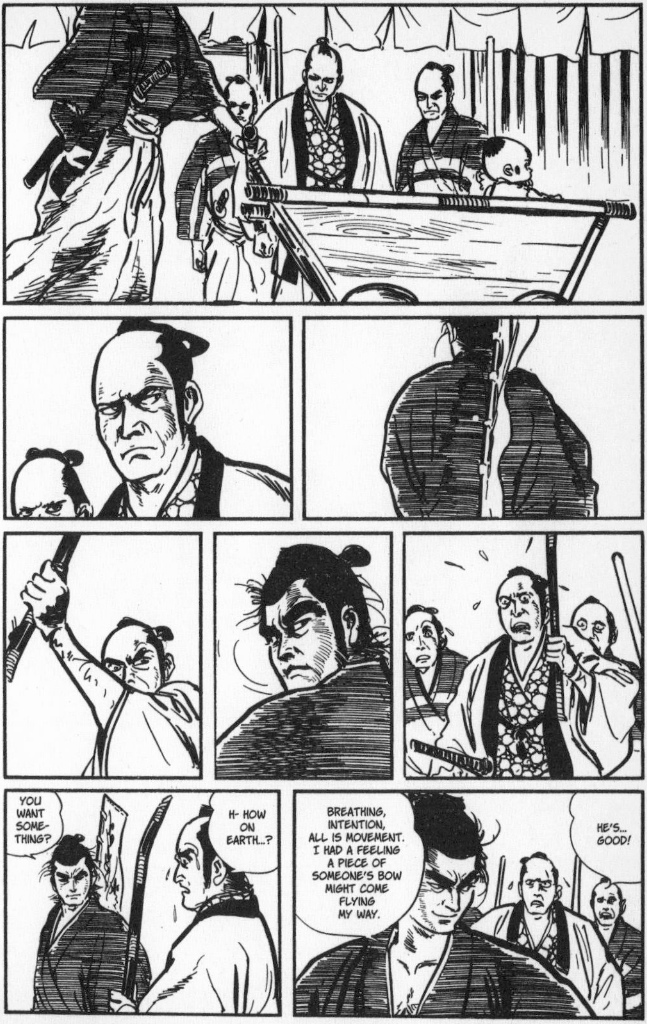
YOU WANT SOME-THING?
H- HOW ON EARTH...?
BREATHING, INTENTION, ALL IS MOVEMENT. I HAD A FEELING A PIECE OF SOMEONE'S BOW MIGHT COME FLYING MY WAY.
HE'S... GOOD!

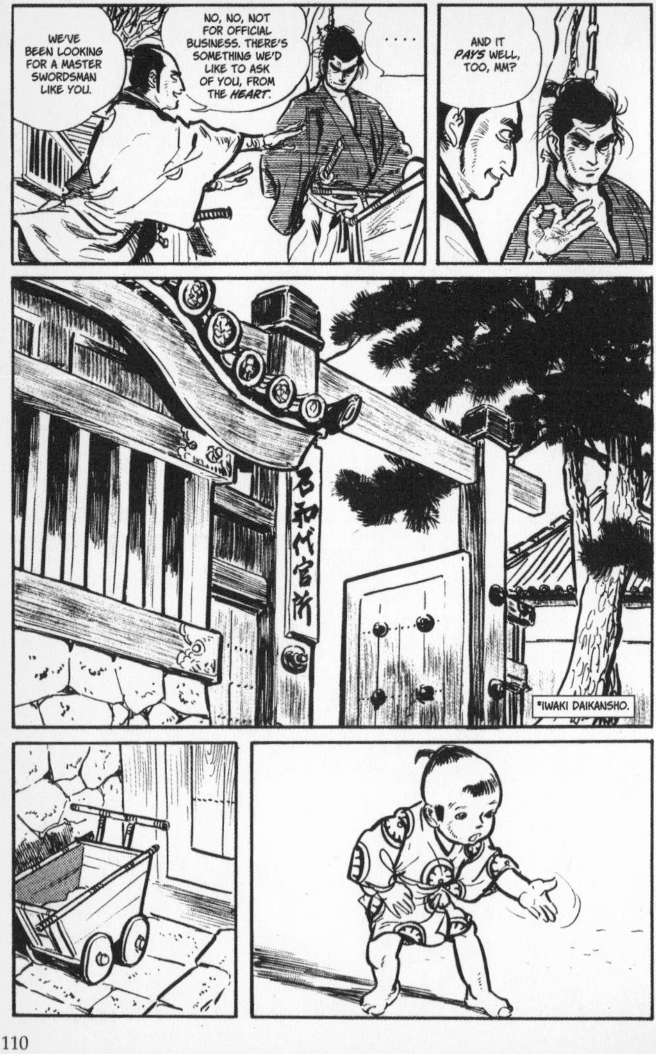
WE'VE BEEN LOOKING FOR A MASTER SWORDSMAN LIKE YOU.
NO, NO, NOT FOR OFFICIAL BUSINESS. THERE'S SOMETHING WE'D LIKE TO ASK OF YOU, FROM THE *HEART*.
....
AND IT *PAYS* WELL, TOO, MM?
*IWAKI DAIKANSHO.

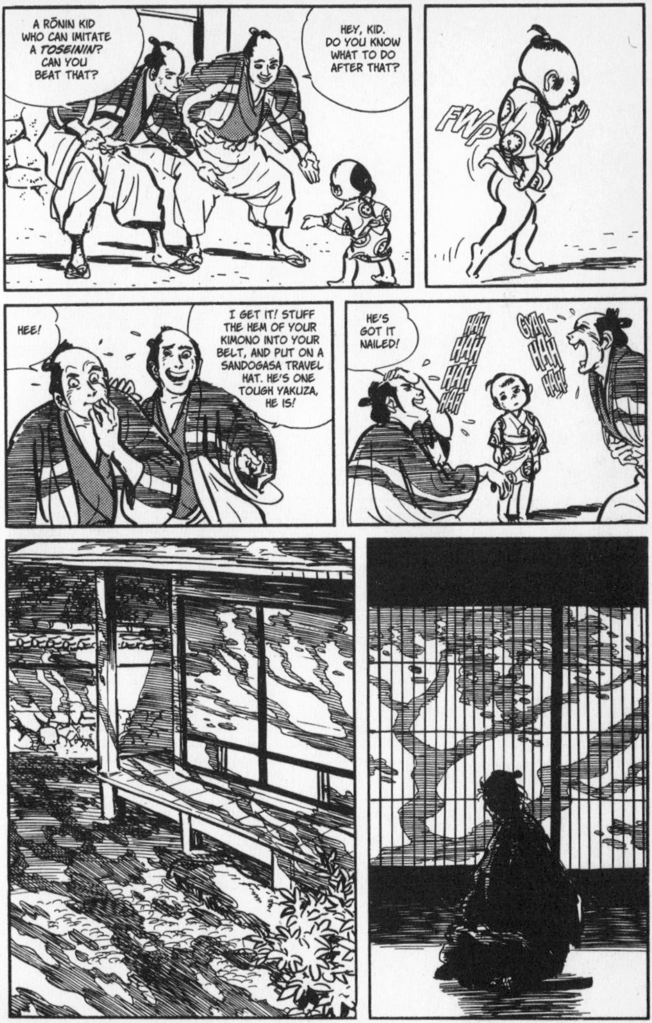
A RŌNIN KID WHO CAN IMITATE A *TOSEININ*? CAN YOU BEAT THAT?
HEY, KID. DO YOU KNOW WHAT TO DO AFTER THAT?
FWP
HEE!
I GET IT! STUFF THE HEM OF YOUR KIMONO INTO YOUR BELT, AND PUT ON A SANDOGASA TRAVEL HAT. HE'S ONE TOUGH YAKUZA, HE IS!
HE'S GOT IT NAILED!
HAH HAH HAH HAH HAH
GYAH HAH HAH

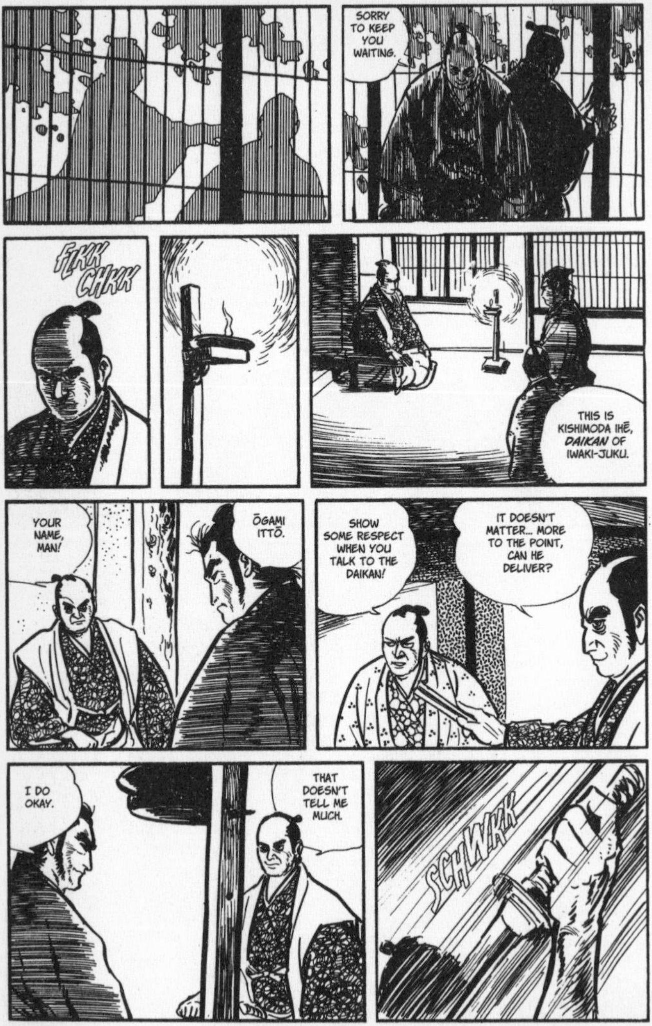
SORRY TO KEEP YOU WAITING.
FLKK CHKK
THIS IS KISHIMODA IHĒ, *DAIKAN* OF IWAKI-JUKU.
YOUR NAME, MAN!
ŌGAMI ITTŌ.
SHOW SOME RESPECT WHEN YOU TALK TO THE DAIKAN!
IT DOESN'T MATTER... MORE TO THE POINT, CAN HE DELIVER?
I DO OKAY.
THAT DOESN'T TELL ME MUCH.
SCHWKK

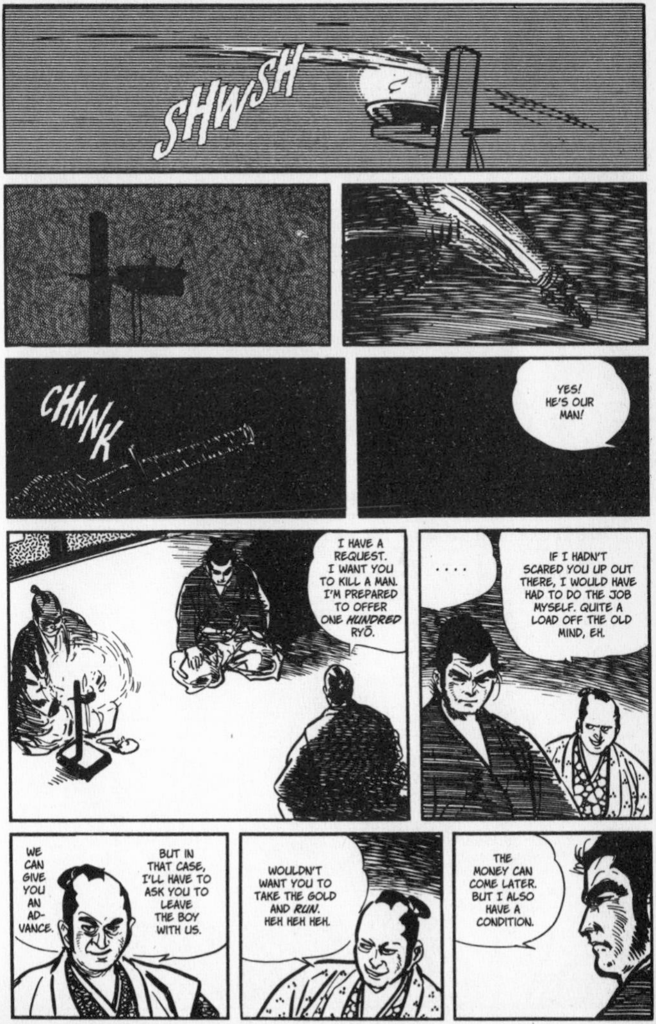
SHWSH
CHNNK
YES! HE'S OUR MAN!
I HAVE A REQUEST. I WANT YOU TO KILL A MAN. I'M PREPARED TO OFFER ONE HUNDRED RYŌ.
....
IF I HADN'T SCARED YOU UP OUT THERE, I WOULD HAVE HAD TO DO THE JOB MYSELF. QUITE A LOAD OFF THE OLD MIND, EH.
WE CAN GIVE YOU AN AD-VANCE.
BUT IN THAT CASE, I'LL HAVE TO ASK YOU TO LEAVE THE BOY WITH US.
WOULDN'T WANT YOU TO TAKE THE GOLD AND RUN. HEH HEH HEH.
THE MONEY CAN COME LATER. BUT I ALSO HAVE A CONDITION.

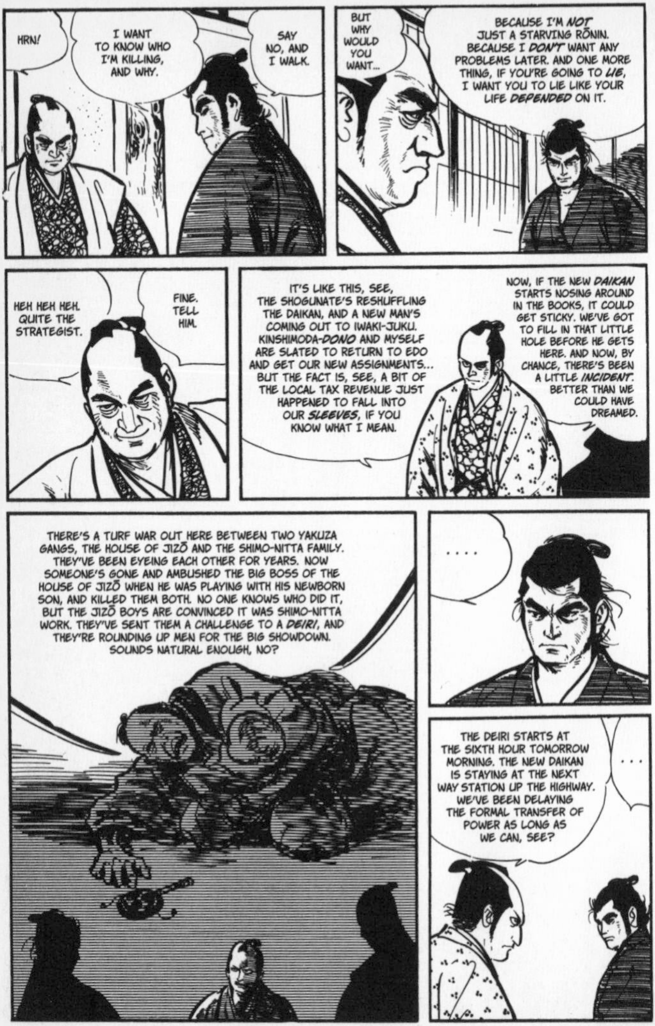
HRN!
I WANT TO KNOW WHO I'M KILLING, AND WHY.
SAY NO, AND I WALK.
BUT WHY WOULD YOU WANT...
BECAUSE I'M *NOT* JUST A STARVING RŌNIN. BECAUSE I *DON'T* WANT ANY PROBLEMS LATER. AND ONE MORE THING, IF YOU'RE GOING TO *LIE*, I WANT YOU TO LIE LIKE YOUR LIFE *DEPENDED* ON IT.
HEH HEH HEH. QUITE THE STRATEGIST.
FINE. TELL HIM.
IT'S LIKE THIS, SEE, THE SHOGUNATE'S RESHUFFLING THE DAIKAN, AND A NEW MAN'S COMING OUT TO IWAKI-JUKU. KINSHIMODA-*DONO* AND MYSELF ARE SLATED TO RETURN TO EDO AND GET OUR NEW ASSIGNMENTS... BUT THE FACT IS, SEE, A BIT OF THE LOCAL TAX REVENUE JUST HAPPENED TO FALL INTO OUR *SLEEVES*, IF YOU KNOW WHAT I MEAN.
NOW, IF THE NEW *DAIKAN* STARTS NOSING AROUND IN THE BOOKS, IT COULD GET STICKY. WE'VE GOT TO FILL IN THAT LITTLE HOLE BEFORE HE GETS HERE. AND NOW, BY CHANCE, THERE'S BEEN A LITTLE *INCIDENT*. BETTER THAN WE COULD HAVE DREAMED.
THERE'S A TURF WAR OUT HERE BETWEEN TWO YAKUZA GANGS, THE HOUSE OF JIZŌ AND THE SHIMO-NITTA FAMILY. THEY'VE BEEN EYEING EACH OTHER FOR YEARS. NOW SOMEONE'S GONE AND AMBUSHED THE BIG BOSS OF THE HOUSE OF JIZŌ WHEN HE WAS PLAYING WITH HIS NEWBORN SON, AND KILLED THEM BOTH. NO ONE KNOWS WHO DID IT, BUT THE JIZŌ BOYS ARE CONVINCED IT WAS SHIMO-NITTA WORK. THEY'VE SENT THEM A CHALLENGE TO A *DEIRI*, AND THEY'RE ROUNDING UP MEN FOR THE BIG SHOWDOWN. SOUNDS NATURAL ENOUGH, NO?
....
THE DEIRI STARTS AT THE SIXTH HOUR TOMORROW MORNING. THE NEW DAIKAN IS STAYING AT THE NEXT WAY STATION UP THE HIGHWAY. WE'VE BEEN DELAYING THE FORMAL TRANSFER OF POWER AS LONG AS WE CAN, SEE?
...

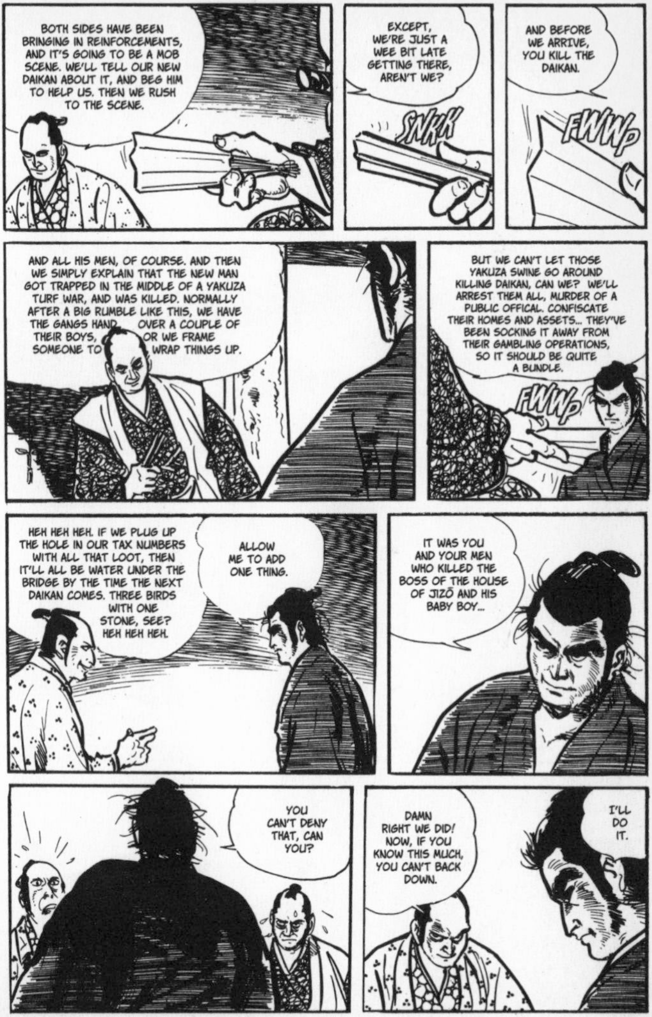
BOTH SIDES HAVE BEEN BRINGING IN REINFORCEMENTS, AND IT'S GOING TO BE A MOB SCENE. WE'LL TELL OUR NEW DAIKAN ABOUT IT, AND BEG HIM TO HELP US. THEN WE RUSH TO THE SCENE.
EXCEPT, WE'RE JUST A WEE BIT LATE GETTING THERE, AREN'T WE?
SNKK
AND BEFORE WE ARRIVE, YOU KILL THE DAIKAN.
FWWP
AND ALL HIS MEN, OF COURSE. AND THEN WE SIMPLY EXPLAIN THAT THE NEW MAN GOT TRAPPED IN THE MIDDLE OF A YAKUZA TURF WAR, AND WAS KILLED. NORMALLY AFTER A BIG RUMBLE LIKE THIS, WE HAVE THE GANGS HAND OVER A COUPLE OF THEIR BOYS, OR WE FRAME SOMEONE TO WRAP THINGS UP.
BUT WE CAN'T LET THOSE YAKUZA SWINE GO AROUND KILLING DAIKAN, CAN WE? WE'LL ARREST THEM ALL, MURDER OF A PUBLIC OFFICAL. CONFISCATE THEIR HOMES AND ASSETS... THEY'VE BEEN SOCKING IT AWAY FROM THEIR GAMBLING OPERATIONS, SO IT SHOULD BE QUITE A BUNDLE.
FWWP
HEH HEH HEH. IF WE PLUG UP THE HOLE IN OUR TAX NUMBERS WITH ALL THAT LOOT, THEN IT'LL ALL BE WATER UNDER THE BRIDGE BY THE TIME THE NEXT DAIKAN COMES. THREE BIRDS WITH ONE STONE, SEE? HEH HEH HEH.
ALLOW ME TO ADD ONE THING.
IT WAS YOU AND YOUR MEN WHO KILLED THE BOSS OF THE HOUSE OF JIZŌ AND HIS BABY BOY...
YOU CAN'T DENY THAT, CAN YOU?
DAMN RIGHT WE DID! NOW, IF YOU KNOW THIS MUCH, YOU CAN'T BACK DOWN.
I'LL DO IT.

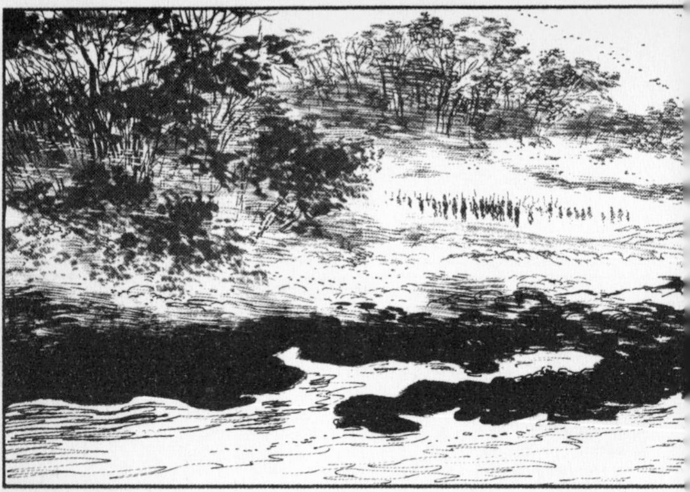
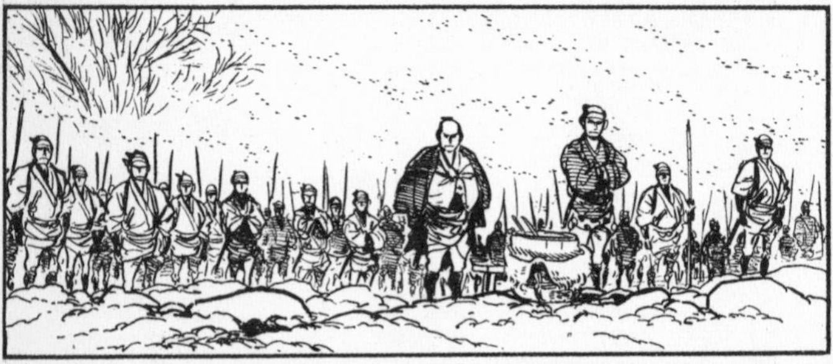
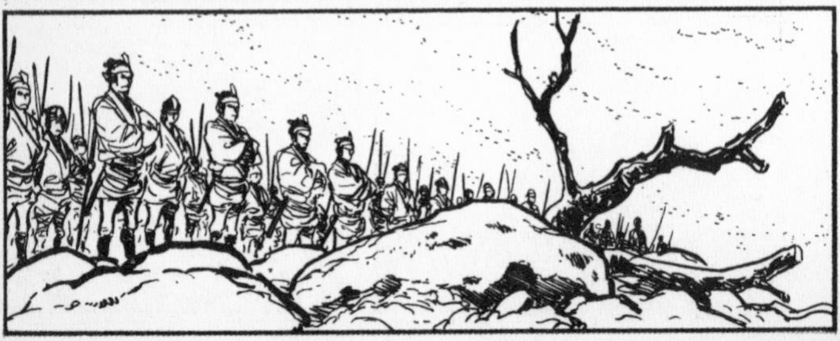

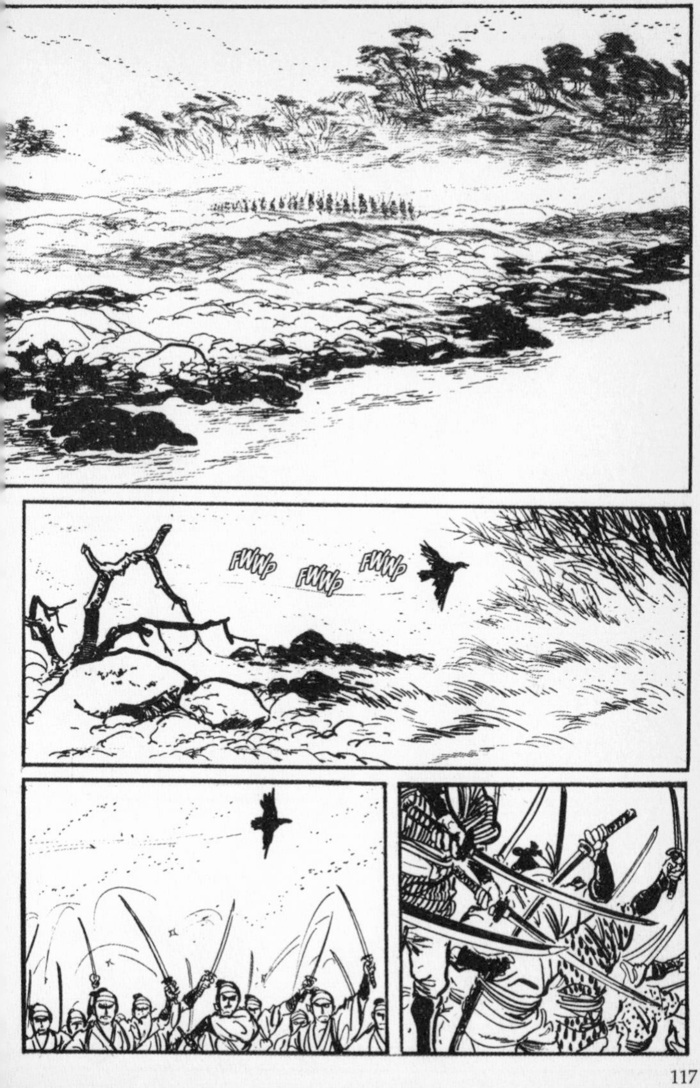
FWWP
FWWP
FWWP

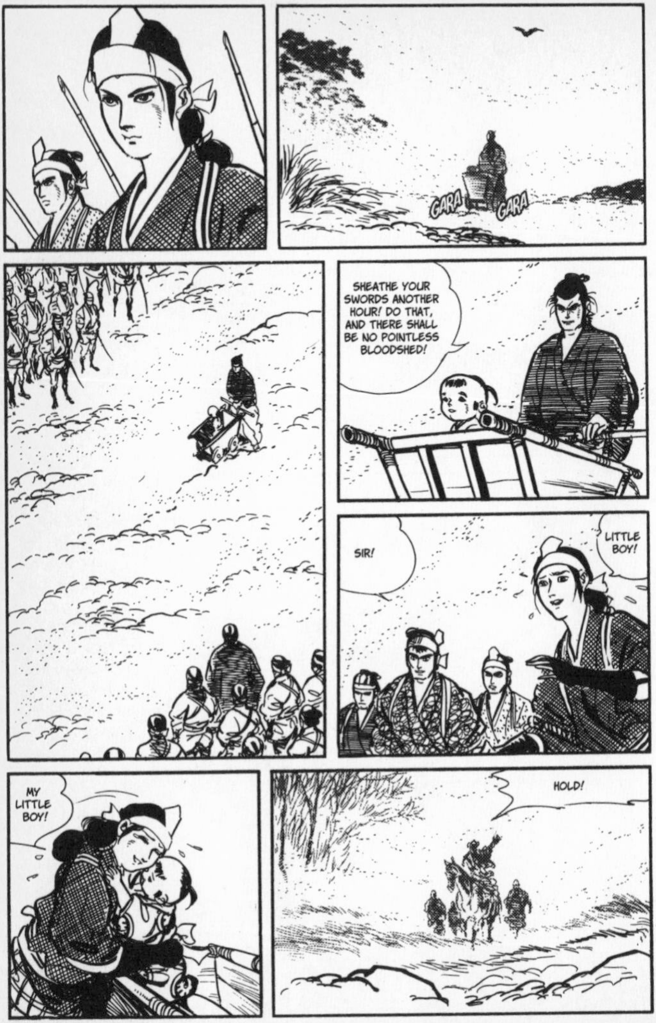
GARA
GARA
SHEATHE YOUR SWORDS ANOTHER HOUR! DO THAT, AND THERE SHALL BE NO POINTLESS BLOODSHED!
SIR!
LITTLE BOY!
MY LITTLE BOY!
HOLD!

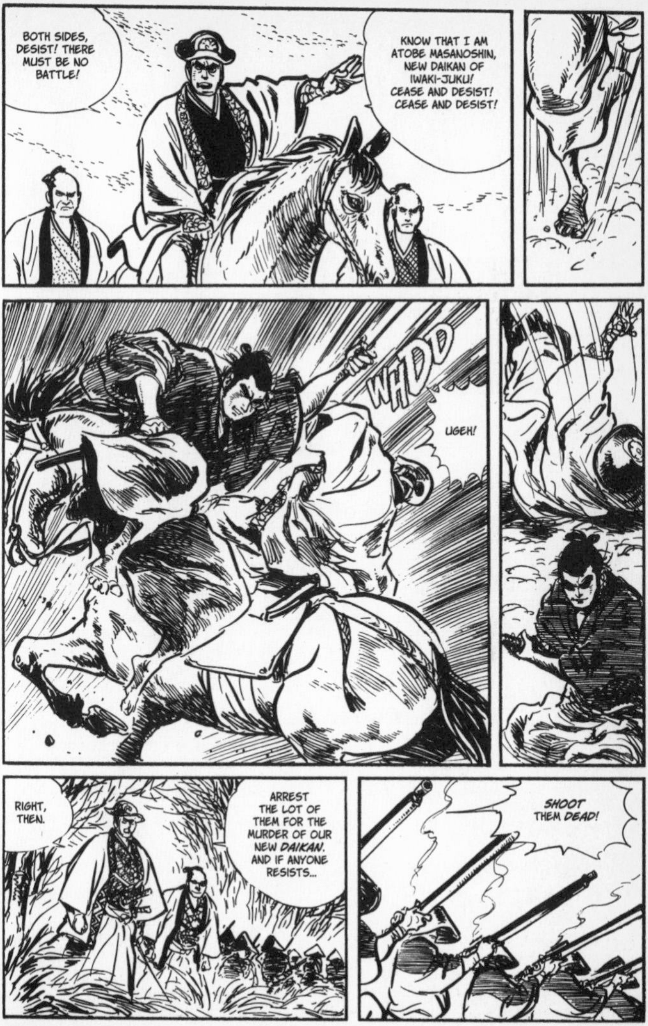
BOTH SIDES, DESIST! THERE MUST BE NO BATTLE!
KNOW THAT I AM ATOBE MASANOSHIN, NEW DAIKAN OF IWAKI-JUKU! CEASE AND DESIST! CEASE AND DESIST!
WHDD
UGEH!
RIGHT, THEN.
ARREST THE LOT OF THEM FOR THE MURDER OF OUR NEW *DAIKAN*. AND IF ANYONE RESISTS...
SHOOT THEM *DEAD!*

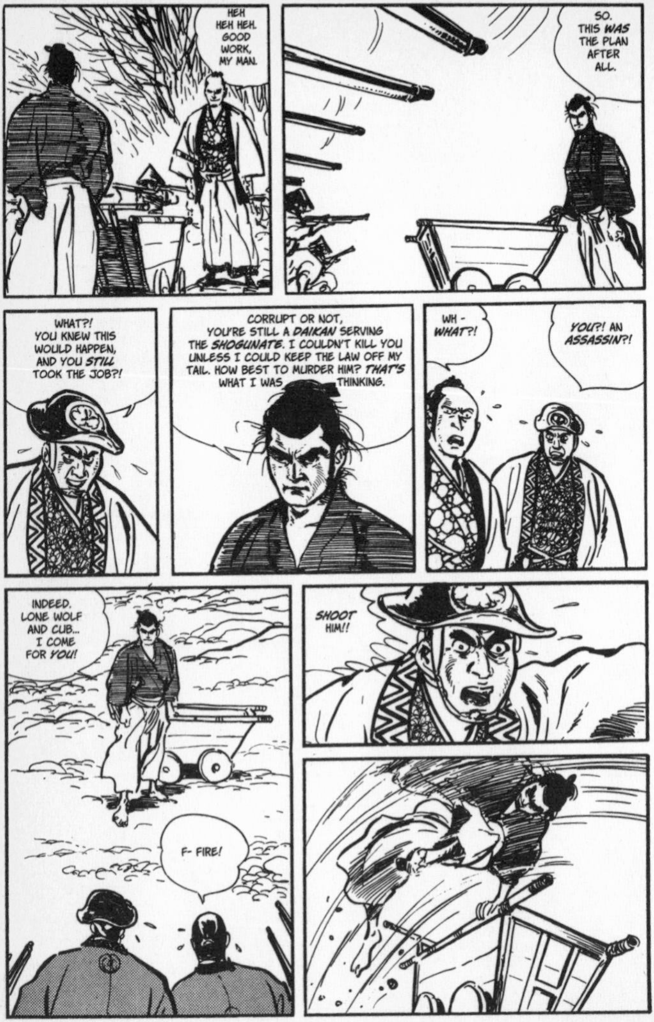
HEH HEH HEH. GOOD WORK, MY MAN.
SO. THIS WAS THE PLAN AFTER ALL.
WHAT?! YOU KNEW THIS WOULD HAPPEN, AND YOU STILL TOOK THE JOB?!
CORRUPT OR NOT, YOU'RE STILL A DAIKAN SERVING THE SHOGUNATE. I COULDN'T KILL YOU UNLESS I COULD KEEP THE LAW OFF MY TAIL. HOW BEST TO MURDER HIM? THAT'S WHAT I WAS THINKING.
WH - WHAT?!
YOU?! AN ASSASSIN?!
INDEED. LONE WOLF AND CUB... I COME FOR YOU!
F- FIRE!
SHOOT HIM!!

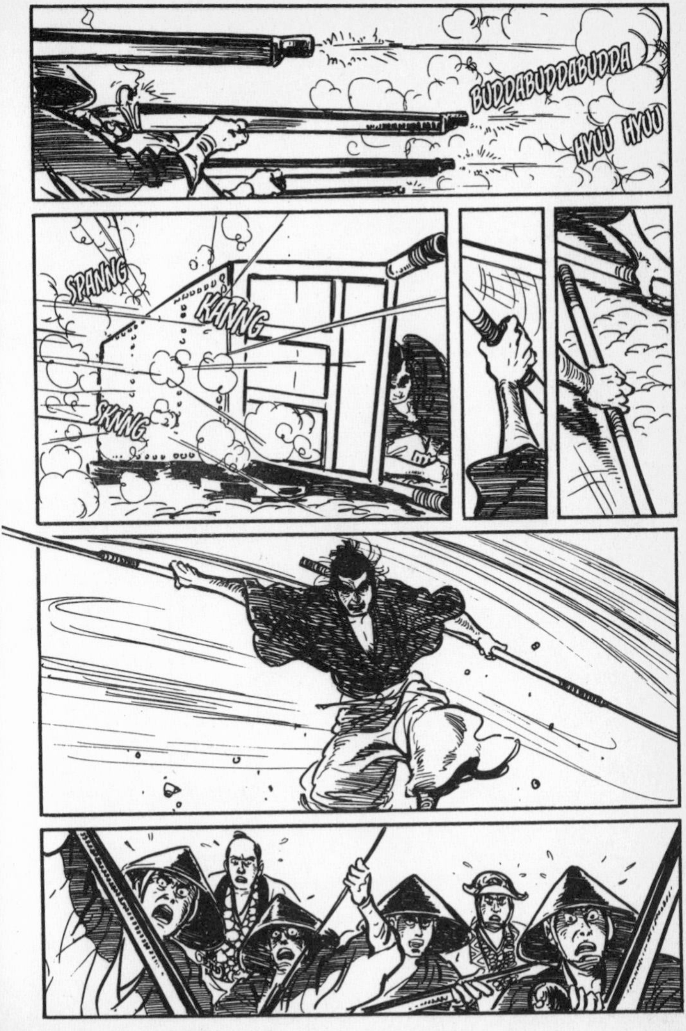
BUDDABUDDABUDDA
HYUU HYUU
SPANNG
KANNG
SKNNG

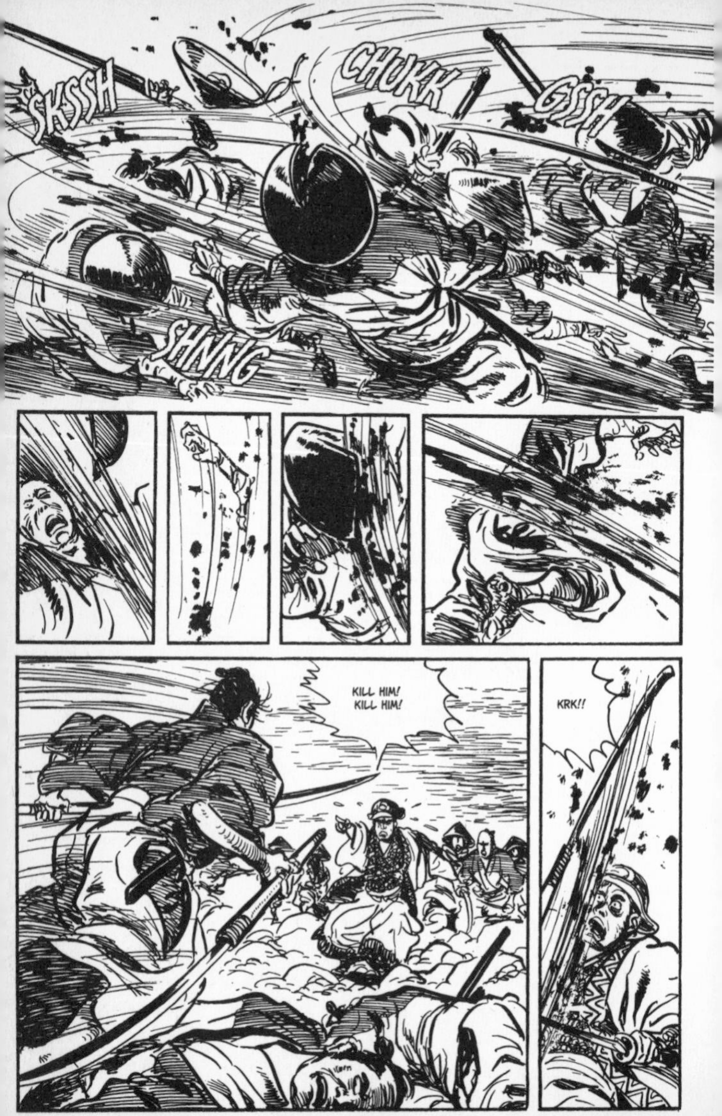
SKSSH
CHUKK
GSSH
SHNNG
KILL HIM!
KILL HIM!
KRK!!

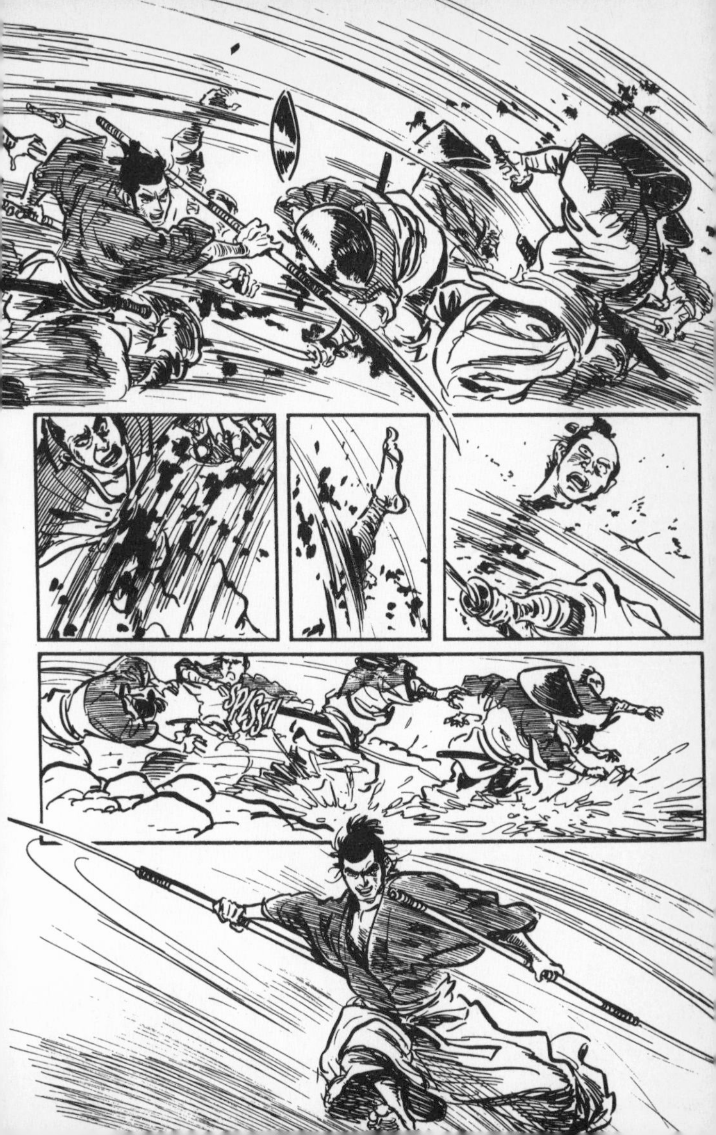
SPLSSH

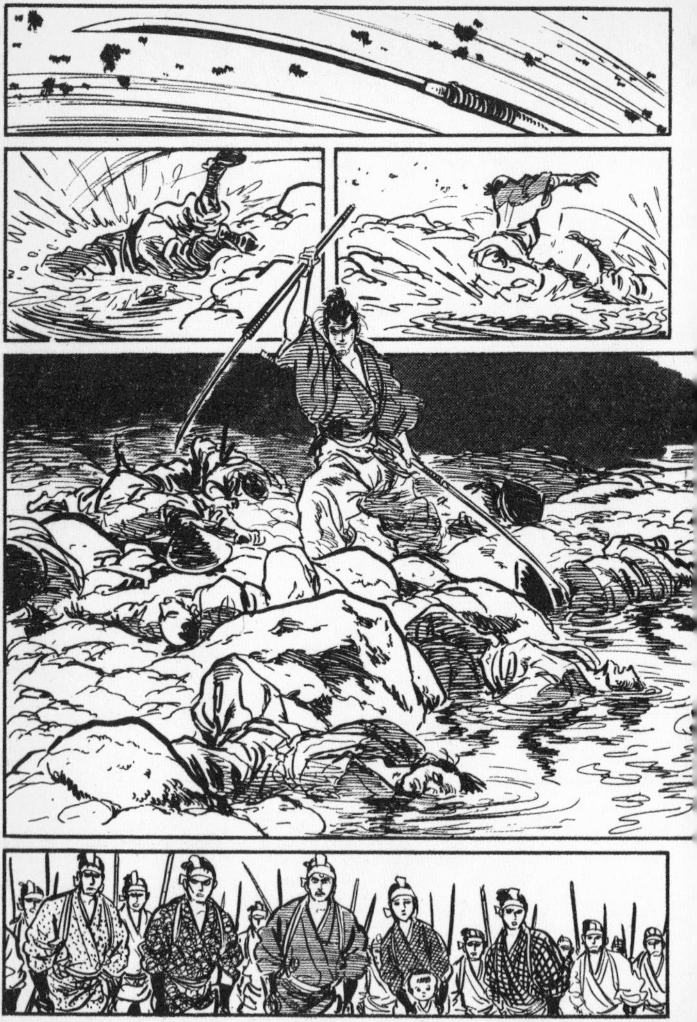

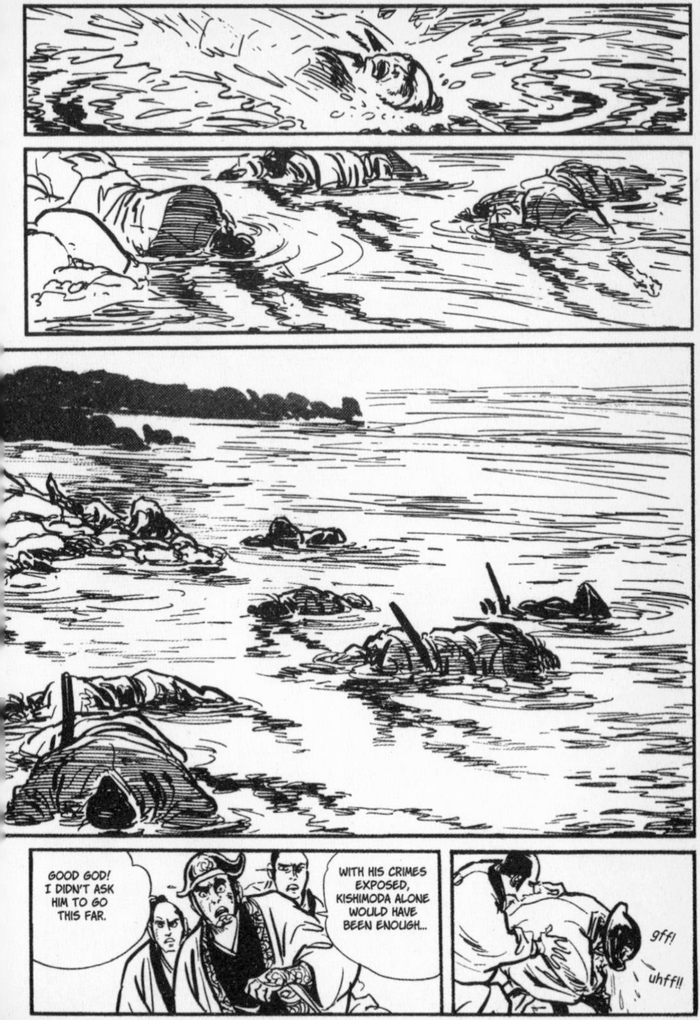
GOOD GOD! I DIDN'T ASK HIM TO GO THIS FAR.
WITH HIS CRIMES EXPOSED, KISHIMODA ALONE WOULD HAVE BEEN ENOUGH...
gff!
uhff!!

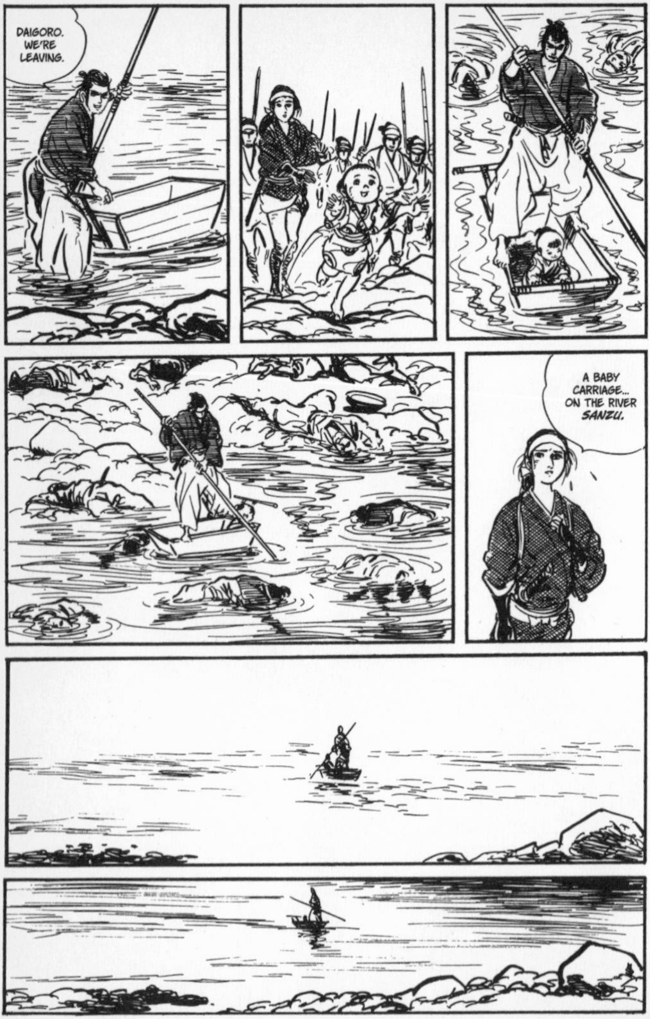
DAIGORO. WE'RE LEAVING.
A BABY CARRIAGE... ON THE RIVER SANZU.

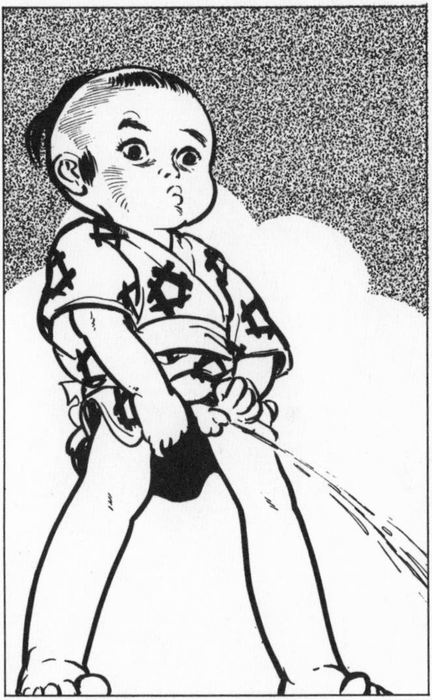

the fifth

Suiō School Zanbatō

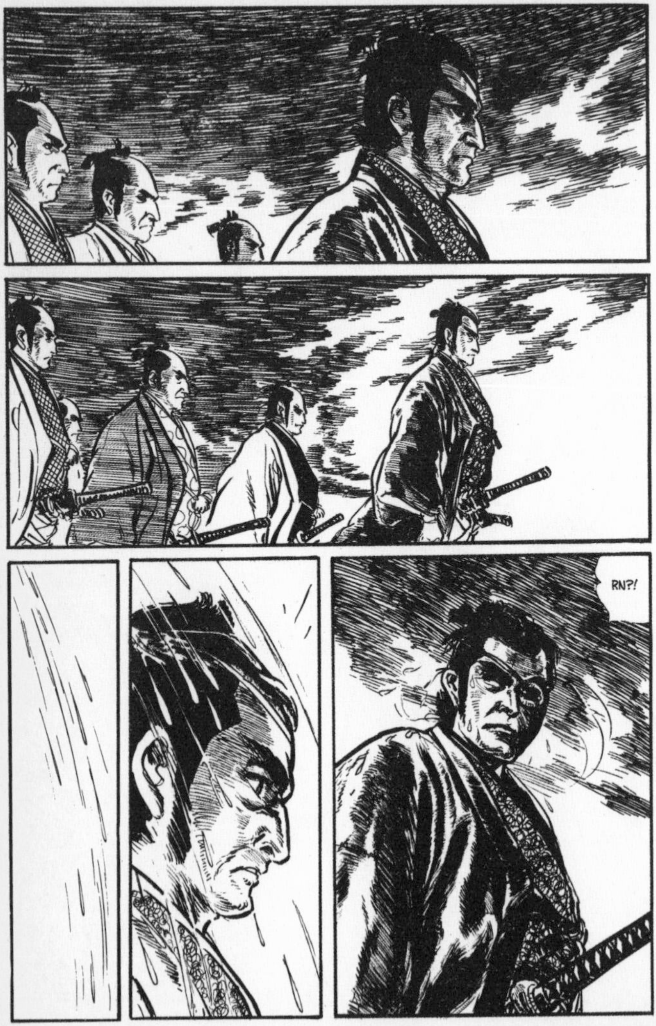
RN?!

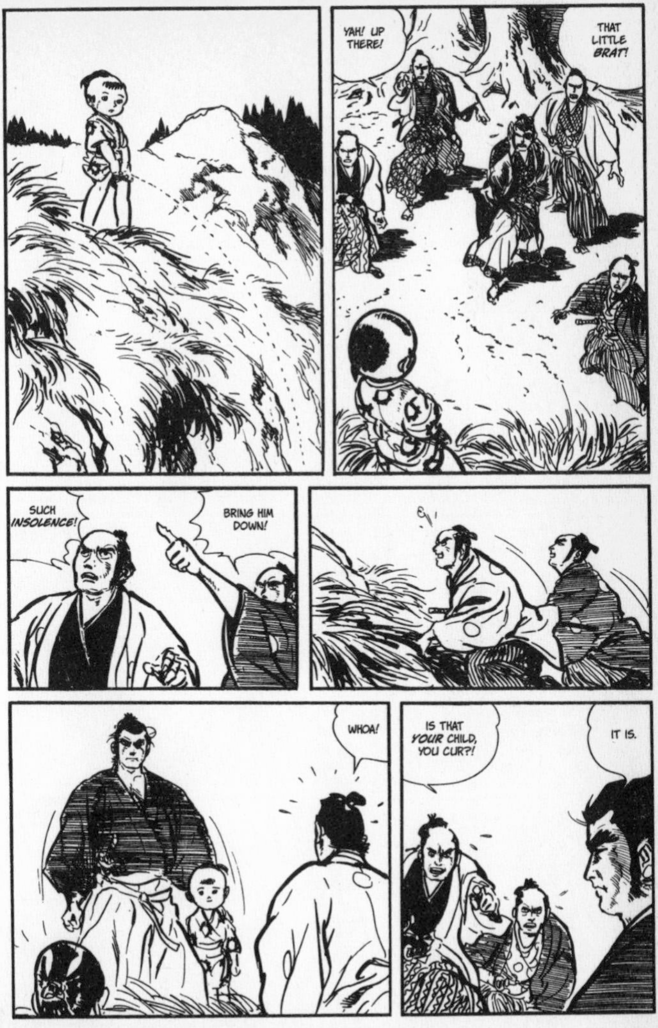
YAH! UP THERE!
THAT LITTLE BRAT!
SUCH INSOLENCE!
BRING HIM DOWN!
WHOA!
IS THAT YOUR CHILD, YOU CUR?!
IT IS.

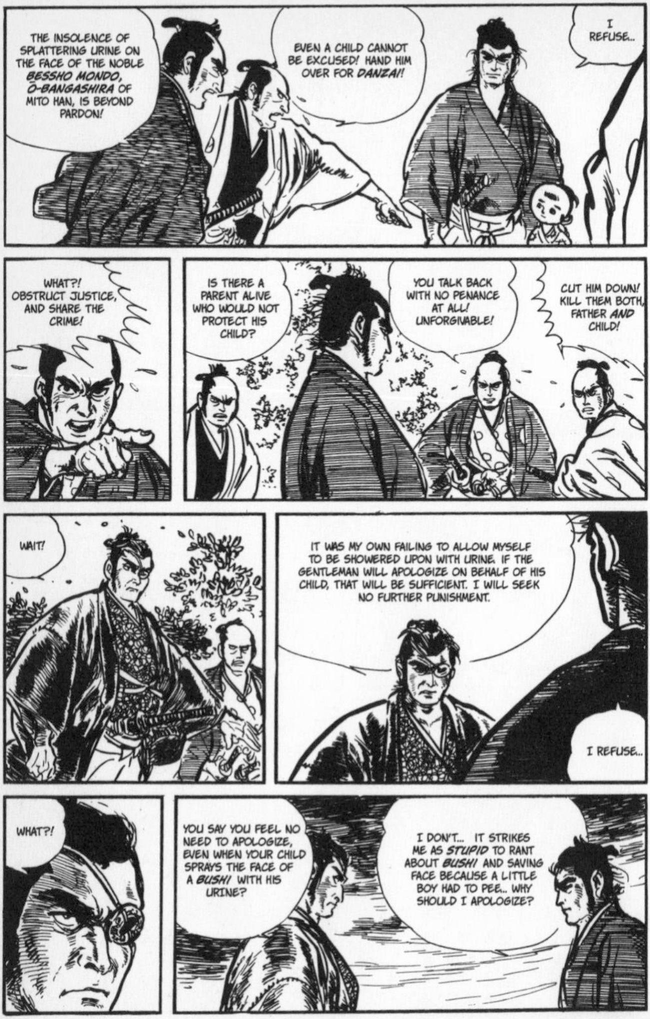
THE INSOLENCE OF SPLATTERING URINE ON THE FACE OF THE NOBLE *BESSHO MONDO, Ō-BANGASHIRA* OF MITO HAN, IS BEYOND PARDON!
EVEN A CHILD CANNOT BE EXCUSED! HAND HIM OVER FOR *DANZAI!*
I REFUSE...
WHAT?! OBSTRUCT JUSTICE, AND SHARE THE CRIME!
IS THERE A PARENT ALIVE WHO WOULD NOT PROTECT HIS CHILD?
YOU TALK BACK WITH NO PENANCE AT ALL! UNFORGIVABLE!
CUT HIM DOWN! KILL THEM BOTH, FATHER *AND* CHILD!
WAIT!
IT WAS MY OWN FAILING TO ALLOW MYSELF TO BE SHOWERED UPON WITH URINE. IF THE GENTLEMAN WILL APOLOGIZE ON BEHALF OF HIS CHILD, THAT WILL BE SUFFICIENT. I WILL SEEK NO FURTHER PUNISHMENT.
I REFUSE...
WHAT?!
YOU SAY YOU FEEL NO NEED TO APOLOGIZE, EVEN WHEN YOUR CHILD SPRAYS THE FACE OF A *BUSHI* WITH HIS URINE?
I DON'T... IT STRIKES ME AS *STUPID* TO RANT ABOUT *BUSHI* AND SAVING FACE BECAUSE A LITTLE BOY HAD TO PEE... WHY SHOULD I APOLOGIZE?

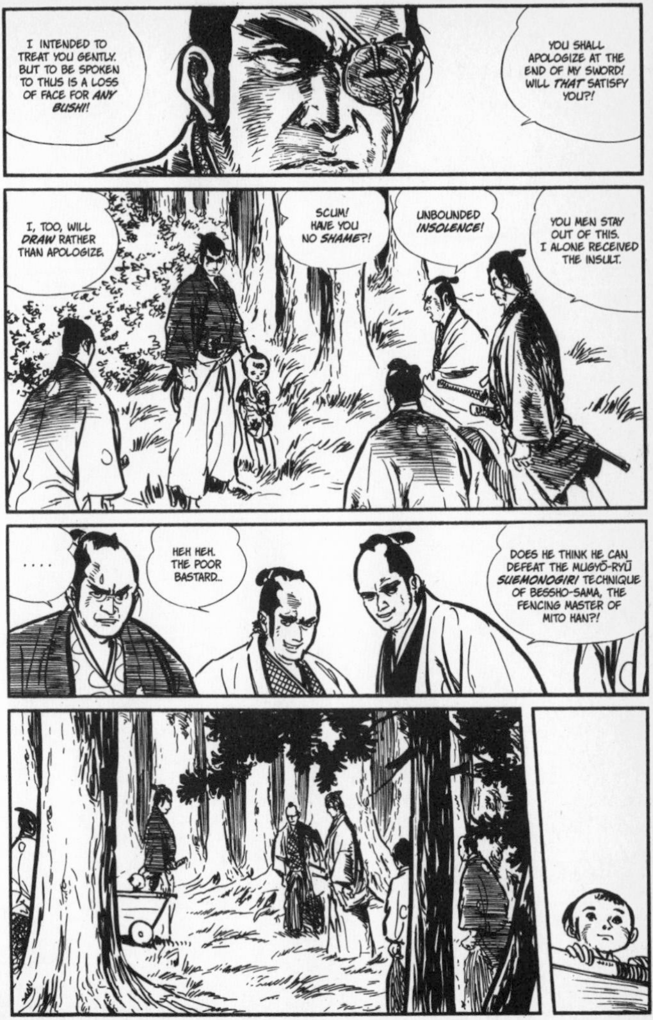
I INTENDED TO TREAT YOU GENTLY. BUT TO BE SPOKEN TO THUS IS A LOSS OF FACE FOR *ANY BUSHI!*
YOU SHALL APOLOGIZE AT THE END OF MY SWORD! WILL *THAT* SATISFY YOU?!
I, TOO, WILL *DRAW* RATHER THAN APOLOGIZE.
SCUM! HAVE YOU NO *SHAME*?!
UNBOUNDED *INSOLENCE!*
YOU MEN STAY OUT OF THIS. I ALONE RECEIVED THE INSULT.
. . . .
HEH HEH. THE POOR BASTARD...
DOES HE THINK HE CAN DEFEAT THE MUGYŌ-RYŪ *SUEMONOGIRI* TECHNIQUE OF BESSHO-SAMA, THE FENCING MASTER OF MITO HAN?!

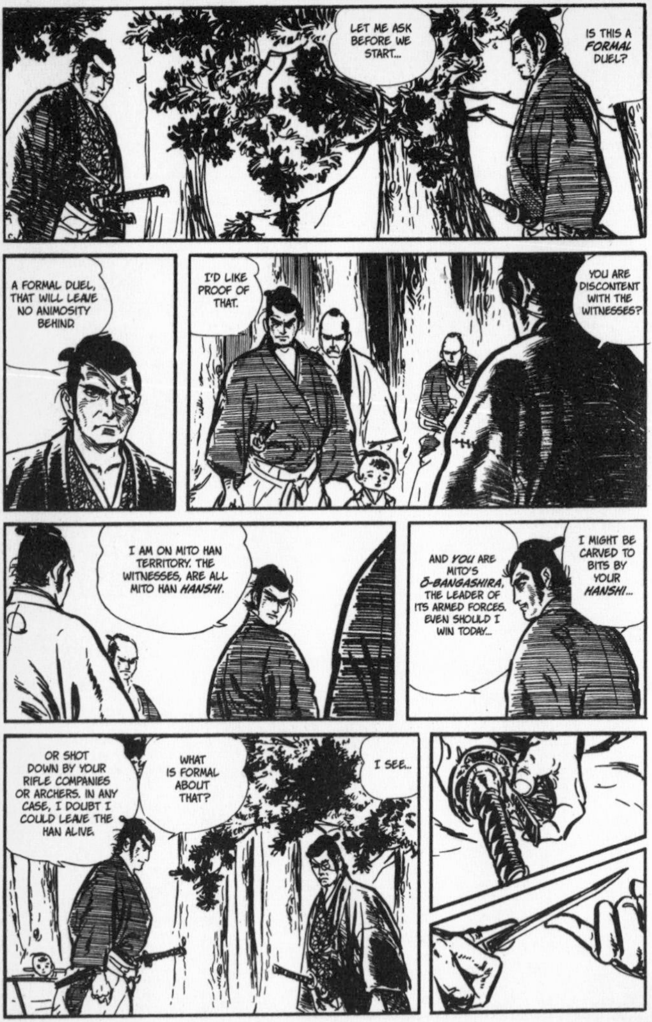
LET ME ASK BEFORE WE START...
IS THIS A *FORMAL* DUEL?
A FORMAL DUEL, THAT WILL LEAVE NO ANIMOSITY BEHIND.
I'D LIKE PROOF OF THAT.
YOU ARE DISCONTENT WITH THE WITNESSES?
I AM ON MITO HAN TERRITORY. THE WITNESSES, ARE ALL MITO HAN *HANSHI*.
AND *YOU* ARE MITO'S *Ō-BANGASHIRA*, THE LEADER OF ITS ARMED FORCES. EVEN SHOULD I WIN TODAY...
I MIGHT BE CARVED TO BITS BY YOUR *HANSHI*...
OR SHOT DOWN BY YOUR RIFLE COMPANIES OR ARCHERS. IN ANY CASE, I DOUBT I COULD LEAVE THE HAN ALIVE.
WHAT IS FORMAL ABOUT THAT?
I SEE...

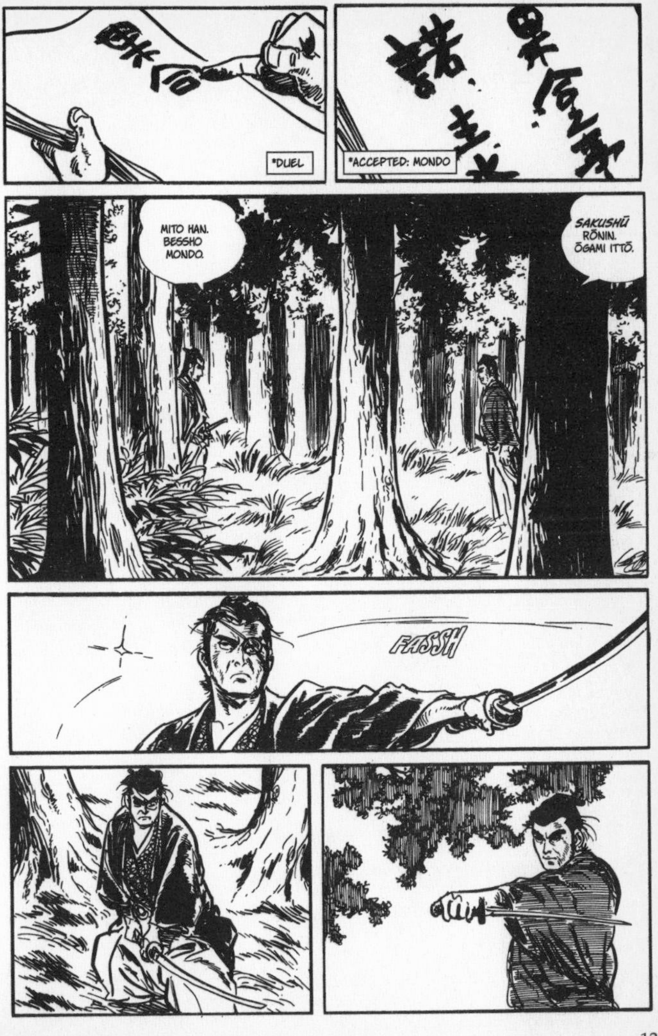
*DUEL
*ACCEPTED: MONDO
MITO HAN. BESSHO MONDO.
SAKUSHŪ RŌNIN. ŌGAMI ITTŌ.
FASSH

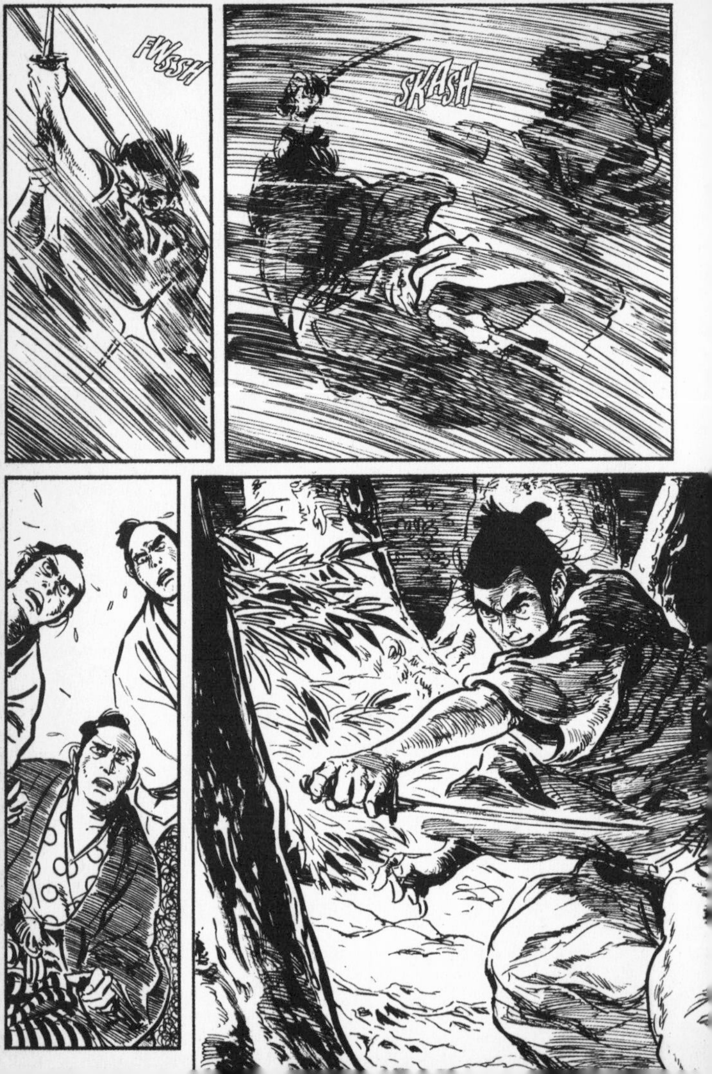
FWSSH
SKASH

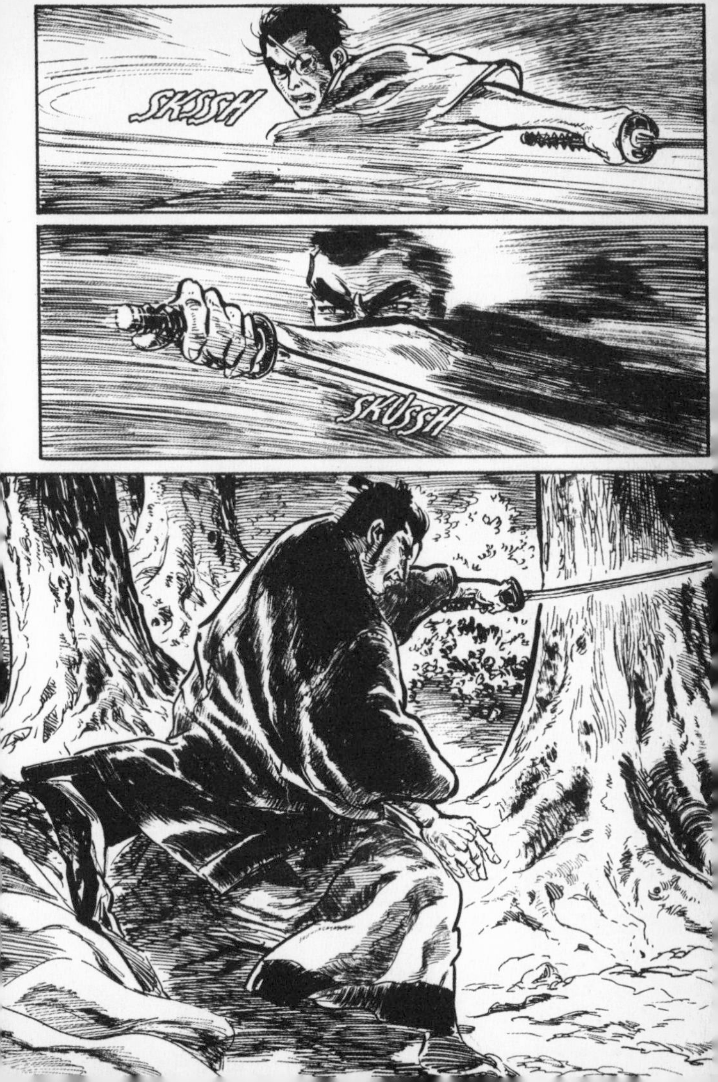
SKSSH
SKUSSH

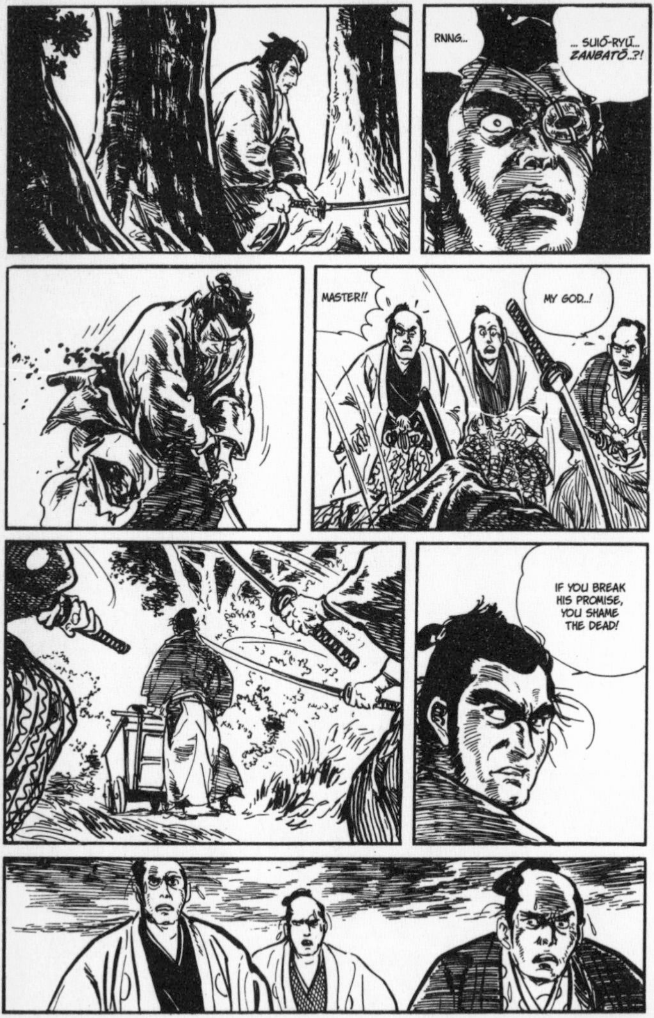
RNNG...
... SUIŌ-RYŪ... ZANBATŌ..?!
MY GOD..!
MASTER!!
IF YOU BREAK HIS PROMISE, YOU SHAME THE DEAD!

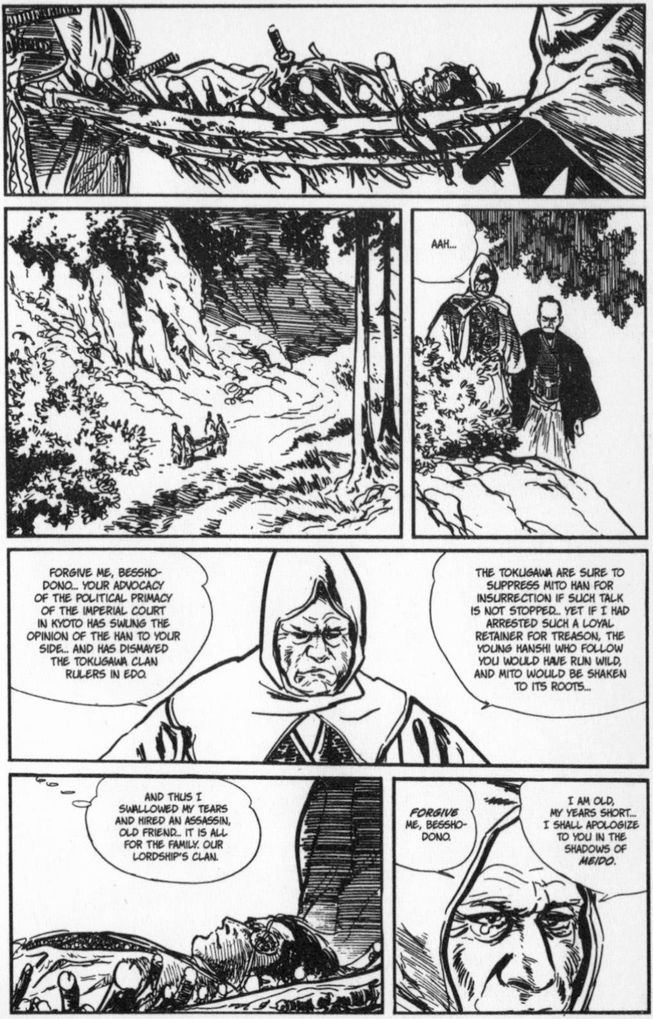
AAH...
FORGIVE ME, BESSHO-DONO... YOUR ADVOCACY OF THE POLITICAL PRIMACY OF THE IMPERIAL COURT IN KYOTO HAS SWUNG THE OPINION OF THE HAN TO YOUR SIDE... AND HAS DISMAYED THE TOKUGAWA CLAN RULERS IN EDO.
THE TOKUGAWA ARE SURE TO SUPPRESS MITO HAN FOR INSURRECTION IF SUCH TALK IS NOT STOPPED... YET IF I HAD ARRESTED SUCH A LOYAL RETAINER FOR TREASON, THE YOUNG HANSHI WHO FOLLOW YOU WOULD HAVE RUN WILD, AND MITO WOULD BE SHAKEN TO ITS ROOTS...
AND THUS I SWALLOWED MY TEARS AND HIRED AN ASSASSIN, OLD FRIEND... IT IS ALL FOR THE FAMILY. OUR LORDSHIP'S CLAN.
FORGIVE ME, BESSHO-DONO.
I AM OLD, MY YEARS SHORT... I SHALL APOLOGIZE TO YOU IN THE SHADOWS OF *MEIDO*.

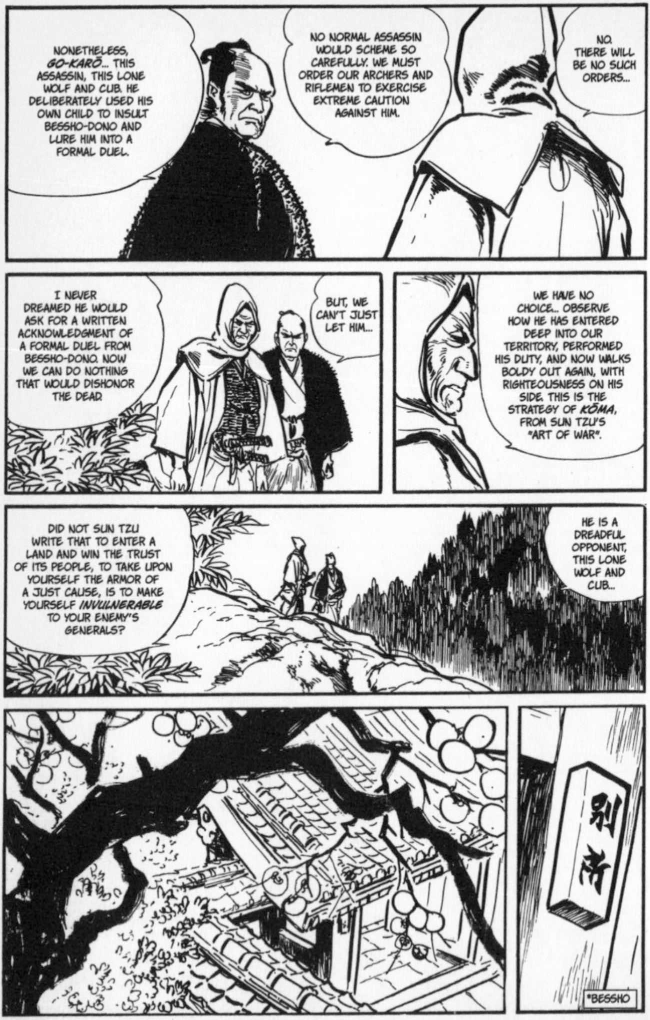
NONETHELESS, *GO-KARŌ*... THIS ASSASSIN, THIS LONE WOLF AND CUB. HE DELIBERATELY USED HIS OWN CHILD TO INSULT BESSHO-DONO AND LURE HIM INTO A FORMAL DUEL.
NO NORMAL ASSASSIN WOULD SCHEME SO CAREFULLY. WE MUST ORDER OUR ARCHERS AND RIFLEMEN TO EXERCISE EXTREME CAUTION AGAINST HIM.
NO. THERE WILL BE NO SUCH ORDERS...
I NEVER DREAMED HE WOULD ASK FOR A WRITTEN ACKNOWLEDGMENT OF A FORMAL DUEL FROM BESSHO-DONO. NOW WE CAN DO NOTHING THAT WOULD DISHONOR THE DEAD.
BUT, WE CAN'T JUST LET HIM...
WE HAVE NO CHOICE... OBSERVE HOW HE HAS ENTERED DEEP INTO OUR TERRITORY, PERFORMED HIS DUTY, AND NOW WALKS BOLDY OUT AGAIN, WITH RIGHTEOUSNESS ON HIS SIDE. THIS IS THE STRATEGY OF *KŌMA*, FROM SUN TZU'S "ART OF WAR".
DID NOT SUN TZU WRITE THAT TO ENTER A LAND AND WIN THE TRUST OF ITS PEOPLE, TO TAKE UPON YOURSELF THE ARMOR OF A JUST CAUSE, IS TO MAKE YOURSELF *INVULNERABLE* TO YOUR ENEMY'S GENERALS?
HE IS A DREADFUL OPPONENT, THIS LONE WOLF AND CUB...
別所
*BESSHO

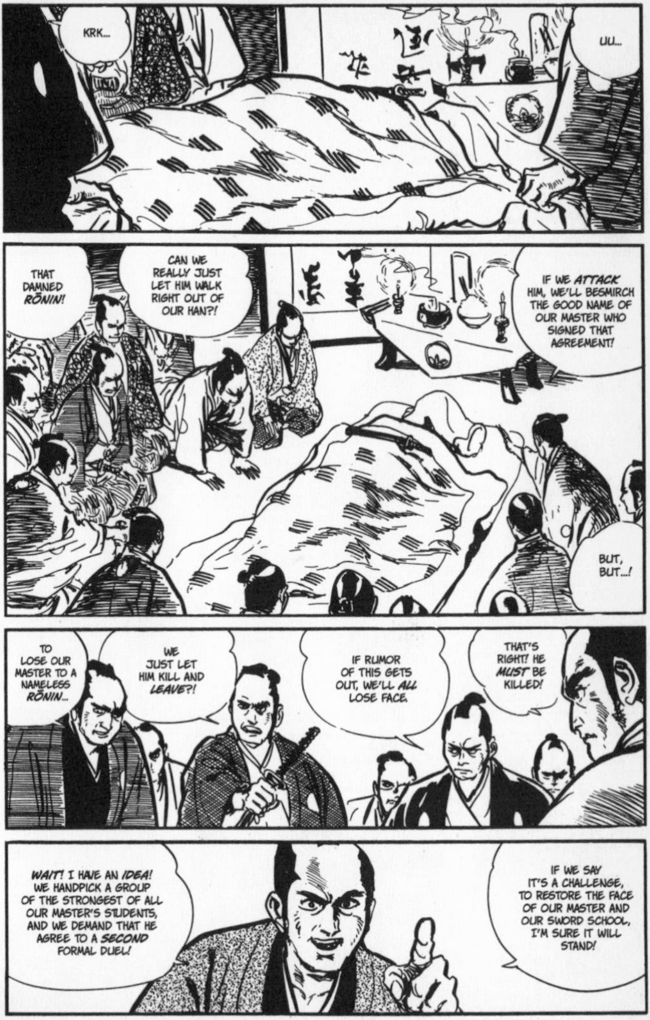
KRK...
UU...
THAT DAMNED *RŌNIN*!
CAN WE REALLY JUST LET HIM WALK RIGHT OUT OF OUR HAN?!
IF WE *ATTACK* HIM, WE'LL BESMIRCH THE GOOD NAME OF OUR MASTER WHO SIGNED THAT AGREEMENT!
BUT, BUT...!
TO LOSE OUR MASTER TO A NAMELESS *RŌNIN*...
WE JUST LET HIM KILL AND *LEAVE*?!
IF RUMOR OF THIS GETS OUT, WE'LL *ALL* LOSE FACE.
THAT'S RIGHT! HE *MUST* BE KILLED!
WAIT! I HAVE AN *IDEA!* WE HANDPICK A GROUP OF THE STRONGEST OF ALL OUR MASTER'S STUDENTS, AND WE DEMAND THAT HE AGREE TO A *SECOND* FORMAL DUEL!
IF WE SAY IT'S A CHALLENGE, TO RESTORE THE FACE OF OUR MASTER AND OUR SWORD SCHOOL, I'M SURE IT WILL STAND!

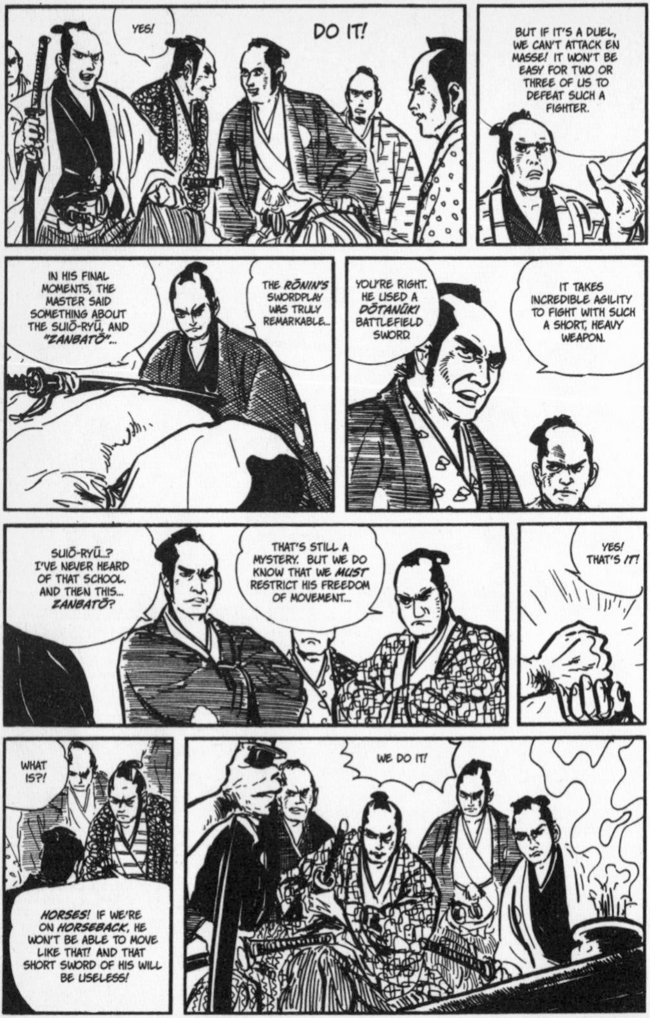
YES!
DO IT!
BUT IF IT'S A DUEL, WE CAN'T ATTACK EN MASSE! IT WON'T BE EASY FOR TWO OR THREE OF US TO DEFEAT SUCH A FIGHTER.
IN HIS FINAL MOMENTS, THE MASTER SAID SOMETHING ABOUT THE SUIŌ-RYŪ, AND "ZANBATŌ"...
THE RŌNIN'S SWORDPLAY WAS TRULY REMARKABLE...
YOU'RE RIGHT. HE USED A DŌTANŪKI BATTLEFIELD SWORD.
IT TAKES INCREDIBLE AGILITY TO FIGHT WITH SUCH A SHORT, HEAVY WEAPON.
SUIŌ-RYŪ...? I'VE NEVER HEARD OF THAT SCHOOL. AND THEN THIS... ZANBATŌ?
THAT'S STILL A MYSTERY. BUT WE DO KNOW THAT WE MUST RESTRICT HIS FREEDOM OF MOVEMENT...
YES! THAT'S IT!
WHAT IS?!
HORSES! IF WE'RE ON HORSEBACK, HE WON'T BE ABLE TO MOVE LIKE THAT! AND THAT SHORT SWORD OF HIS WILL BE USELESS!
WE DO IT!

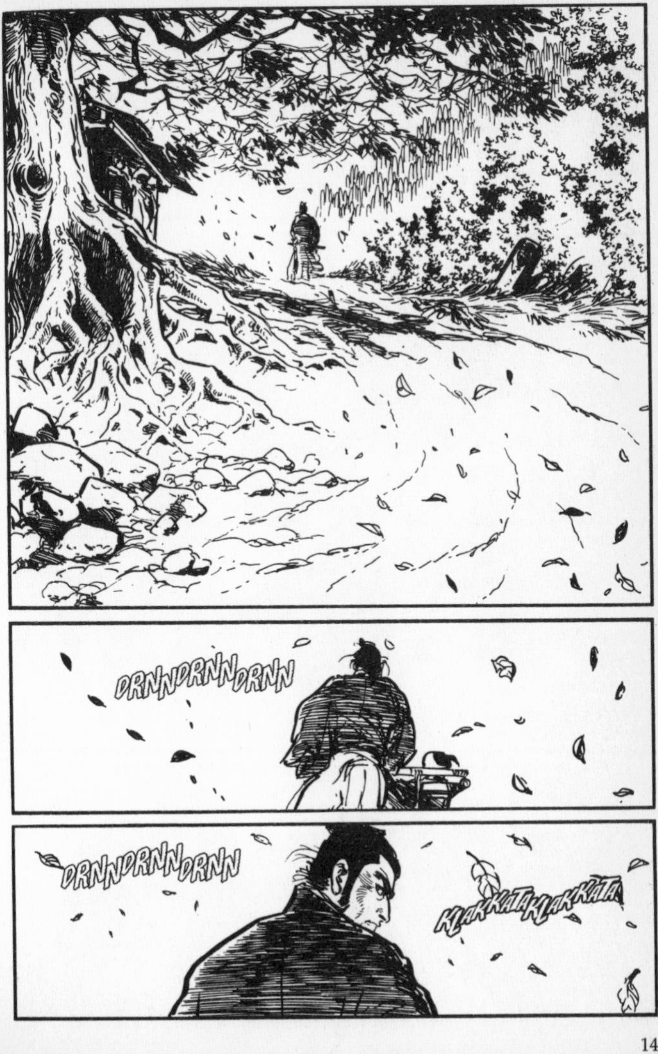
DRNNDRNNDRNN
DRNNDRNNDRNN
KLAKKATAKLAKKATA

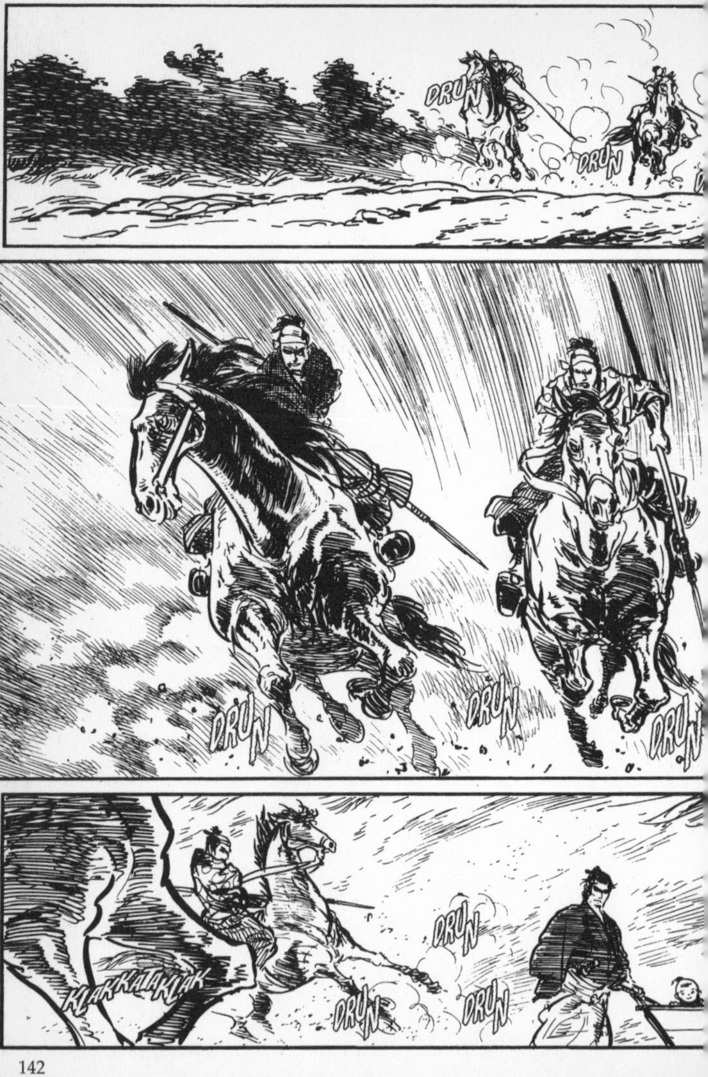
DRUN
DRUN
DRUN
DRUN
DRUN
DRUN
KLAKKATAKLAK
DRUN
DRUN

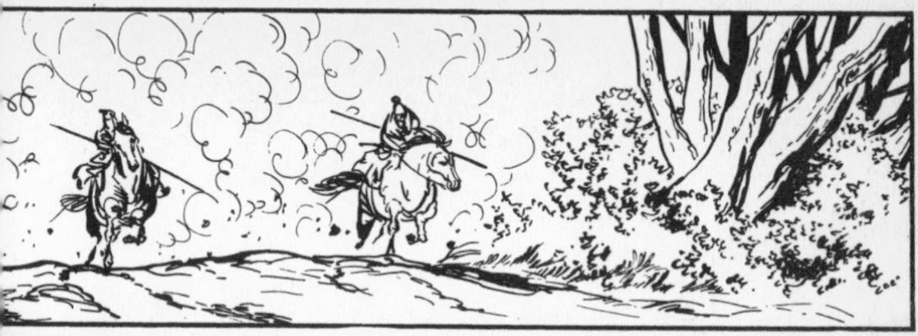

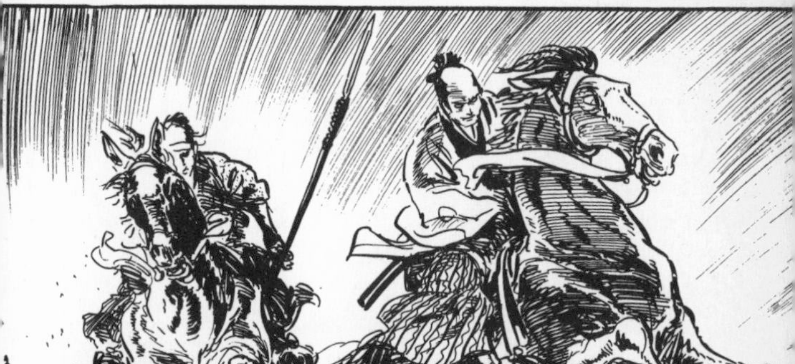

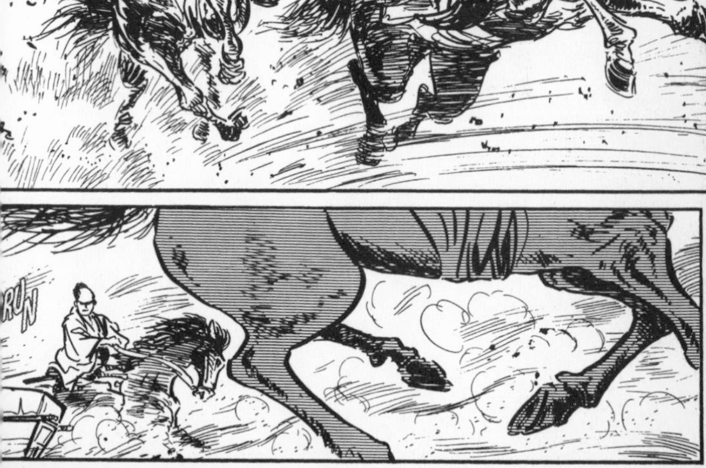
RUN

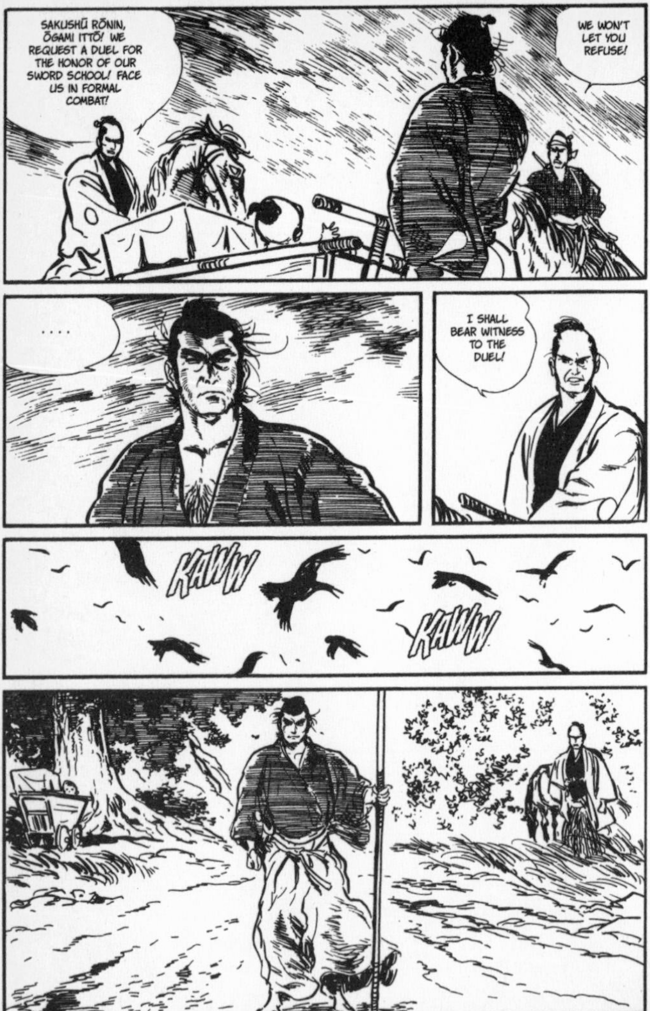
SAKUSHŪ RŌNIN, ŌGAMI ITTŌ! WE REQUEST A DUEL FOR THE HONOR OF OUR SWORD SCHOOL! FACE US IN FORMAL COMBAT!
WE WON'T LET YOU REFUSE!
. . . .
I SHALL BEAR WITNESS TO THE DUEL!
KAWW
KAWW

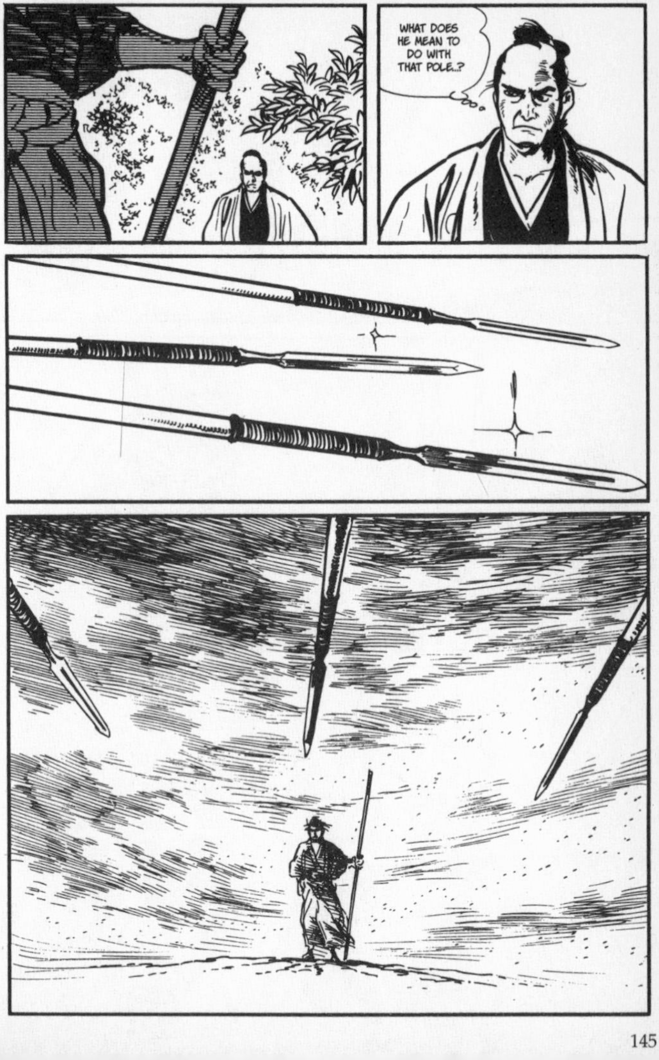
WHAT DOES HE MEAN TO DO WITH THAT POLE..?

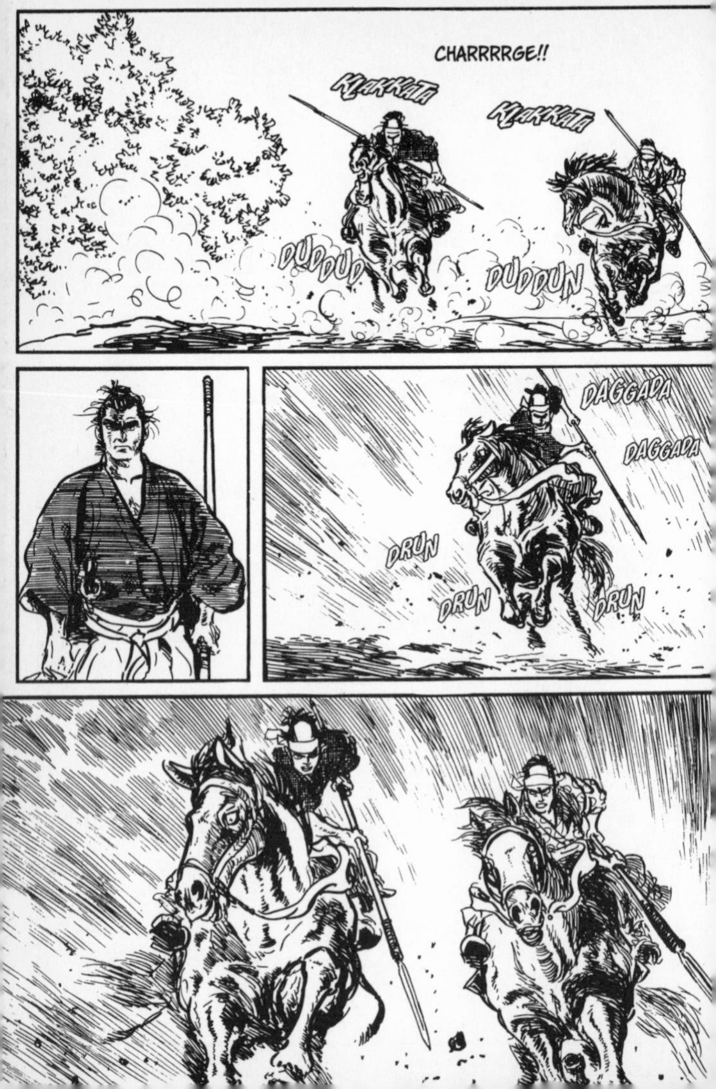
CHARRRRGE!!
KLAKKATA
KLAKKATA
DUDDUD
DUDDUN
DAGGADA
DAGGADA
DRUN
DRUN
DRUN

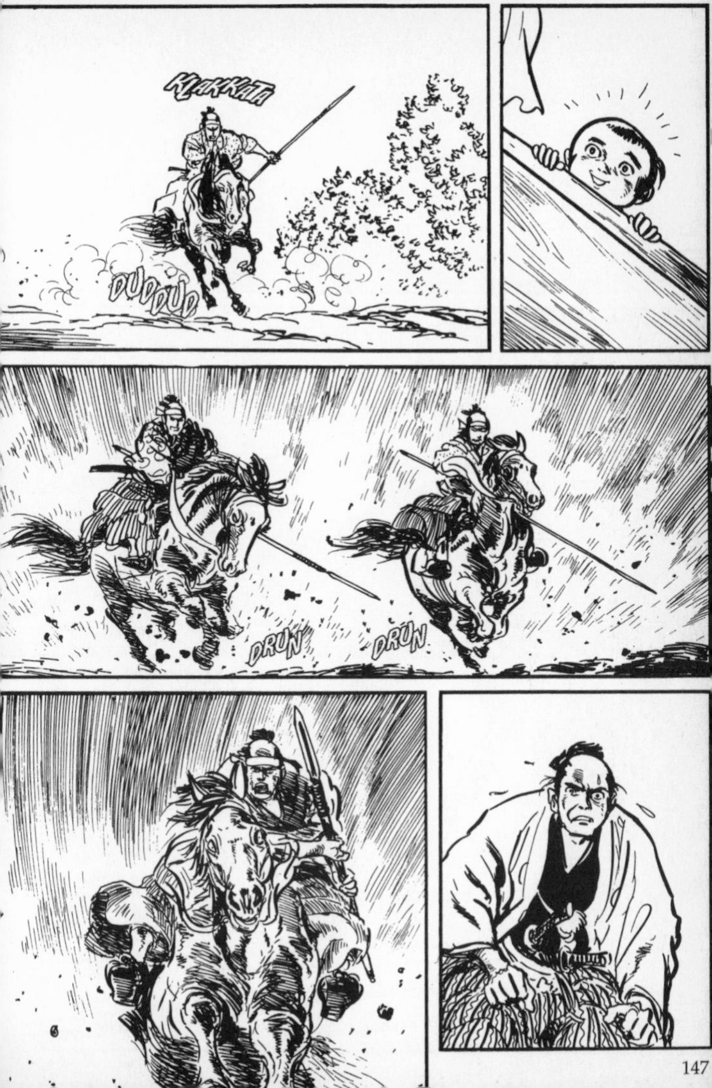
KLAKKATA
DUDDUD
DRUN
DRUN

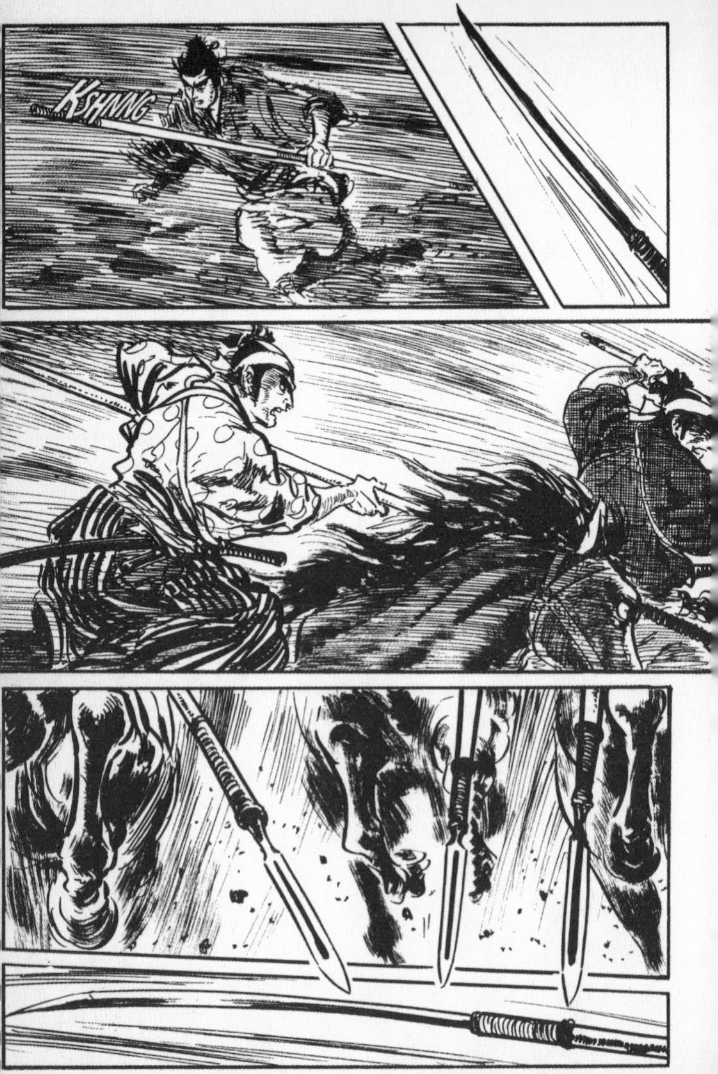
KSHNNG

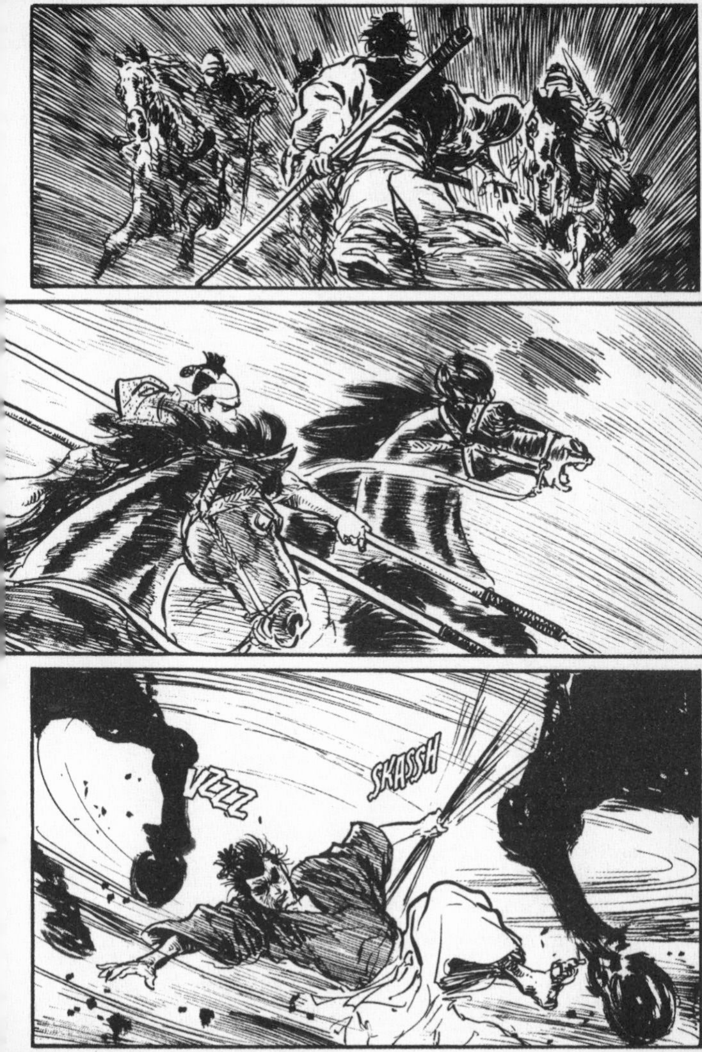
VZZZ
SKASSH

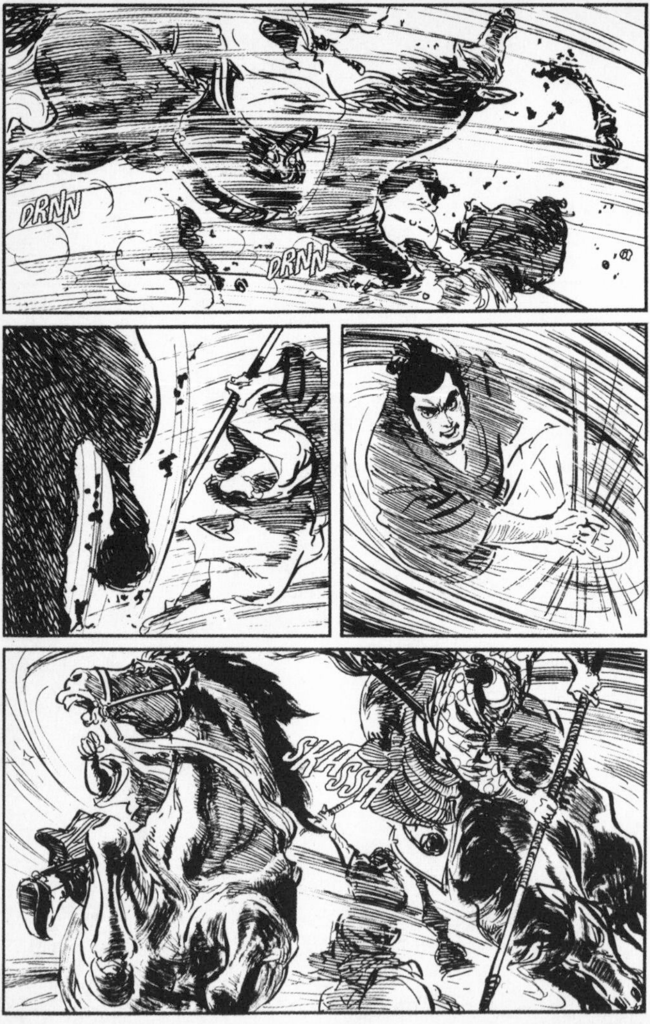
DRNN
DRNN
SKASSH

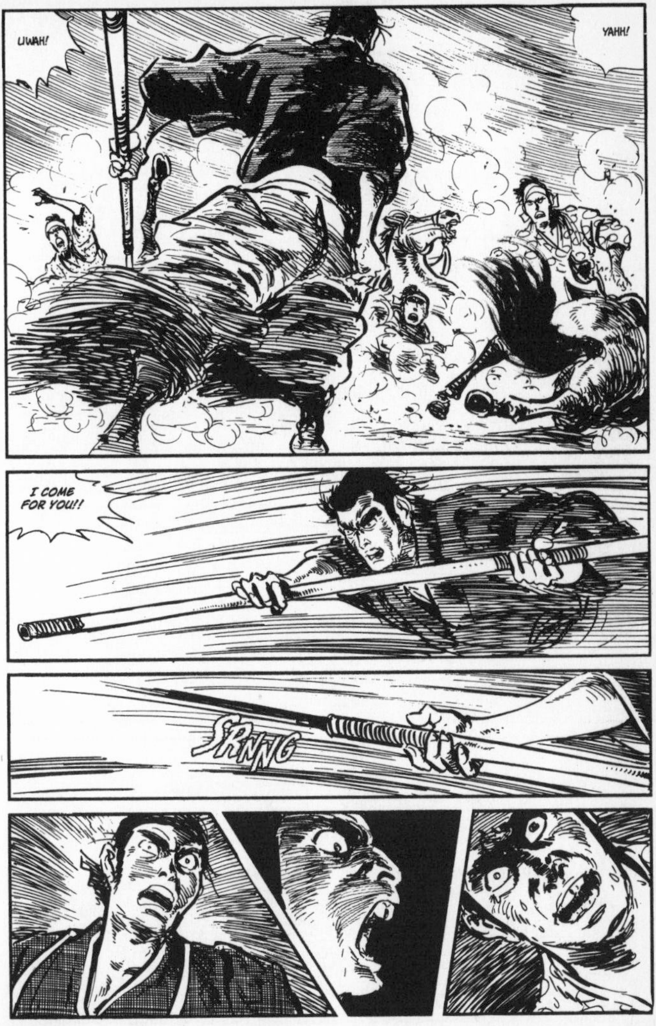
UWAH!
YAHH!
I COME FOR YOU!!
SRNNG

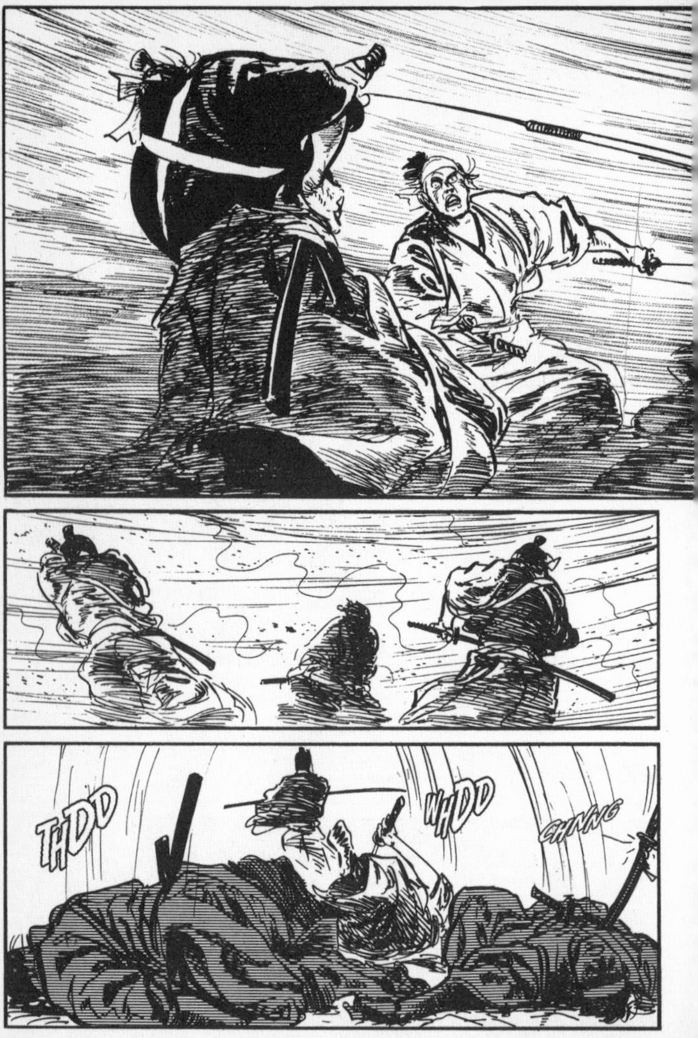
CHINNG
WHDD
THDD

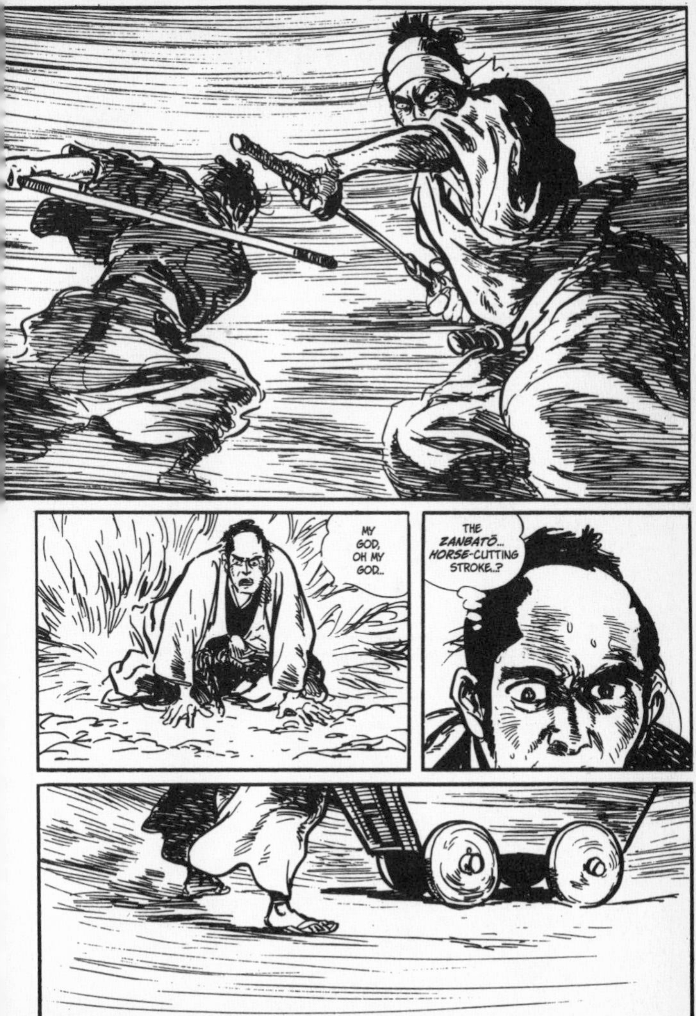
MY GOD, OH MY GOD...
THE ZANBATŌ... HORSE-CUTTING STROKE..?

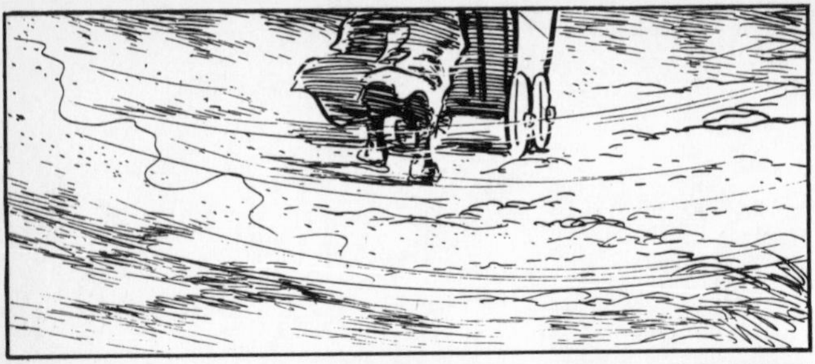
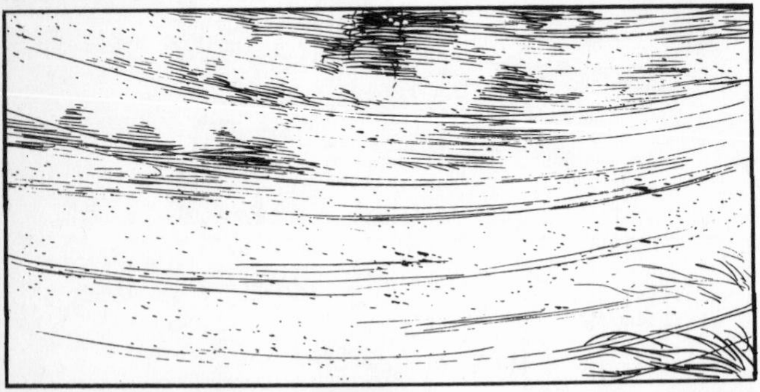
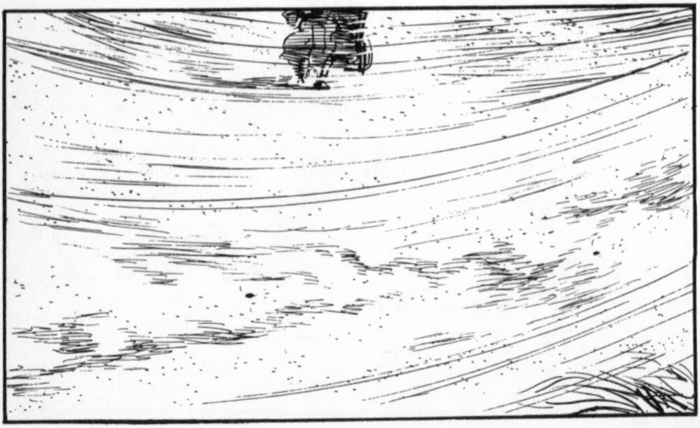

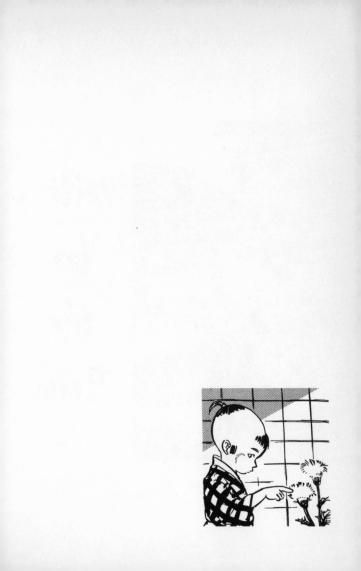

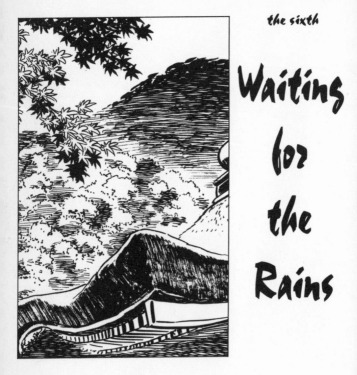

the sixth

Waiting for the Rains

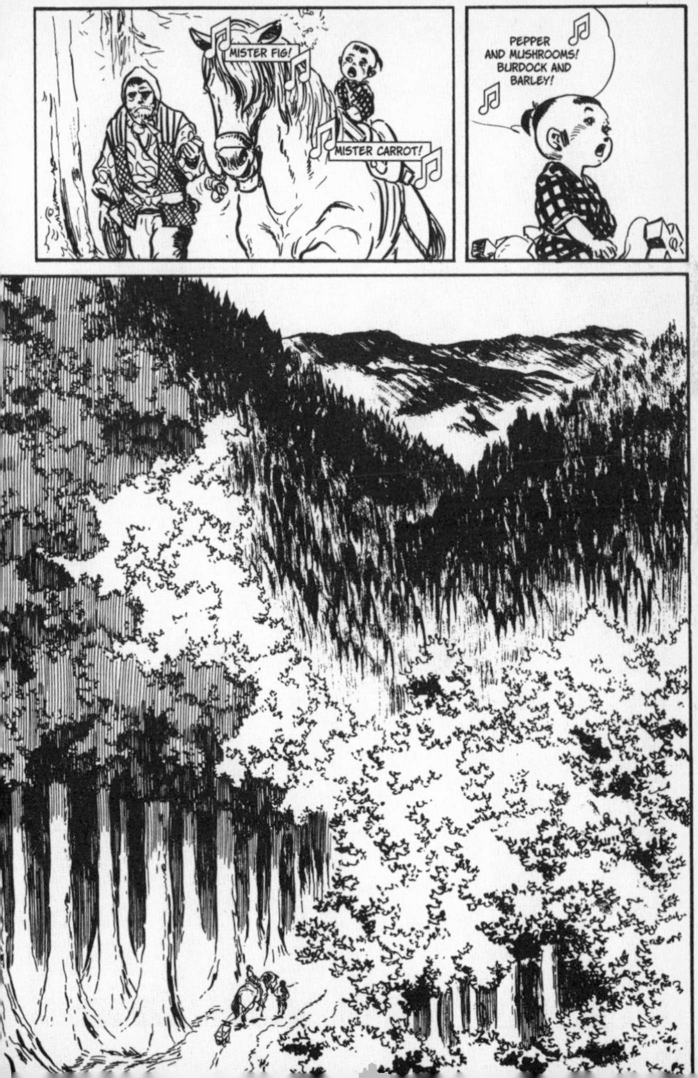
MISTER FIG!
MISTER CARROT!
PEPPER AND MUSHROOMS! BURDOCK AND BARLEY!

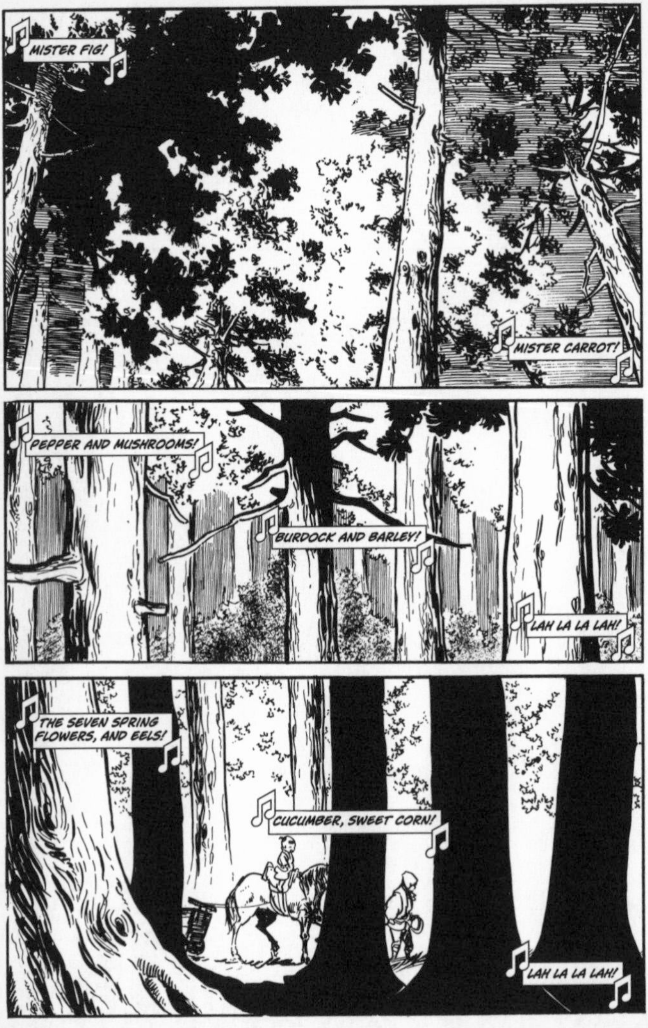
MISTER FIG!
MISTER CARROT!
PEPPER AND MUSHROOMS!
BURDOCK AND BARLEY!
LAH LA LA LAH!
THE SEVEN SPRING FLOWERS, AND EELS!
CUCUMBER, SWEET CORN!
LAH LA LA LAH!

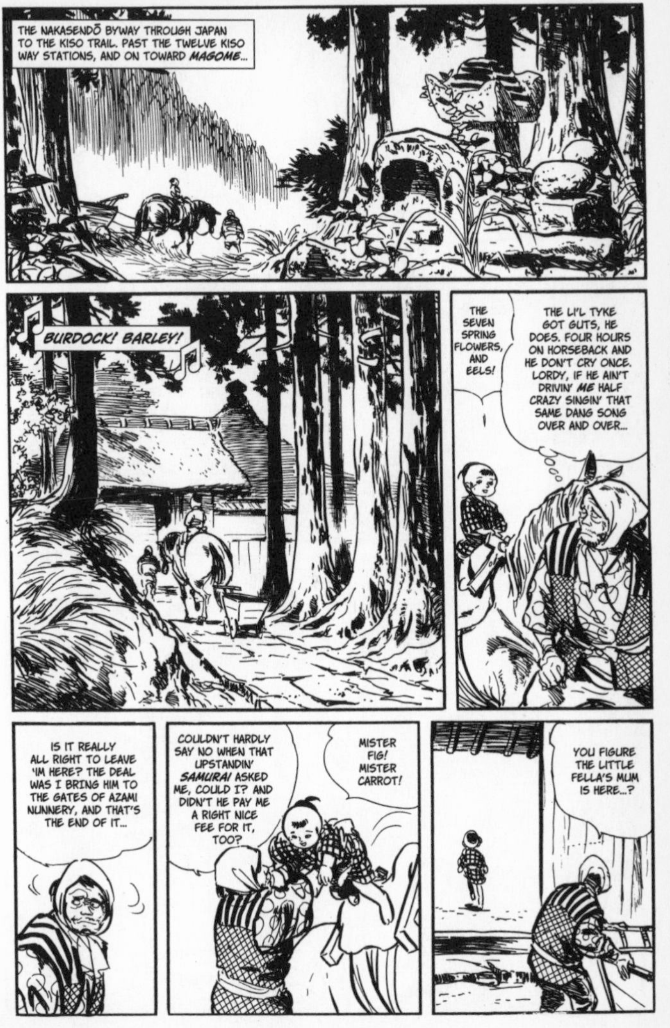
THE NAKASENDŌ BYWAY THROUGH JAPAN TO THE KISO TRAIL. PAST THE TWELVE KISO WAY STATIONS, AND ON TOWARD *MAGOME*...
BURDOCK! BARLEY!
THE SEVEN SPRING FLOWERS, AND EELS!
THE LI'L TYKE GOT GUTS, HE DOES. FOUR HOURS ON HORSEBACK AND HE DON'T CRY ONCE. LORDY, IF HE AIN'T DRIVIN' *ME* HALF CRAZY SINGIN' THAT SAME DANG SONG OVER AND OVER...
IS IT REALLY ALL RIGHT TO LEAVE 'IM HERE? THE DEAL WAS I BRING HIM TO THE GATES OF AZAMI NUNNERY, AND THAT'S THE END OF IT...
COULDN'T HARDLY SAY NO WHEN THAT UPSTANDIN' *SAMURAI* ASKED ME, COULD I? AND DIDN'T HE PAY ME A RIGHT NICE FEE FOR IT, TOO?
MISTER FIG! MISTER CARROT!
YOU FIGURE THE LITTLE FELLA'S MUM IS HERE...?

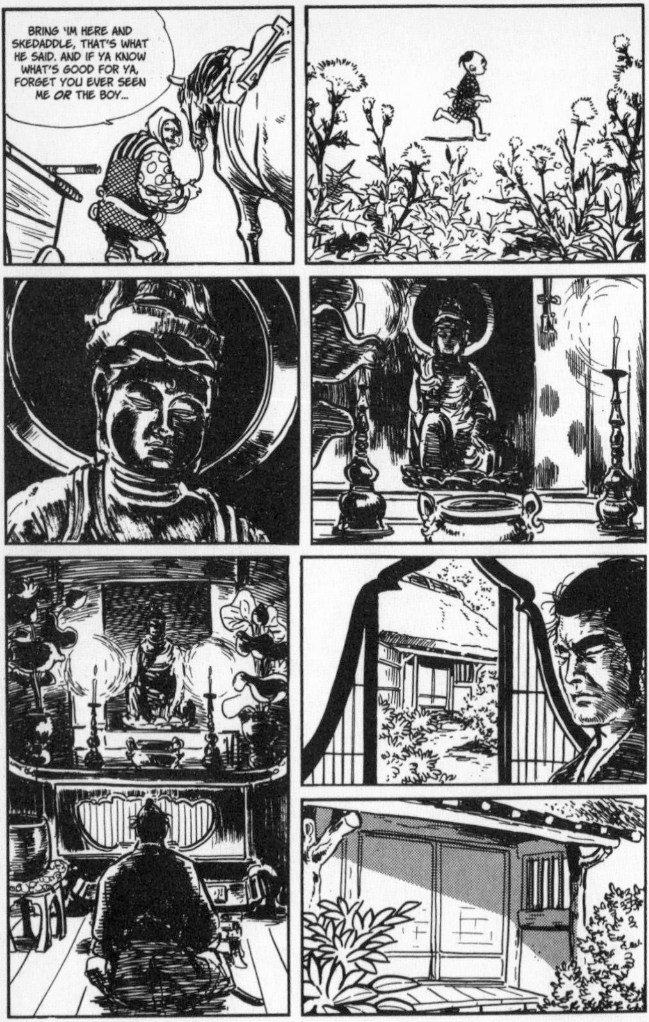
BRING 'IM HERE AND SKEDADDLE, THAT'S WHAT HE SAID. AND IF YA KNOW WHAT'S GOOD FOR YA, FORGET YOU EVER SEEN ME OR THE BOY...

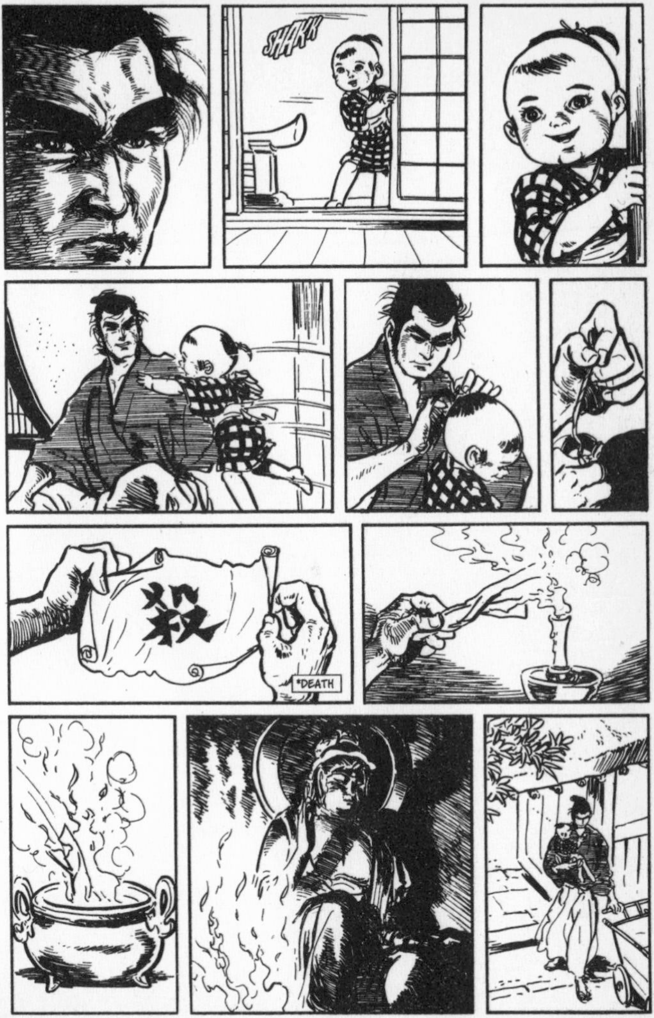
SHAK'K
殺
*DEATH

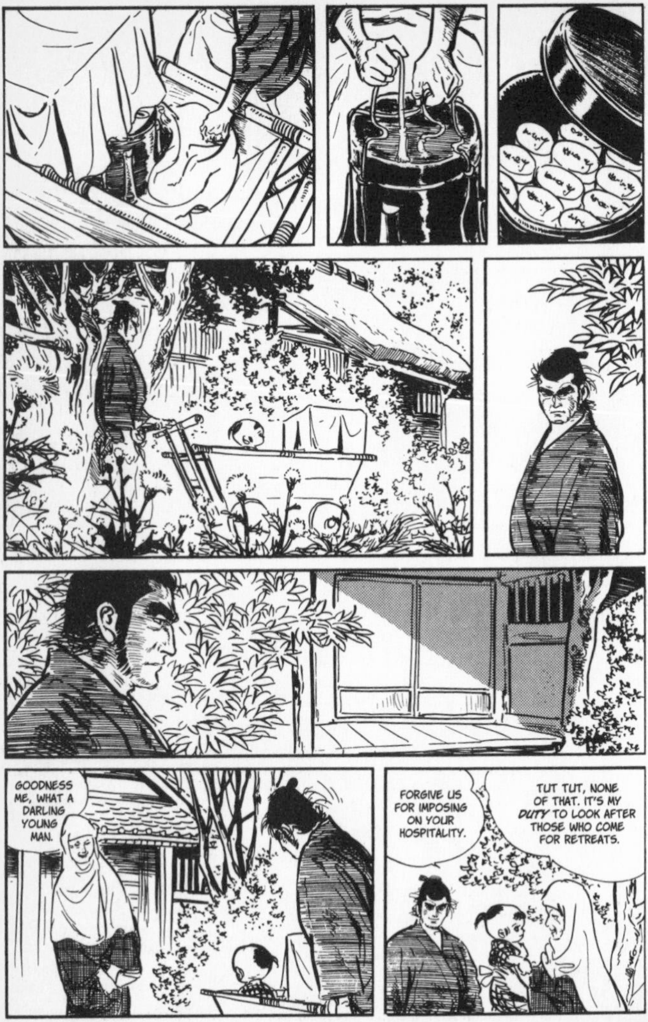

GOODNESS ME, WHAT A DARLING YOUNG MAN.
FORGIVE US FOR IMPOSING ON YOUR HOSPITALITY.
TUT TUT, NONE OF THAT. IT'S MY *DUTY* TO LOOK AFTER THOSE WHO COME FOR RETREATS.

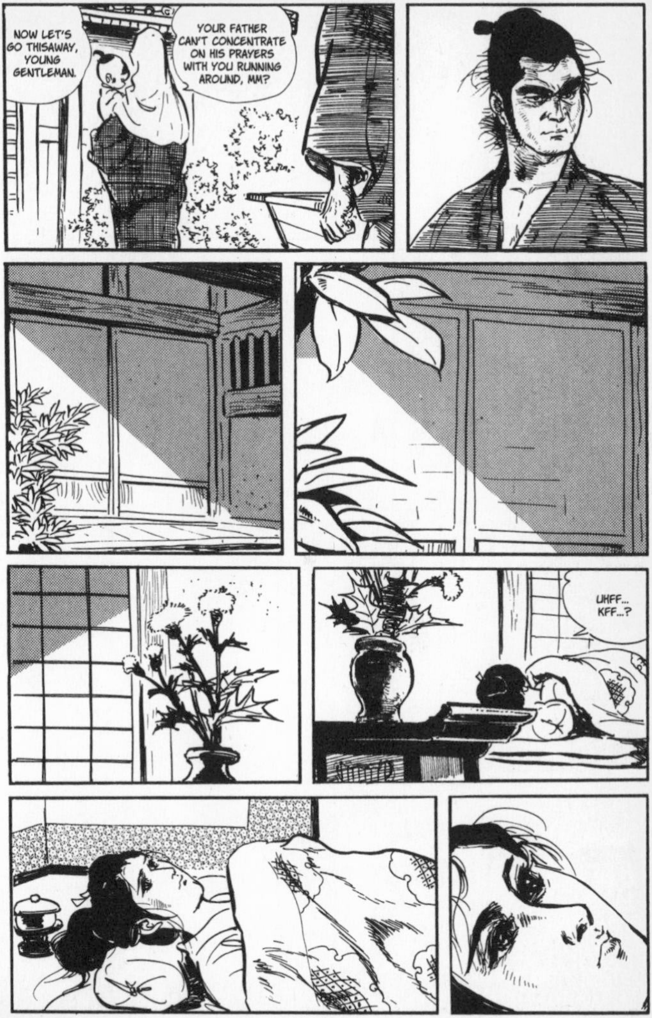
NOW LET'S GO THISAWAY, YOUNG GENTLEMAN.
YOUR FATHER CAN'T CONCENTRATE ON HIS PRAYERS WITH YOU RUNNING AROUND, MM?
UHFF... KFF...?

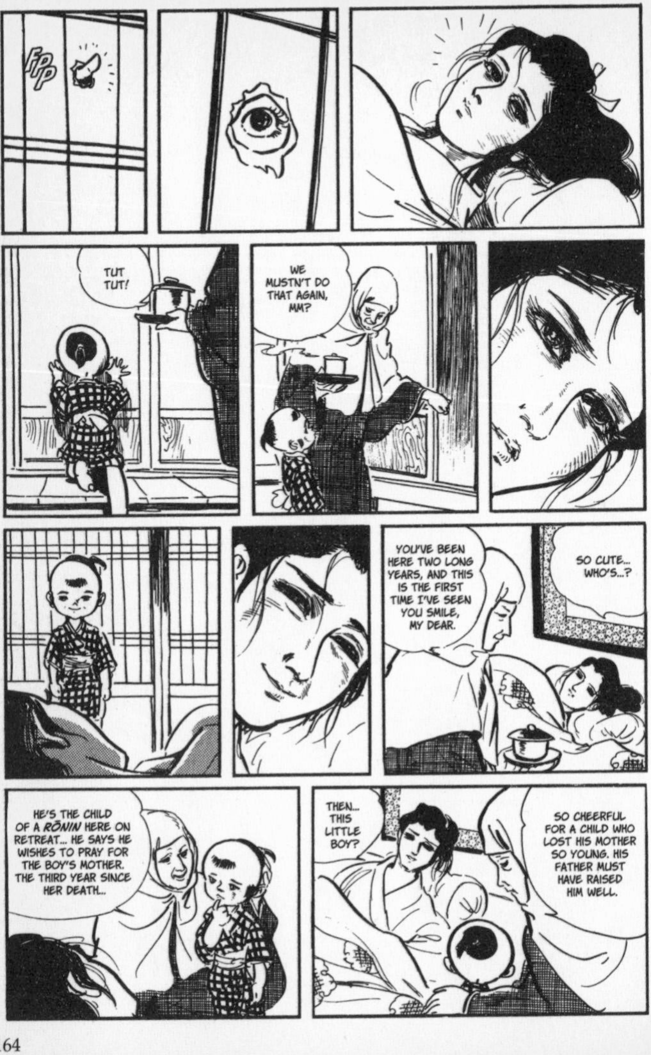
FPP
TUT TUT!
WE MUSTN'T DO THAT AGAIN, MM?
YOU'VE BEEN HERE TWO LONG YEARS, AND THIS IS THE FIRST TIME I'VE SEEN YOU SMILE, MY DEAR.
SO CUTE... WHO'S...?
HE'S THE CHILD OF A *RŌNIN* HERE ON RETREAT... HE SAYS HE WISHES TO PRAY FOR THE BOY'S MOTHER. THE THIRD YEAR SINCE HER DEATH...
THEN... THIS LITTLE BOY?
SO CHEERFUL FOR A CHILD WHO LOST HIS MOTHER SO YOUNG. HIS FATHER MUST HAVE RAISED HIM WELL.

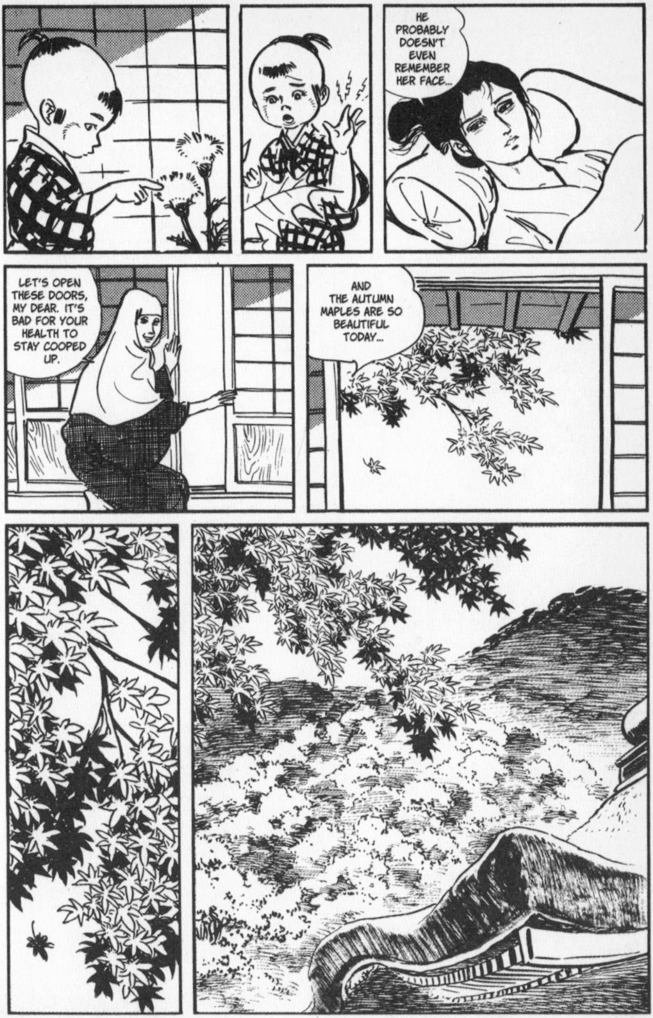
HE PROBABLY DOESN'T EVEN REMEMBER HER FACE...
LET'S OPEN THESE DOORS, MY DEAR. IT'S BAD FOR YOUR HEALTH TO STAY COOPED UP.
AND THE AUTUMN MAPLES ARE SO BEAUTIFUL TODAY...

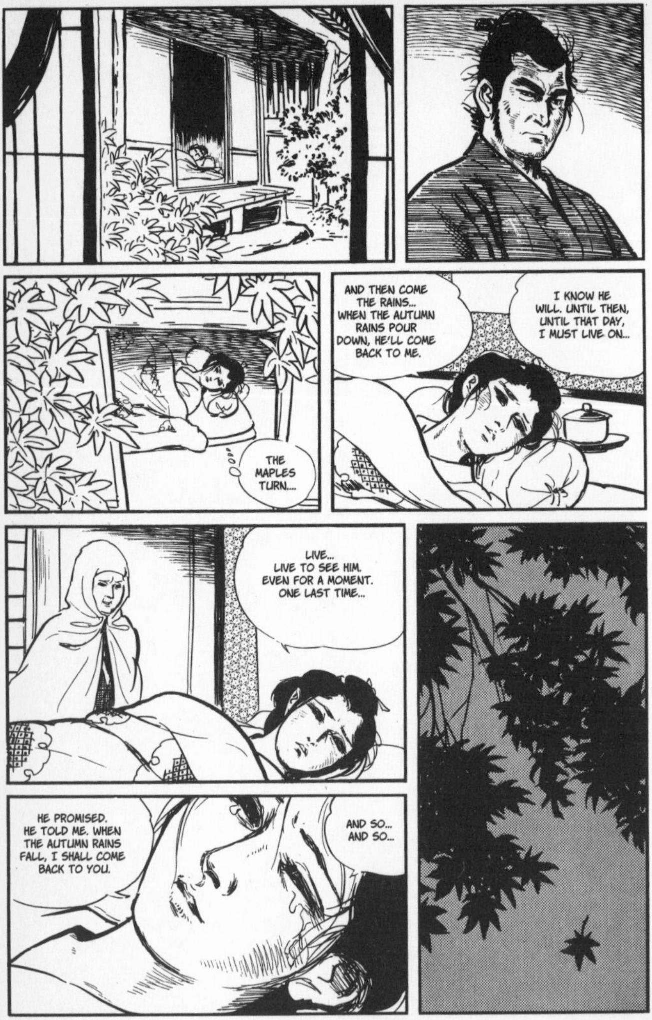
THE MAPLES TURN....
AND THEN COME THE RAINS... WHEN THE AUTUMN RAINS POUR DOWN, HE'LL COME BACK TO ME.
I KNOW HE WILL. UNTIL THEN, UNTIL THAT DAY, I MUST LIVE ON...
LIVE... LIVE TO SEE HIM. EVEN FOR A MOMENT. ONE LAST TIME...
HE PROMISED. HE TOLD ME. WHEN THE AUTUMN RAINS FALL, I SHALL COME BACK TO YOU.
AND SO... AND SO...

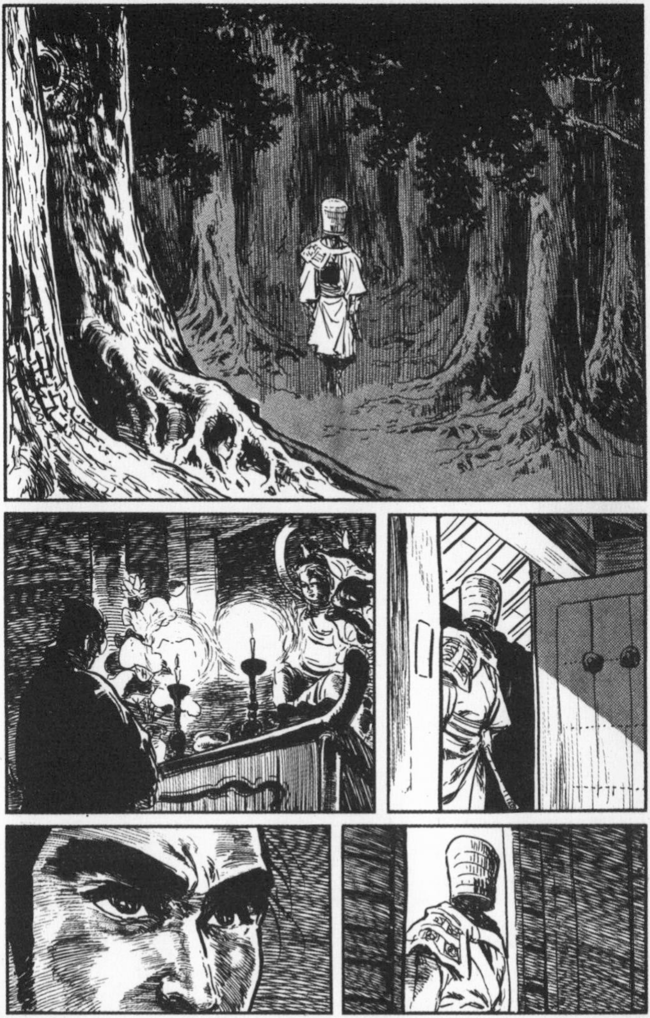

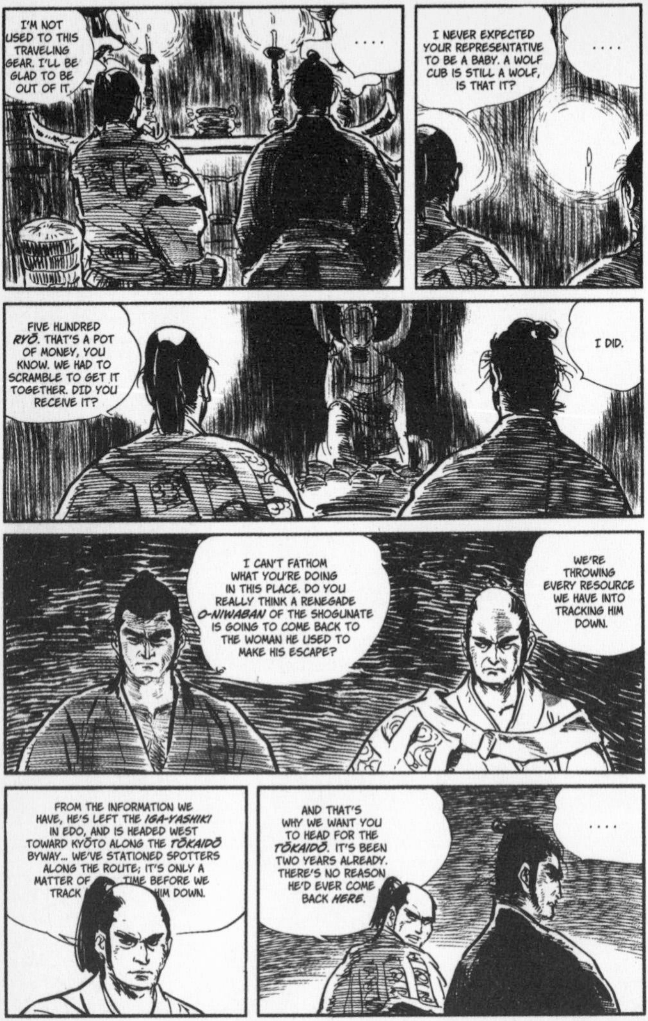
I'M NOT USED TO THIS TRAVELING GEAR. I'LL BE GLAD TO BE OUT OF IT.
. . . .
I NEVER EXPECTED YOUR REPRESENTATIVE TO BE A BABY. A WOLF CUB IS STILL A WOLF, IS THAT IT?
. . . .
FIVE HUNDRED *RYŌ*. THAT'S A POT OF MONEY, YOU KNOW. WE HAD TO SCRAMBLE TO GET IT TOGETHER. DID YOU RECEIVE IT?
I DID.
I CAN'T FATHOM WHAT YOU'RE DOING IN THIS PLACE. DO YOU REALLY THINK A RENEGADE *O-NIWABAN* OF THE SHOGUNATE IS GOING TO COME BACK TO THE WOMAN HE USED TO MAKE HIS ESCAPE?
WE'RE THROWING EVERY RESOURCE WE HAVE INTO TRACKING HIM DOWN.
FROM THE INFORMATION WE HAVE, HE'S LEFT THE *IGA-YASHIKI* IN EDO, AND IS HEADED WEST TOWARD KYŌTO ALONG THE *TŌKAIDŌ* BYWAY... WE'VE STATIONED SPOTTERS ALONG THE ROUTE; IT'S ONLY A MATTER OF TIME BEFORE WE TRACK HIM DOWN.
AND THAT'S WHY WE WANT YOU TO HEAD FOR THE *TŌKAIDŌ*. IT'S BEEN TWO YEARS ALREADY. THERE'S NO REASON HE'D EVER COME BACK *HERE*.
. . . .

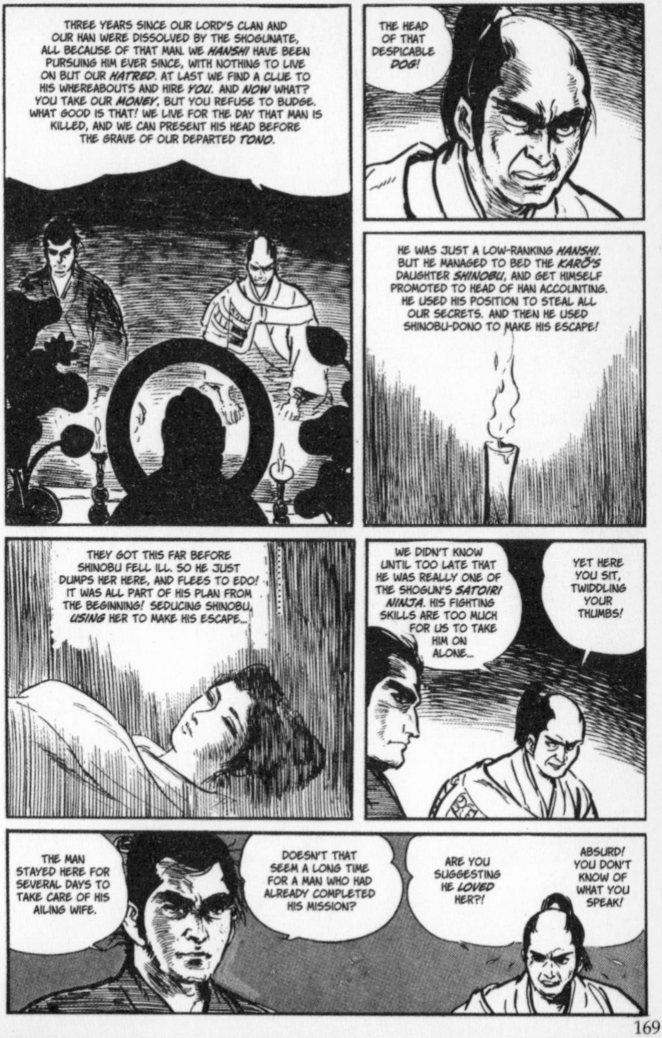
THREE YEARS SINCE OUR LORD'S CLAN AND OUR HAN WERE DISSOLVED BY THE SHOGUNATE, ALL BECAUSE OF THAT MAN. WE HANSHI HAVE BEEN PURSUING HIM EVER SINCE, WITH NOTHING TO LIVE ON BUT OUR HATRED. AT LAST WE FIND A CLUE TO HIS WHEREABOUTS AND HIRE YOU. AND NOW WHAT? YOU TAKE OUR MONEY, BUT YOU REFUSE TO BUDGE. WHAT GOOD IS THAT! WE LIVE FOR THE DAY THAT MAN IS KILLED, AND WE CAN PRESENT HIS HEAD BEFORE THE GRAVE OF OUR DEPARTED TONO.
THE HEAD OF THAT DESPICABLE DOG!
HE WAS JUST A LOW-RANKING HANSHI. BUT HE MANAGED TO BED THE KARŌ'S DAUGHTER SHINOBU, AND GET HIMSELF PROMOTED TO HEAD OF HAN ACCOUNTING. HE USED HIS POSITION TO STEAL ALL OUR SECRETS. AND THEN HE USED SHINOBU-DONO TO MAKE HIS ESCAPE!
THEY GOT THIS FAR BEFORE SHINOBU FELL ILL. SO HE JUST DUMPS HER HERE, AND FLEES TO EDO! IT WAS ALL PART OF HIS PLAN FROM THE BEGINNING! SEDUCING SHINOBU, USING HER TO MAKE HIS ESCAPE...
WE DIDN'T KNOW UNTIL TOO LATE THAT HE WAS REALLY ONE OF THE SHOGUN'S SATOIRI NINJA. HIS FIGHTING SKILLS ARE TOO MUCH FOR US TO TAKE HIM ON ALONE...
YET HERE YOU SIT, TWIDDLING YOUR THUMBS!
THE MAN STAYED HERE FOR SEVERAL DAYS TO TAKE CARE OF HIS AILING WIFE.
DOESN'T THAT SEEM A LONG TIME FOR A MAN WHO HAD ALREADY COMPLETED HIS MISSION?
ARE YOU SUGGESTING HE LOVED HER?!
ABSURD! YOU DON'T KNOW OF WHAT YOU SPEAK!

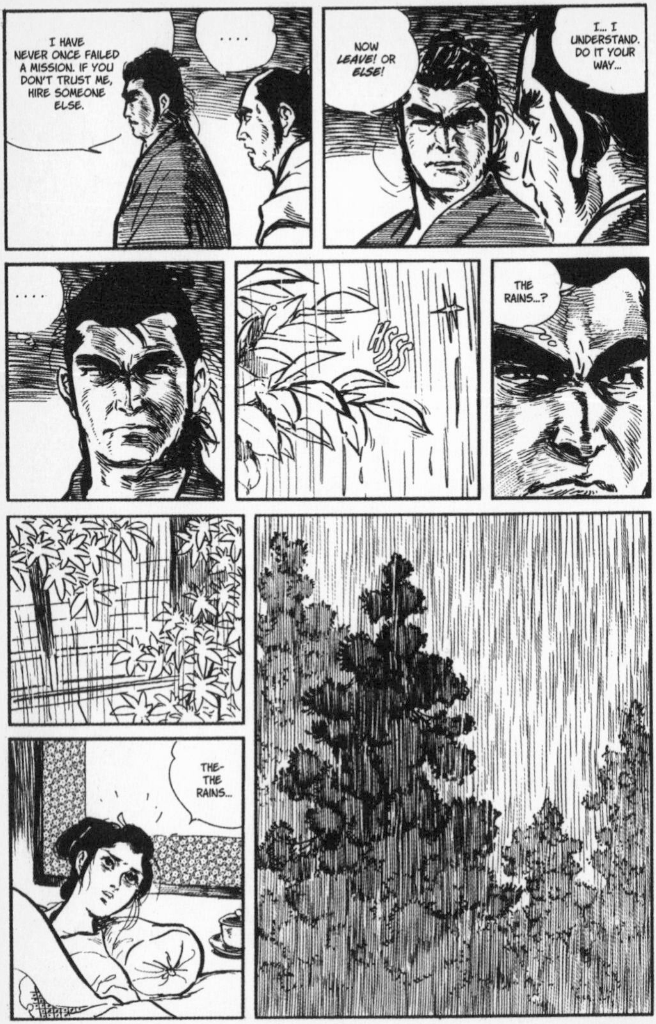
I HAVE NEVER ONCE FAILED A MISSION. IF YOU DON'T TRUST ME, HIRE SOMEONE ELSE.
....
NOW LEAVE! OR ELSE!
I... I UNDERSTAND. DO IT YOUR WAY...
....
HSSS
THE RAINS...?
THE- THE RAINS...

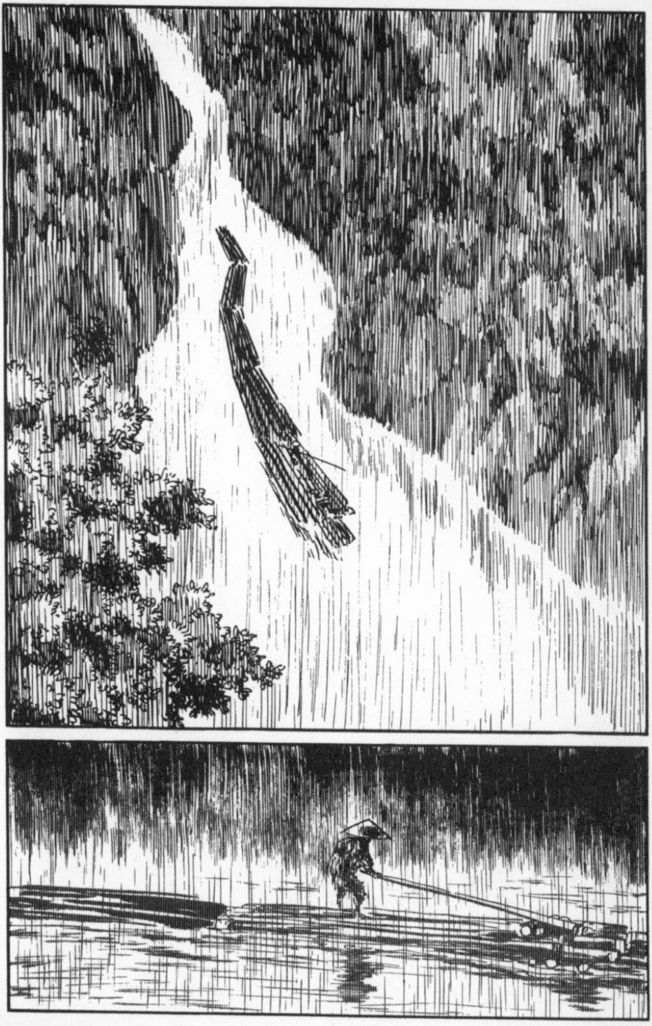

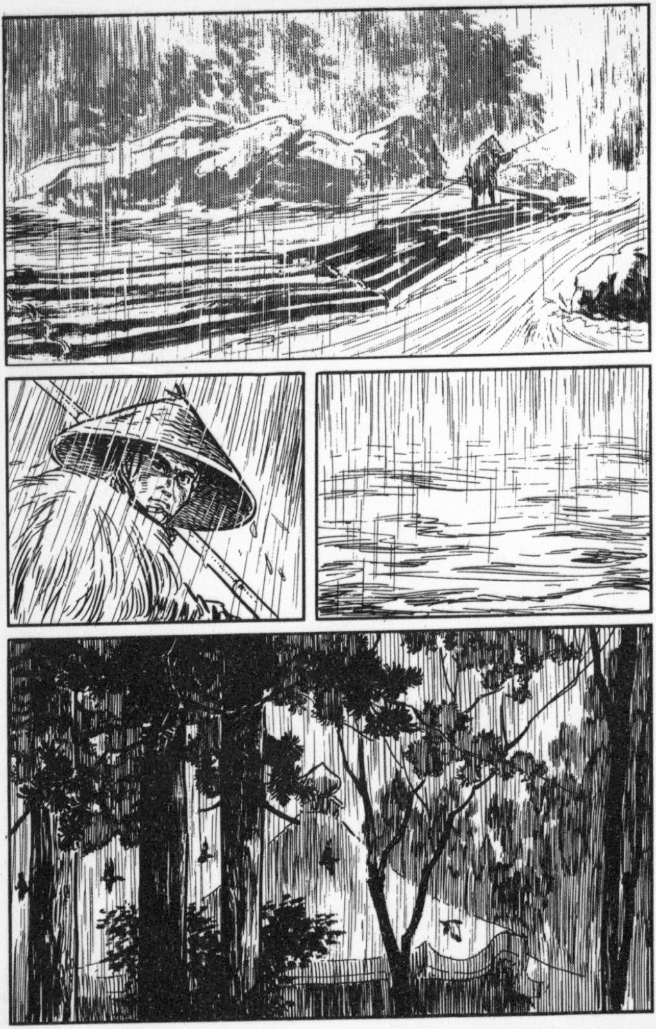

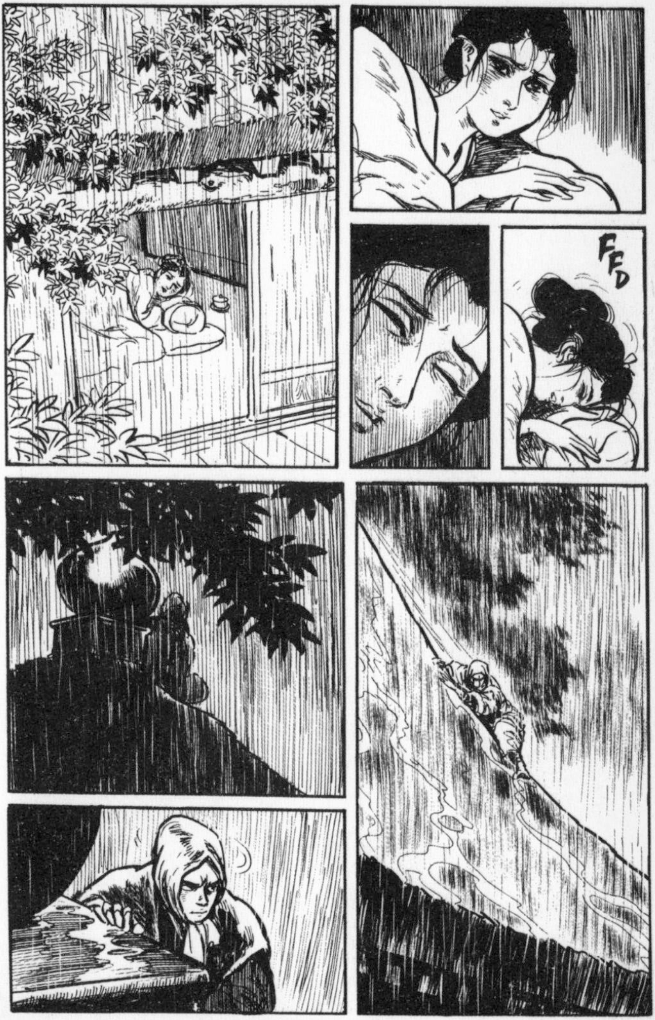
FFD

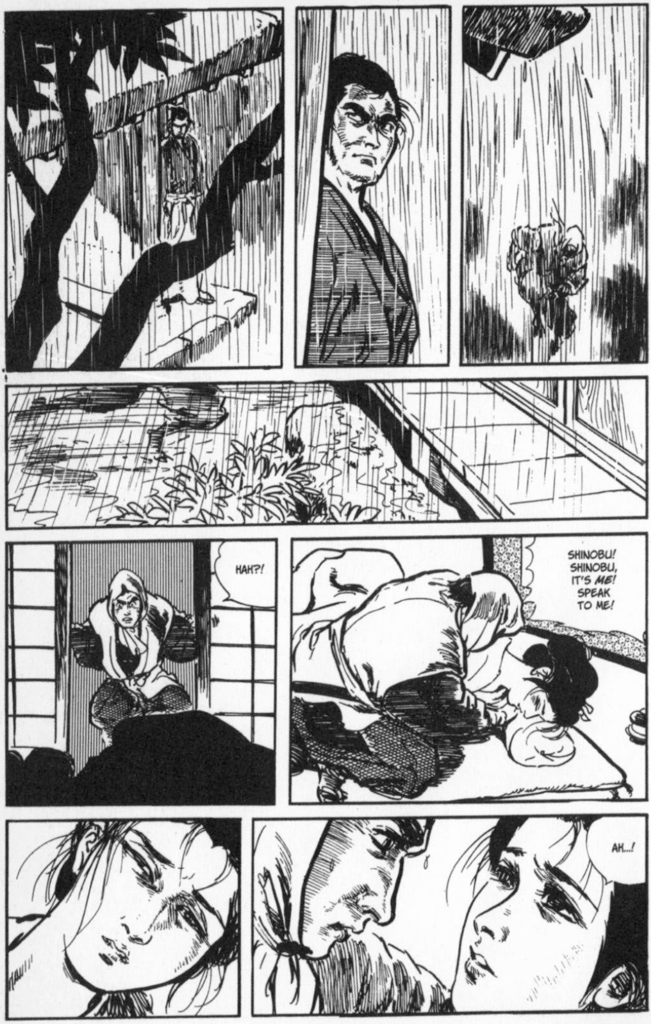
HAH?!
SHINOBU! SHINOBU, IT'S *ME!* SPEAK TO ME!
AH...!

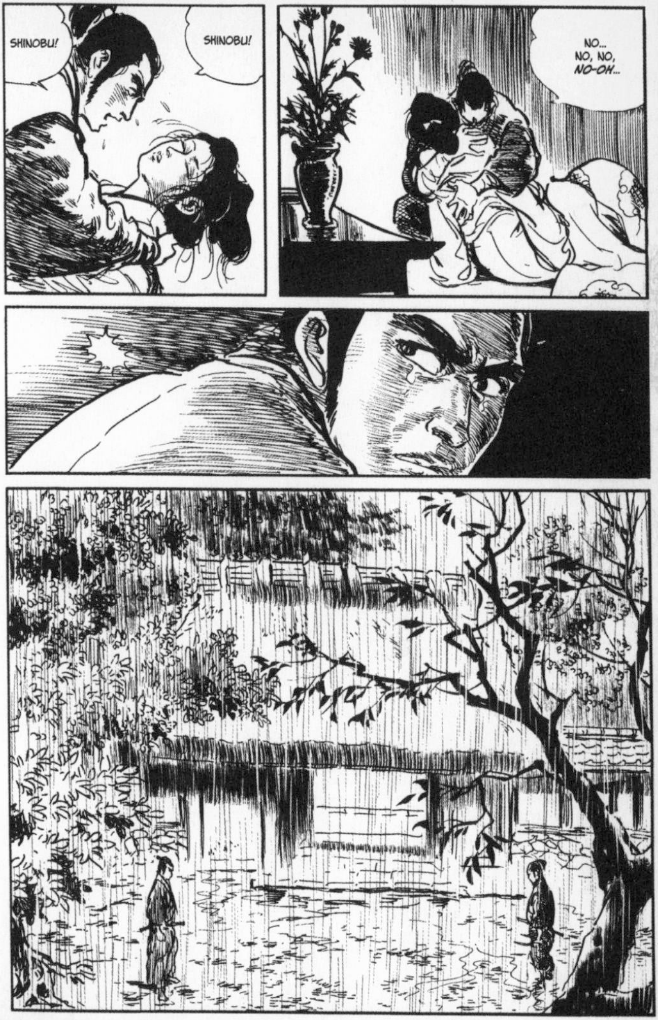
SHINOBU!
SHINOBU!
NO... NO, NO, NO-OH...

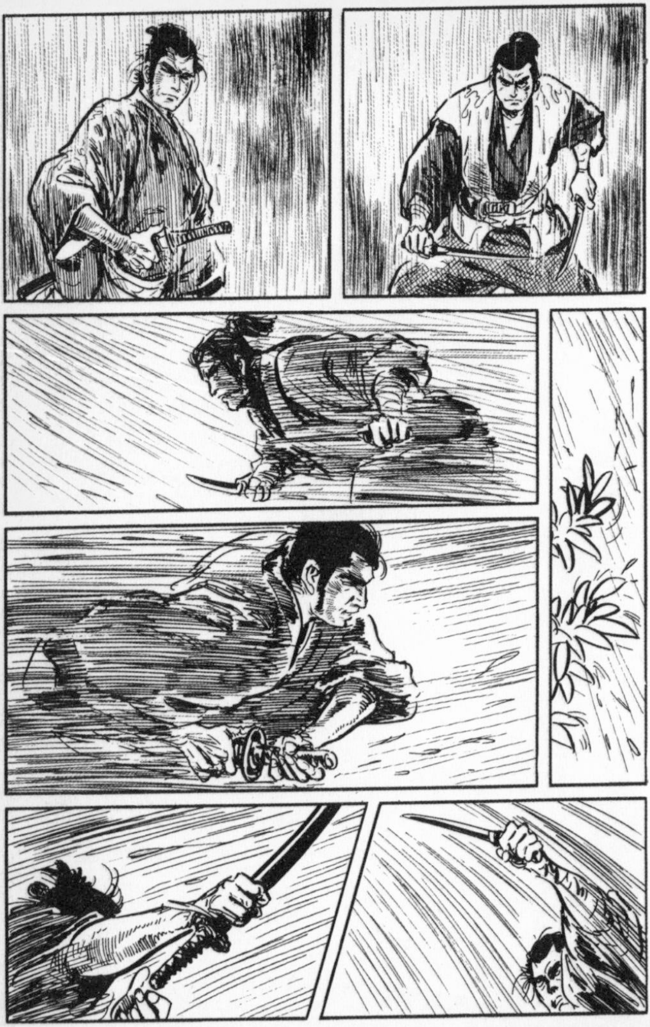

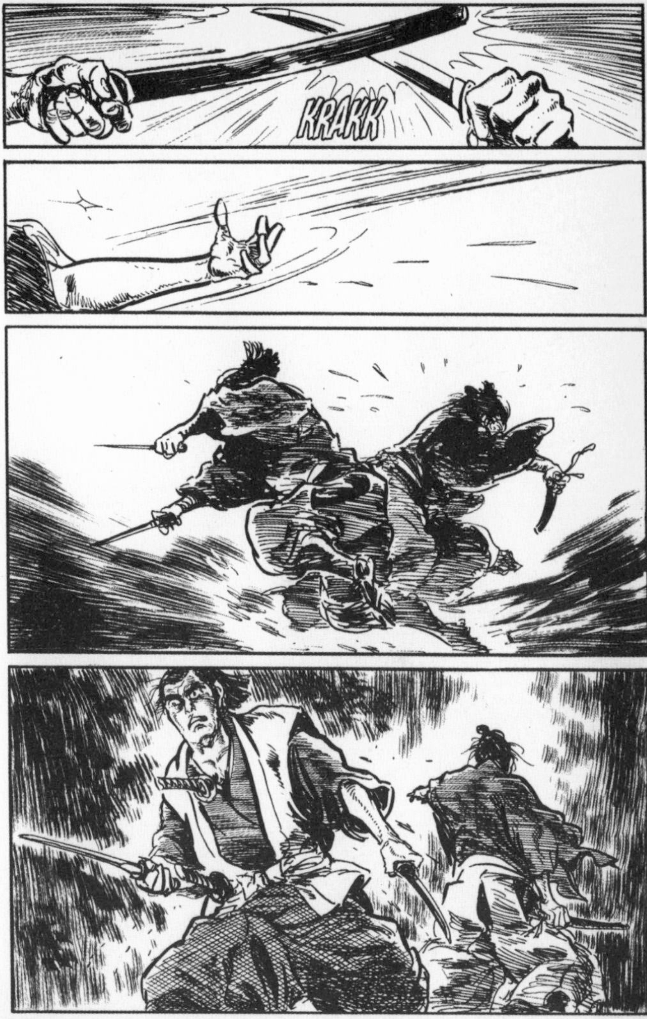
KRAKK

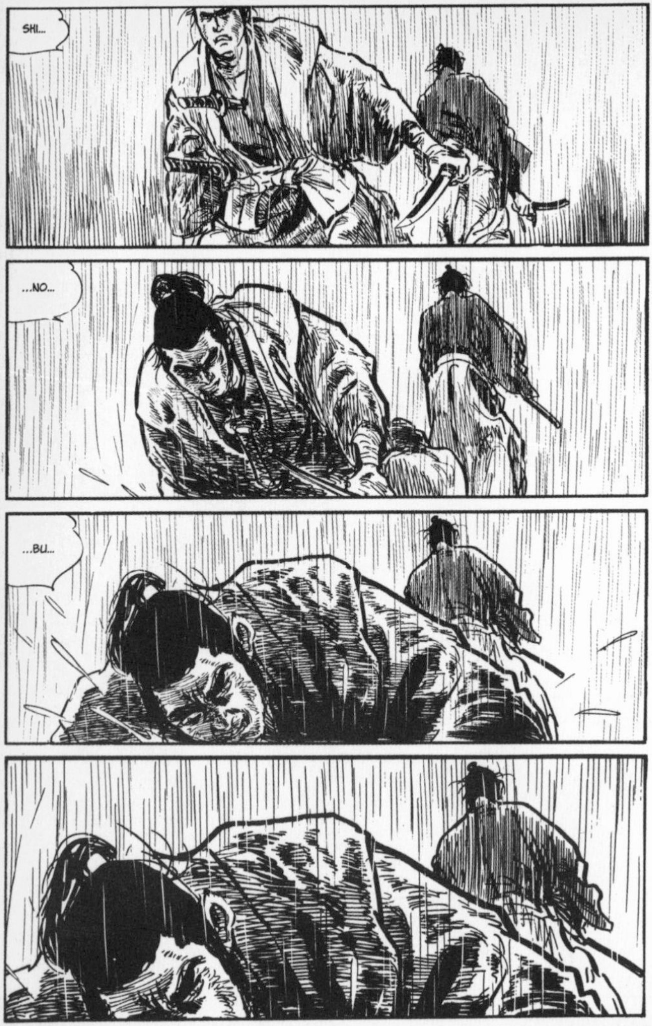
SHI...
...NO...
...BU...

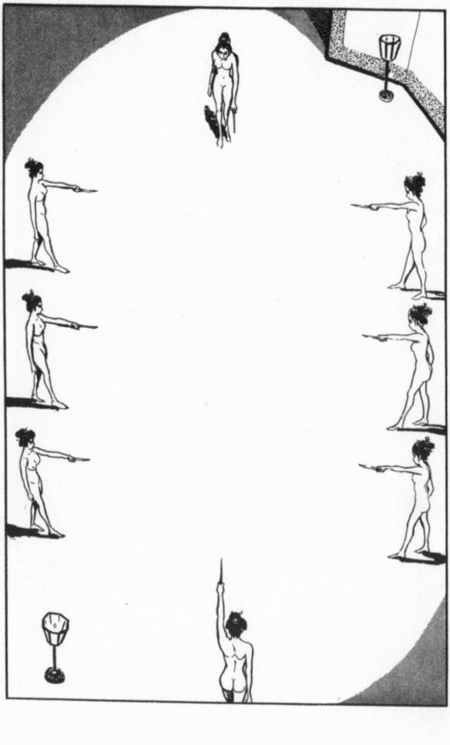

the seventh

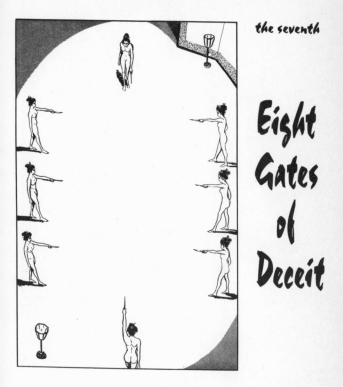

Eight Gates of Deceit

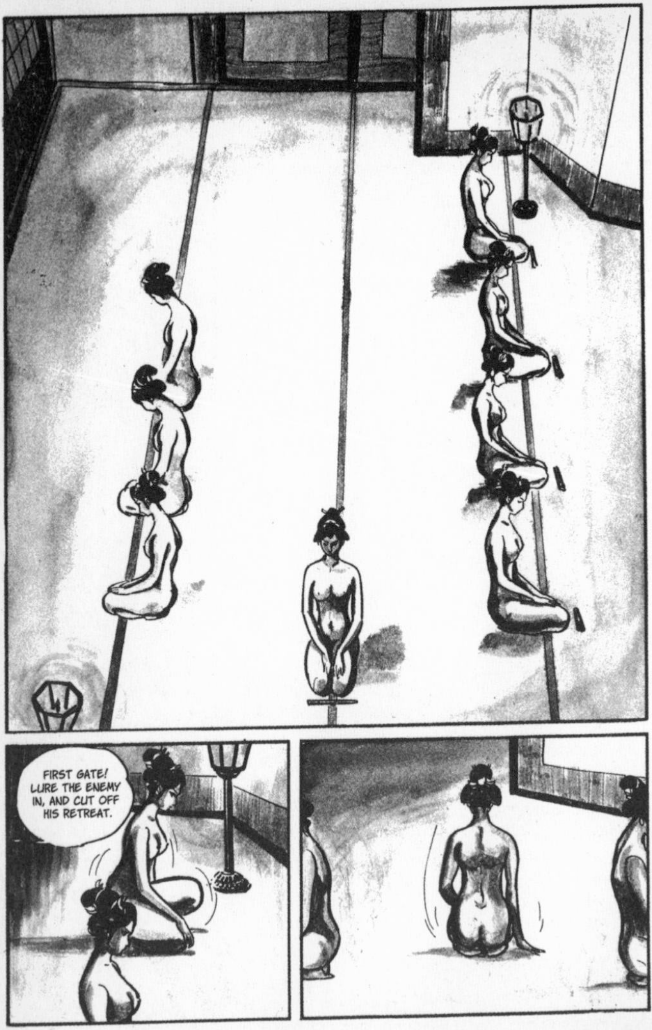
FIRST GATE! LURE THE ENEMY IN, AND CUT OFF HIS RETREAT.

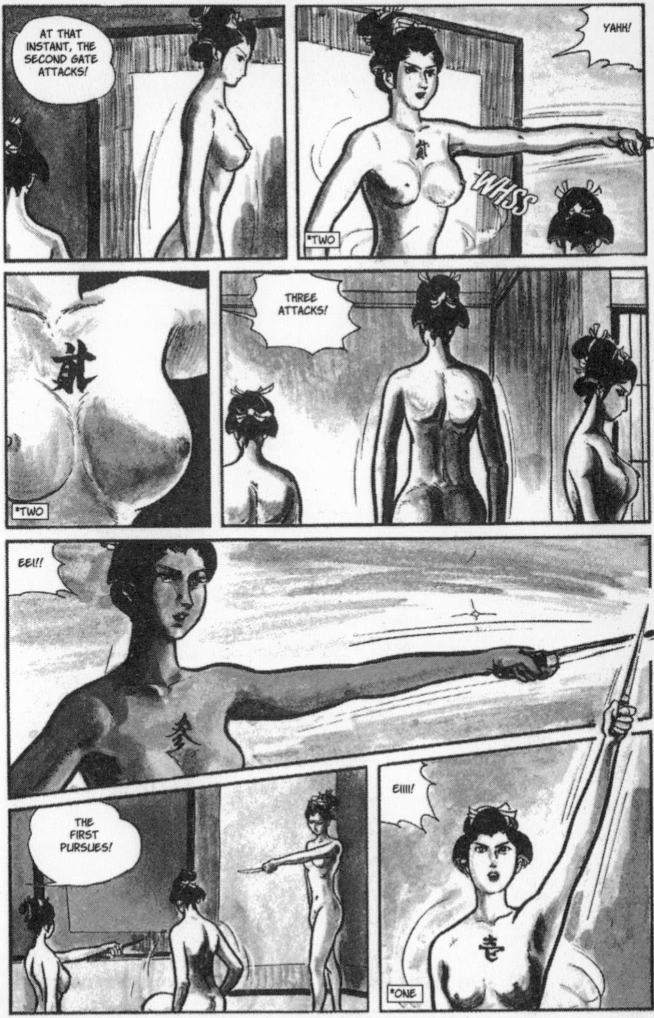
AT THAT INSTANT, THE SECOND GATE ATTACKS!
YAHH!
WHSS
*TWO
*TWO
THREE ATTACKS!
EEI!!
THE FIRST PURSUES!
EIIII!
*ONE

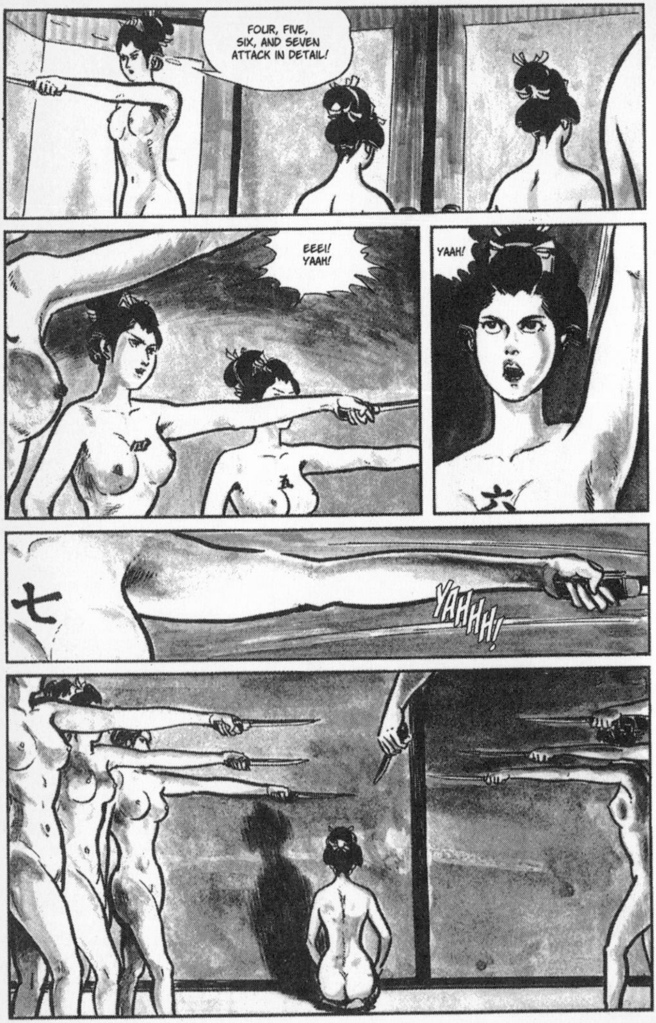
FOUR, FIVE, SIX, AND SEVEN ATTACK IN DETAIL!
EEEI! YAAH!
YAAH!
YAHHH!

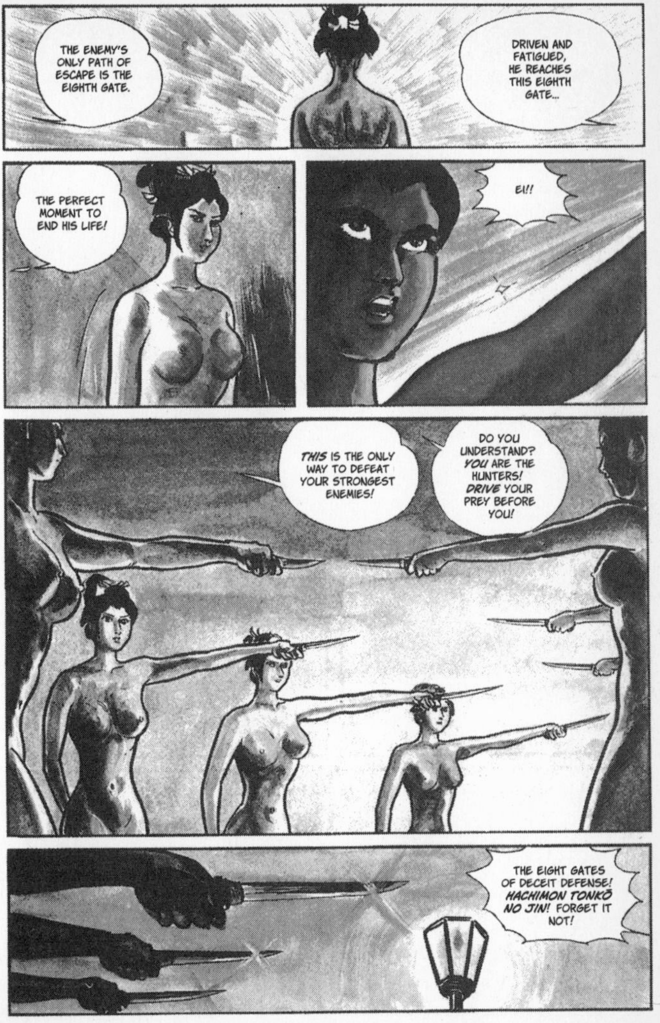
THE ENEMY'S ONLY PATH OF ESCAPE IS THE EIGHTH GATE.
DRIVEN AND FATIGUED, HE REACHES THIS EIGHTH GATE...
THE PERFECT MOMENT TO END HIS LIFE!
EI!!
THIS IS THE ONLY WAY TO DEFEAT YOUR STRONGEST ENEMIES!
DO YOU UNDERSTAND? YOU ARE THE HUNTERS! DRIVE YOUR PREY BEFORE YOU!
THE EIGHT GATES OF DECEIT DEFENSE! HACHIMON TONKŌ NO JIN! FORGET IT NOT!

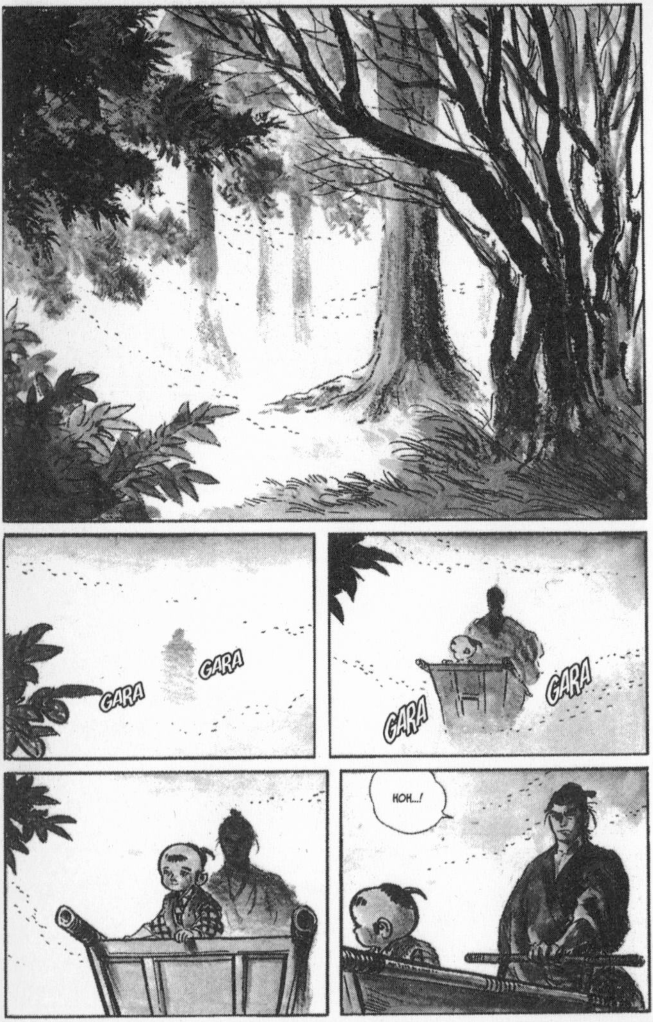
GARA
GARA
GARA
GARA
HOH...!

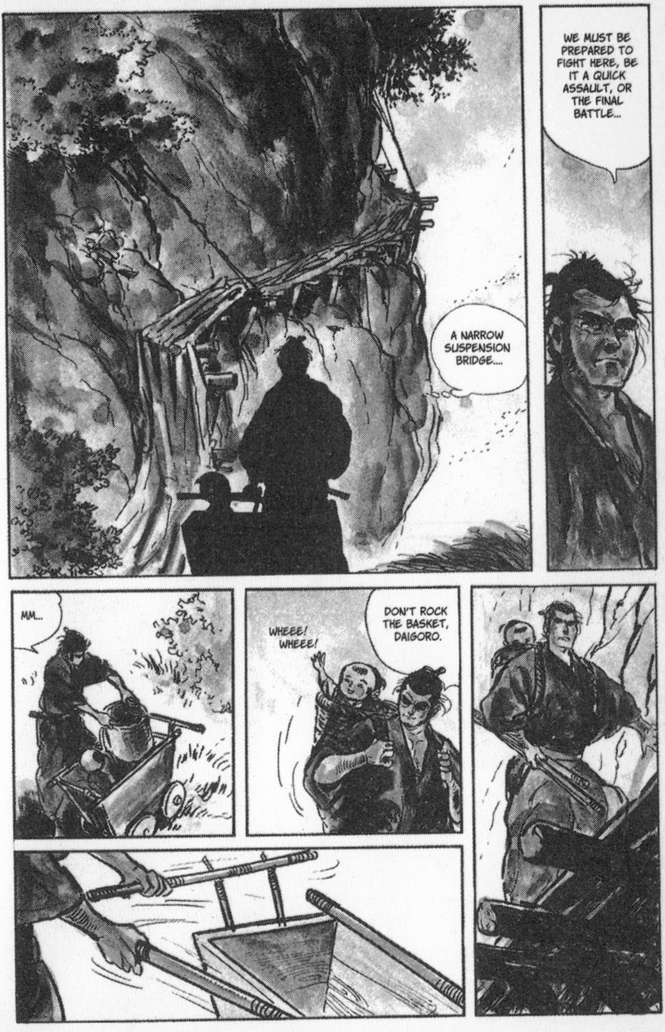
A NARROW SUSPENSION BRIDGE....
WE MUST BE PREPARED TO FIGHT HERE, BE IT A QUICK ASSAULT, OR THE FINAL BATTLE...
MM...
WHEEE! WHEEE!
DON'T ROCK THE BASKET, DAIGORO.

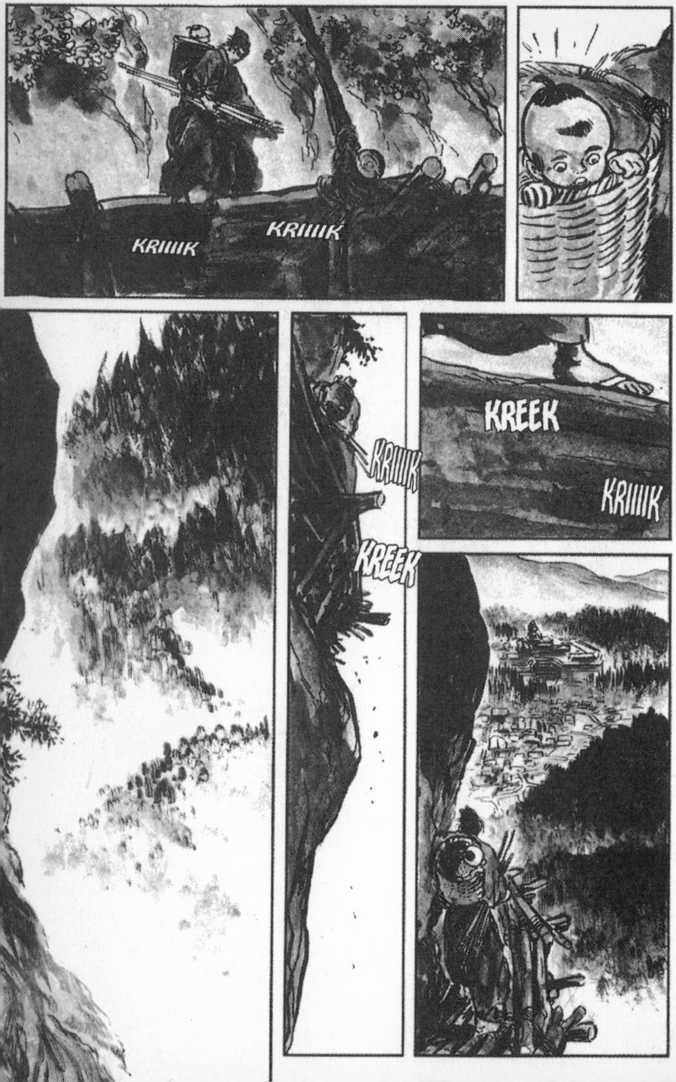
KRIIIIK
KRIIIIK
KRIIIIK
KREEK
KREEK
KRIIIIK

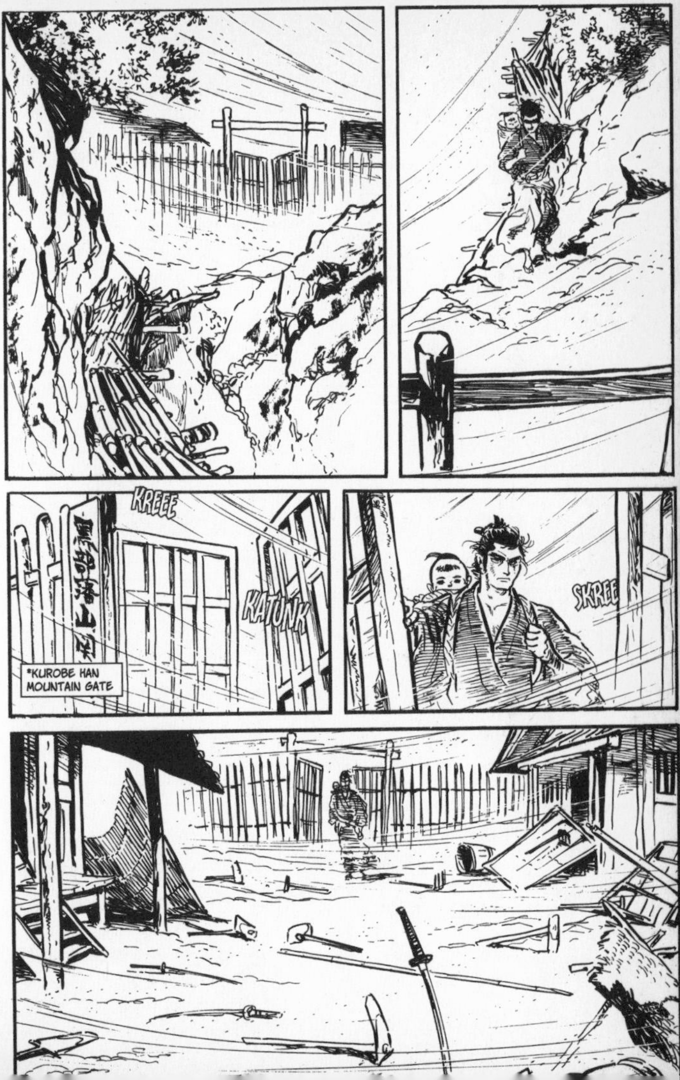
KREEE
KATUNK
*KUROBE HAN
MOUNTAIN GATE
SKREE

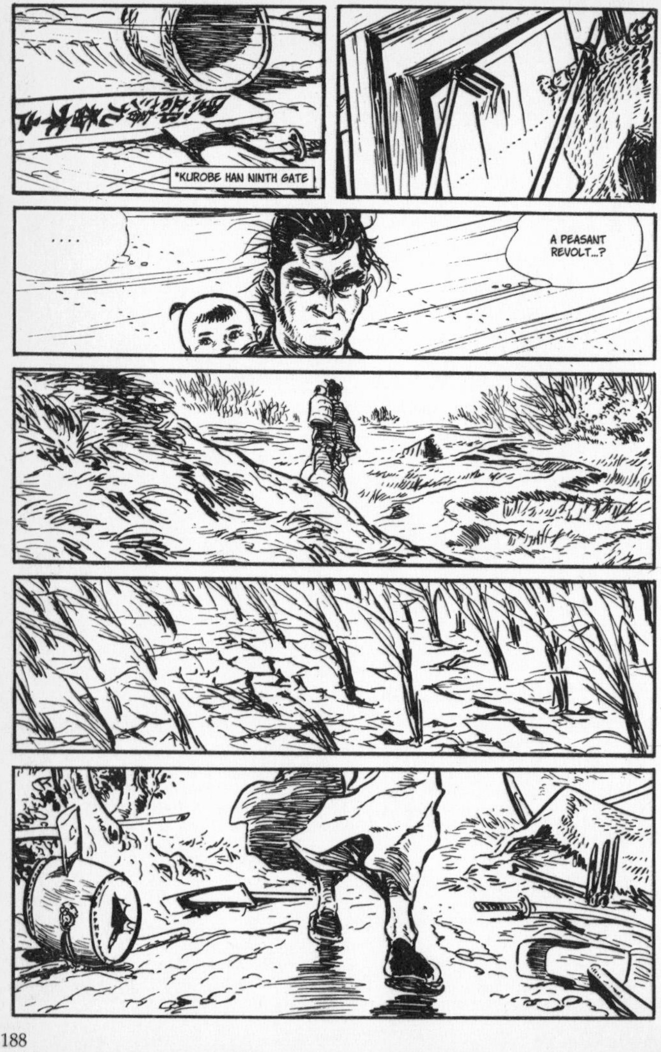
*KUROBE HAN NINTH GATE
....
A PEASANT REVOLT...?

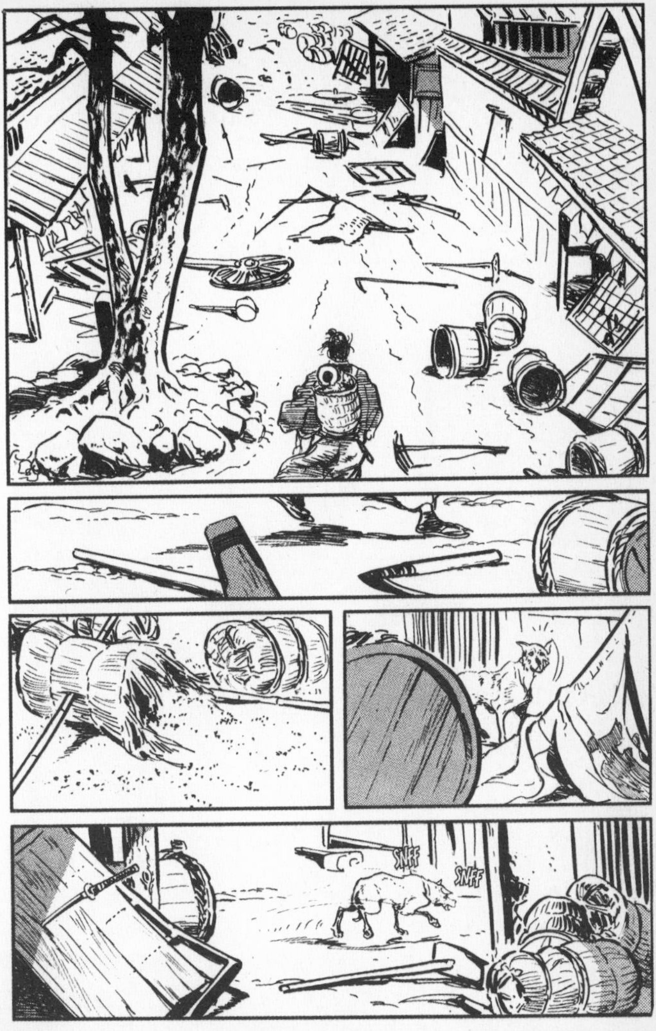
SNFF
SNFF

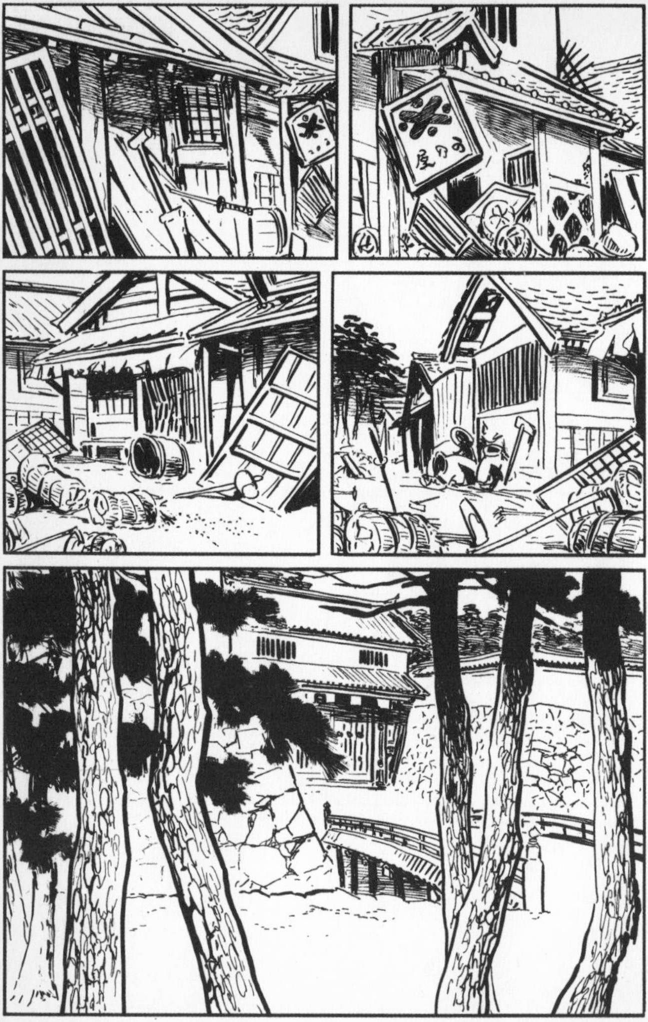

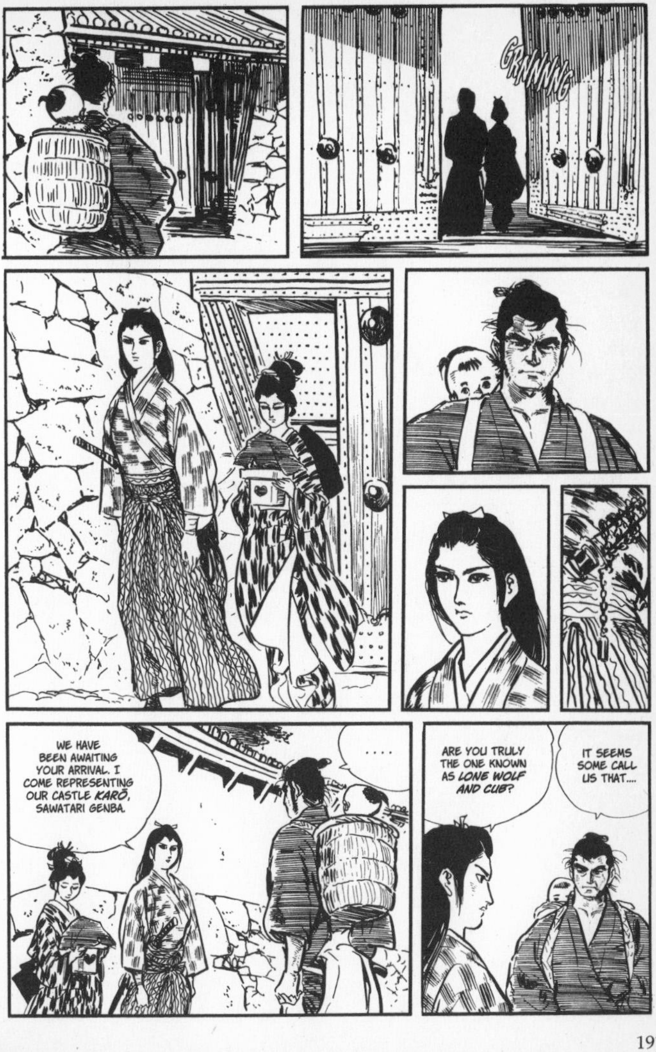
GRNNNNG
WE HAVE BEEN AWAITING YOUR ARRIVAL. I COME REPRESENTING OUR CASTLE *KARŌ*, SAWATARI GENBA.
....
ARE YOU TRULY THE ONE KNOWN AS *LONE WOLF AND CUB*?
IT SEEMS SOME CALL US THAT....

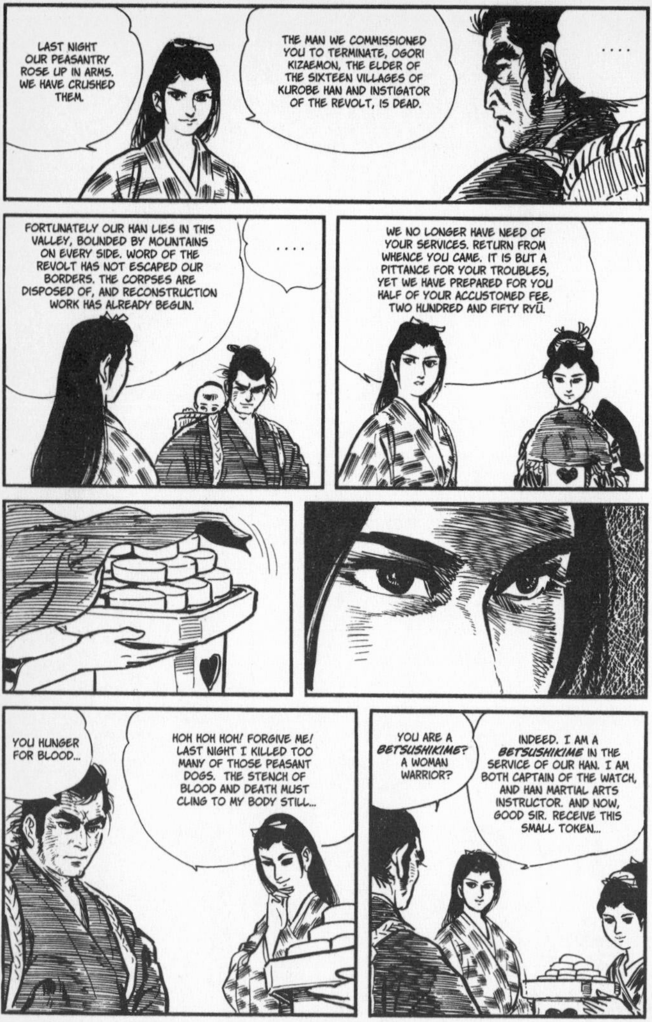
LAST NIGHT OUR PEASANTRY ROSE UP IN ARMS. WE HAVE CRUSHED THEM.
THE MAN WE COMMISSIONED YOU TO TERMINATE, OGORI KIZAEMON, THE ELDER OF THE SIXTEEN VILLAGES OF KUROBE HAN AND INSTIGATOR OF THE REVOLT, IS DEAD.
....
FORTUNATELY OUR HAN LIES IN THIS VALLEY, BOUNDED BY MOUNTAINS ON EVERY SIDE. WORD OF THE REVOLT HAS NOT ESCAPED OUR BORDERS. THE CORPSES ARE DISPOSED OF, AND RECONSTRUCTION WORK HAS ALREADY BEGUN.
....
WE NO LONGER HAVE NEED OF YOUR SERVICES. RETURN FROM WHENCE YOU CAME. IT IS BUT A PITTANCE FOR YOUR TROUBLES, YET WE HAVE PREPARED FOR YOU HALF OF YOUR ACCUSTOMED FEE, TWO HUNDRED AND FIFTY RYŪ.
YOU HUNGER FOR BLOOD...
HOH HOH HOH! FORGIVE ME! LAST NIGHT I KILLED TOO MANY OF THOSE PEASANT DOGS. THE STENCH OF BLOOD AND DEATH MUST CLING TO MY BODY STILL...
YOU ARE A *BETSUSHIKIME*? A WOMAN WARRIOR?
INDEED. I AM A *BETSUSHIKIME* IN THE SERVICE OF OUR HAN. I AM BOTH CAPTAIN OF THE WATCH, AND HAN MARTIAL ARTS INSTRUCTOR. AND NOW, GOOD SIR. RECEIVE THIS SMALL TOKEN...

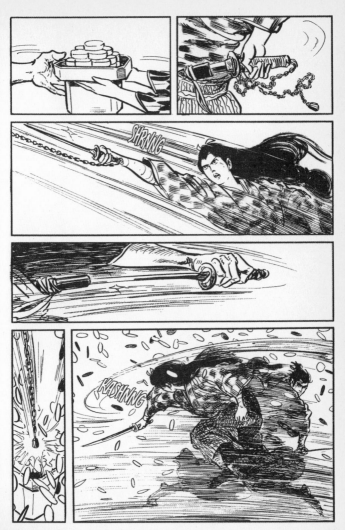

SHRNNG

KASHNNG

193

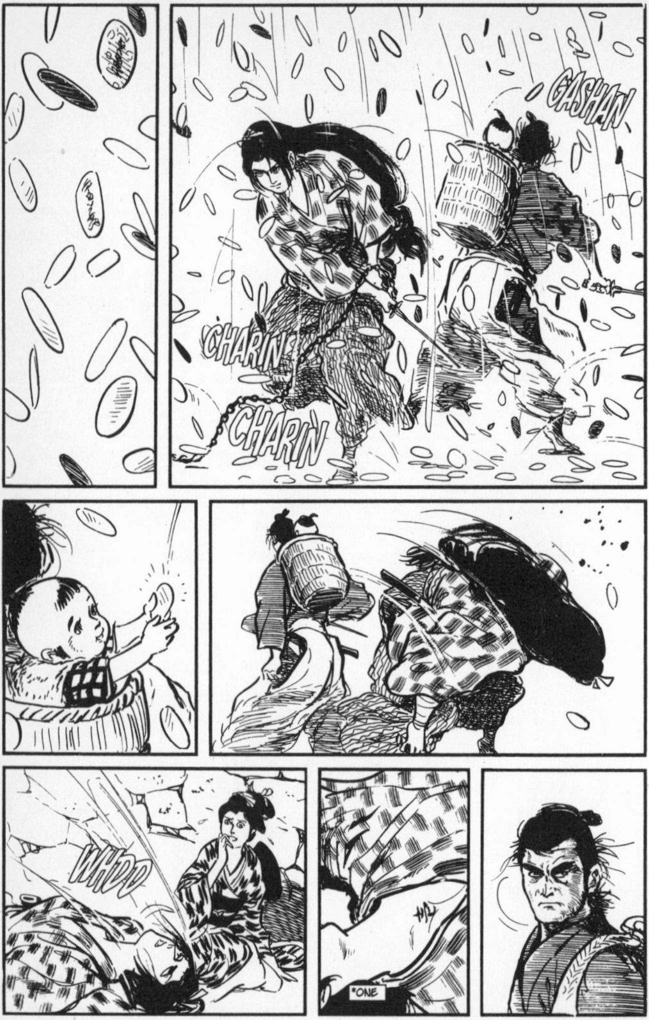
GASHAN
CHARIN
CHARIN
WHOO
*ONE

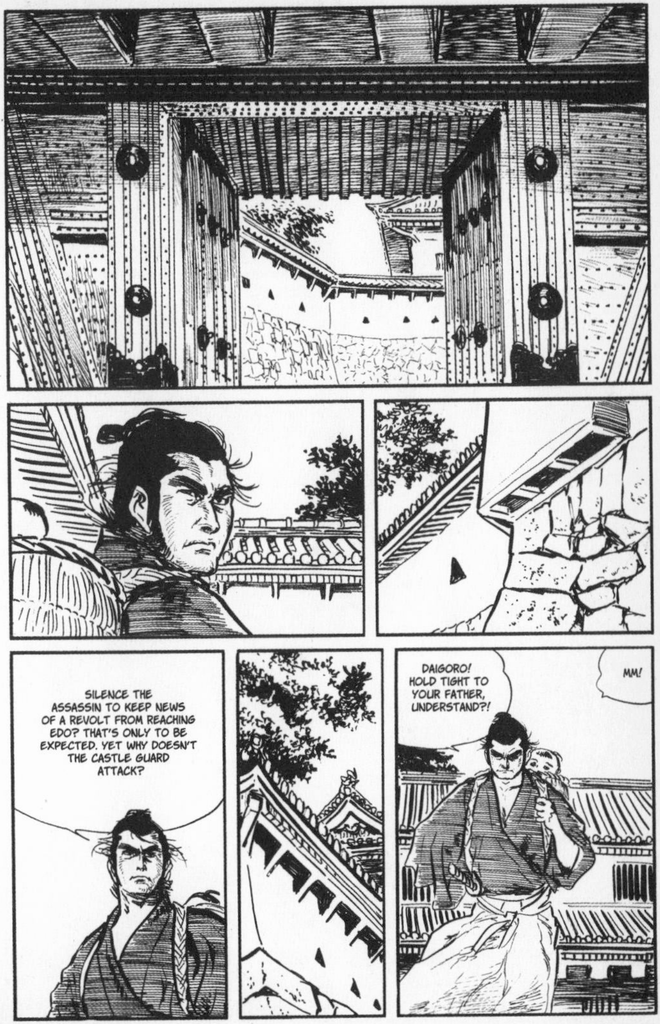

SILENCE THE ASSASSIN TO KEEP NEWS OF A REVOLT FROM REACHING EDO? THAT'S ONLY TO BE EXPECTED. YET WHY DOESN'T THE CASTLE GUARD ATTACK?
DAIGORO! HOLD TIGHT TO YOUR FATHER, UNDERSTAND?!
MM!

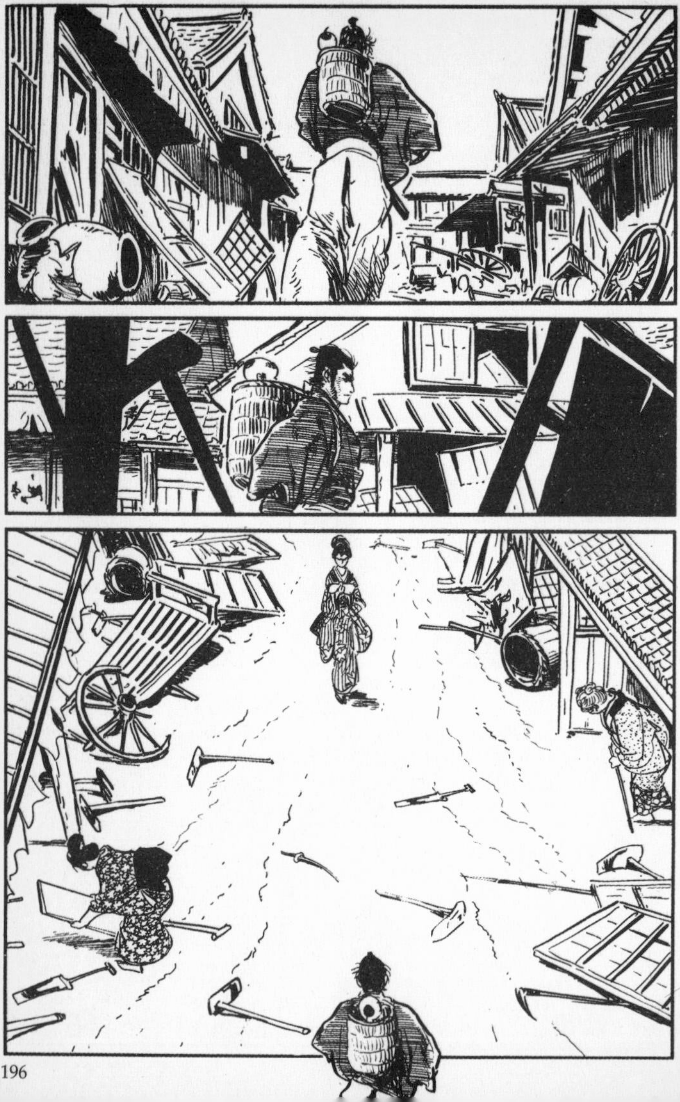

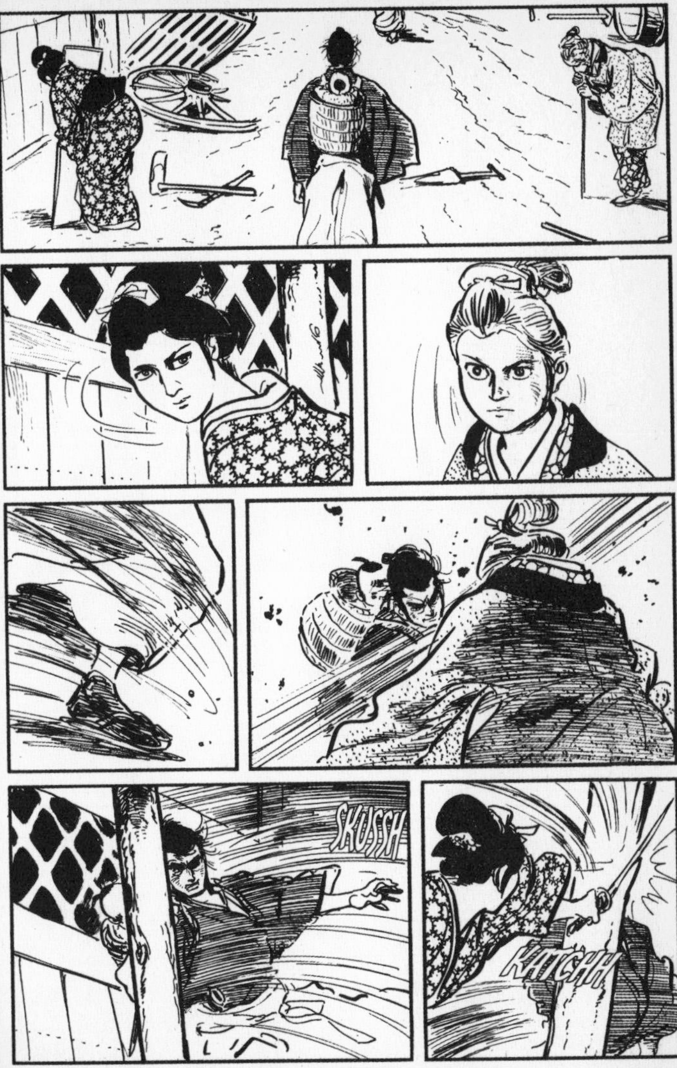
SKUSSH
KATCHH

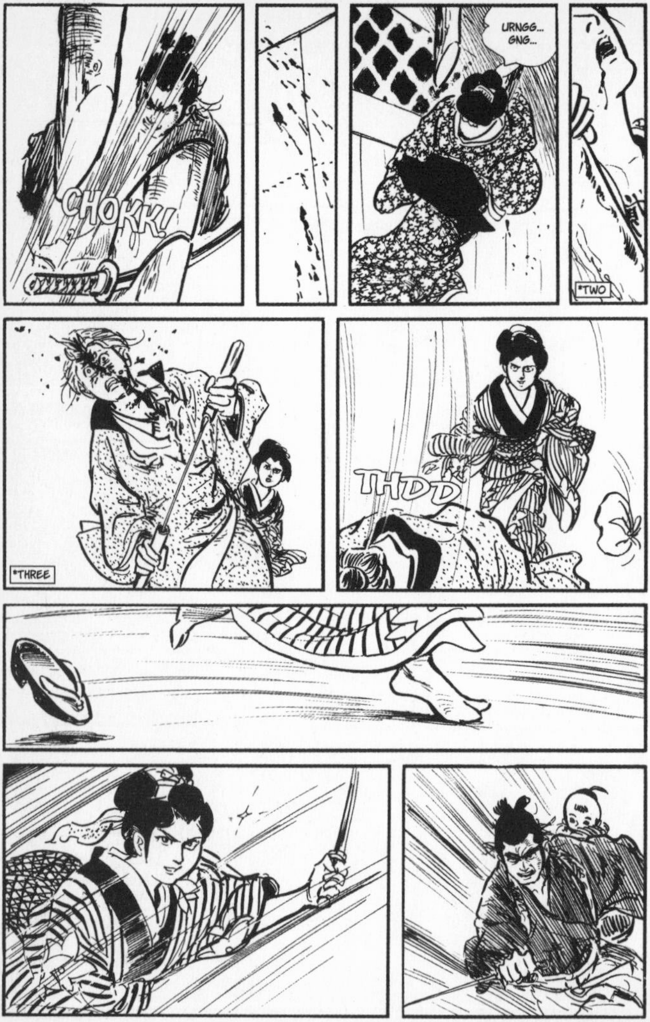
CHOKK!
URNGG... GNG...
*TWO
*THREE
THDD

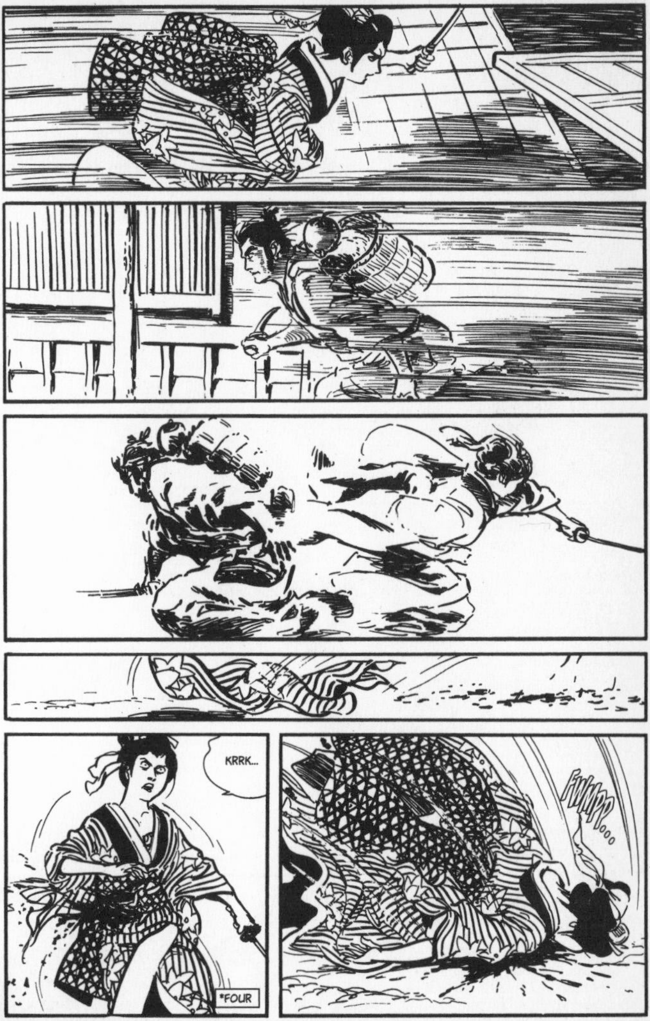
KRRK...
*FOUR
FWMPPoooo

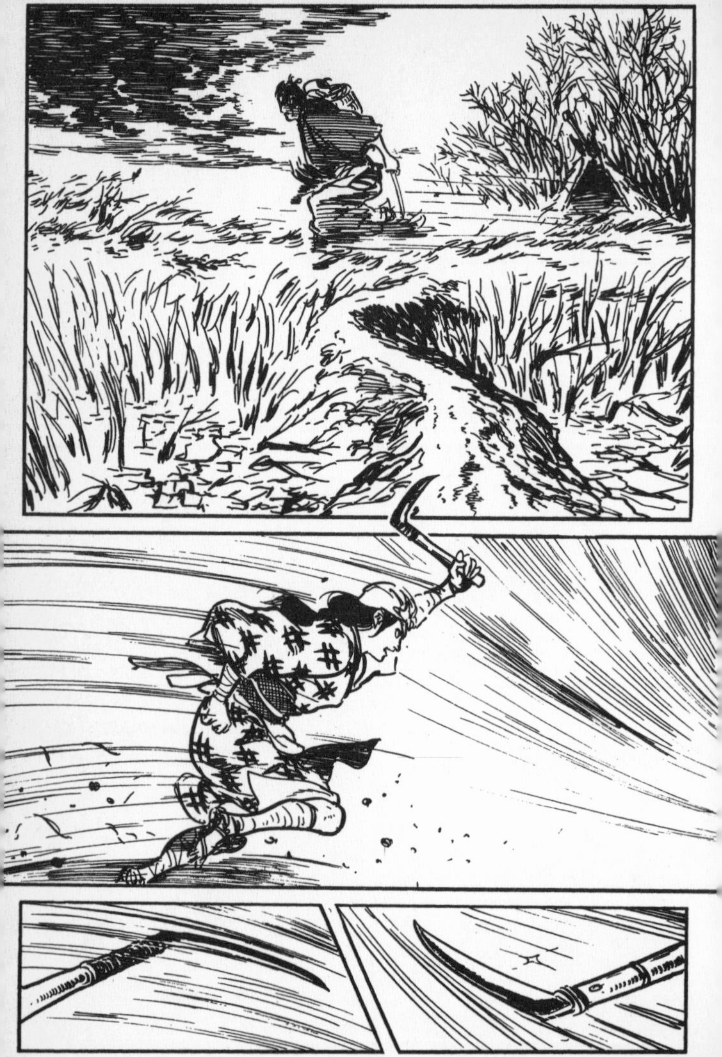

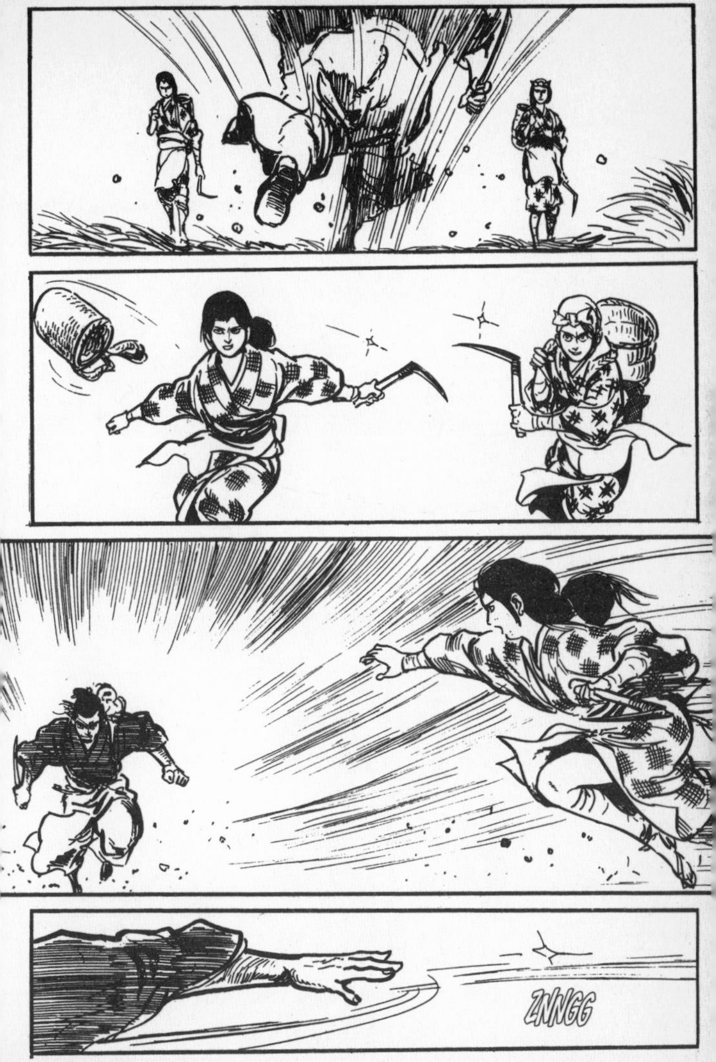
ZNNGG

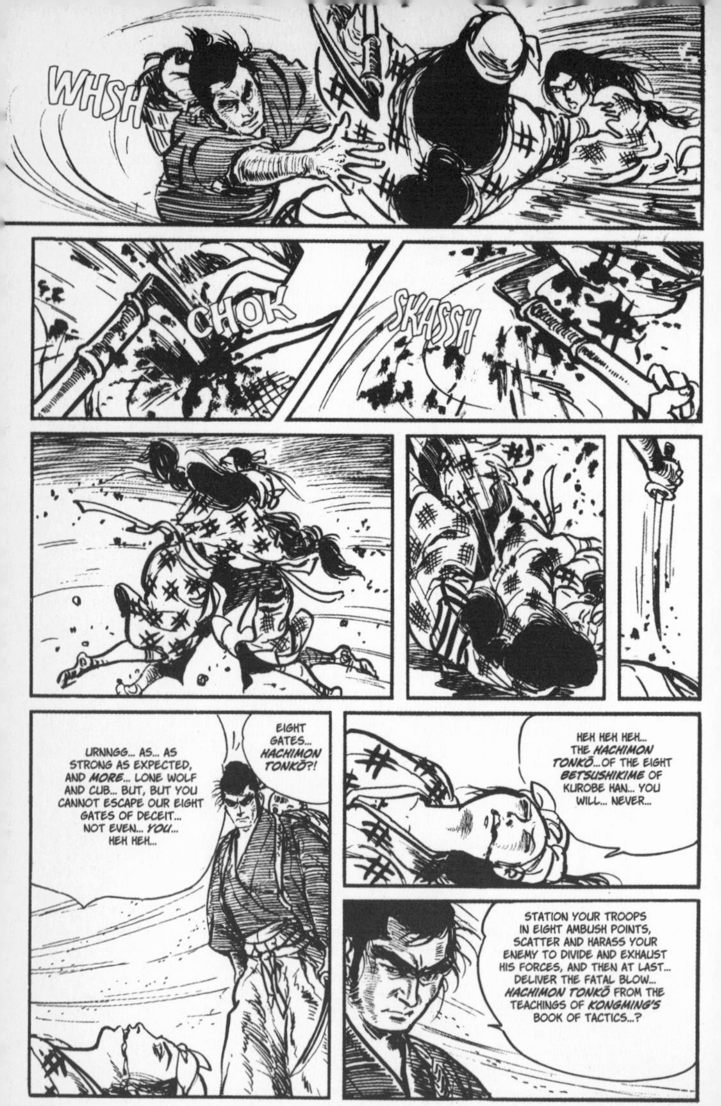

WHSH
CHOK
SKASSH
URNNGG... AS... AS STRONG AS EXPECTED, AND MORE... LONE WOLF AND CUB... BUT, BUT YOU CANNOT ESCAPE OUR EIGHT GATES OF DECEIT... NOT EVEN... YOU... HEH HEH...
EIGHT GATES... HACHIMON TONKŌ?!
HEH HEH HEH... THE HACHIMON TONKŌ...OF THE EIGHT BETSUSHIKIME OF KUROBE HAN... YOU WILL... NEVER...
STATION YOUR TROOPS IN EIGHT AMBUSH POINTS, SCATTER AND HARASS YOUR ENEMY TO DIVIDE AND EXHAUST HIS FORCES, AND THEN AT LAST... DELIVER THE FATAL BLOW... HACHIMON TONKŌ FROM THE TEACHINGS OF KONGMING'S BOOK OF TACTICS...?

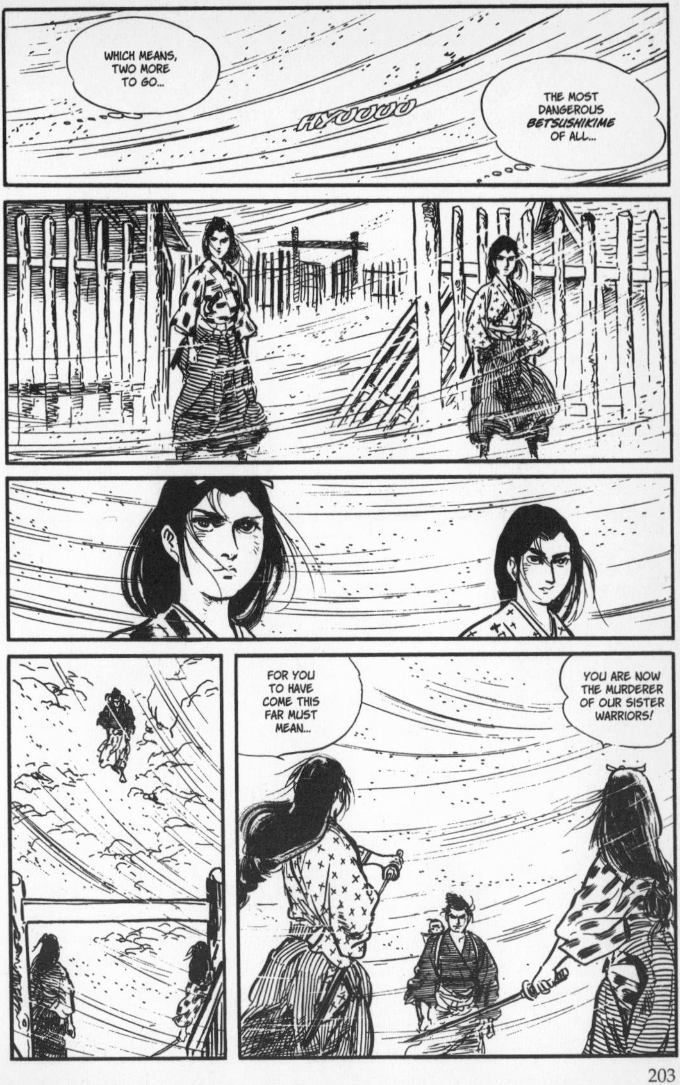
WHICH MEANS, TWO MORE TO GO...
HYUUUU
THE MOST DANGEROUS *BETSUSHIKIME* OF ALL...
FOR YOU TO HAVE COME THIS FAR MUST MEAN...
YOU ARE NOW THE MURDERER OF OUR SISTER WARRIORS!

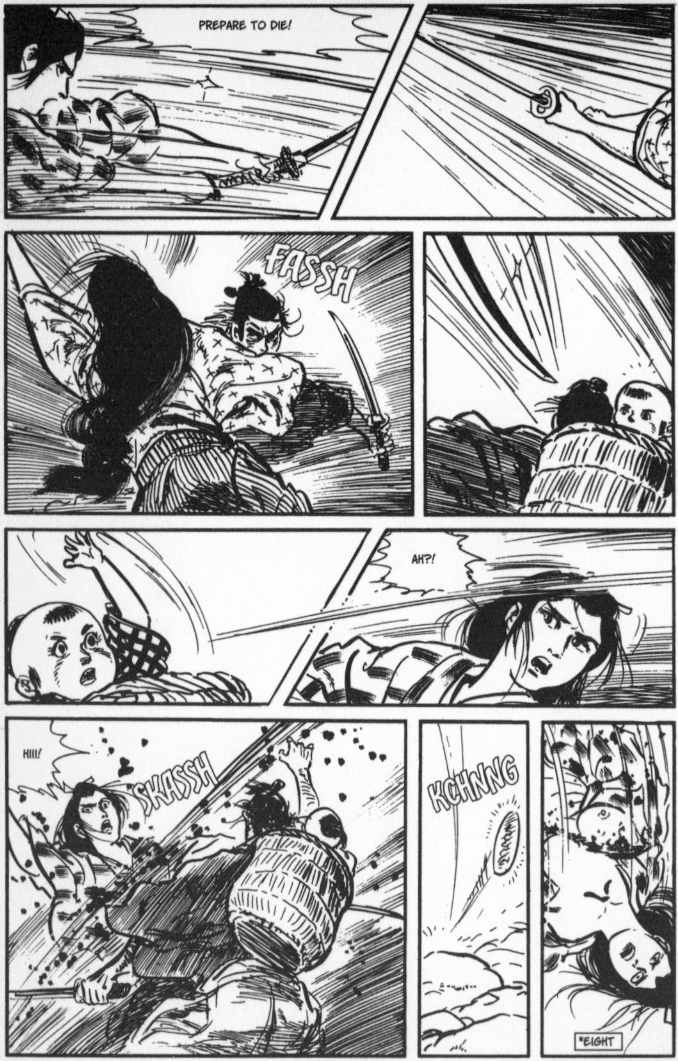
PREPARE TO DIE!
FASSH
AH?!
HIII!
SKASSH
KCHNNG
*EIGHT

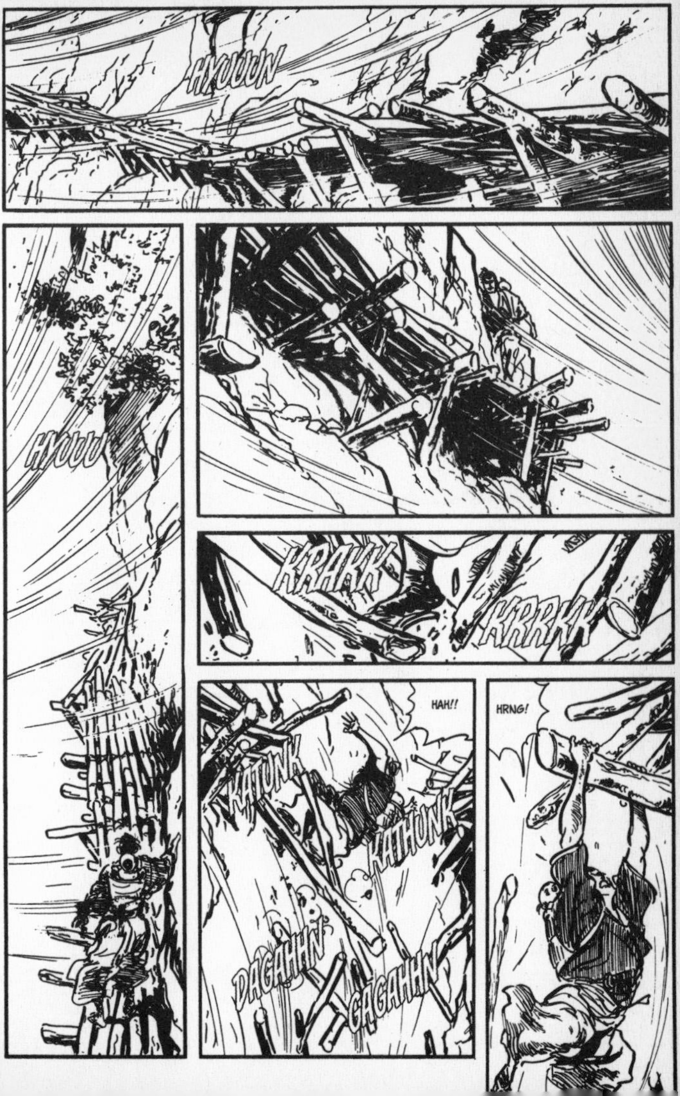
HYUUUN
HYUUU
KRAKK
KRRKK
KATUNK
HAH!!
KATHUNK
DAGAHHN
GAGAHHN
HRNG!

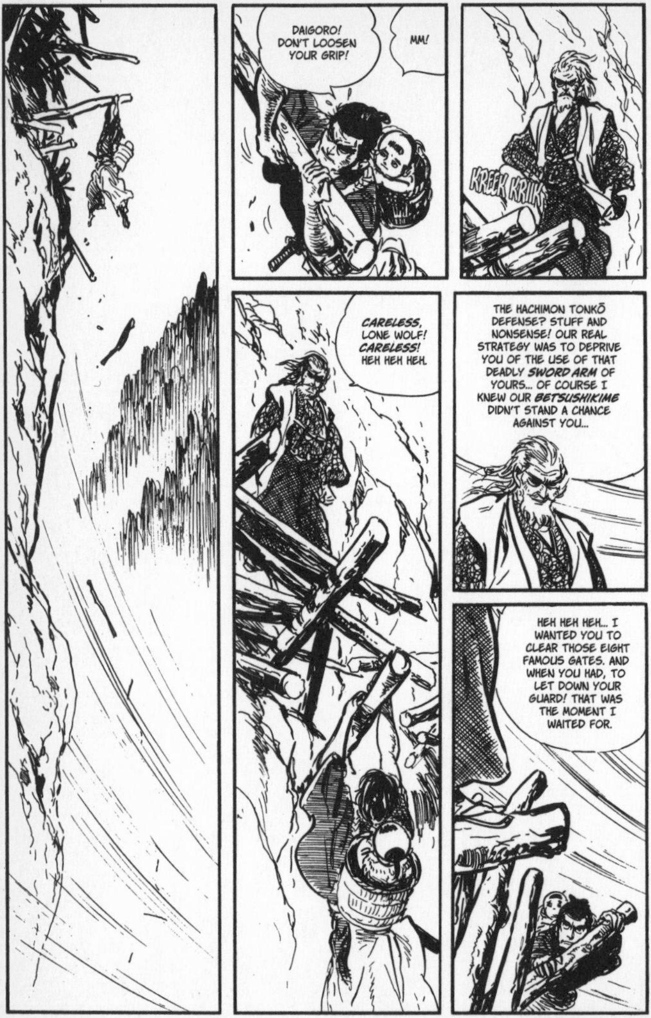
DAIGORO! DON'T LOOSEN YOUR GRIP!
MM!
KREEK KRIIK
CARELESS, LONE WOLF! CARELESS! HEH HEH HEH.
THE HACHIMON TONKŌ DEFENSE? STUFF AND NONSENSE! OUR REAL STRATEGY WAS TO DEPRIVE YOU OF THE USE OF THAT DEADLY SWORD ARM OF YOURS... OF COURSE I KNEW OUR BETSUSHIKIME DIDN'T STAND A CHANCE AGAINST YOU...
HEH HEH HEH... I WANTED YOU TO CLEAR THOSE EIGHT FAMOUS GATES. AND WHEN YOU HAD, TO LET DOWN YOUR GUARD! THAT WAS THE MOMENT I WAITED FOR.

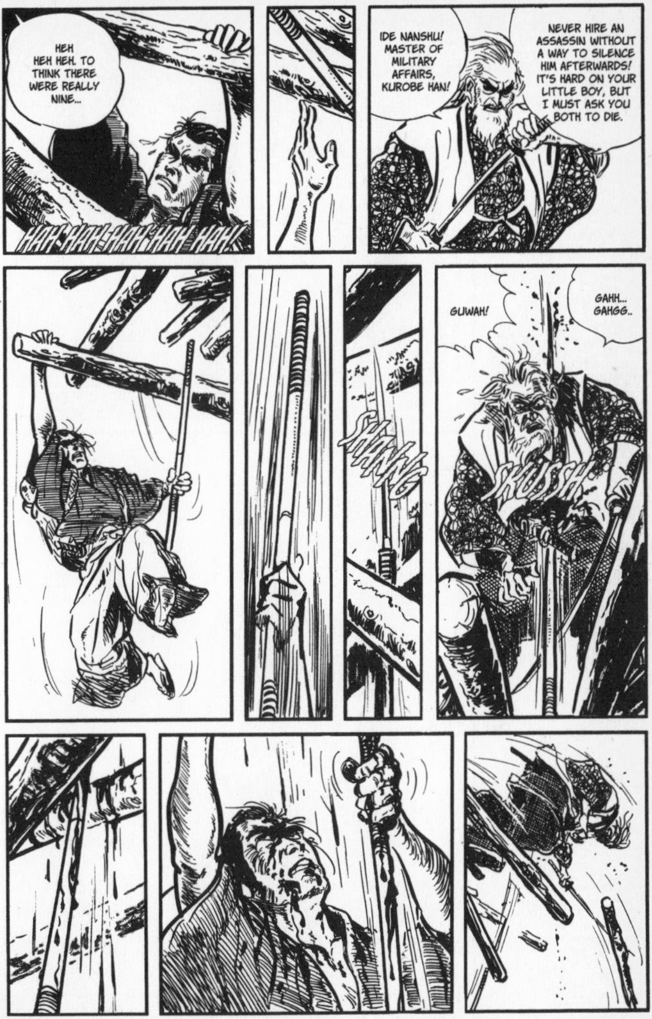
HEH HEH HEH. TO THINK THERE WERE REALLY NINE...
HAH HAH HAH HAH HAH!
IDE NANSHU! MASTER OF MILITARY AFFAIRS, KUROBE HAN!
NEVER HIRE AN ASSASSIN WITHOUT A WAY TO SILENCE HIM AFTERWARDS! IT'S HARD ON YOUR LITTLE BOY, BUT I MUST ASK YOU BOTH TO DIE.
SHING
GUWAH!
GAHH... GAHGG..
SKUSH

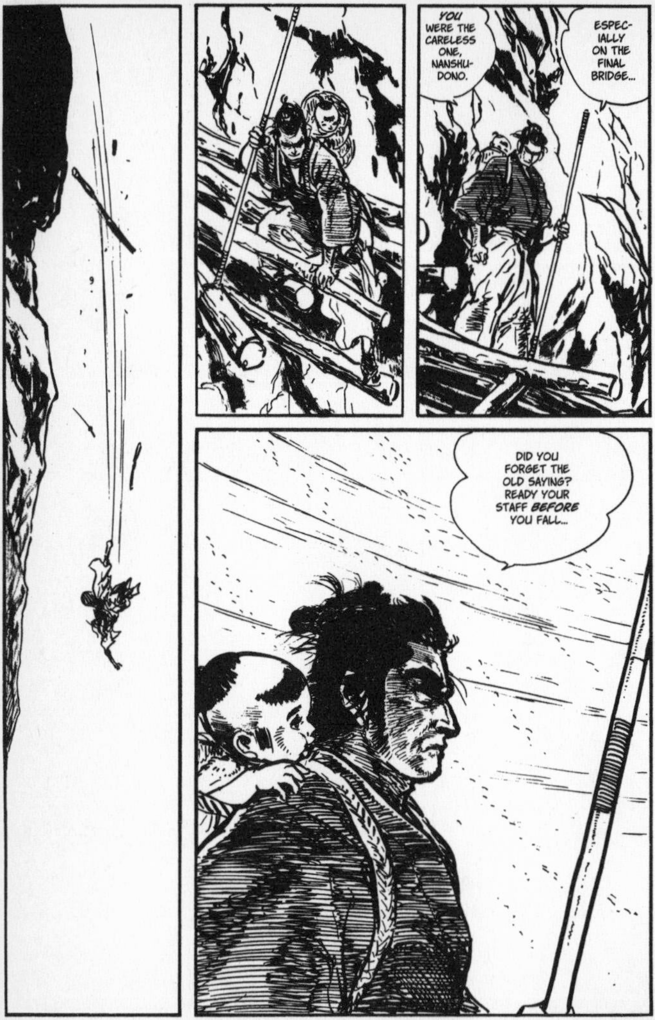
YOU WERE THE CARELESS ONE, NANSHU-DONO.
ESPEC-IALLY ON THE FINAL BRIDGE...
DID YOU FORGET THE OLD SAYING? READY YOUR STAFF BEFORE YOU FALL...

the eighth

Wings to the Bird, Fangs to the Beast

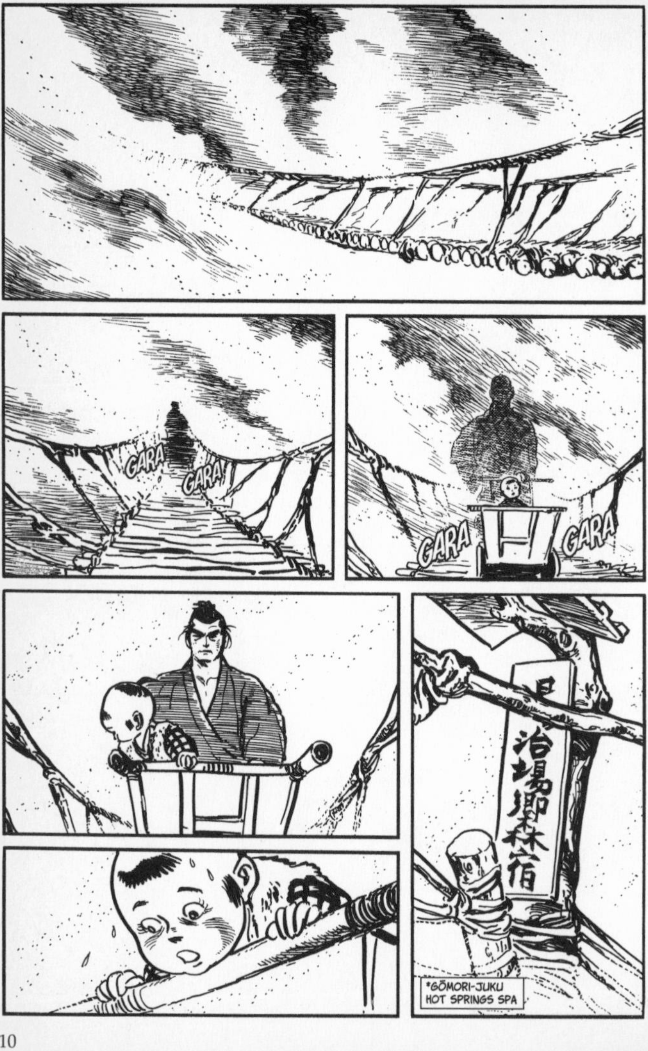
GARA
GARA
GARA
GARA
治場郷森宿
*GŌMORI-JUKU HOT SPRINGS SPA

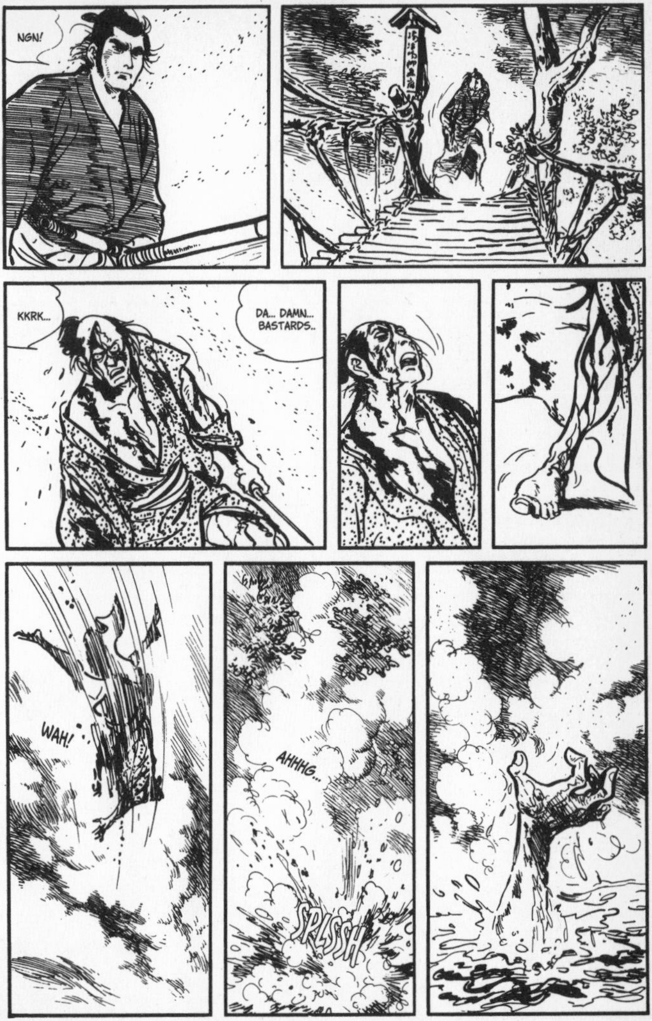
NGN!
KKRK...
DA... DAMN... BASTARDS..
WAH!
AHHHG...
SPLSSH

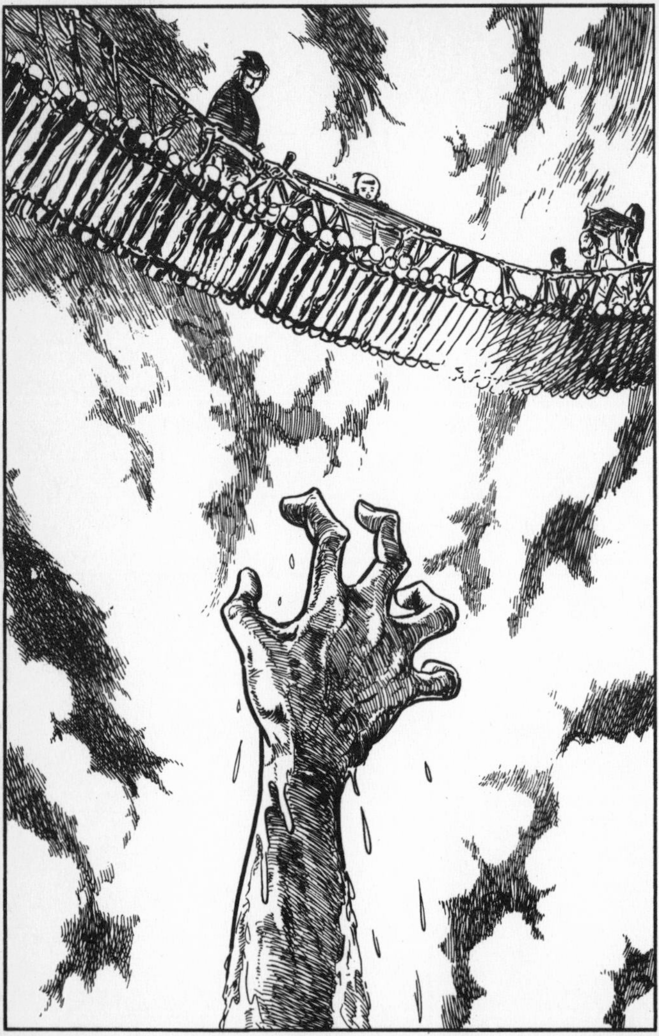

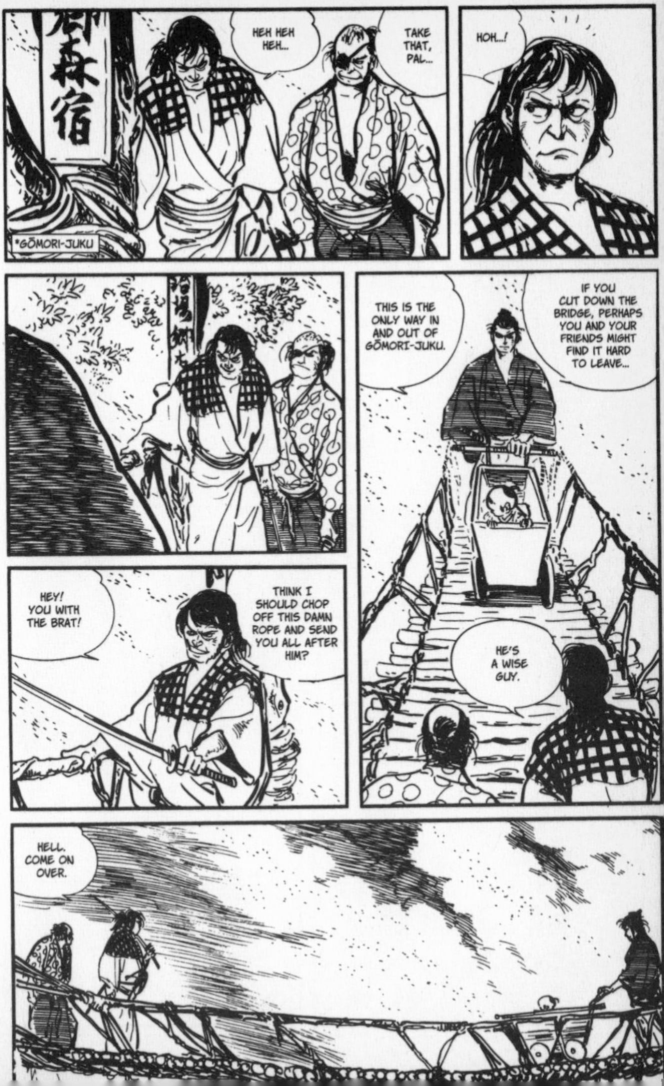
HEH HEH HEH...
TAKE THAT, PAL...
*GŌMORI-JUKU
HOH...!
HEY! YOU WITH THE BRAT!
THINK I SHOULD CHOP OFF THIS DAMN ROPE AND SEND YOU ALL AFTER HIM?
THIS IS THE ONLY WAY IN AND OUT OF GŌMORI-JUKU.
IF YOU CUT DOWN THE BRIDGE, PERHAPS YOU AND YOUR FRIENDS MIGHT FIND IT HARD TO LEAVE...
HE'S A WISE GUY.
HELL. COME ON OVER.

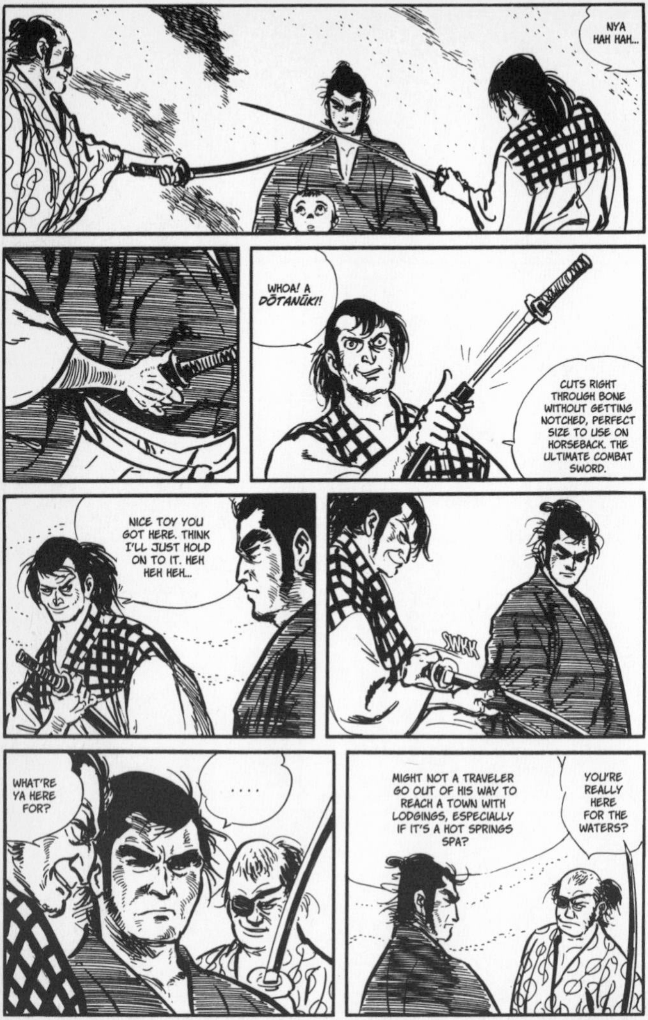
NYA HAH HAH...
WHOA! A DŌTANUKI!!
CUTS RIGHT THROUGH BONE WITHOUT GETTING NOTCHED, PERFECT SIZE TO USE ON HORSEBACK. THE ULTIMATE COMBAT SWORD.
NICE TOY YOU GOT HERE. THINK I'LL JUST HOLD ON TO IT. HEH HEH HEH...
SWKK
WHAT'RE YA HERE FOR?
....
MIGHT NOT A TRAVELER GO OUT OF HIS WAY TO REACH A TOWN WITH LODGINGS, ESPECIALLY IF IT'S A HOT SPRINGS SPA?
YOU'RE REALLY HERE FOR THE WATERS?

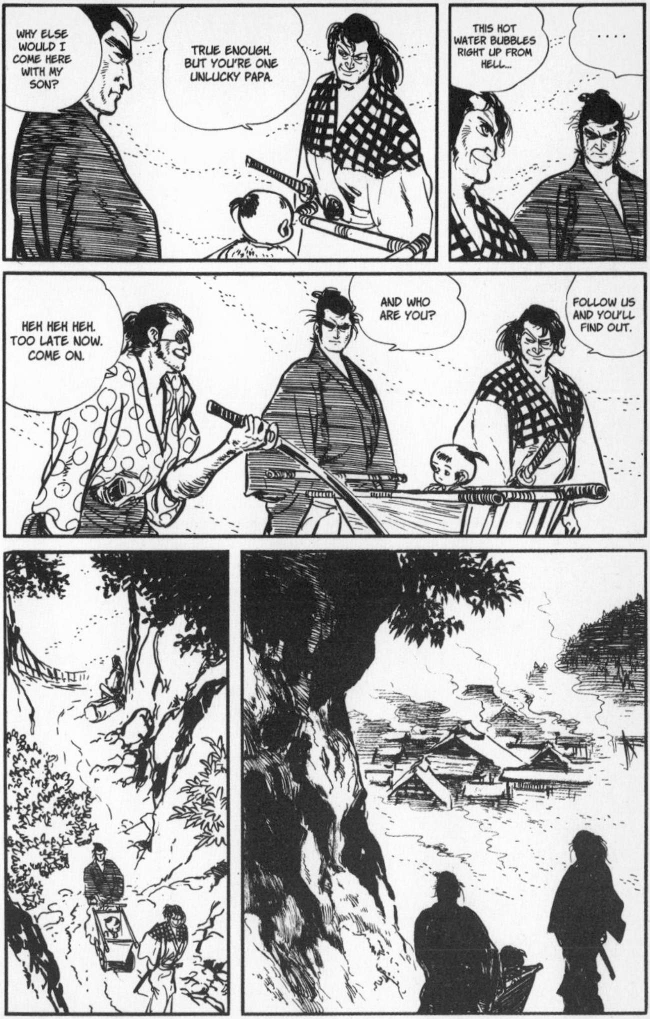
WHY ELSE WOULD I COME HERE WITH MY SON?
TRUE ENOUGH. BUT YOU'RE ONE UNLUCKY PAPA.
THIS HOT WATER BUBBLES RIGHT UP FROM HELL...
....
HEH HEH HEH. TOO LATE NOW. COME ON.
AND WHO ARE YOU?
FOLLOW US AND YOU'LL FIND OUT.

EEK!

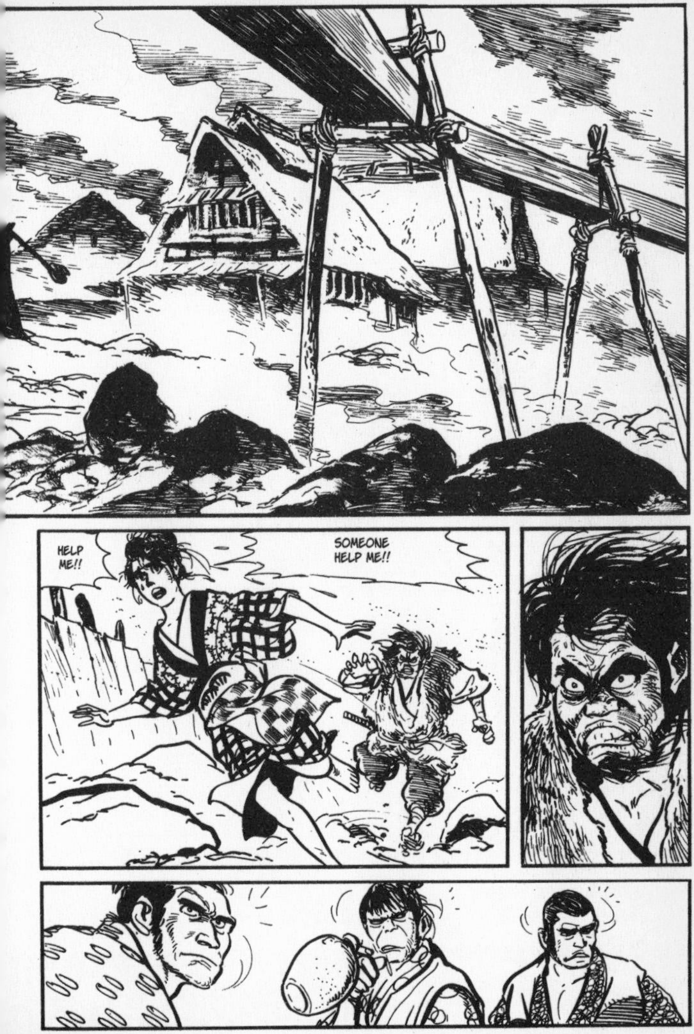
HELP ME!!
SOMEONE HELP ME!!

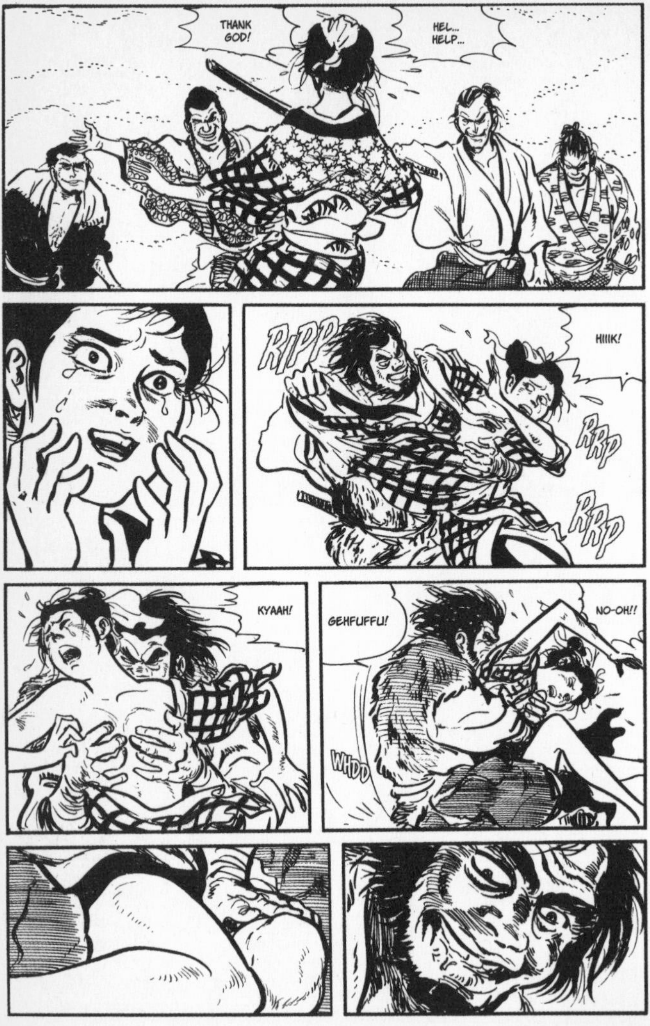
THANK GOD!
HEL... HELP...
RIPP
HIIIK!
RRP
RRP
KYAAH!
GEHFUFFU!
NO-OH!!
WHDD

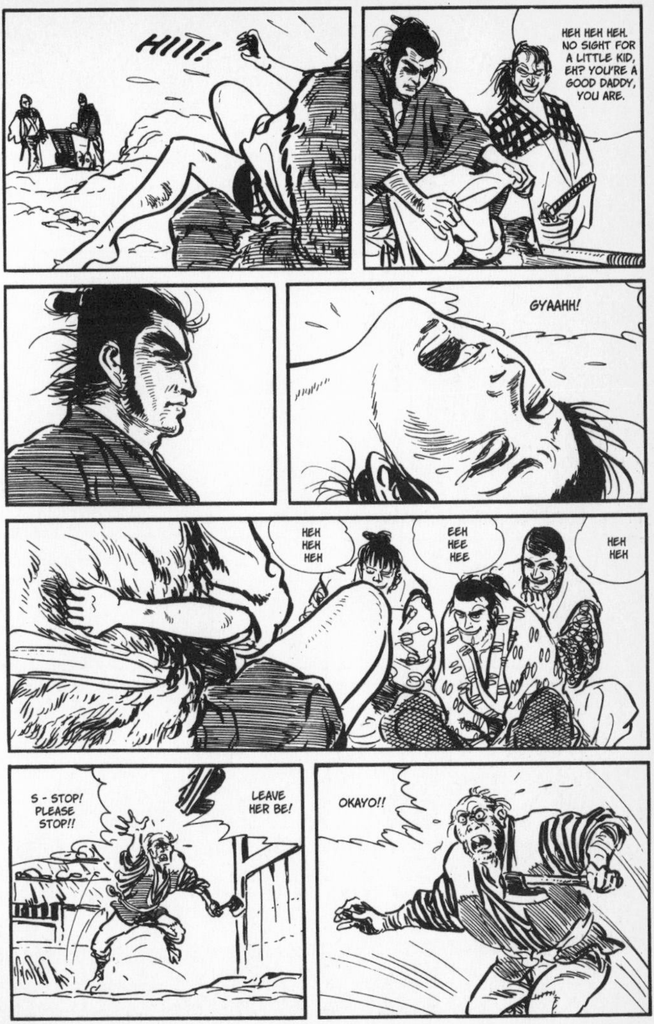
HIII!
HEH HEH HEH. NO SIGHT FOR A LITTLE KID, EH? YOU'RE A GOOD DADDY, YOU ARE.
GYAAHH!
HEH HEH HEH
EEH HEE HEE
HEH HEH
S - STOP! PLEASE STOP!!
LEAVE HER BE!
OKAYO!!

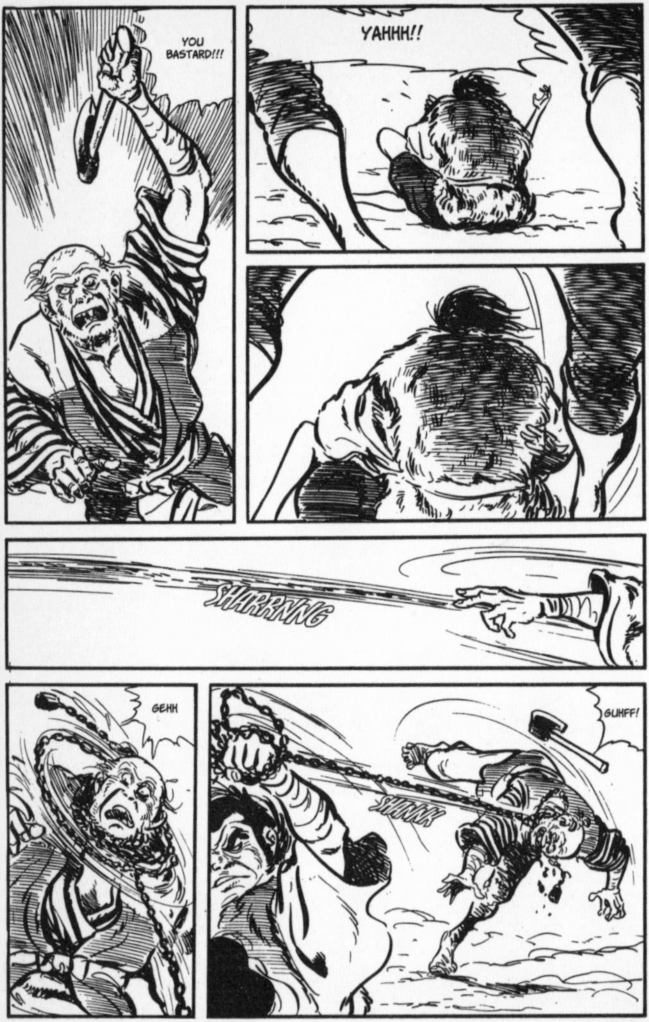
YOU BASTARD!!!
YAHHH!!
SHARRNNG
GEHH
SHINK
GUHFF!

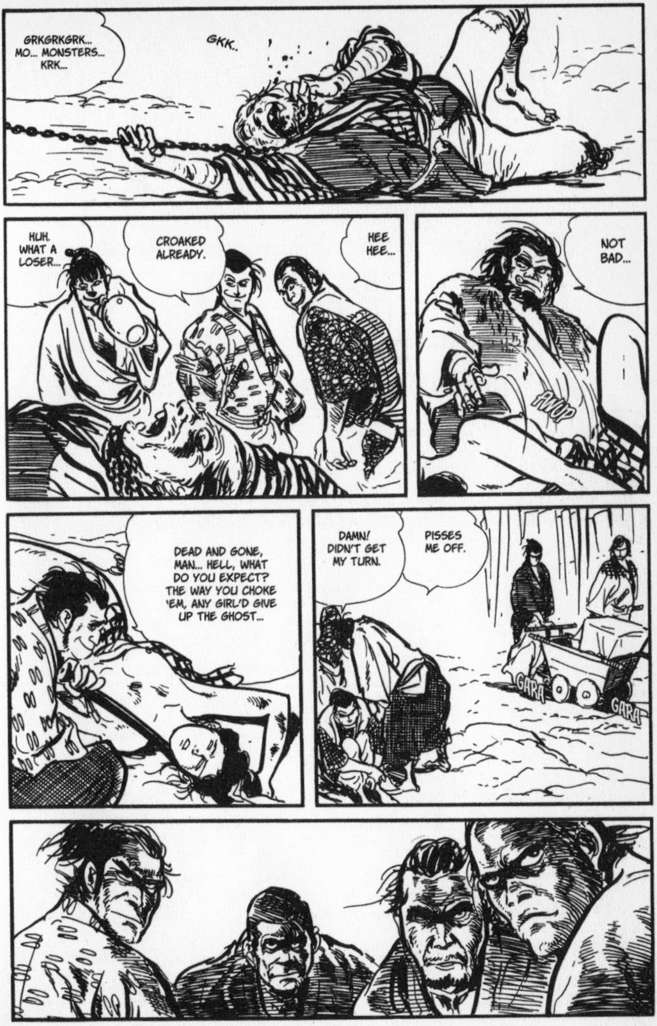
GRKGRKGRK... MO... MONSTERS... KRK...
GKK..
HUH. WHAT A LOSER...
CROAKED ALREADY.
HEE HEE...
NOT BAD...
AWOP
DEAD AND GONE, MAN... HELL, WHAT DO YOU EXPECT? THE WAY YOU CHOKE 'EM, ANY GIRL'D GIVE UP THE GHOST...
DAMN! DIDN'T GET MY TURN.
PISSES ME OFF.
GARA
GARA

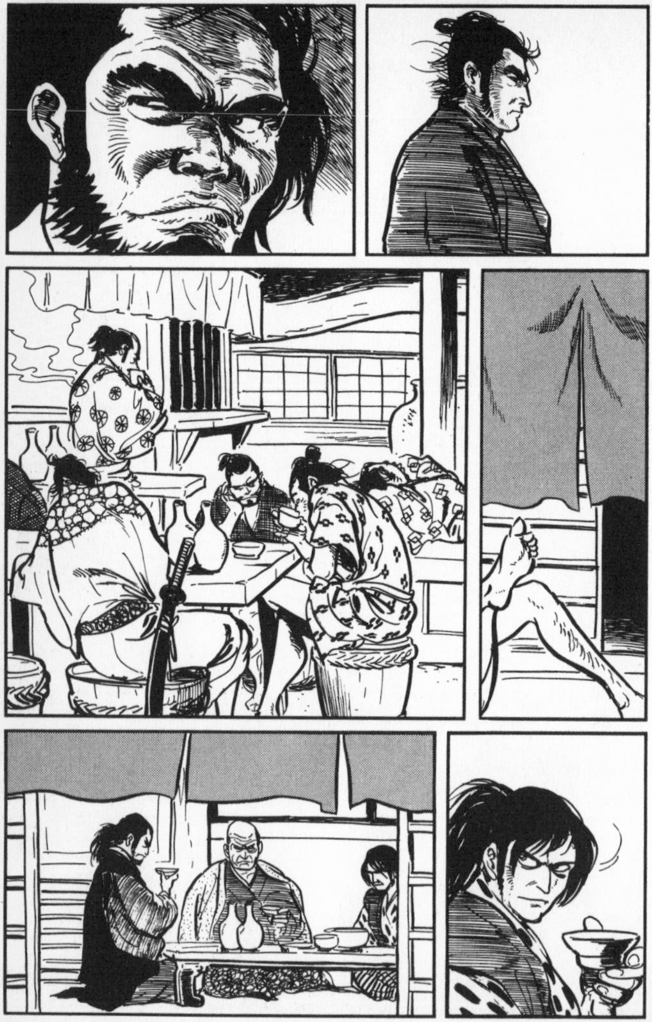

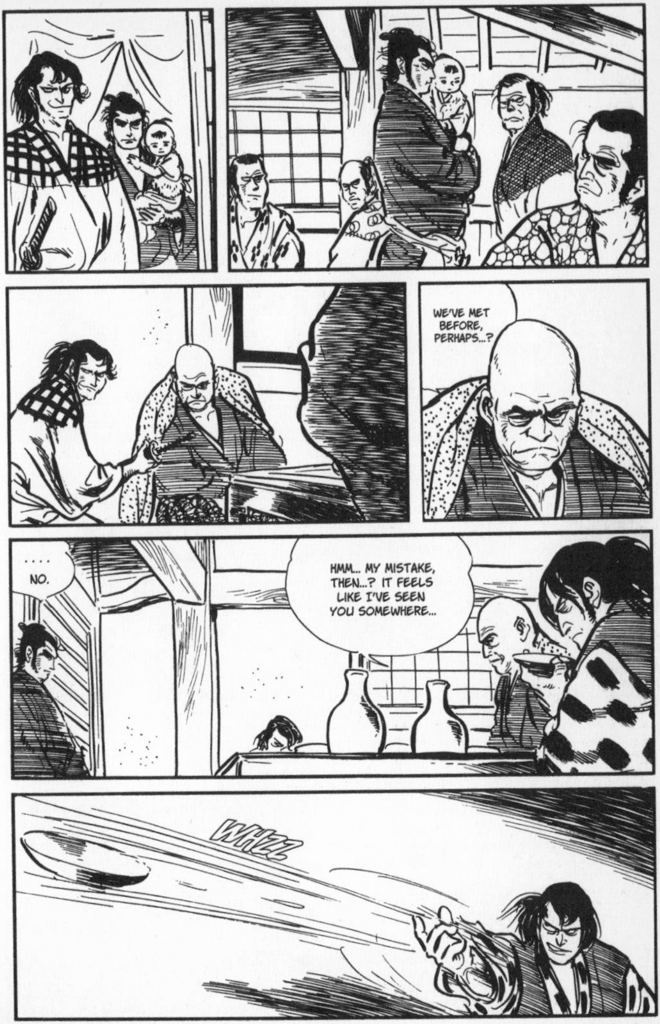
WE'VE MET BEFORE, PERHAPS...?
....
NO.
HMM... MY MISTAKE, THEN...? IT FEELS LIKE I'VE SEEN YOU SOMEWHERE...
WHZZ

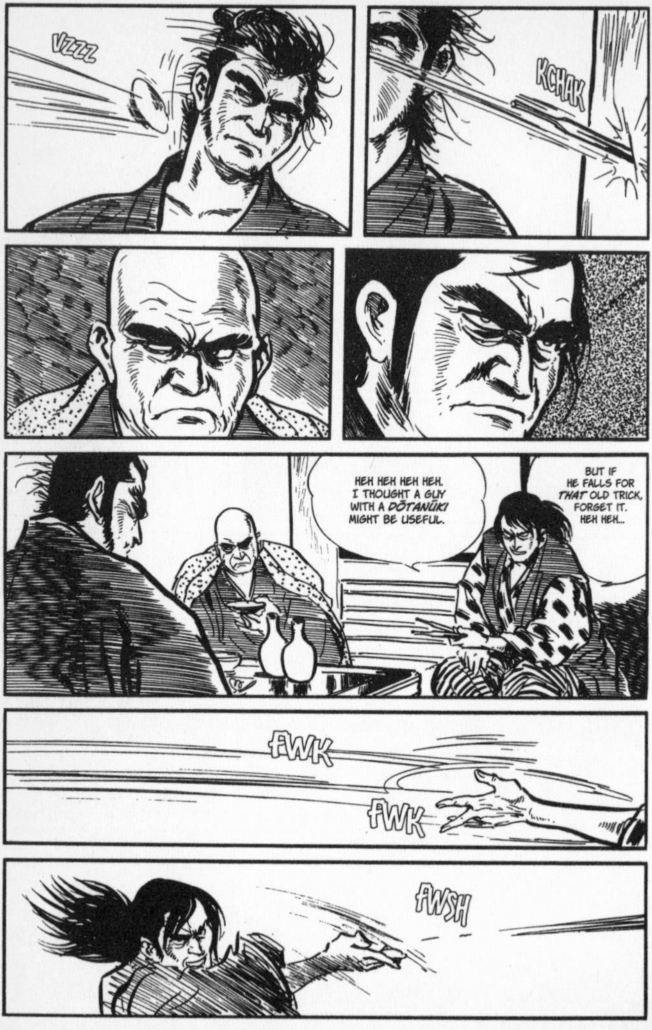
VZZZ
KCHAK
HEH HEH HEH HEH. I THOUGHT A GUY WITH A DŌTANŪKI MIGHT BE USEFUL.
BUT IF HE FALLS FOR THAT OLD TRICK, FORGET IT. HEH HEH...
FWK
FWK
FWSH

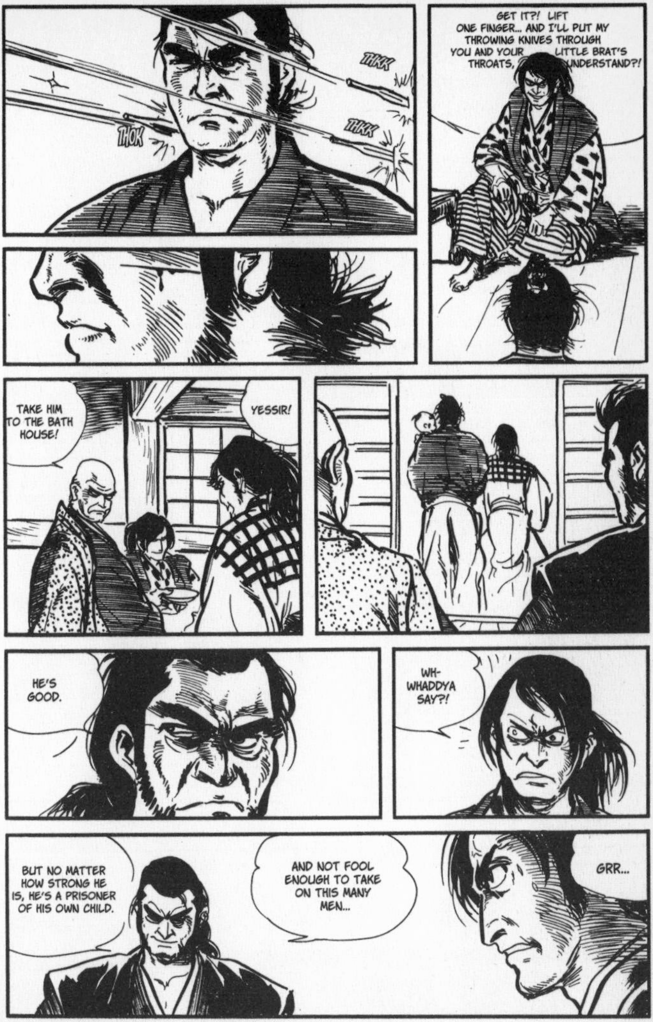
THKK
THOK
THKK
GET IT?! LIFT ONE FINGER... AND I'LL PUT MY THROWING KNIVES THROUGH YOU AND YOUR LITTLE BRAT'S THROATS, UNDERSTAND?!
TAKE HIM TO THE BATH HOUSE!
YESSIR!
HE'S GOOD.
WH- WHADDYA SAY?!
BUT NO MATTER HOW STRONG HE IS, HE'S A PRISONER OF HIS OWN CHILD.
AND NOT FOOL ENOUGH TO TAKE ON THIS MANY MEN...
GRR...

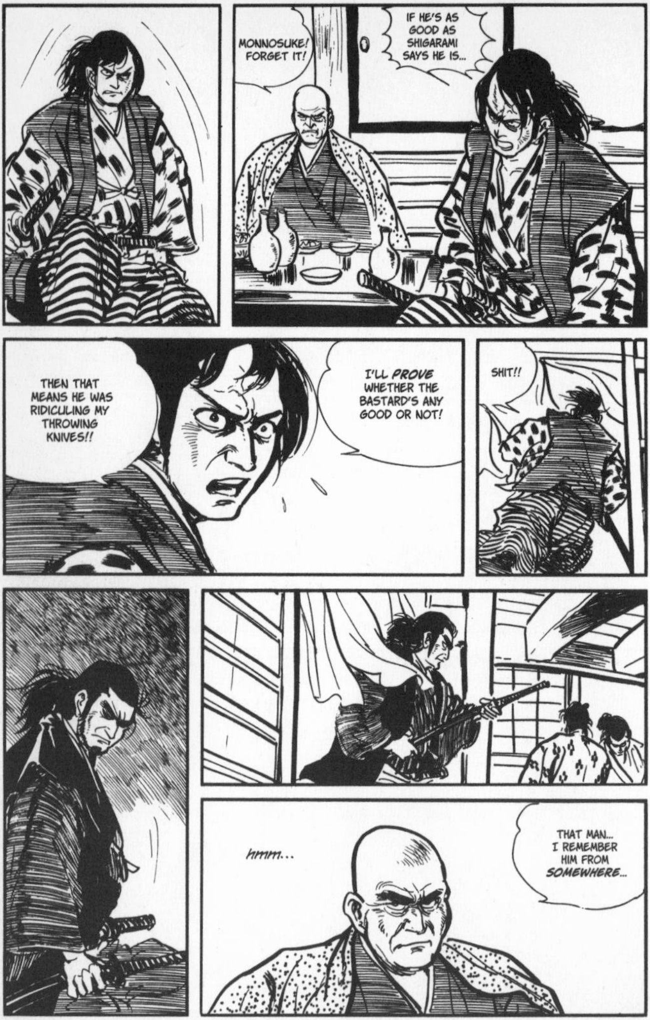
MONNOSUKE! FORGET IT!
IF HE'S AS GOOD AS SHIGARAMI SAYS HE IS...
THEN THAT MEANS HE WAS RIDICULING MY THROWING KNIVES!!
I'LL *PROVE* WHETHER THE BASTARD'S ANY GOOD OR NOT!
SHIT!!
hmm...
THAT MAN... I REMEMBER HIM FROM *SOMEWHERE*...

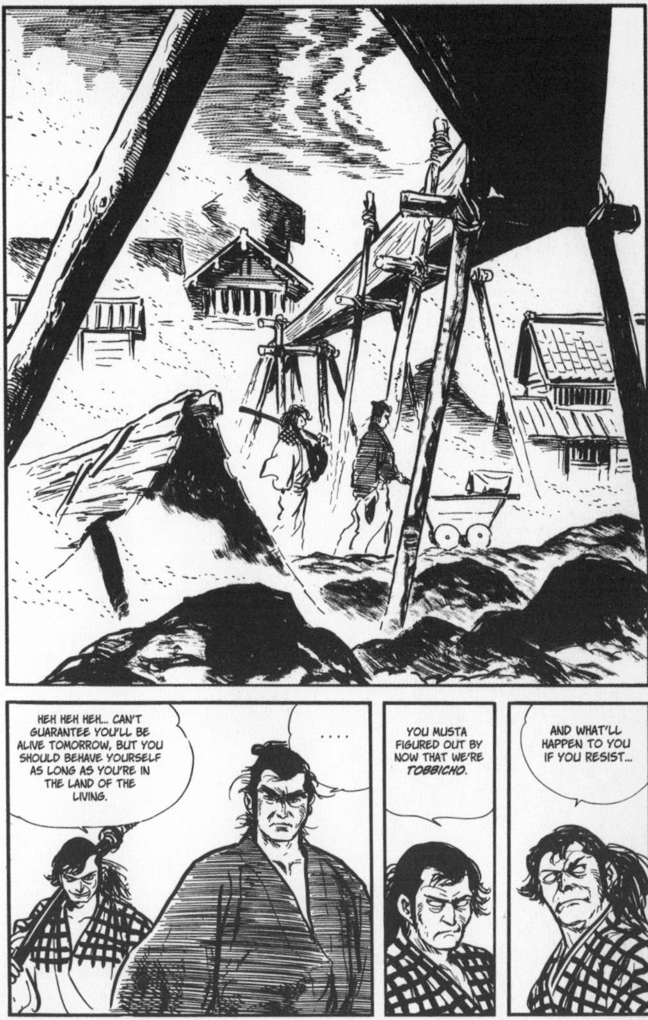
HEH HEH HEH... CAN'T GUARANTEE YOU'LL BE ALIVE TOMORROW, BUT YOU SHOULD BEHAVE YOURSELF AS LONG AS YOU'RE IN THE LAND OF THE LIVING.
....
YOU MUSTA FIGURED OUT BY NOW THAT WE'RE *TOBBICHO*.
AND WHAT'LL HAPPEN TO YOU IF YOU RESIST...

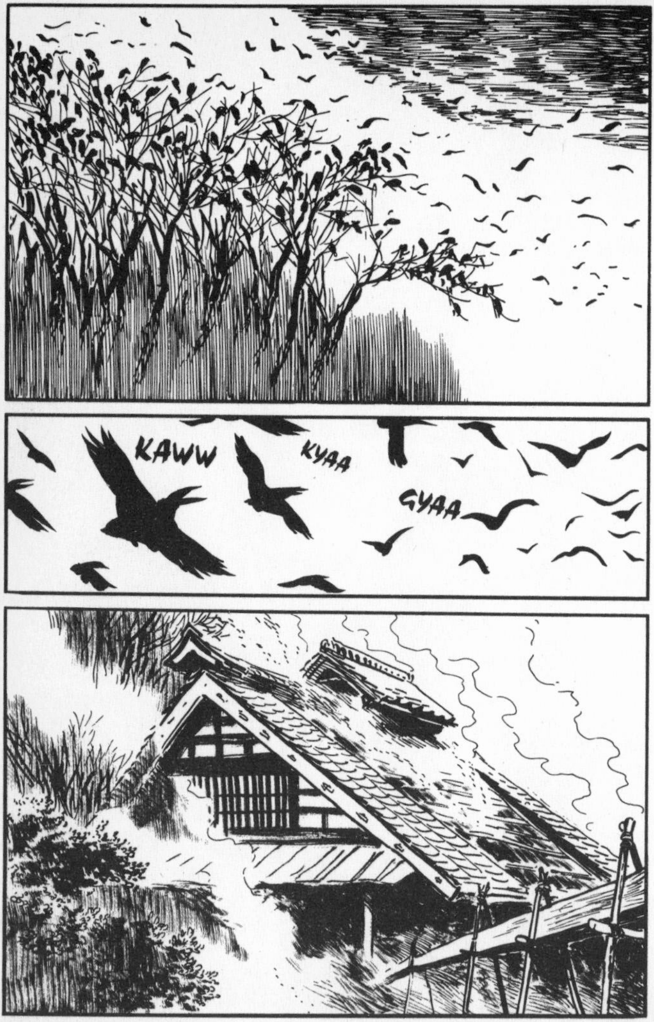
KAWW
KYAA
GYAA

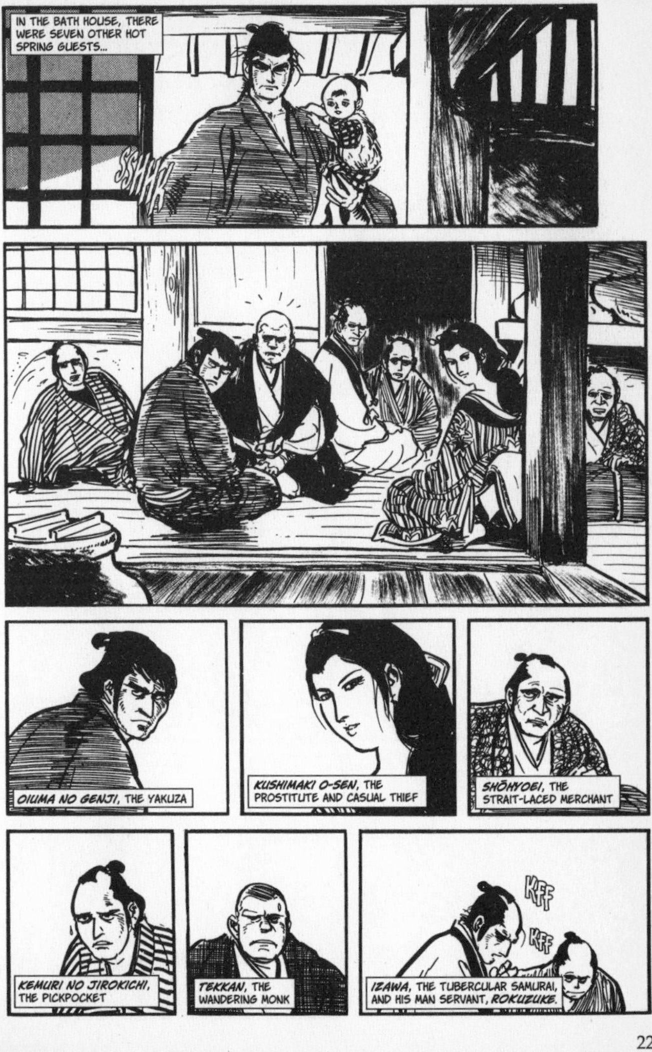
IN THE BATH HOUSE, THERE WERE SEVEN OTHER HOT SPRING GUESTS...
SSHHK
OIUMA NO GENJI, THE YAKUZA
KUSHIMAKI O-SEN, THE PROSTITUTE AND CASUAL THIEF
SHŌHYOEI, THE STRAIT-LACED MERCHANT
KEMURI NO JIROKICHI, THE PICKPOCKET
TEKKAN, THE WANDERING MONK
IZAWA, THE TUBERCULAR SAMURAI, AND HIS MAN SERVANT, ROKUZUKE.
KFF
KFF

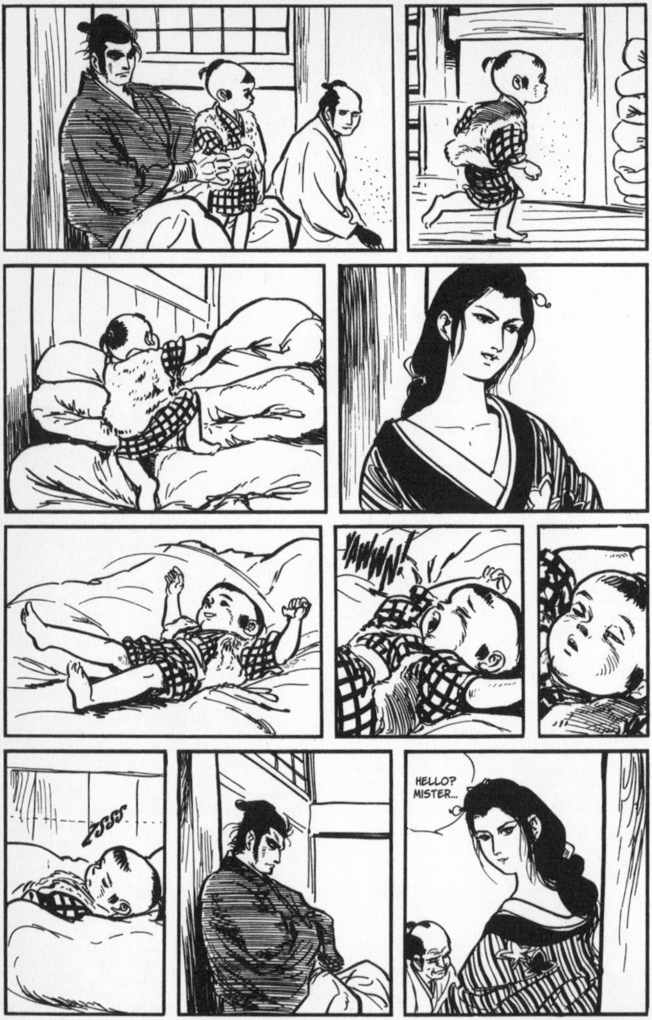
YAWWN!
ZSSS
HELLO? MISTER...

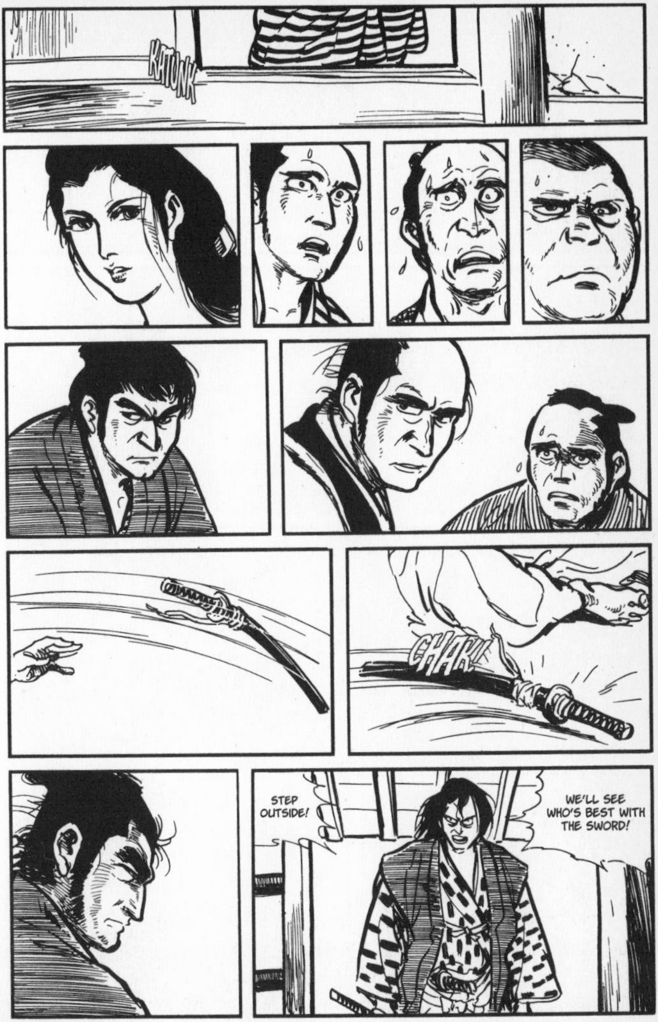
KATUNK
CHAK!
STEP OUTSIDE!
WE'LL SEE WHO'S BEST WITH THE SWORD!

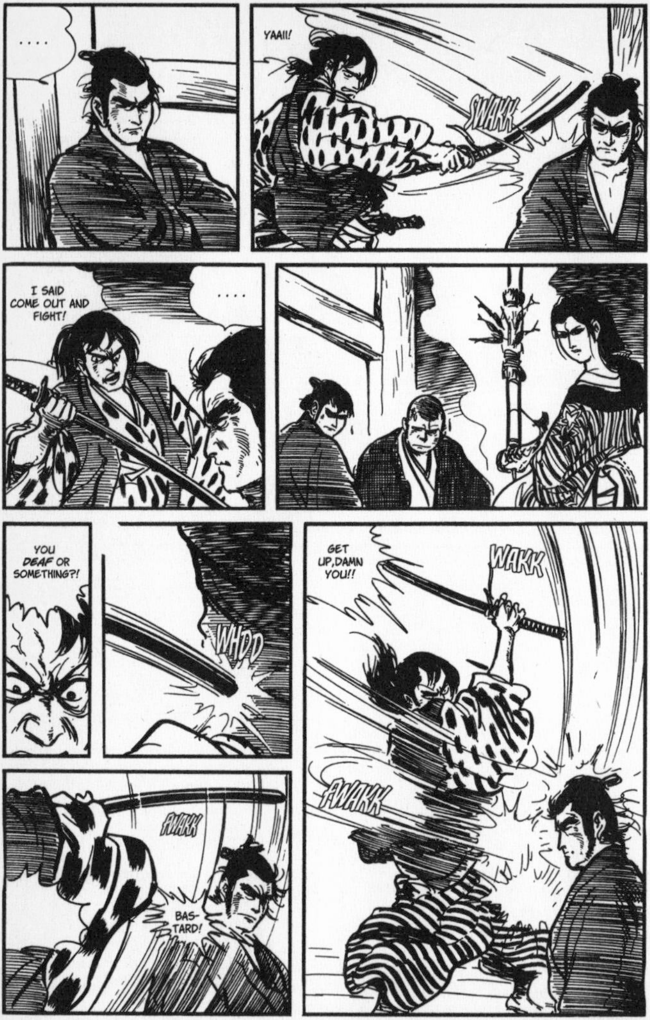
....
YAAII!
SWAKK
I SAID COME OUT AND FIGHT!
....
YOU *DEAF* OR SOMETHING?!
WHDD
AWAKK
BAS-TARD!
GET UP, DAMN YOU!!
WAKK
AWAKK

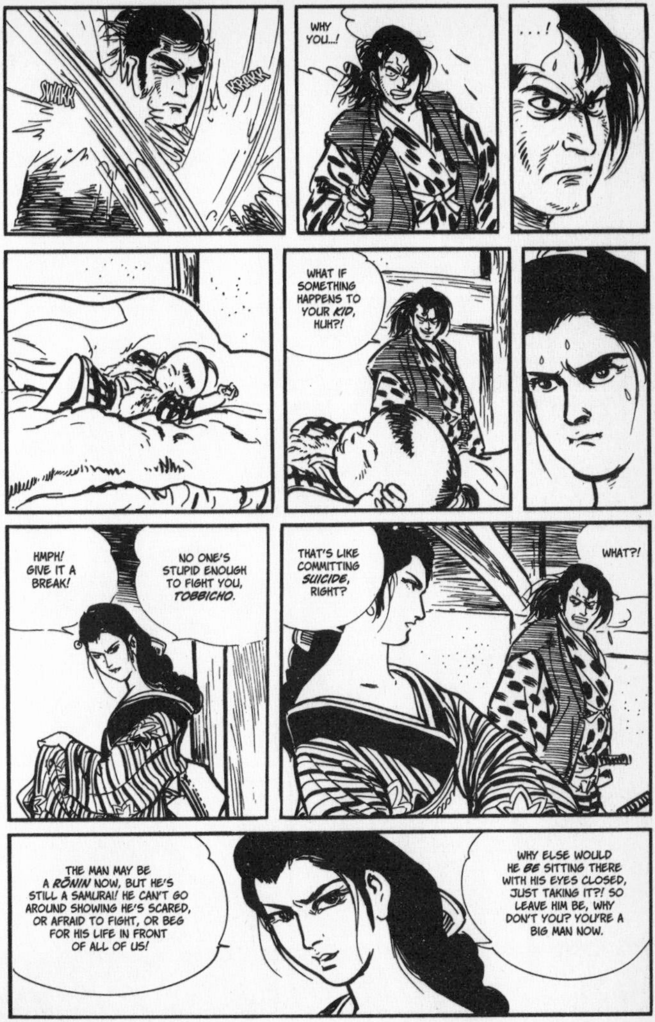
SWAKK
KRAKK
WHY YOU...!
...!
WHAT IF SOMETHING HAPPENS TO YOUR *KID*, HUH?!
HMPH! GIVE IT A BREAK!
NO ONE'S STUPID ENOUGH TO FIGHT YOU, *TOBBICHO*.
THAT'S LIKE COMMITTING *SUICIDE*, RIGHT?
WHAT?!
THE MAN MAY BE A *RŌNIN* NOW, BUT HE'S STILL A SAMURAI! HE CAN'T GO AROUND SHOWING HE'S SCARED, OR AFRAID TO FIGHT, OR BEG FOR HIS LIFE IN FRONT OF ALL OF US!
WHY ELSE WOULD HE *BE* SITTING THERE WITH HIS EYES CLOSED, JUST TAKING IT?! SO LEAVE HIM BE, WHY DON'T YOU? YOU'RE A BIG MAN NOW.

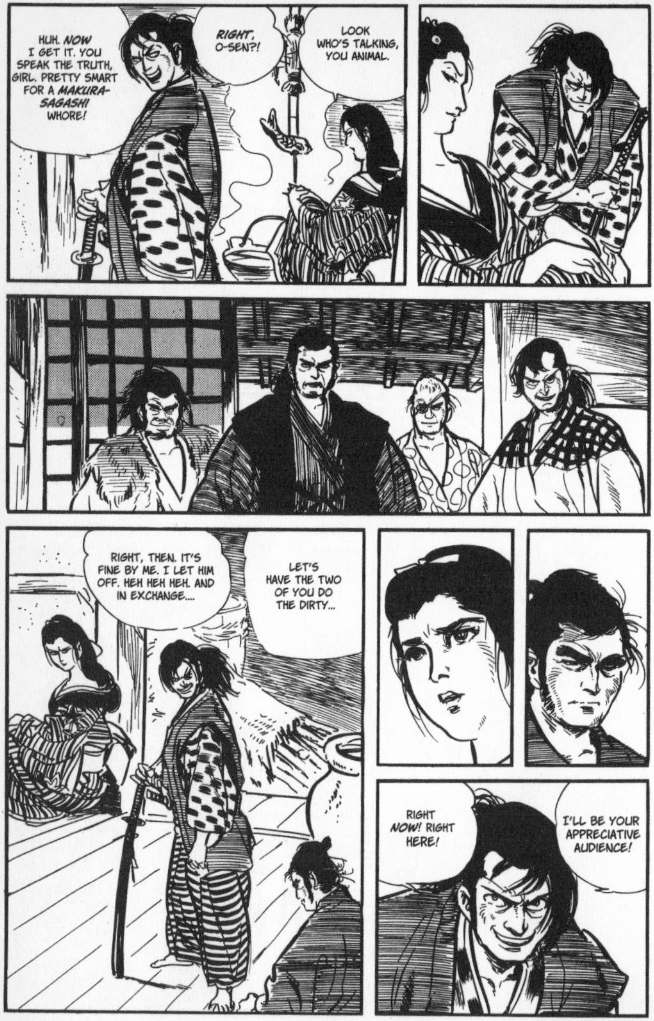
HUH. *NOW* I GET IT. YOU SPEAK THE TRUTH, GIRL. PRETTY SMART FOR A *MAKURA-SAGASHI* WHORE!
RIGHT, O-SEN?!
LOOK WHO'S TALKING, YOU ANIMAL.
RIGHT, THEN. IT'S FINE BY ME. I LET HIM OFF. HEH HEH HEH. AND IN EXCHANGE....
LET'S HAVE THE TWO OF YOU DO THE DIRTY...
RIGHT *NOW!* RIGHT HERE!
I'LL BE YOUR APPRECIATIVE AUDIENCE!

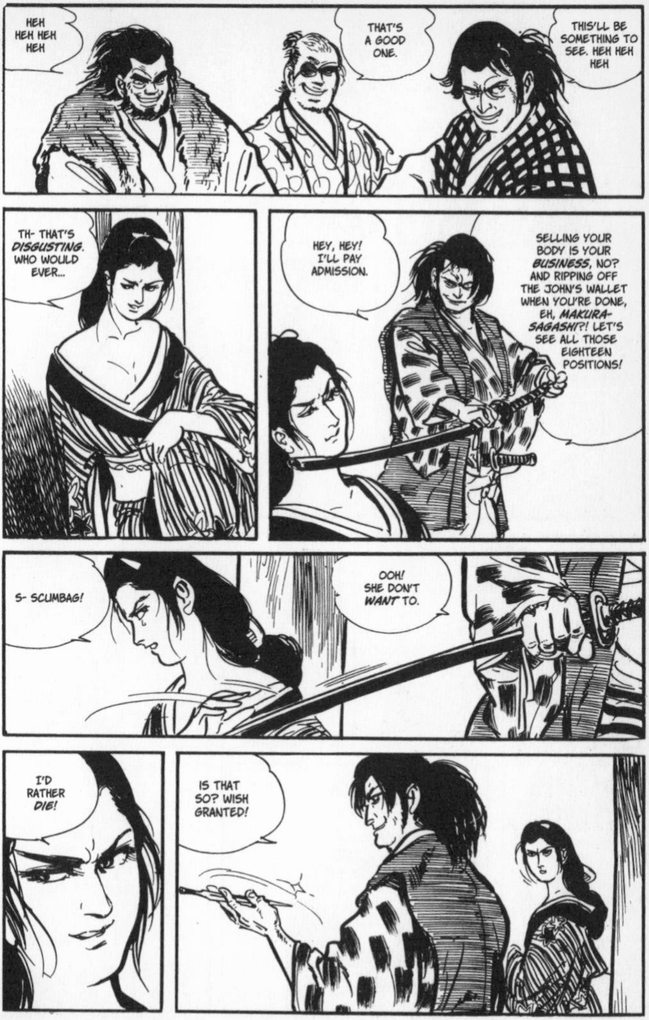

HEH HEH HEH HEH
THAT'S A GOOD ONE.
THIS'LL BE SOMETHING TO SEE. HEH HEH HEH
TH- THAT'S *DISGUSTING*. WHO WOULD EVER...
HEY, HEY! I'LL PAY ADMISSION.
SELLING YOUR BODY IS YOUR *BUSINESS*, NO? AND RIPPING OFF THE JOHN'S WALLET WHEN YOU'RE DONE, EH, *MAKURA-SAGASHI*?! LET'S SEE ALL THOSE EIGHTEEN POSITIONS!
S- SCUMBAG!
OOH! SHE DON'T *WANT* TO.
I'D RATHER *DIE*!
IS THAT SO? WISH GRANTED!

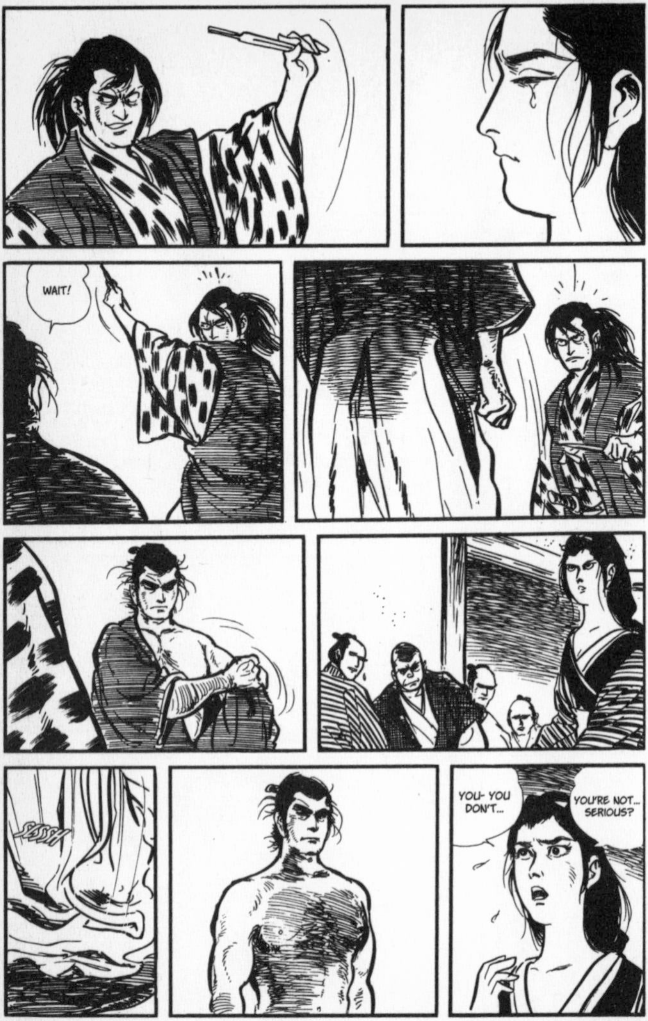
WAIT!
SSSH
YOU- YOU DON'T...
YOU'RE NOT... SERIOUS?

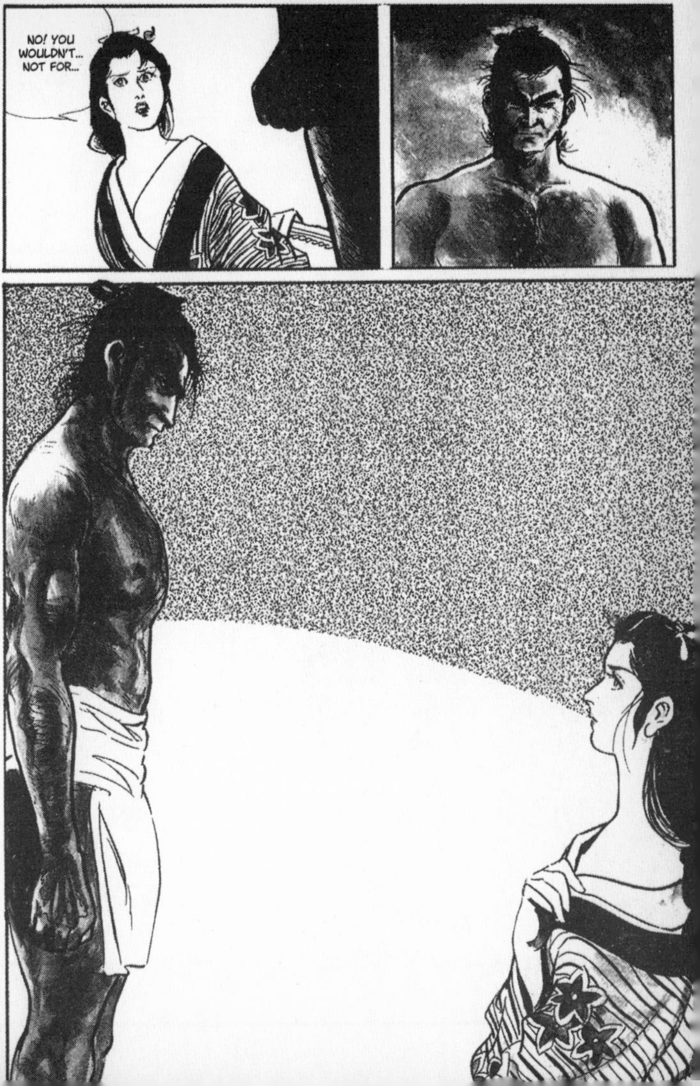
NO! YOU WOULDN'T... NOT FOR...

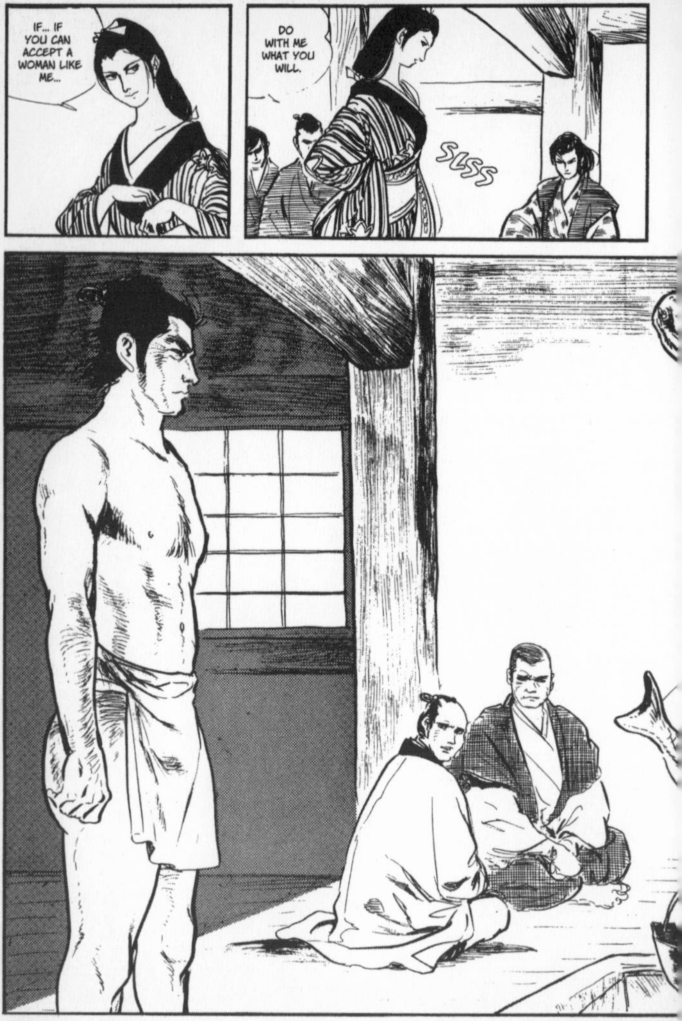
IF... IF YOU CAN ACCEPT A WOMAN LIKE ME...
DO WITH ME WHAT YOU WILL.
SLSS

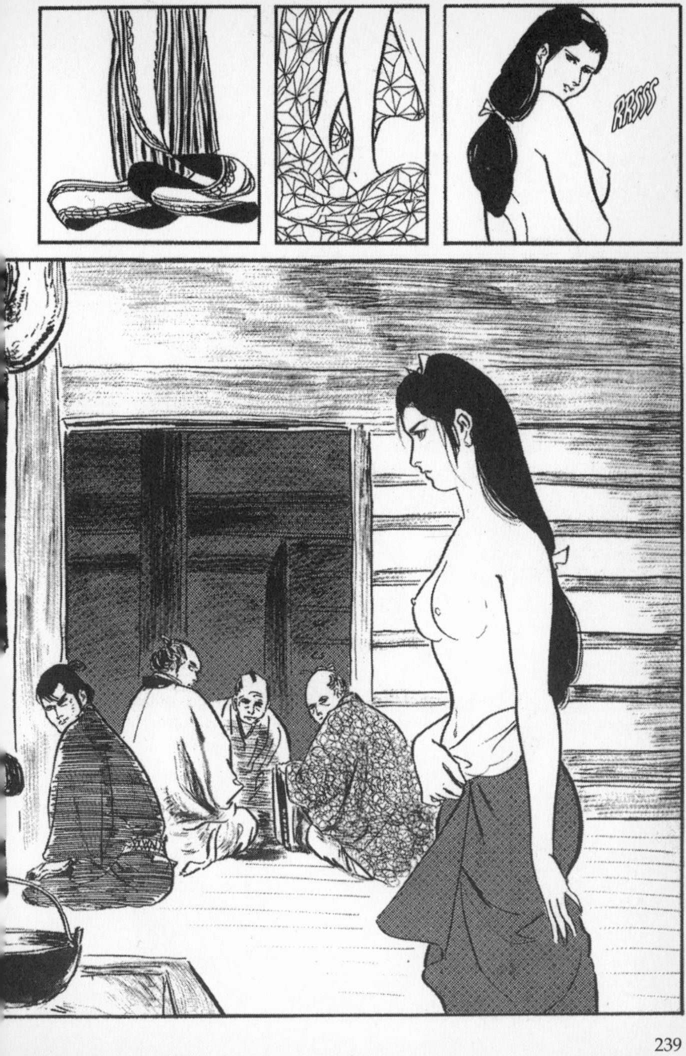
RRSSS

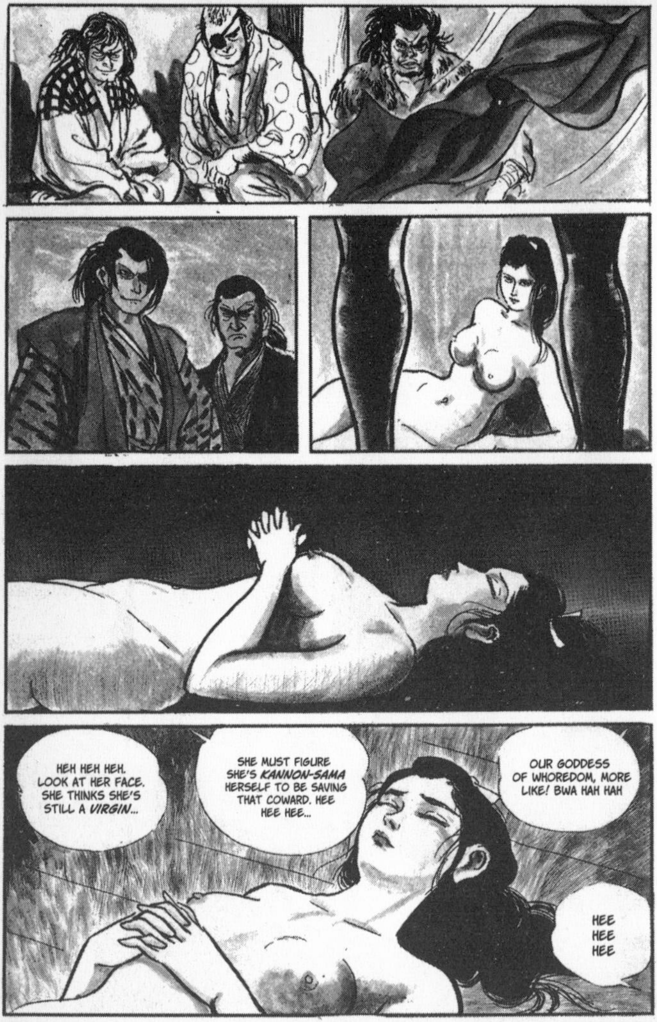

HEH HEH HEH. LOOK AT HER FACE. SHE THINKS SHE'S STILL A *VIRGIN*...
SHE MUST FIGURE SHE'S *KANNON-SAMA* HERSELF TO BE SAVING THAT COWARD. HEE HEE HEE...
OUR GODDESS OF WHOREDOM, MORE LIKE! BWA HAH HAH
HEE HEE HEE

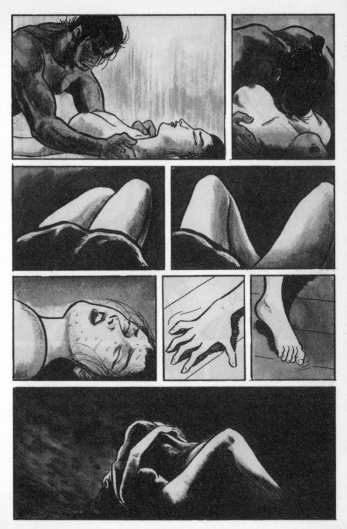

241

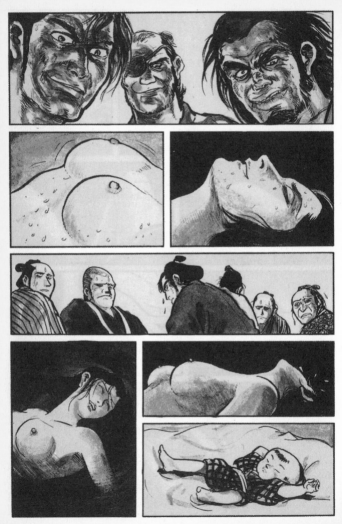

242

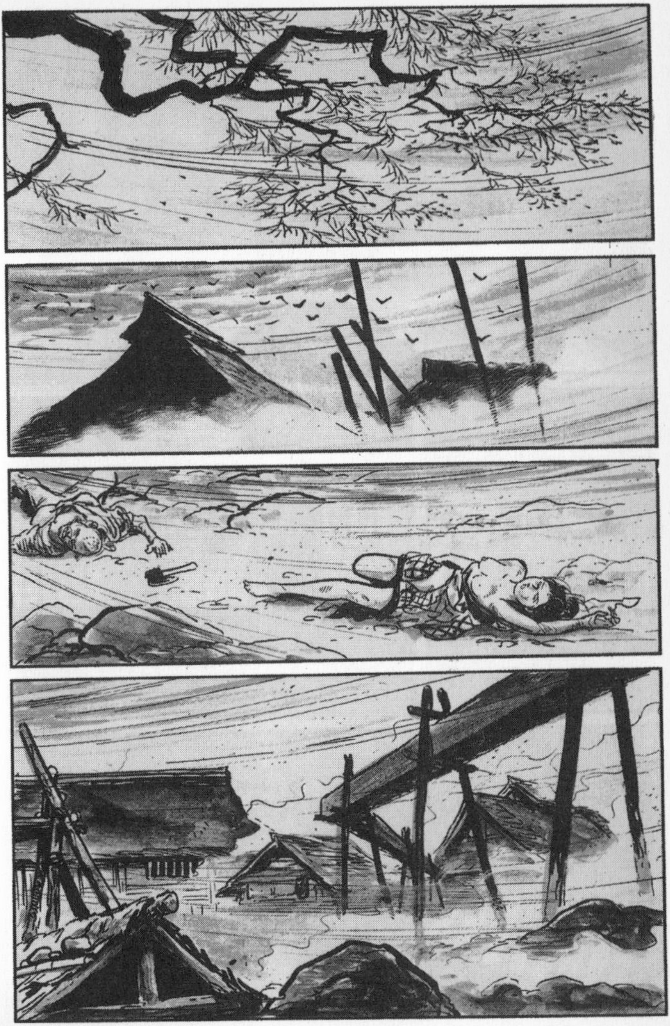

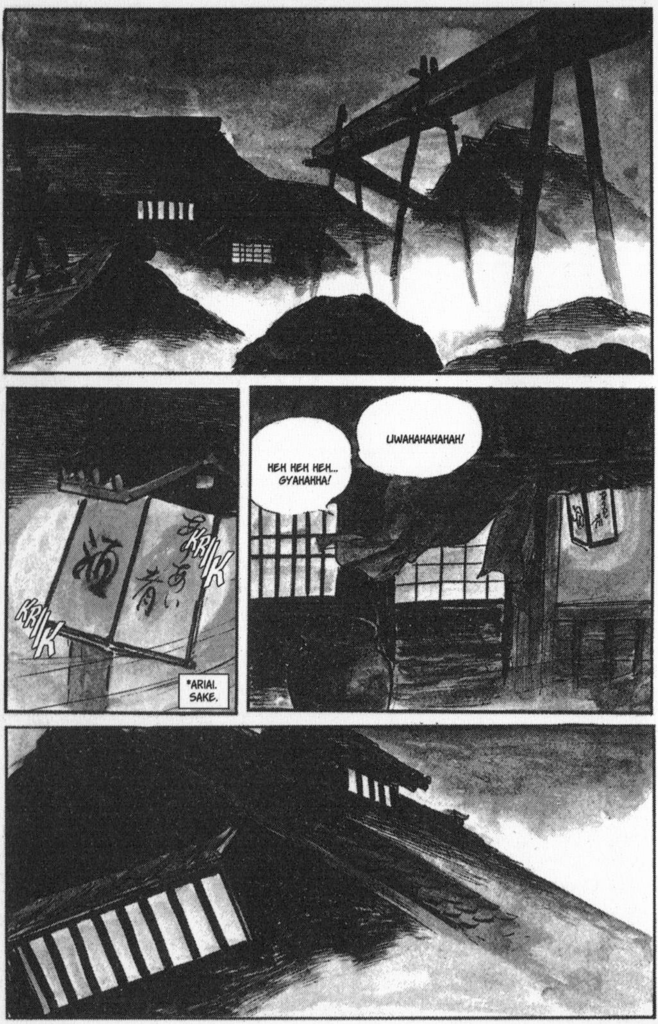
KRIIK
KRIIK
*ARIAI. SAKE.
HEH HEH HEH... GYAHAHHA!
UWAHAHAHAHAH!

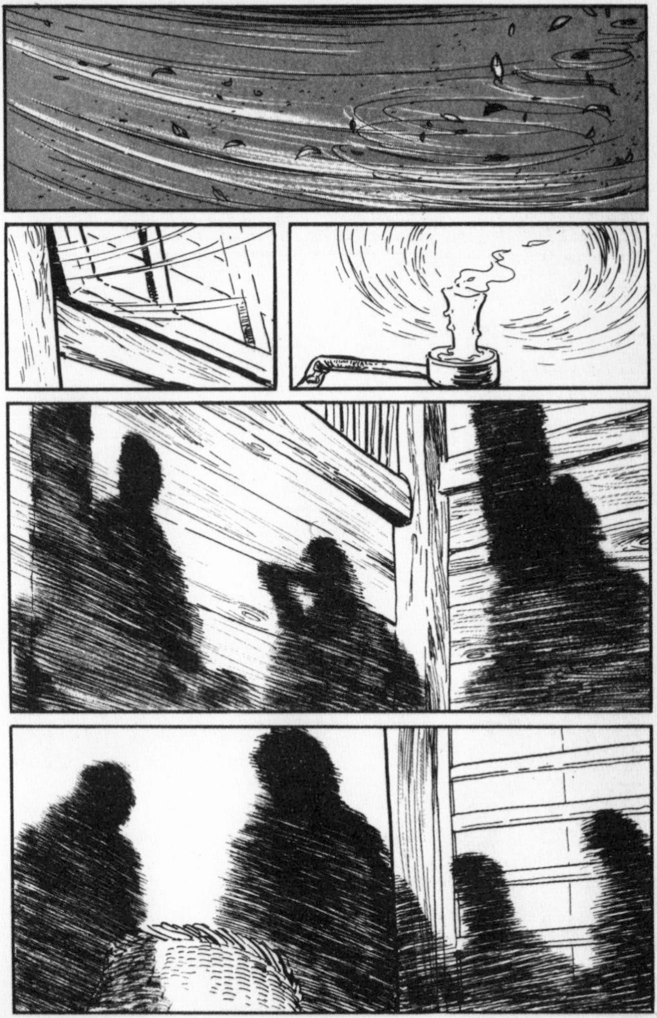

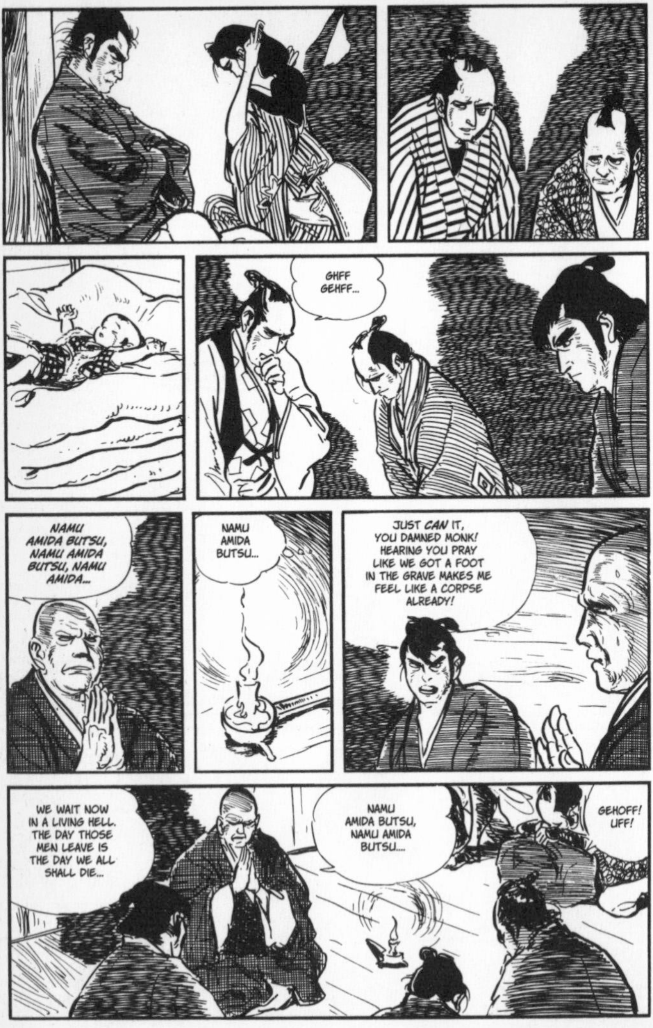
GHFF GEHFF...
NAMU AMIDA BUTSU, NAMU AMIDA BUTSU, NAMU AMIDA...
NAMU AMIDA BUTSU...
JUST CAN IT, YOU DAMNED MONK! HEARING YOU PRAY LIKE WE GOT A FOOT IN THE GRAVE MAKES ME FEEL LIKE A CORPSE ALREADY!
WE WAIT NOW IN A LIVING HELL. THE DAY THOSE MEN LEAVE IS THE DAY WE ALL SHALL DIE...
NAMU AMIDA BUTSU, NAMU AMIDA BUTSU....
GEHOFF! UFF!

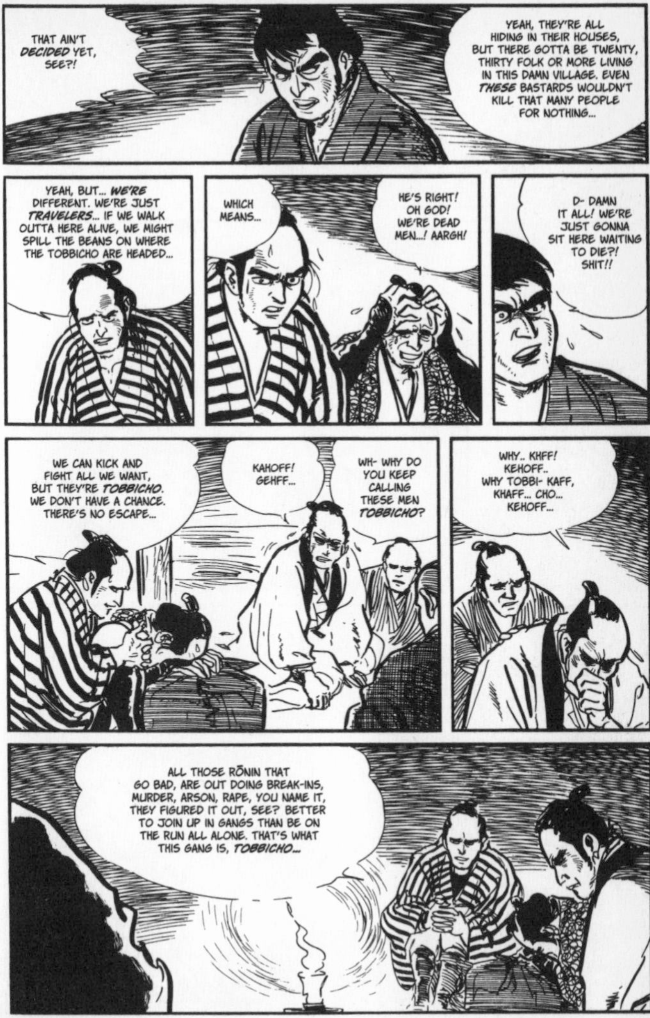
THAT AIN'T *DECIDED* YET, SEE?!
YEAH, THEY'RE ALL HIDING IN THEIR HOUSES, BUT THERE GOTTA BE TWENTY, THIRTY FOLK OR MORE LIVING IN THIS DAMN VILLAGE. EVEN *THESE* BASTARDS WOULDN'T KILL THAT MANY PEOPLE FOR NOTHING...
YEAH, BUT... *WE'RE* DIFFERENT. WE'RE JUST *TRAVELERS*... IF WE WALK OUTTA HERE ALIVE, WE MIGHT SPILL THE BEANS ON WHERE THE TOBBICHO ARE HEADED...
WHICH MEANS...
HE'S RIGHT! OH GOD! WE'RE DEAD MEN...! AARGH!
D- DAMN IT ALL! WE'RE JUST GONNA SIT HERE WAITING TO DIE?! SHIT!!
WE CAN KICK AND FIGHT ALL WE WANT, BUT THEY'RE *TOBBICHO*. WE DON'T HAVE A CHANCE. THERE'S NO ESCAPE...
KAHOFF! GEHFF...
WH- WHY DO YOU KEEP CALLING THESE MEN *TOBBICHO*?
WHY.. KHFF! KEHOFF.. WHY TOBBI- KAFF, KHAFF... CHO... KEHOFF...
ALL THOSE RŌNIN THAT GO BAD, ARE OUT DOING BREAK-INS, MURDER, ARSON, RAPE, YOU NAME IT, THEY FIGURED IT OUT, SEE? BETTER TO JOIN UP IN GANGS THAN BE ON THE RUN ALL ALONE. THAT'S WHAT THIS GANG IS, *TOBBICHO*...

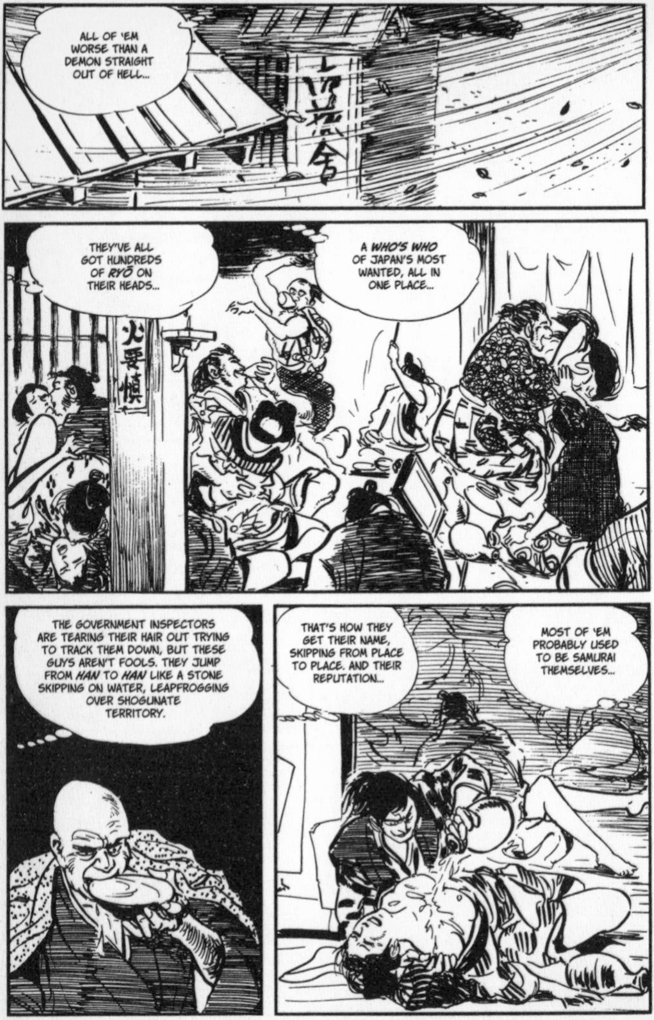
ALL OF 'EM WORSE THAN A DEMON STRAIGHT OUT OF HELL...
THEY'VE ALL GOT HUNDREDS OF *RYŌ* ON THEIR HEADS...
A *WHO'S WHO* OF JAPAN'S MOST WANTED, ALL IN ONE PLACE...
火要慎
THE GOVERNMENT INSPECTORS ARE TEARING THEIR HAIR OUT TRYING TO TRACK THEM DOWN, BUT THESE GUYS AREN'T FOOLS. THEY JUMP FROM *HAN* TO *HAN* LIKE A STONE SKIPPING ON WATER, LEAPFROGGING OVER SHOGUNATE TERRITORY.
THAT'S HOW THEY GET THEIR NAME, SKIPPING FROM PLACE TO PLACE. AND THEIR REPUTATION...
MOST OF 'EM PROBABLY USED TO BE SAMURAI THEMSELVES...

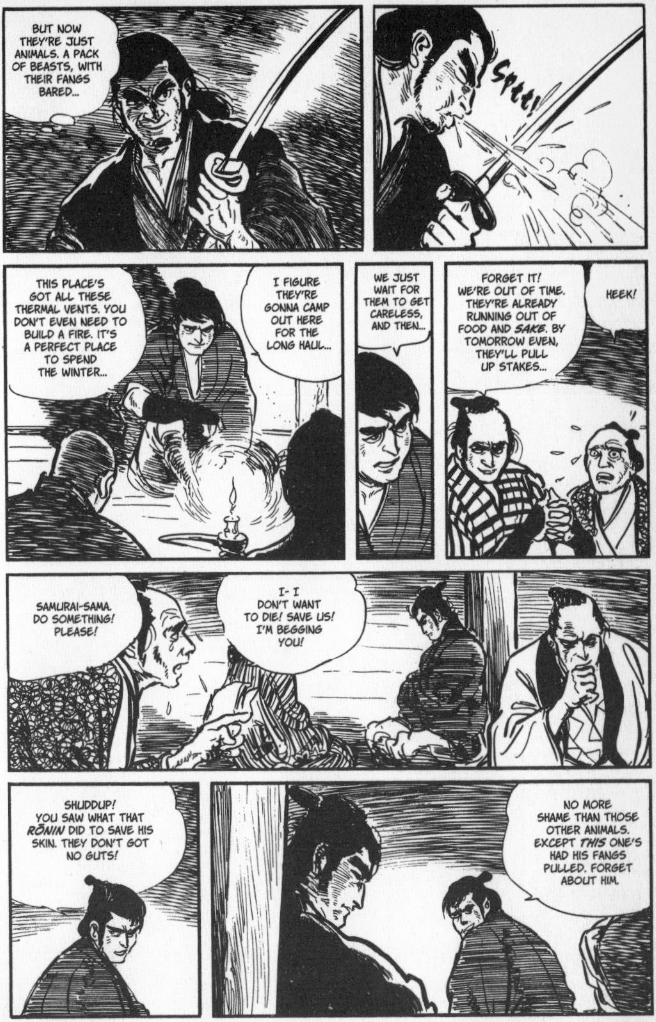
BUT NOW THEY'RE JUST ANIMALS. A PACK OF BEASTS, WITH THEIR FANGS BARED...
SPTTT!
THIS PLACE'S GOT ALL THESE THERMAL VENTS. YOU DON'T EVEN NEED TO BUILD A FIRE. IT'S A PERFECT PLACE TO SPEND THE WINTER...
I FIGURE THEY'RE GONNA CAMP OUT HERE FOR THE LONG HAUL...
WE JUST WAIT FOR THEM TO GET CARELESS, AND THEN...
FORGET IT! WE'RE OUT OF TIME. THEY'RE ALREADY RUNNING OUT OF FOOD AND *SAKE*. BY TOMORROW EVEN, THEY'LL PULL UP STAKES...
HEEK!
SAMURAI-SAMA. DO SOMETHING! PLEASE!
I- I DON'T WANT TO DIE! SAVE US! I'M BEGGING YOU!
SHUDDUP! YOU SAW WHAT THAT *RŌNIN* DID TO SAVE HIS SKIN. THEY DON'T GOT NO GUTS!
NO MORE SHAME THAN THOSE OTHER ANIMALS. EXCEPT *THIS* ONE'S HAD HIS FANGS PULLED. FORGET ABOUT HIM.

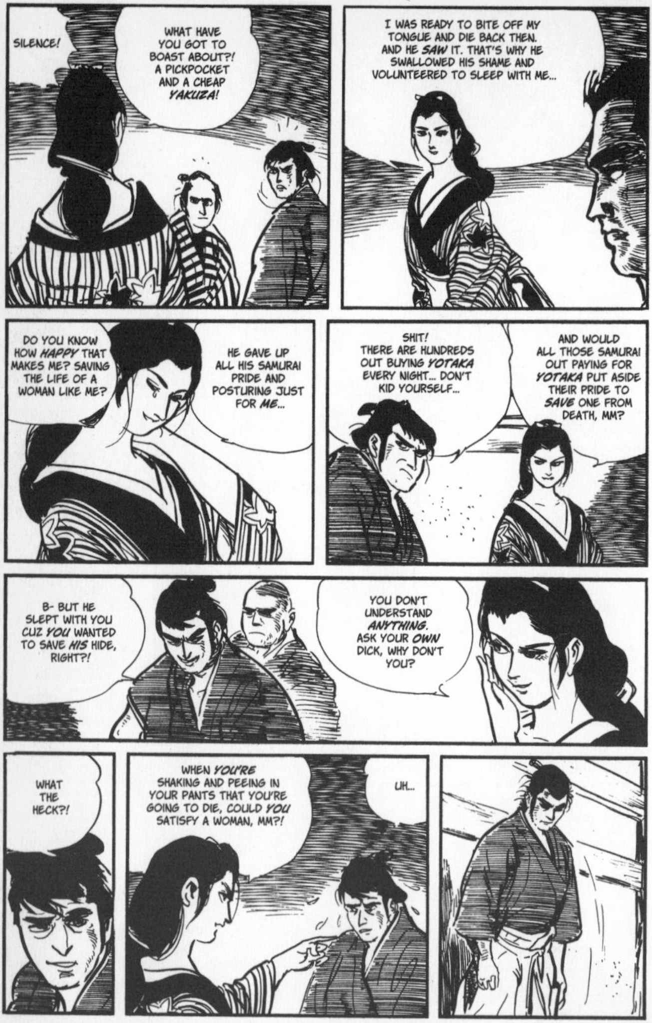
SILENCE!
WHAT HAVE YOU GOT TO BOAST ABOUT?! A PICKPOCKET AND A CHEAP *YAKUZA!*
I WAS READY TO BITE OFF MY TONGUE AND DIE BACK THEN. AND HE *SAW* IT. THAT'S WHY HE SWALLOWED HIS SHAME AND VOLUNTEERED TO SLEEP WITH ME...
DO YOU KNOW HOW *HAPPY* THAT MAKES ME? SAVING THE LIFE OF A WOMAN LIKE ME?
HE GAVE UP ALL HIS SAMURAI PRIDE AND POSTURING JUST FOR *ME*...
SHIT! THERE ARE HUNDREDS OUT BUYING *YOTAKA* EVERY NIGHT... DON'T KID YOURSELF...
AND WOULD ALL THOSE SAMURAI OUT PAYING FOR *YOTAKA* PUT ASIDE THEIR PRIDE TO *SAVE* ONE FROM DEATH, MM?
B- BUT HE SLEPT WITH YOU CUZ *YOU* WANTED TO SAVE *HIS* HIDE, RIGHT?!
YOU DON'T UNDERSTAND *ANYTHING*. ASK YOUR *OWN* DICK, WHY DON'T YOU?
WHAT THE HECK?!
WHEN *YOU'RE* SHAKING AND PEEING IN YOUR PANTS THAT YOU'RE GOING TO DIE, COULD *YOU* SATISFY A WOMAN, MM?!
UH...

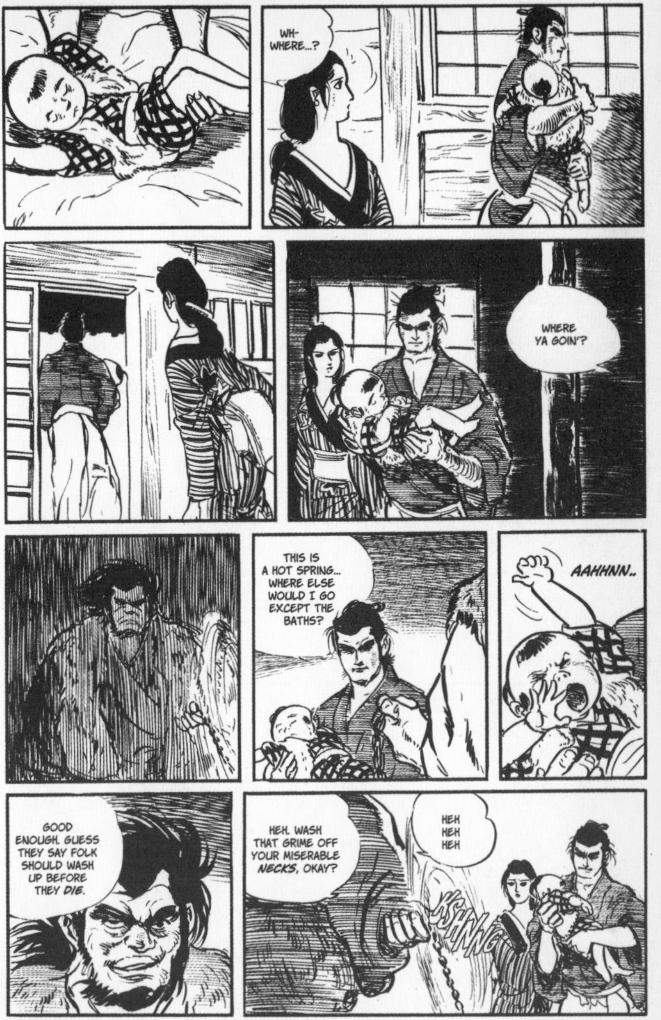
WH- WHERE...?
WHERE YA GOIN'?
THIS IS A HOT SPRING... WHERE ELSE WOULD I GO EXCEPT THE BATHS?
AAHHNN..
GOOD ENOUGH. GUESS THEY SAY FOLK SHOULD WASH UP BEFORE THEY *DIE*.
HEH. WASH THAT GRIME OFF YOUR MISERABLE *NECKS*, OKAY?
HEH HEH HEH
KSHNNG

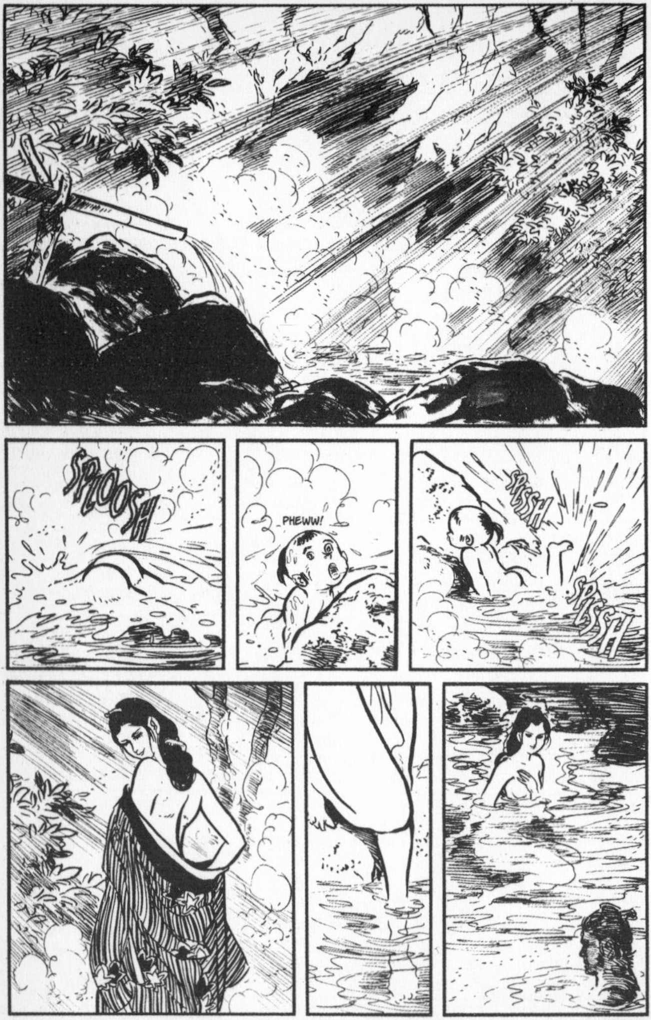
SPLOOSH
PHEWW!
SPISSH
SPISSH

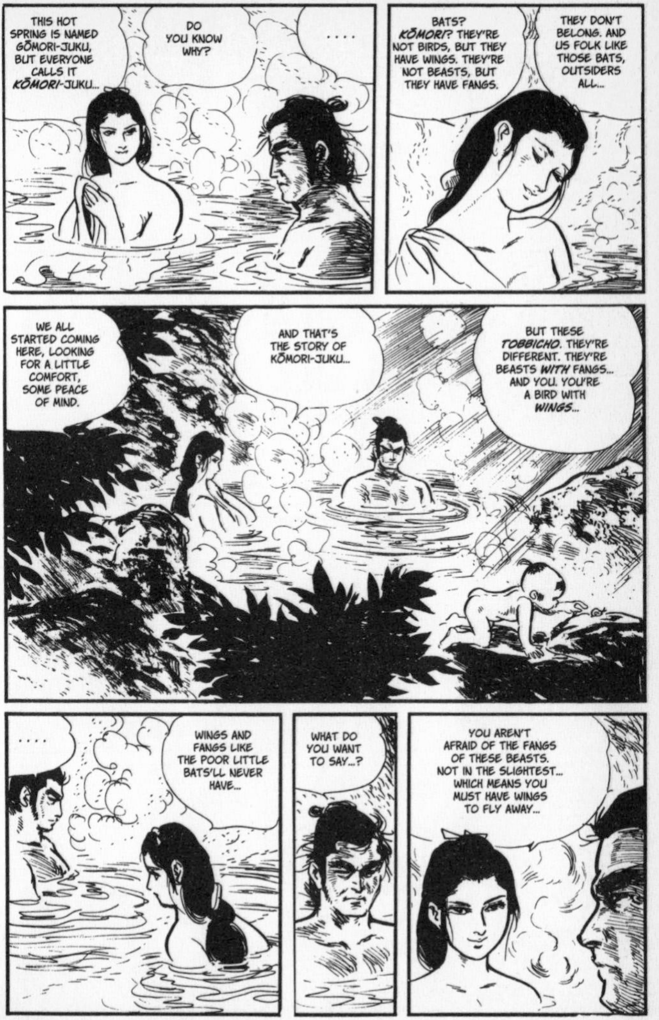
THIS HOT SPRING IS NAMED GŌMORI-JUKU, BUT EVERYONE CALLS IT *KŌMORI*-JUKU...
DO YOU KNOW WHY?
....
BATS? *KŌMORI*? THEY'RE NOT BIRDS, BUT THEY HAVE WINGS. THEY'RE NOT BEASTS, BUT THEY HAVE FANGS.
THEY DON'T BELONG. AND US FOLK LIKE THOSE BATS, OUTSIDERS ALL...
WE ALL STARTED COMING HERE, LOOKING FOR A LITTLE COMFORT, SOME PEACE OF MIND.
AND THAT'S THE STORY OF KŌMORI-JUKU...
BUT THESE *TOBBICHO*. THEY'RE DIFFERENT. THEY'RE BEASTS *WITH* FANGS... AND YOU. YOU'RE A BIRD WITH *WINGS*...
....
WINGS AND FANGS LIKE THE POOR LITTLE BATS'LL NEVER HAVE...
WHAT DO YOU WANT TO SAY...?
YOU AREN'T AFRAID OF THE FANGS OF THESE BEASTS. NOT IN THE SLIGHTEST... WHICH MEANS YOU MUST HAVE WINGS TO FLY AWAY...

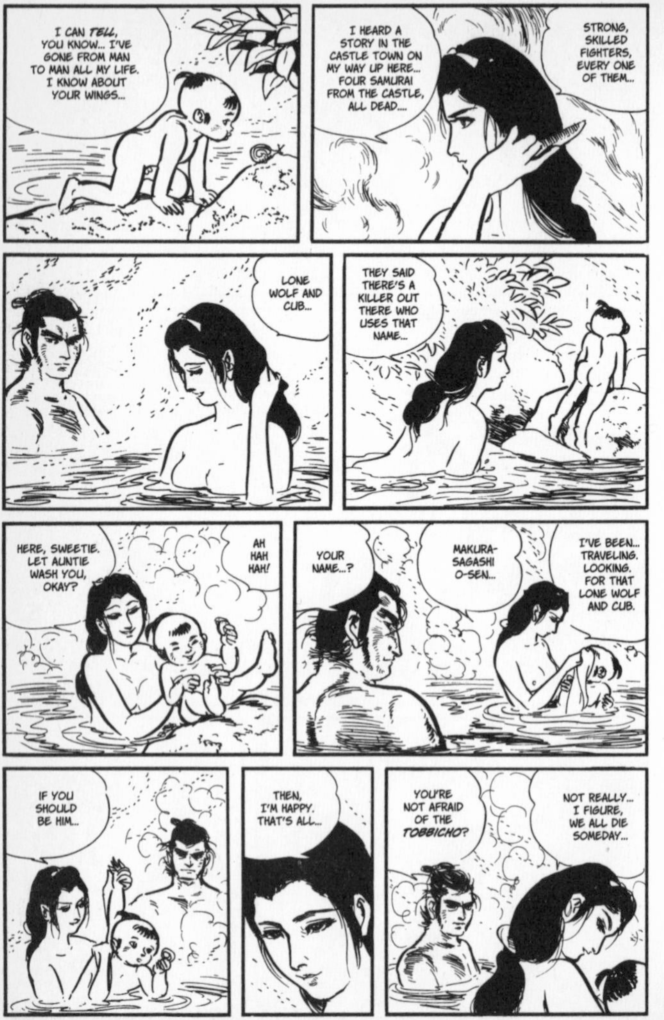
I CAN TELL, YOU KNOW... I'VE GONE FROM MAN TO MAN ALL MY LIFE. I KNOW ABOUT YOUR WINGS...
I HEARD A STORY IN THE CASTLE TOWN ON MY WAY UP HERE... FOUR SAMURAI FROM THE CASTLE, ALL DEAD....
STRONG, SKILLED FIGHTERS, EVERY ONE OF THEM...
LONE WOLF AND CUB...
THEY SAID THERE'S A KILLER OUT THERE WHO USES THAT NAME...
HERE, SWEETIE. LET AUNTIE WASH YOU, OKAY?
AH HAH HAH!
YOUR NAME...?
MAKURA-SAGASHI O-SEN...
I'VE BEEN... TRAVELING. LOOKING. FOR THAT LONE WOLF AND CUB.
IF YOU SHOULD BE HIM...
THEN, I'M HAPPY. THAT'S ALL...
YOU'RE NOT AFRAID OF THE TOBBICHO?
NOT REALLY... I FIGURE, WE ALL DIE SOMEDAY...

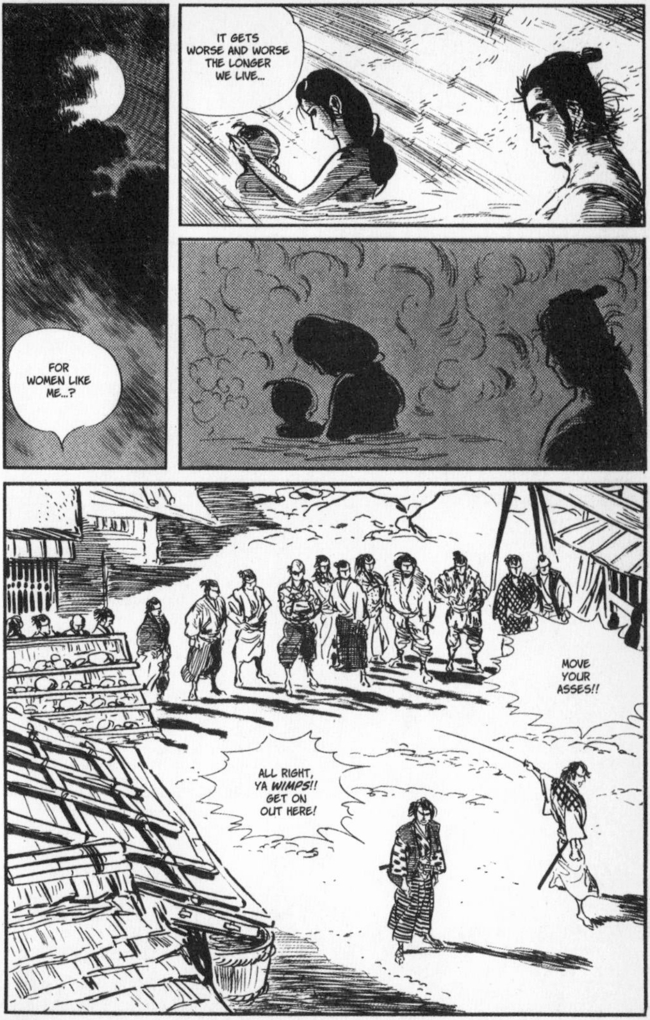
IT GETS WORSE AND WORSE THE LONGER WE LIVE...
FOR WOMEN LIKE ME...?
MOVE YOUR ASSES!!
ALL RIGHT, YA *WIMPS!!* GET ON OUT HERE!

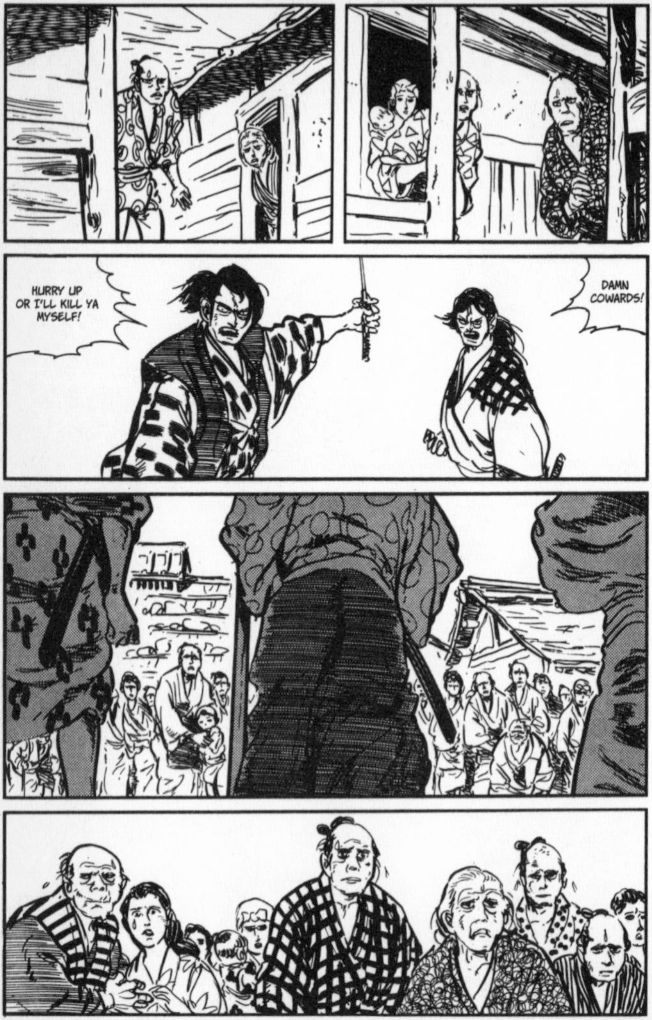
HURRY UP OR I'LL KILL YA MYSELF!
DAMN COWARDS!

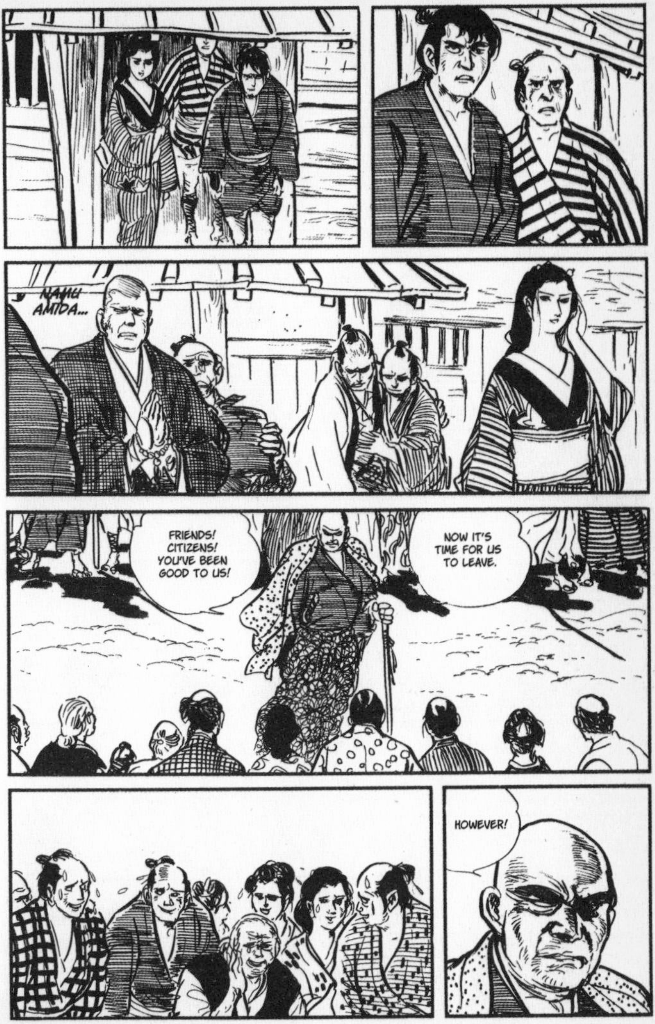
NAMU AMIDA...
FRIENDS! CITIZENS! YOU'VE BEEN GOOD TO US!
NOW IT'S TIME FOR US TO LEAVE.
HOWEVER!

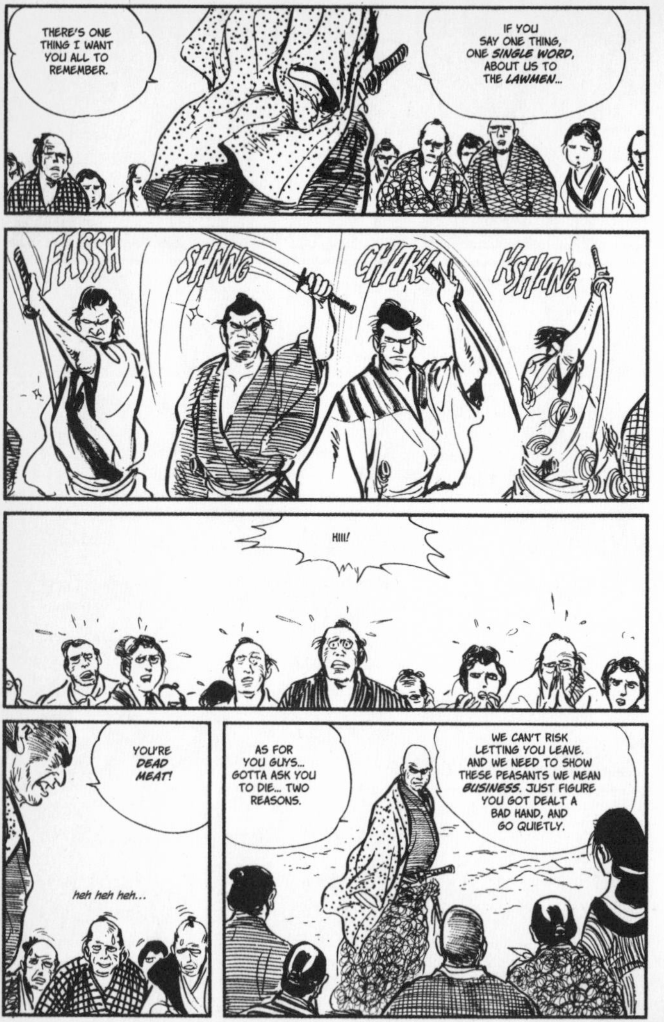

THERE'S ONE THING I WANT YOU ALL TO REMEMBER.
IF YOU SAY ONE THING, ONE SINGLE WORD, ABOUT US TO THE LAWMEN...
FASSH
SHNNG
CHAK!
KSHANG
HIII!
YOU'RE DEAD MEAT!
heh heh heh...
AS FOR YOU GUYS... GOTTA ASK YOU TO DIE... TWO REASONS.
WE CAN'T RISK LETTING YOU LEAVE. AND WE NEED TO SHOW THESE PEASANTS WE MEAN BUSINESS. JUST FIGURE YOU GOT DEALT A BAD HAND, AND GO QUIETLY.

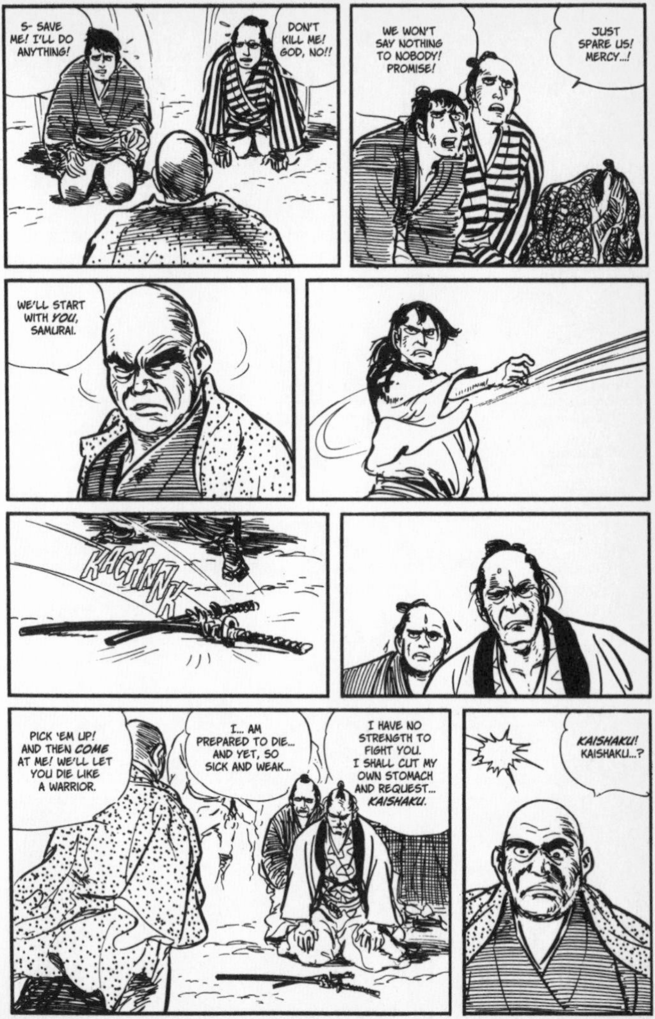
S- SAVE ME! I'LL DO ANYTHING!
DON'T KILL ME! GOD, NO!!
WE WON'T SAY NOTHING TO NOBODY! PROMISE!
JUST SPARE US! MERCY...!
WE'LL START WITH *YOU*, SAMURAI.
KACHINNNK
PICK 'EM UP! AND THEN *COME* AT ME! WE'LL LET YOU DIE LIKE A WARRIOR.
I... AM PREPARED TO DIE... AND YET, SO SICK AND WEAK...
I HAVE NO STRENGTH TO FIGHT YOU. I SHALL CUT MY OWN STOMACH AND REQUEST... *KAISHAKU*.
KAISHAKU! KAISHAKU...?

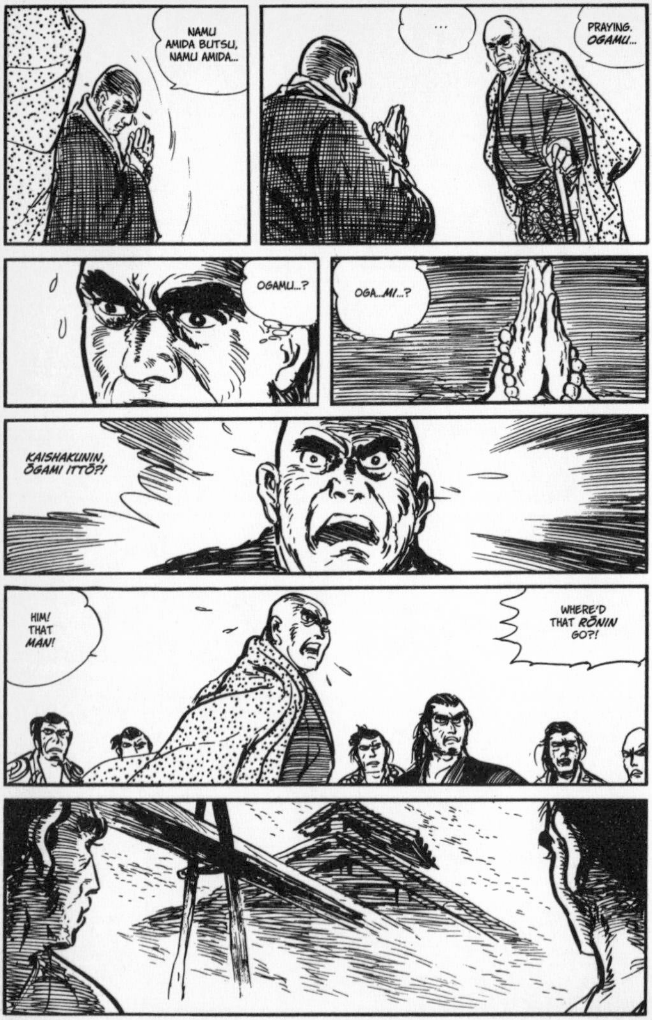
NAMU AMIDA BUTSU, NAMU AMIDA...
...
PRAYING. OGAMU...
OGAMU...?
OGA...MI...?
KAISHAKUNIN, ŌGAMI ITTŌ?!
HIM! THAT MAN!
WHERE'D THAT RŌNIN GO?!

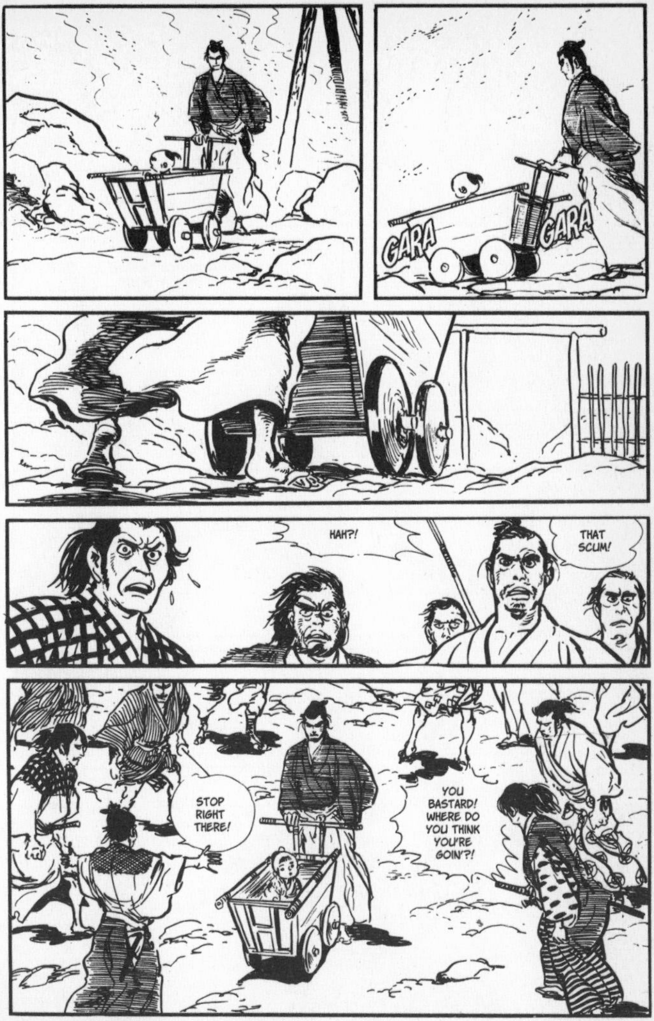
GARA
GARA
HAH?!
THAT SCUM!
STOP RIGHT THERE!
YOU BASTARD! WHERE DO YOU THINK YOU'RE GOIN'?!

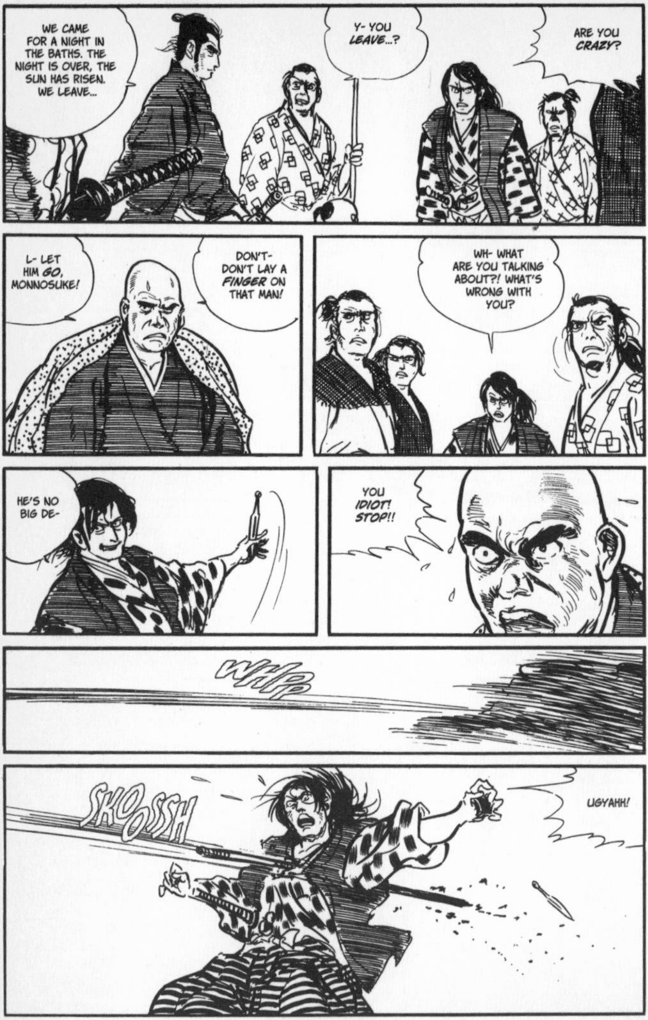
WE CAME FOR A NIGHT IN THE BATHS. THE NIGHT IS OVER, THE SUN HAS RISEN. WE LEAVE...
Y- YOU *LEAVE*...?
ARE YOU *CRAZY?*
L- LET HIM *GO*, MONNOSUKE!
DON'T- DON'T LAY A *FINGER* ON THAT MAN!
WH- WHAT ARE YOU TALKING ABOUT?! WHAT'S WRONG WITH YOU?
HE'S NO BIG DE-
YOU *IDIOT! STOP!!*
WHIP
SKOOSSH
UGYAHH!

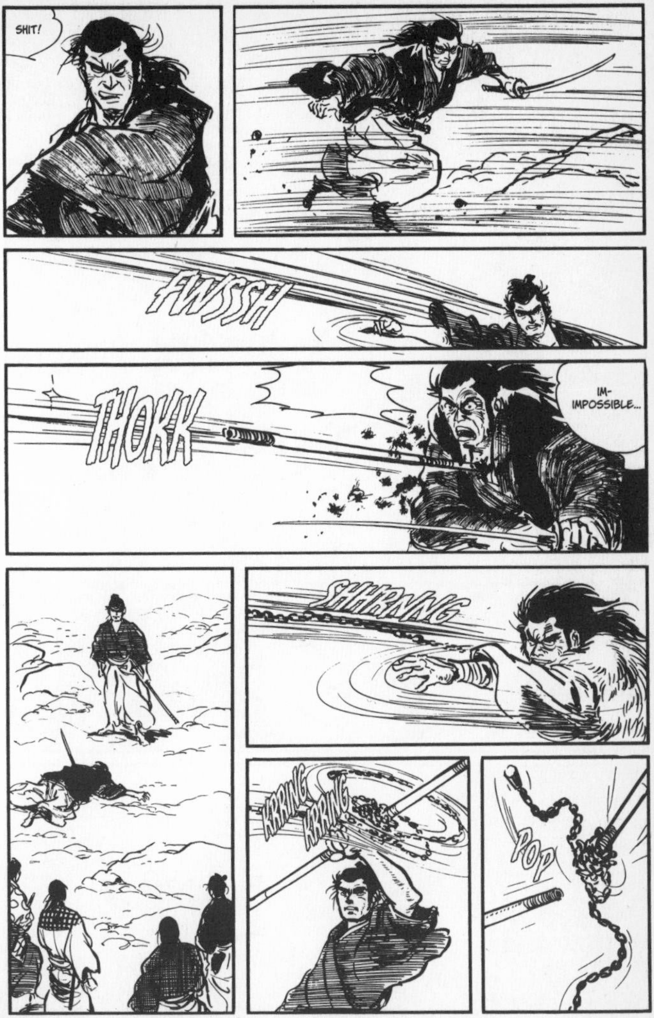
SHIT!
FWSSH
THOKK
IM-IMPOSSIBLE...
SHHRNNG
KRRING KRRING
POP

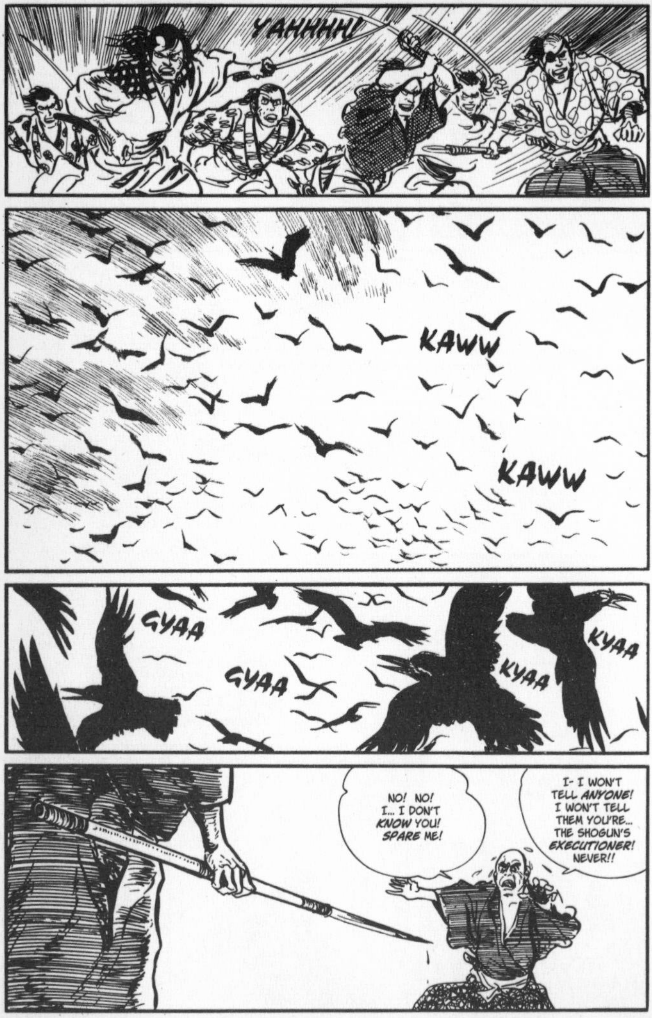
YAHHHH!
KAWW
KAWW
GYAA
GYAA
KYAA
KYAA
NO! NO! I... I DON'T *KNOW* YOU! *SPARE* ME!
I- I WON'T TELL *ANYONE*! I WON'T TELL THEM YOU'RE... THE SHOGUN'S *EXECUTIONER*! NEVER!!

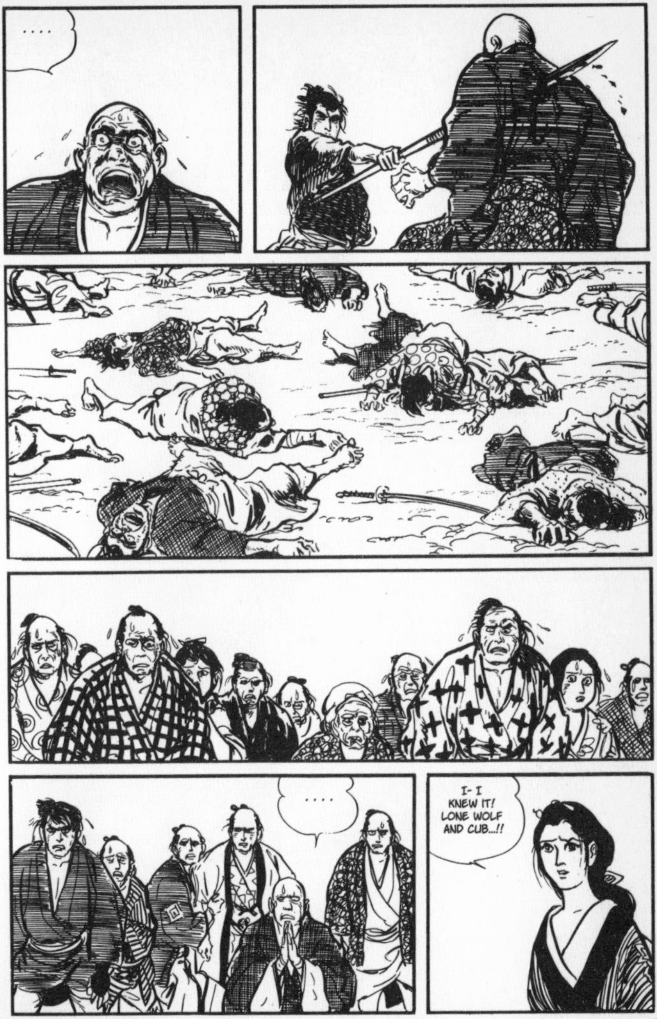
....
....
I- I KNEW IT! LONE WOLF AND CUB...!!

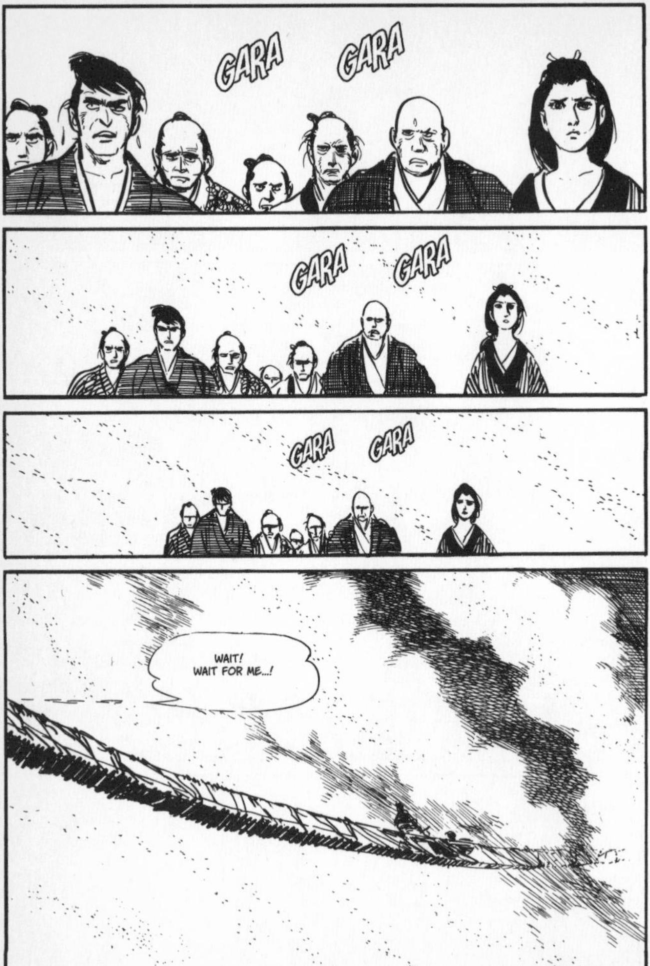
GARA
GARA
GARA
GARA
GARA
GARA
WAIT!
WAIT FOR ME...!

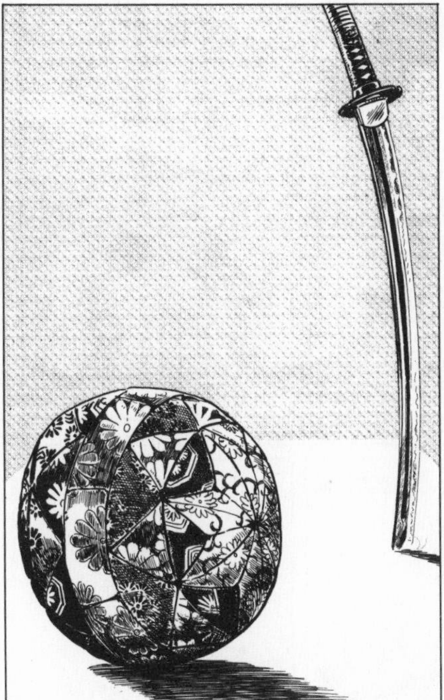

the ninth

The Assassin's Road

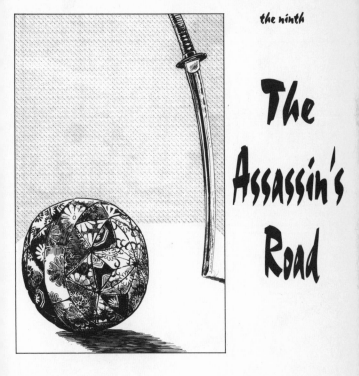

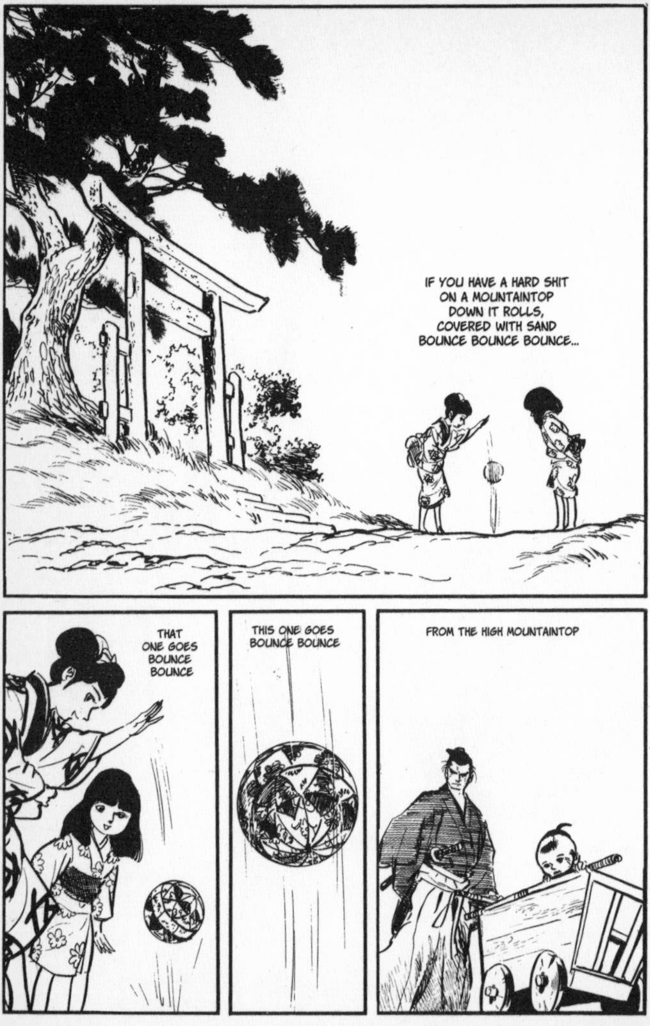
IF YOU HAVE A HARD SHIT
ON A MOUNTAINTOP
DOWN IT ROLLS,
COVERED WITH SAND
BOUNCE BOUNCE BOUNCE...
THAT ONE GOES BOUNCE BOUNCE
THIS ONE GOES BOUNCE BOUNCE
FROM THE HIGH MOUNTAINTOP

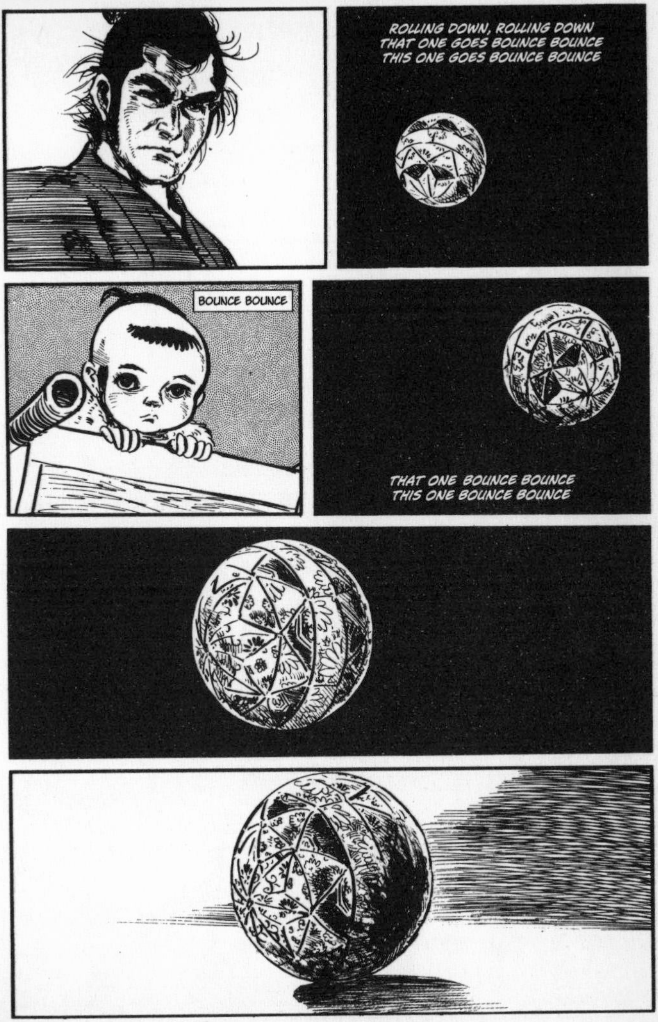
ROLLING DOWN, ROLLING DOWN
THAT ONE GOES BOUNCE BOUNCE
THIS ONE GOES BOUNCE BOUNCE
BOUNCE BOUNCE
THAT ONE BOUNCE BOUNCE
THIS ONE BOUNCE BOUNCE

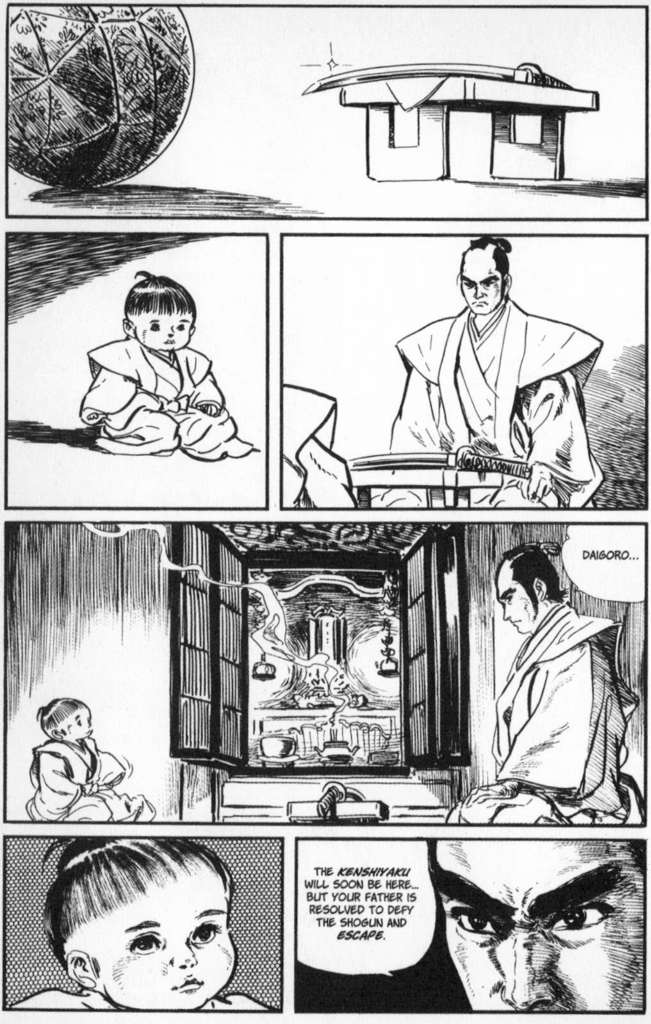
DAIGORO...
THE *KENSHIYAKU* WILL SOON BE HERE... BUT YOUR FATHER IS RESOLVED TO DEFY THE SHOGUN AND *ESCAPE*.

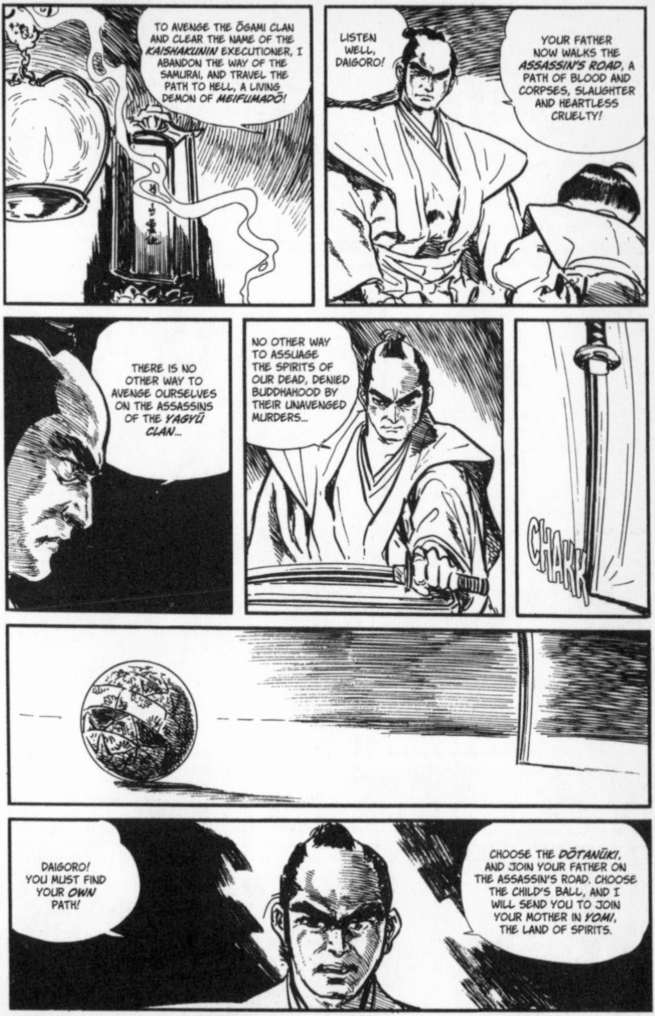
TO AVENGE THE ŌGAMI CLAN AND CLEAR THE NAME OF THE *KAISHAKUNIN* EXECUTIONER, I ABANDON THE WAY OF THE SAMURAI, AND TRAVEL THE PATH TO HELL, A LIVING DEMON OF *MEIFUMADŌ*!
LISTEN WELL, DAIGORO!
YOUR FATHER NOW WALKS THE *ASSASSIN'S ROAD*, A PATH OF BLOOD AND CORPSES, SLAUGHTER AND HEARTLESS CRUELTY!
THERE IS NO OTHER WAY TO AVENGE OURSELVES ON THE ASSASSINS OF THE *YAGYŪ CLAN*...
NO OTHER WAY TO ASSUAGE THE SPIRITS OF OUR DEAD, DENIED BUDDHAHOOD BY THEIR UNAVENGED MURDERS...
CHAKK
DAIGORO! YOU MUST FIND YOUR *OWN* PATH!
CHOOSE THE *DŌTANUKI*, AND JOIN YOUR FATHER ON THE ASSASSIN'S ROAD. CHOOSE THE CHILD'S BALL, AND I WILL SEND YOU TO JOIN YOUR MOTHER IN *YOMI*, THE LAND OF SPIRITS.

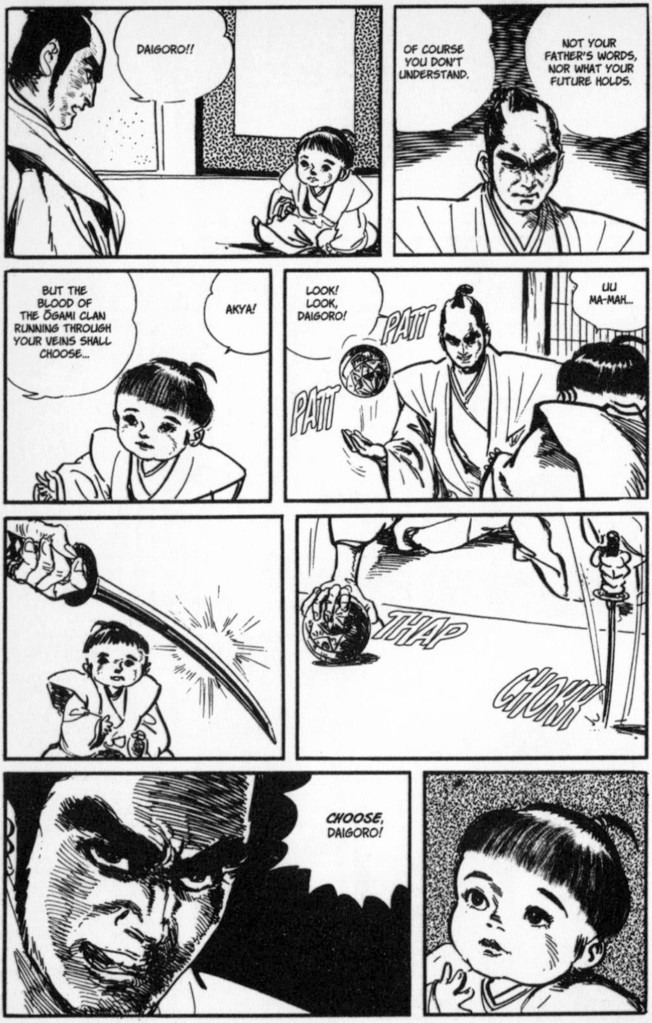

DAIGORO!!
OF COURSE YOU DON'T UNDERSTAND.
NOT YOUR FATHER'S WORDS, NOR WHAT YOUR FUTURE HOLDS.
BUT THE BLOOD OF THE ŌGAMI CLAN RUNNING THROUGH YOUR VEINS SHALL CHOOSE...
AKYA!
LOOK! LOOK, DAIGORO!
PATT
PATT
UU MA-MAH...
THAP
CHOKK
CHOOSE, DAIGORO!

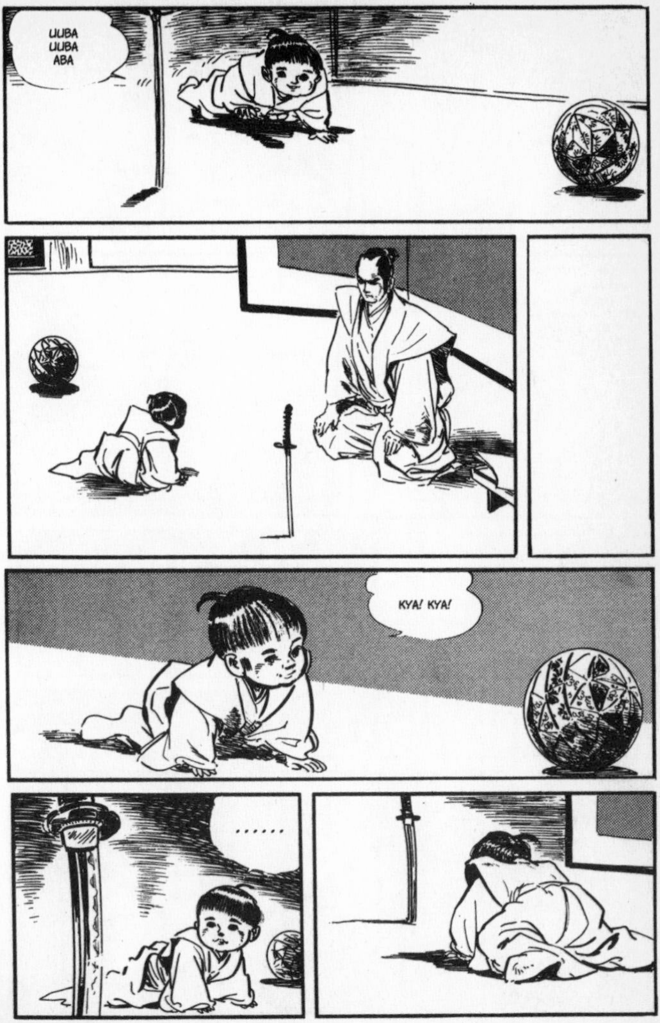
UUBA
UUBA
ABA
KYA! KYA!
......

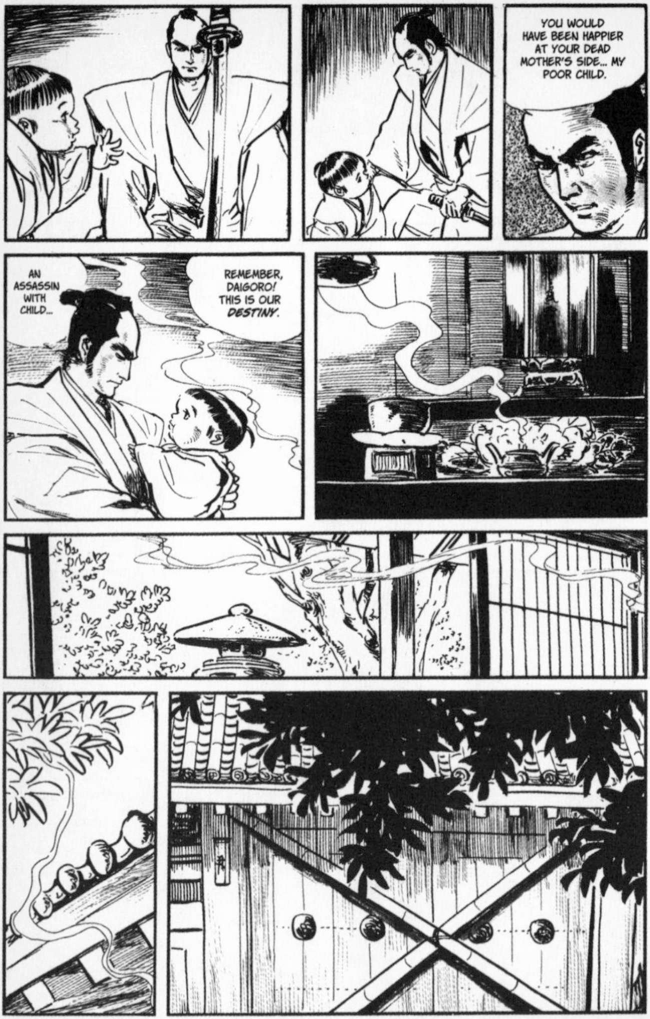
YOU WOULD HAVE BEEN HAPPIER AT YOUR DEAD MOTHER'S SIDE... MY POOR CHILD.
AN ASSASSIN WITH CHILD...
REMEMBER, DAIGORO! THIS IS OUR DESTINY.

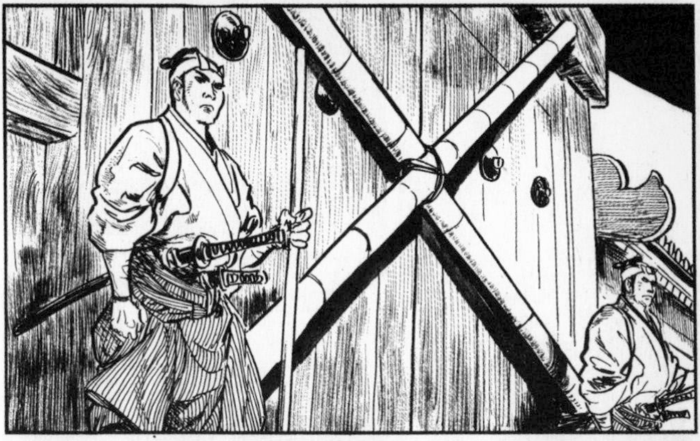

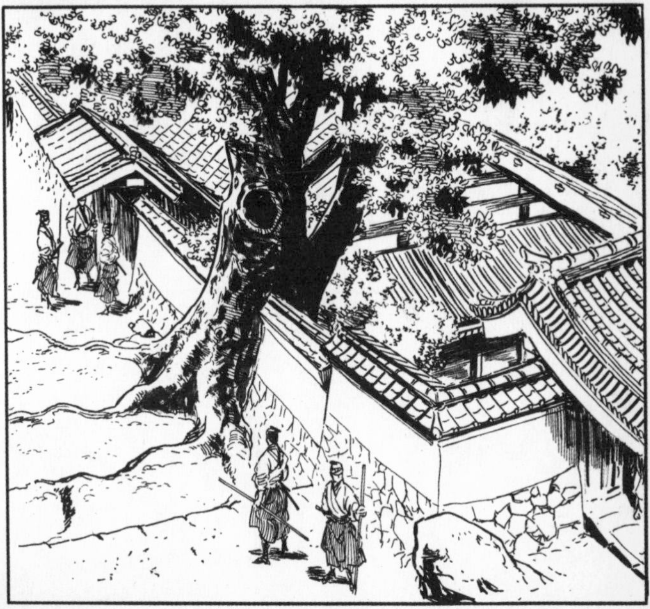

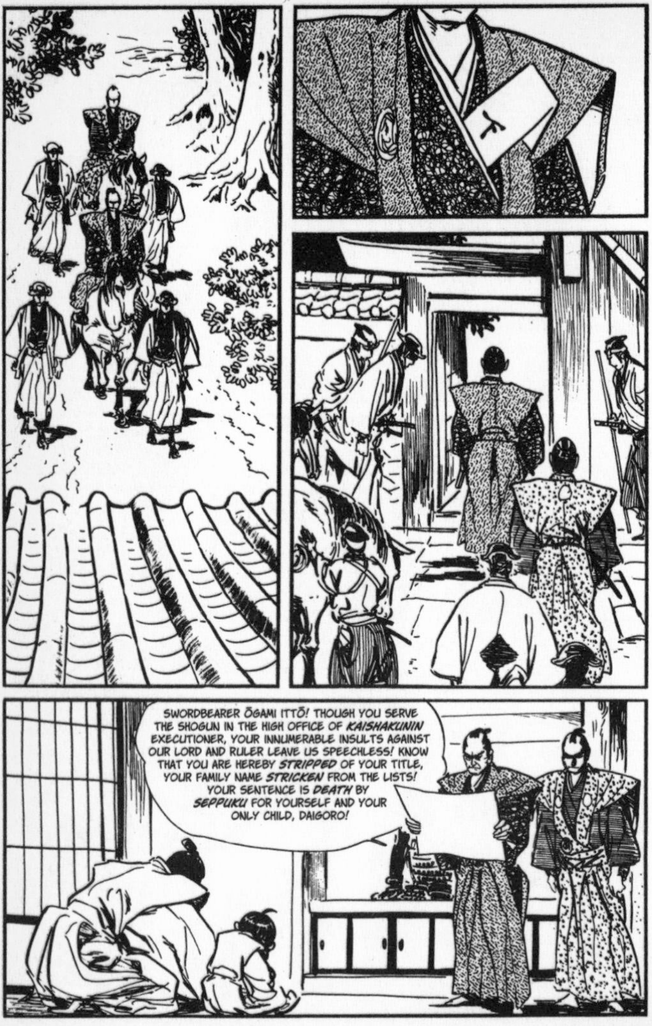
SWORDBEARER ŌGAMI ITTŌ! THOUGH YOU SERVE THE SHOGUN IN THE HIGH OFFICE OF *KAISHAKUNIN* EXECUTIONER, YOUR INNUMERABLE INSULTS AGAINST OUR LORD AND RULER LEAVE US SPEECHLESS! KNOW THAT YOU ARE HEREBY *STRIPPED* OF YOUR TITLE, YOUR FAMILY NAME *STRICKEN* FROM THE LISTS! YOUR SENTENCE IS *DEATH* BY *SEPPUKU* FOR YOURSELF AND YOUR ONLY CHILD, DAIGORO!

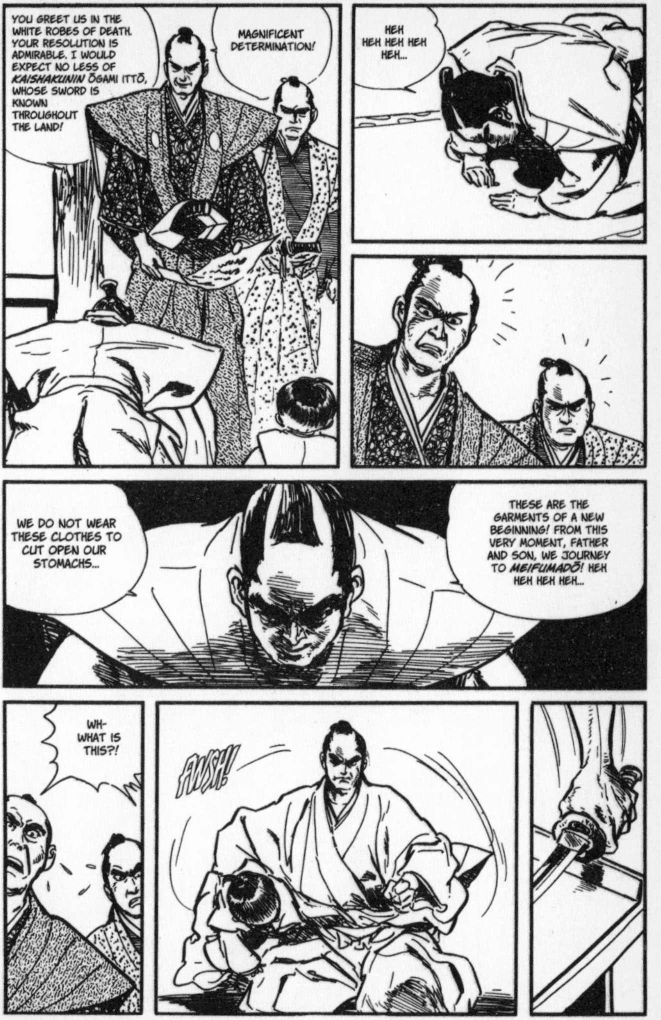
YOU GREET US IN THE WHITE ROBES OF DEATH. YOUR RESOLUTION IS ADMIRABLE. I WOULD EXPECT NO LESS OF *KAISHAKUNIN* ŌGAMI ITTŌ, WHOSE SWORD IS KNOWN THROUGHOUT THE LAND!
MAGNIFICENT DETERMINATION!
HEH HEH HEH HEH HEH...
WE DO NOT WEAR THESE CLOTHES TO CUT OPEN OUR STOMACHS...
THESE ARE THE GARMENTS OF A NEW BEGINNING! FROM THIS VERY MOMENT, FATHER AND SON, WE JOURNEY TO *MEIFUMADŌ*! HEH HEH HEH HEH...
WH-WHAT IS THIS?!
FWSH!

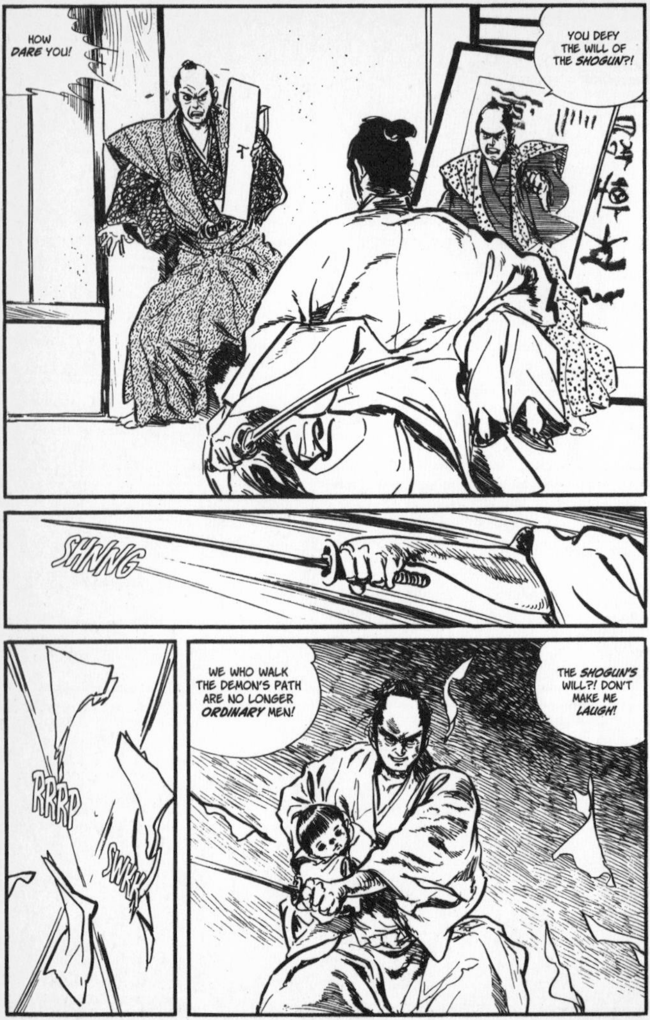
HOW DARE YOU!
YOU DEFY THE WILL OF THE SHOGUN?!
SHNNG
RRRP
SWKK
WE WHO WALK THE DEMON'S PATH ARE NO LONGER ORDINARY MEN!
THE SHOGUN'S WILL?! DON'T MAKE ME LAUGH!

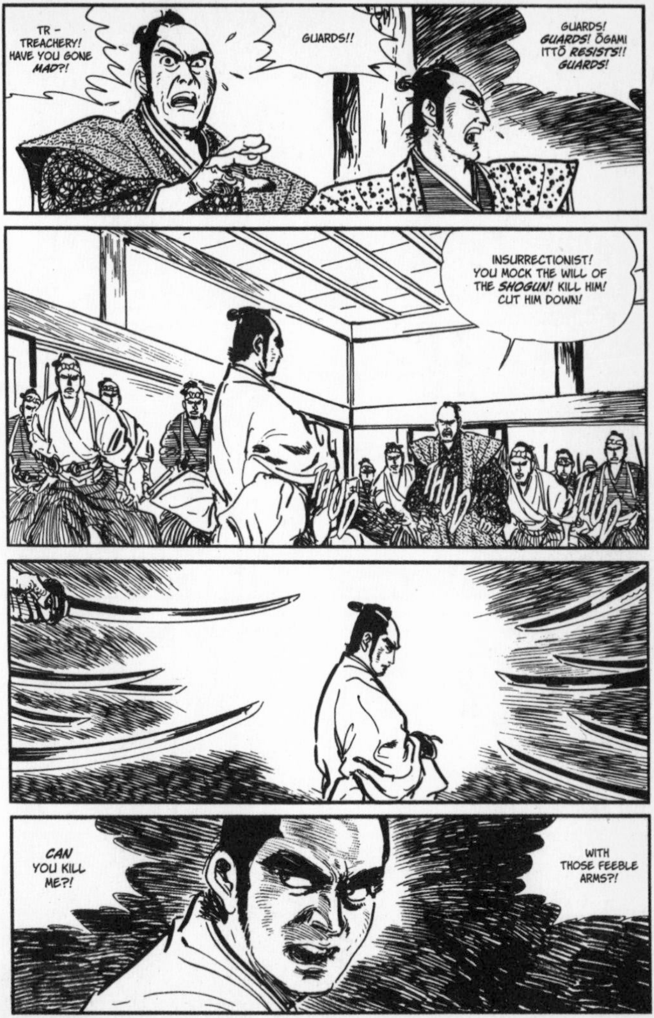
TR - TREACHERY! HAVE YOU GONE *MAD?!*
GUARDS!!
GUARDS! *GUARDS!* ŌGAMI ITTŌ *RESISTS!!* *GUARDS!*
INSURRECTIONIST! YOU MOCK THE WILL OF THE ***SHOGUN!*** KILL HIM! CUT HIM DOWN!
THUD
THUD
THUD
CAN YOU KILL ME?!
WITH THOSE FEEBLE ARMS?!

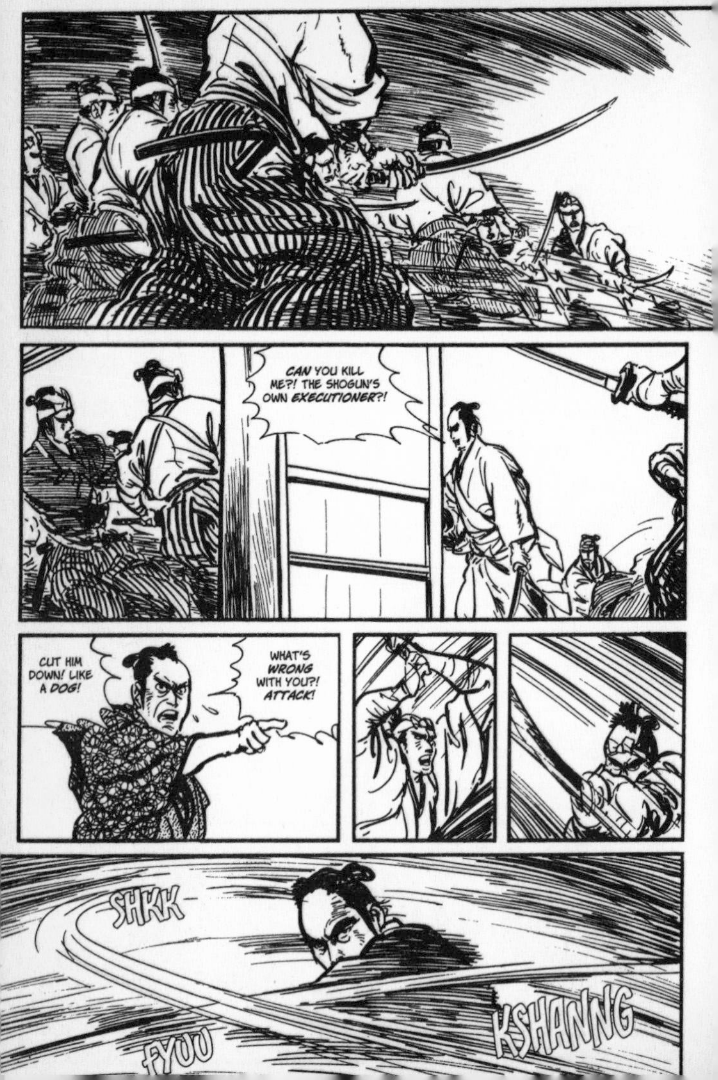
CAN YOU KILL ME?! THE SHOGUN'S OWN EXECUTIONER?!
CUT HIM DOWN! LIKE A DOG!
WHAT'S WRONG WITH YOU?! ATTACK!
SHKK
FYUU
KSHANNG

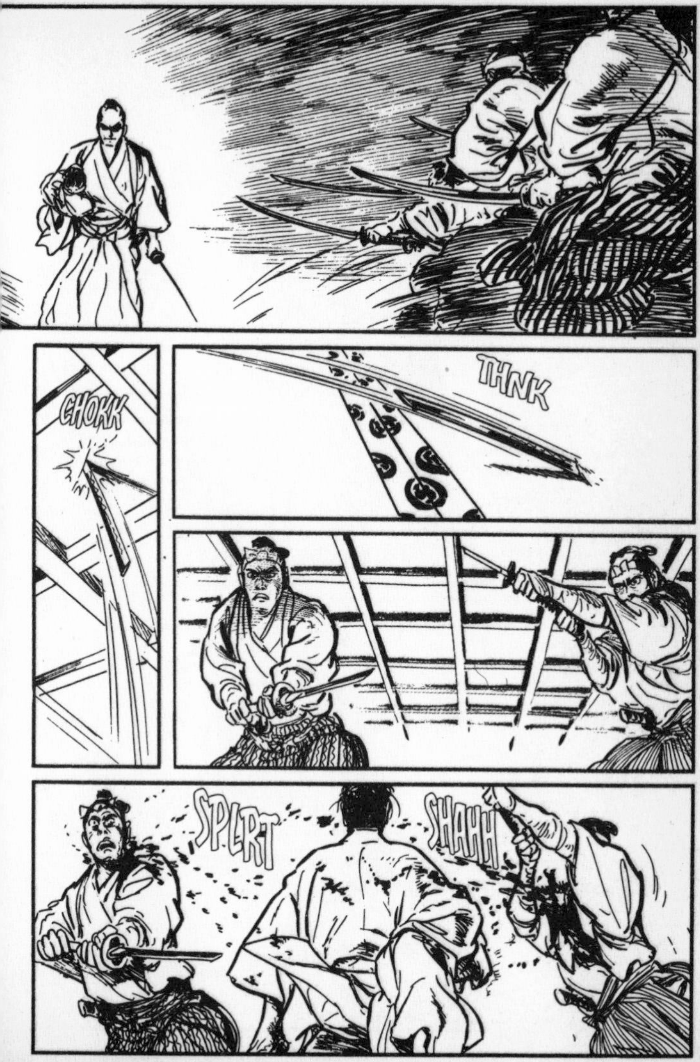
CHOKK
THNK
SPLRT
SHAHH

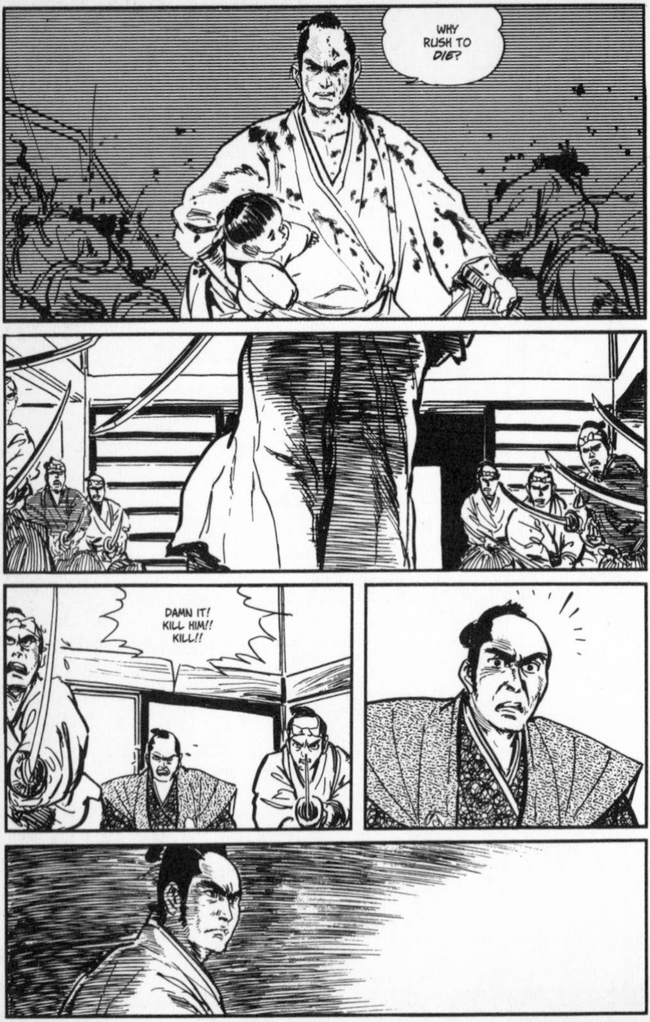
WHY RUSH TO *DIE?*
DAMN IT! KILL HIM!! KILL!!

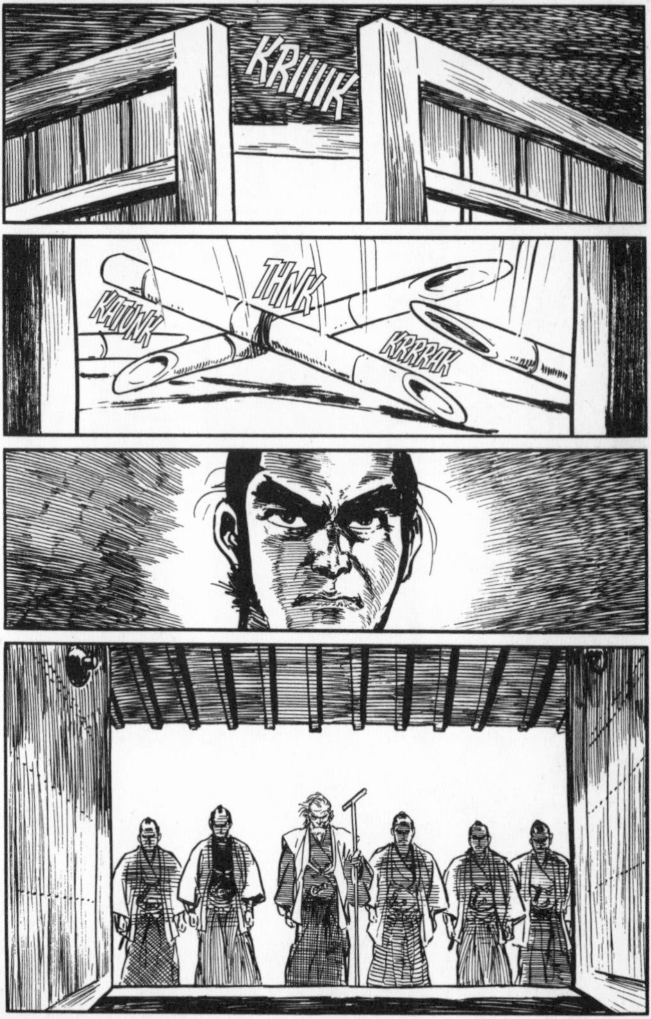
KRIIIIK
KATUNK
THNK
KRRRAK

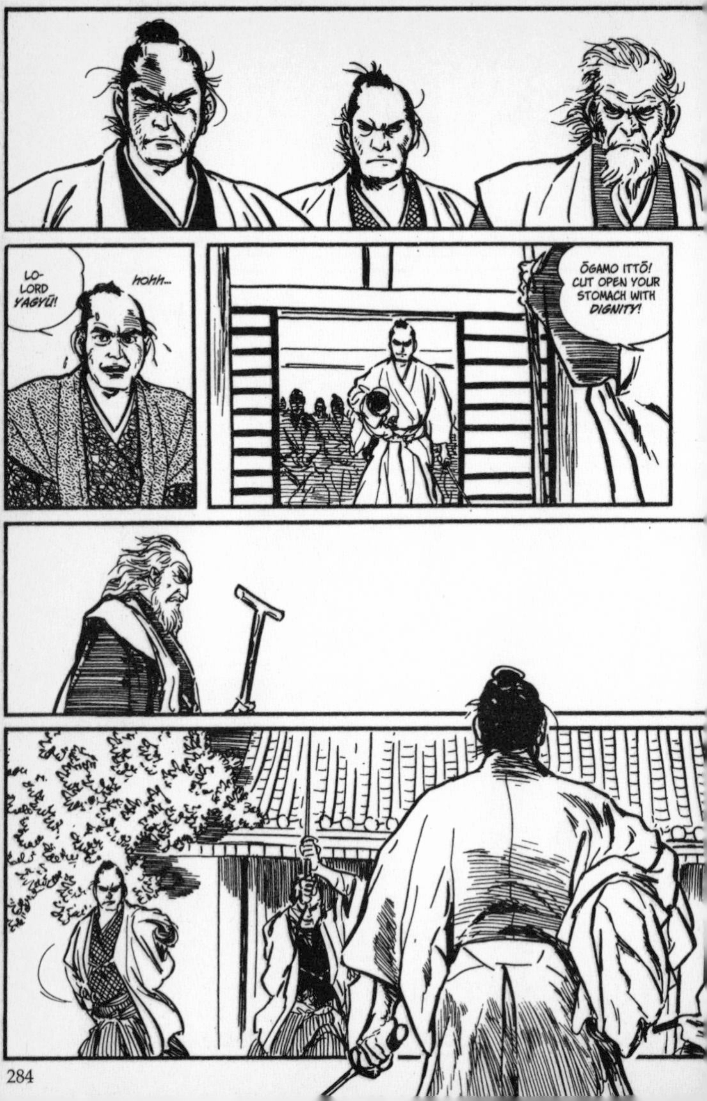
LO-
LORD
YAGYŪ!
hohh...
ŌGAMO ITTŌ!
CUT OPEN YOUR
STOMACH WITH
DIGNITY!

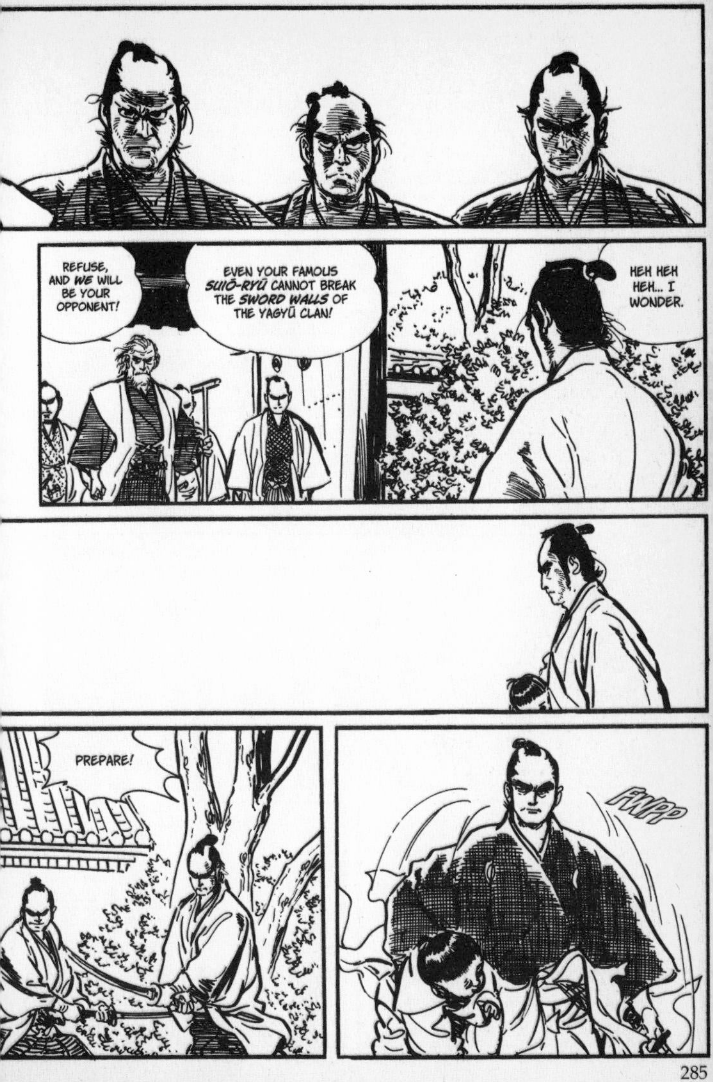
REFUSE, AND WE WILL BE YOUR OPPONENT!
EVEN YOUR FAMOUS SUIŌ-RYŪ CANNOT BREAK THE SWORD WALLS OF THE YAGYŪ CLAN!
HEH HEH HEH... I WONDER.
PREPARE!
FWPP

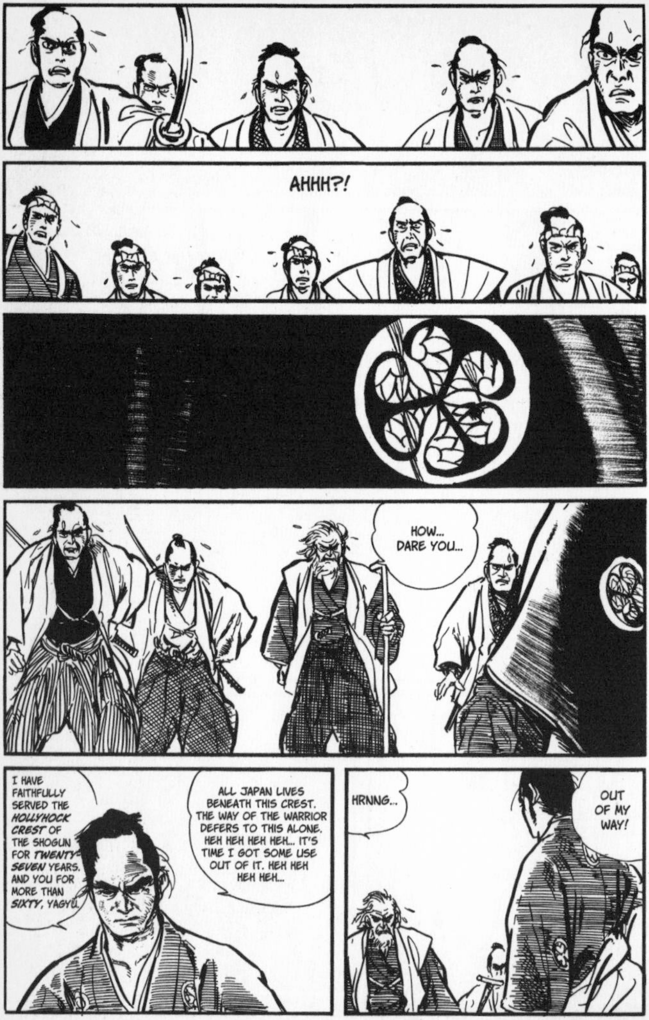
AHHH?!
HOW... DARE YOU...
I HAVE FAITHFULLY SERVED THE HOLLYHOCK CREST OF THE SHOGUN FOR TWENTY-SEVEN YEARS. AND YOU FOR MORE THAN SIXTY, YAGYU.
ALL JAPAN LIVES BENEATH THIS CREST. THE WAY OF THE WARRIOR DEFERS TO THIS ALONE. HEH HEH HEH HEH... IT'S TIME I GOT SOME USE OUT OF IT. HEH HEH HEH HEH...
HRNNG...
OUT OF MY WAY!

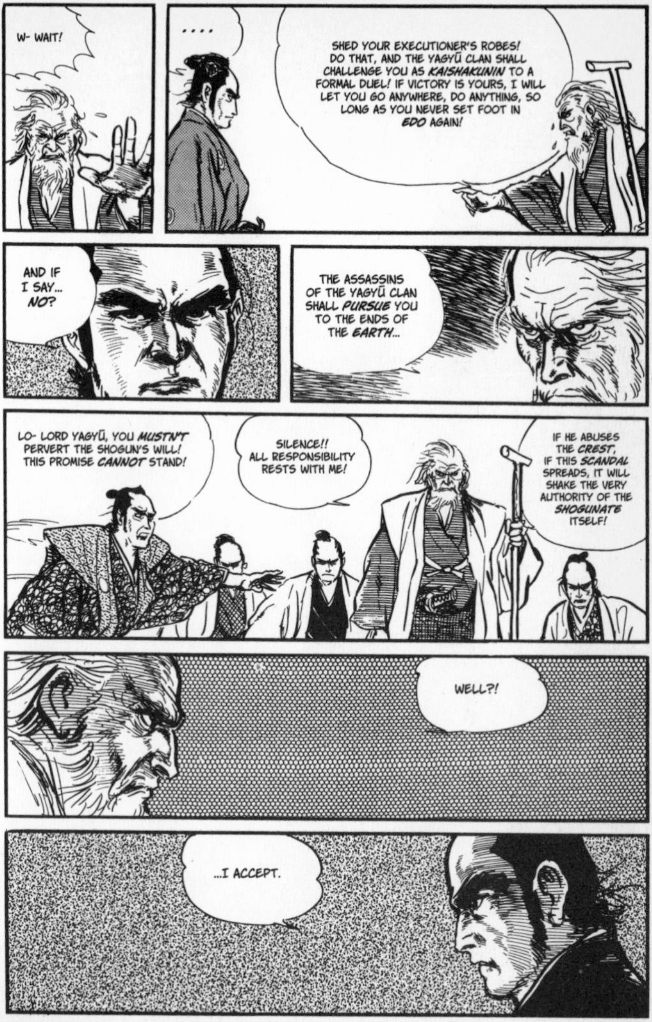
W- WAIT!
....
SHED YOUR EXECUTIONER'S ROBES! DO THAT, AND THE YAGYŪ CLAN SHALL CHALLENGE YOU AS KAISHAKUNIN TO A FORMAL DUEL! IF VICTORY IS YOURS, I WILL LET YOU GO ANYWHERE, DO ANYTHING, SO LONG AS YOU NEVER SET FOOT IN EDO AGAIN!
AND IF I SAY... NO?
THE ASSASSINS OF THE YAGYŪ CLAN SHALL PURSUE YOU TO THE ENDS OF THE EARTH...
LO- LORD YAGYŪ, YOU MUSTN'T PERVERT THE SHOGUN'S WILL! THIS PROMISE CANNOT STAND!
SILENCE!! ALL RESPONSIBILITY RESTS WITH ME!
IF HE ABUSES THE CREST, IF THIS SCANDAL SPREADS, IT WILL SHAKE THE VERY AUTHORITY OF THE SHOGUNATE ITSELF!
WELL?!
...I ACCEPT.

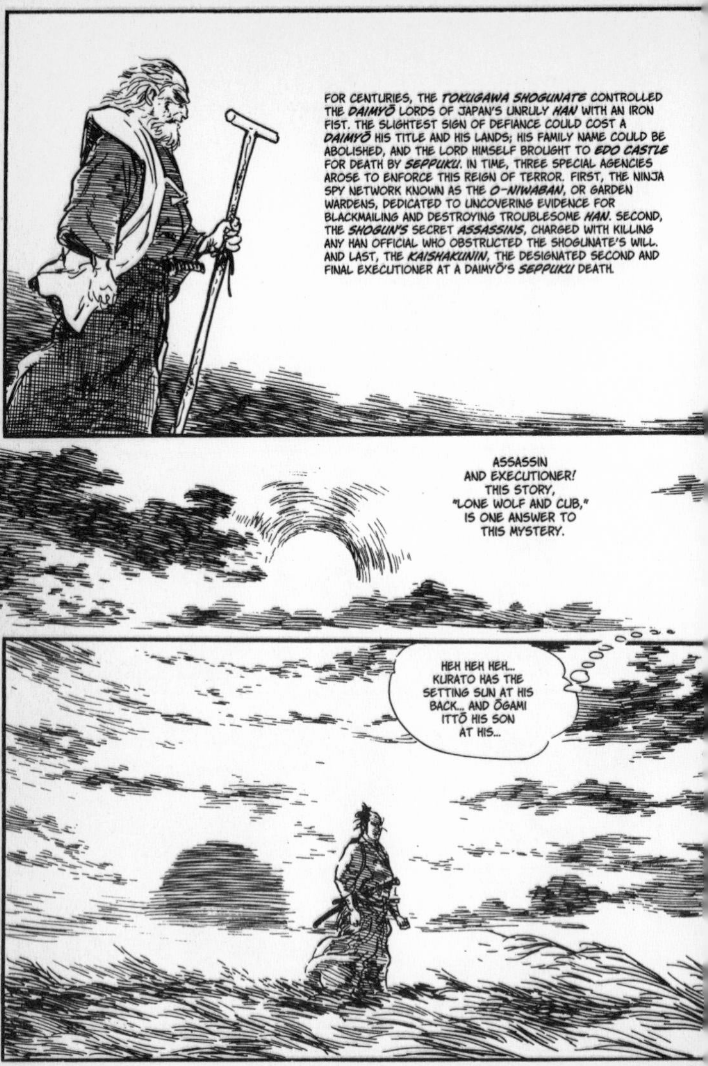
FOR CENTURIES, THE TOKUGAWA SHOGUNATE CONTROLLED THE DAIMYŌ LORDS OF JAPAN'S UNRULY HAN WITH AN IRON FIST. THE SLIGHTEST SIGN OF DEFIANCE COULD COST A DAIMYŌ HIS TITLE AND HIS LANDS; HIS FAMILY NAME COULD BE ABOLISHED, AND THE LORD HIMSELF BROUGHT TO EDO CASTLE FOR DEATH BY SEPPUKU. IN TIME, THREE SPECIAL AGENCIES AROSE TO ENFORCE THIS REIGN OF TERROR. FIRST, THE NINJA SPY NETWORK KNOWN AS THE O-NIWABAN, OR GARDEN WARDENS, DEDICATED TO UNCOVERING EVIDENCE FOR BLACKMAILING AND DESTROYING TROUBLESOME HAN. SECOND, THE SHOGUN'S SECRET ASSASSINS, CHARGED WITH KILLING ANY HAN OFFICIAL WHO OBSTRUCTED THE SHOGUNATE'S WILL. AND LAST, THE KAISHAKUNIN, THE DESIGNATED SECOND AND FINAL EXECUTIONER AT A DAIMYŌ'S SEPPUKU DEATH.
ASSASSIN AND EXECUTIONER! THIS STORY, "LONE WOLF AND CUB," IS ONE ANSWER TO THIS MYSTERY.
HEH HEH HEH... KURATO HAS THE SETTING SUN AT HIS BACK... AND ŌGAMI ITTŌ HIS SON AT HIS...

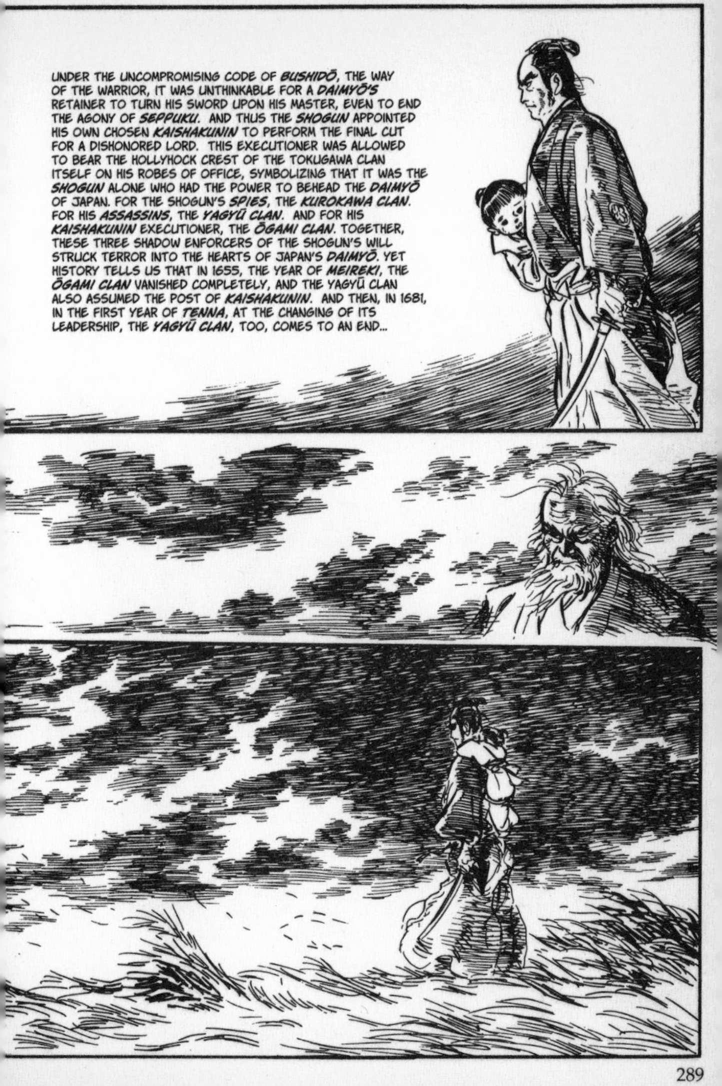
UNDER THE UNCOMPROMISING CODE OF BUSHIDŌ, THE WAY OF THE WARRIOR, IT WAS UNTHINKABLE FOR A DAIMYŌ'S RETAINER TO TURN HIS SWORD UPON HIS MASTER, EVEN TO END THE AGONY OF SEPPUKU. AND THUS THE SHOGUN APPOINTED HIS OWN CHOSEN KAISHAKUNIN TO PERFORM THE FINAL CUT FOR A DISHONORED LORD. THIS EXECUTIONER WAS ALLOWED TO BEAR THE HOLLYHOCK CREST OF THE TOKUGAWA CLAN ITSELF ON HIS ROBES OF OFFICE, SYMBOLIZING THAT IT WAS THE SHOGUN ALONE WHO HAD THE POWER TO BEHEAD THE DAIMYŌ OF JAPAN. FOR THE SHOGUN'S SPIES, THE KUROKAWA CLAN. FOR HIS ASSASSINS, THE YAGYŪ CLAN. AND FOR HIS KAISHAKUNIN EXECUTIONER, THE ŌGAMI CLAN. TOGETHER, THESE THREE SHADOW ENFORCERS OF THE SHOGUN'S WILL STRUCK TERROR INTO THE HEARTS OF JAPAN'S DAIMYŌ. YET HISTORY TELLS US THAT IN 1655, THE YEAR OF MEIREKI, THE ŌGAMI CLAN VANISHED COMPLETELY, AND THE YAGYŪ CLAN ALSO ASSUMED THE POST OF KAISHAKUNIN. AND THEN, IN 1681, IN THE FIRST YEAR OF TENNA, AT THE CHANGING OF ITS LEADERSHIP, THE YAGYŪ CLAN, TOO, COMES TO AN END...

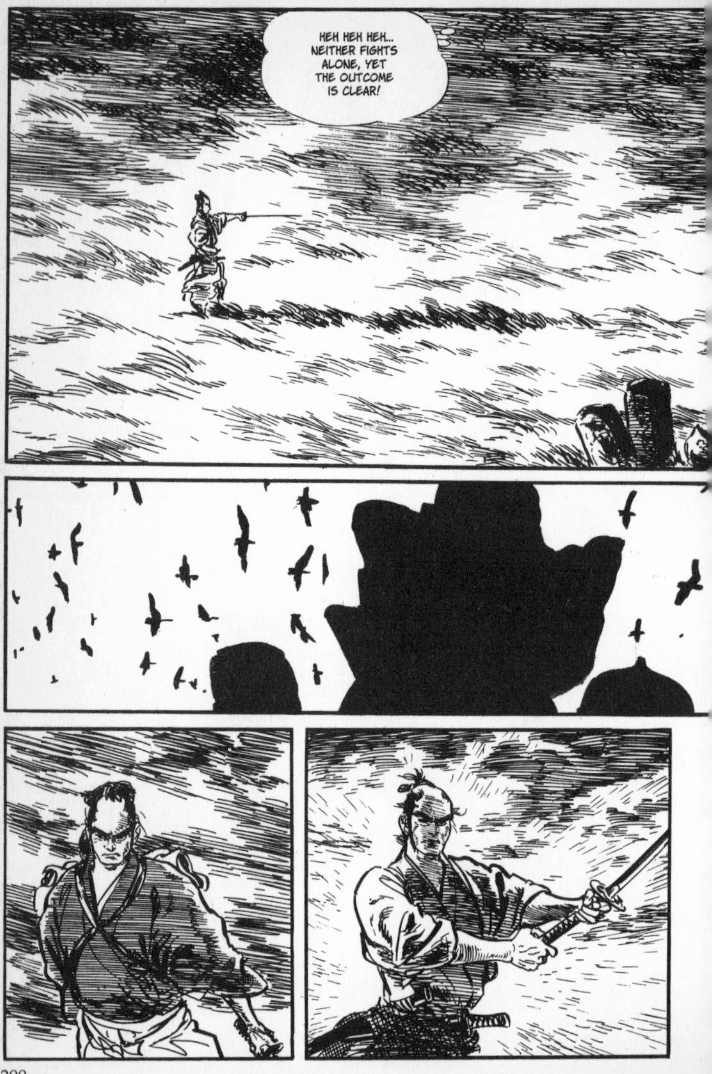
HEH HEH HEH... NEITHER FIGHTS ALONE, YET THE OUTCOME IS CLEAR!

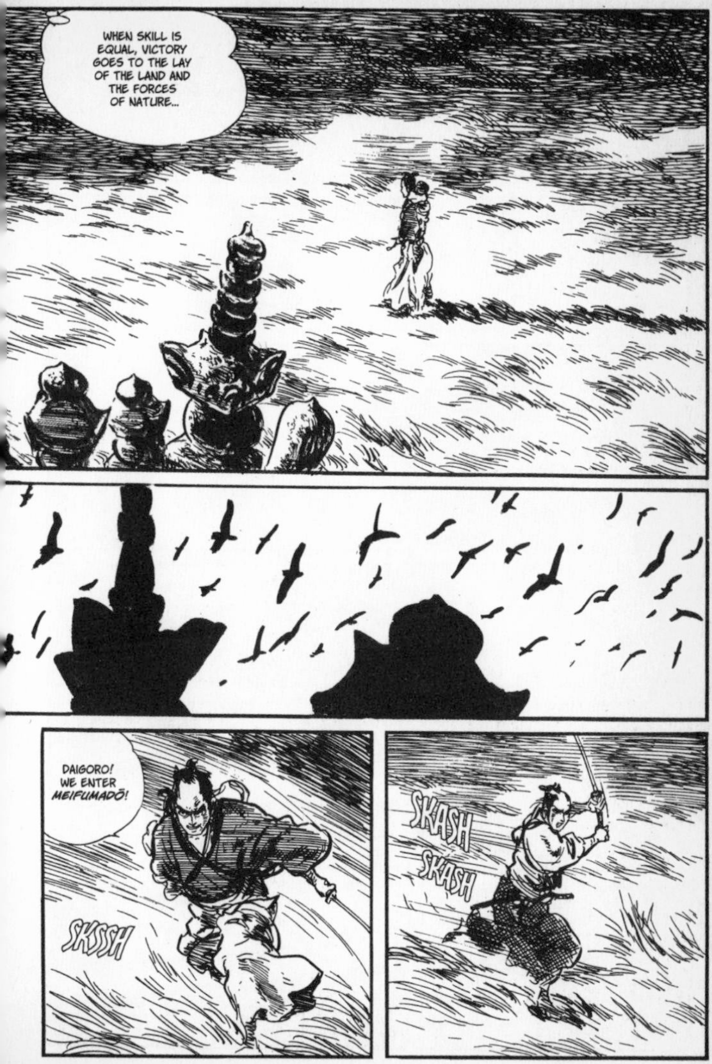
WHEN SKILL IS EQUAL, VICTORY GOES TO THE LAY OF THE LAND AND THE FORCES OF NATURE...
DAIGORO! WE ENTER *MEIFUMADŌ*!
SKSSH
SKASH
SKASH

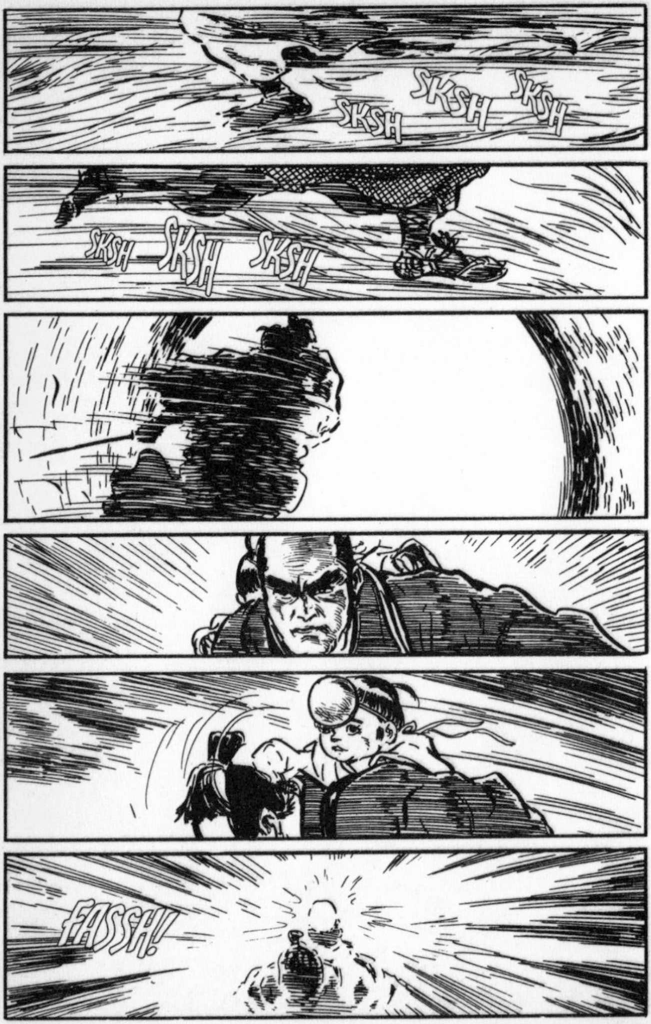
SKSH
SKSH
SKSH
SKSH
SKSH
SKSH
FASSH!

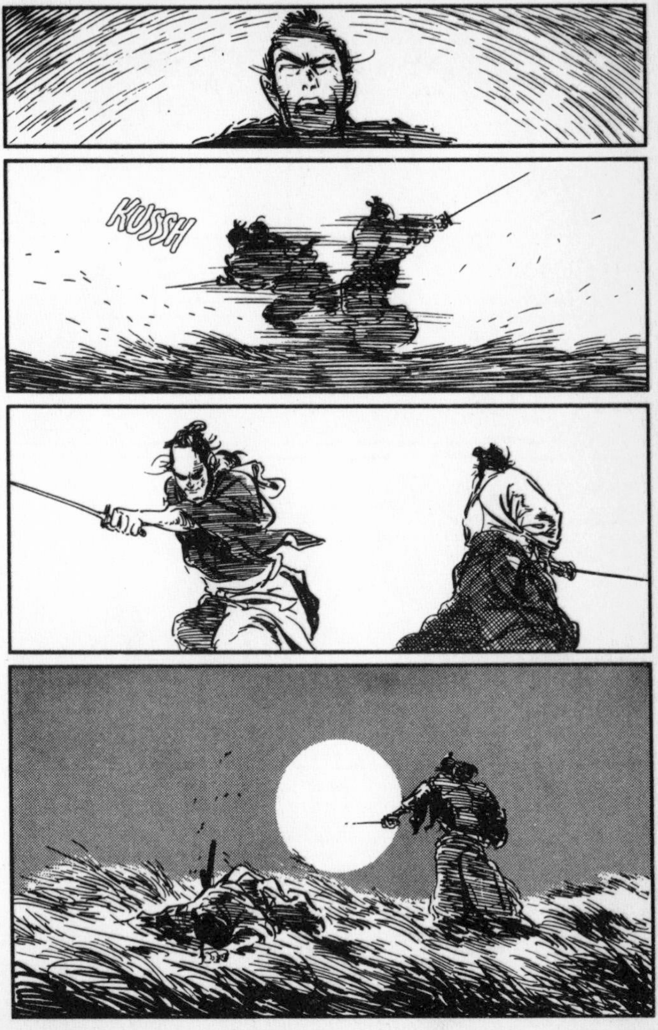
KUSSH

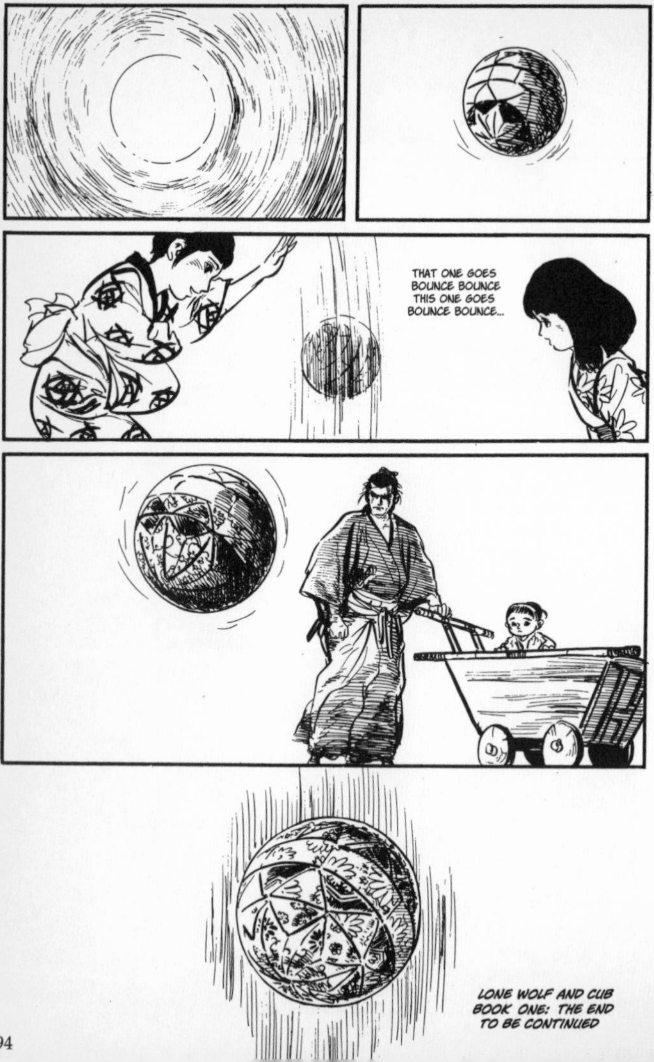
THAT ONE GOES BOUNCE BOUNCE THIS ONE GOES BOUNCE BOUNCE...
LONE WOLF AND CUB BOOK ONE: THE END TO BE CONTINUED

GLOSSARY

ashigaru
A foot soldier in the employ of a *daimyō*. lowest of the warrior ranks.

bangashira
Commander of the guard. Each han had a standing guard — the *ban* — of samurai to protect the lord and castle. The *ō-bangashira* was the supreme commander of the guard, the general of the *han* army.

bushi
A samurai. A member of the warrior class.

ō-metsuke
Chief inspector. The supreme inspector of the shogunate, the J. Edgar Hoover of the Tokugawa power structure.

daikan
The primary local representative of the shogunate in territories outside of the capital of Edo. The *daikan* and his staff collected taxes owed to Edo and oversaw public works, agriculture, and other projects administered by the central government.

daikansho
The office of the *daikan*.

daimyō
A feudal lord.

danzai
The samurai's right to put to death anyone who insulted their honor.

deiri
A fight between rival *yakuza* gangs. From their clothes, speech, and greetings, it is clear that the house of Jizō are *yakuza*, Japan's criminal syndicates. In the Edo period, *yakuza* were a common part of the landscape, running houses of gambling and prostitution. As long as they did not overstep their bounds, they were tolerated by the authorities, a tradition little changed in modern Japan.

dono
A term of respect for a higher-ranking official or aristocrat. A more common term of respect among civilians is *sama*, indicating more respect than the most common *san*.

dōtanuki
A battle sword, literally, "sword that cuts through torsos."

Edo
The capital of medieval Japan.

fudasashi
Merchant houses specializing in rice. They loaned gold to *han* governments, loans secured by the *han's* projected rice revenues.

han
A feudal domain.

hanshi
Samurai in the service of a *han*.

hollyhock crest
Each samurai family had a family crest considered synonymous with the clan itself. The Tokugawa clan crest was a three-leafed hollyhock. To point one's sword toward the shogun's crest was to point your sword toward the shogun himself, an unforgivable act of treason.

honmaru
The large, central keep of a Japanese castle.

Iga-yashiki
There were two main ninja clans in Japan, from the Iga and Kōga regions respectively. The Iga ninja served the shogunate. The Iga-yashiki (residence) was their base in Edo.

jigoku-tabi
Literally, "a journey to hell." When *yakuza* would go ask allies to help them in a fight.

juku
Way station. The major byways through Japan during the Edo period had way stations a day's walk apart with inns, tea houses, and other facilities for the traveler. The names of these old way stations still remain in many Japanese cities.

kaishaku
A second. In the rite of *seppuku*, a samurai was allowed death with honor by cutting up his own abdomen. After the incision was complete, the second would perform *kaishaku*, severing the samurai's head for a quick death. The second was known as a *kaishakunin*.

Kannon
Buddist goddess of mercy.

karō
Elders, usually the senior advisor to a *daimyō*, the lord of a *han*. Since the *daimyō* was required to alternate each year between life in his castle in the *han* and his residence in Edo, the capital and the seat of the Tokugawa shogunate, there was usually an *Edo-karō* (Edo elder) and a *kuni-karō* (*han* elder), who would administer affairs in Edo or in the *han* when their lord was away.

kenshiyaku
The shogunate official present at an execution to confirm the death of the person to be killed.

koku
1. A bale of rice. The traditional measure of a *han's* wealth, a measure of its agricultural land and productivity.
2. Standard time unit in the Edo period. Approximately two hours long, further sub-divided into three equal parts.

kōmori
A bat.

Kongming
A famous general and tactician who lived during the warring states period in ancient China., born 181 A.D., died 234 A.D.

kuramoto
Merchant houses. Under the Confucian social order imposed by the Tokugawa shogunate, merchants ranked a lowly fourth in Japan's four-strata caste society. But, in fact, by the middle Edo period the merchant class had gained tremendous wealth and power by managing the assets of the *han* and selling *han* rice and other products. Many *han* fell deeply into debt to the big merchant houses.

makura-sagashi
Literally, pillow searcher. A wandering thief who preyed on other travelers, stealing their valuables from under their pillows while they slept.

meido
The afterlife. The land after death. Believed to be a place of darkness. Only a few Buddhist sects described a division between heaven and hell.

meifumadō
The Buddhist hell, the way of demons and damnation.

metsuke
Inspector, a post combining the functions of chief of police and chief intelligence officer.

namu amida butsu
One of the most common of all Buddhist chants, calling for mercy in the world to come.

ogamu
To pray.

o-niwaban
"One in the garden." A ninja. The secret agent of the shogunate, heard but never seen.

rōnin
A masterless samurai. Literally, one adrift on the waves. Members of the samurai caste who have lost their masters through the dissolution of *han*, expulsion for misbehavior, or other reasons. Prohibited from working as farmers or merchants under the strict Confucian caste system imposed by the Tokugawa shogunate, many impoverished *rōnin* became "hired guns" for whom the code of the samurai was nothing but empty words.

ryō
A gold piece.

ryū
Often translated as "school." The many variations on swordsmanship and other martial arts were passed down from generation to generation to the offspring of the originator of the technique or set of techniques, and to any *deishi* students that sought to learn from the master. The largest schools had their own *dōjō* training centers, and scores of students. An effective swordsman had to study the different techniques of the different schools to know how to block them in combat. Many ryū also had a set

of special, secret techniques that were
only taught to school initiates.

Sakushū

A town in what is today Okayama
prefecture.

Sanzu-no-kawa

The river Sanzu, the Japanese
equivalent of the river Styx. On their
way to the afterlife, the dead must
take boats across the river Sanzu.

satoiri ninja

Ninja in the sato (homeland). In
addition to the ninja based in Edo,
the shogunate placed ninja undercover
in the various *han* of rival lords. These
moles would monitor dissident han
and gather evidence that could be used
to blackmail or dissolve a *han* when
it stepped out of line.

seppuku

The right to kill oneself with honor to
atone for failure, or to follow one's
master into death. Only the samurai
class was allowed this glorious but
excruciating death. The abdomen was
cut horizontally, followed by an
upward cut to spill out the intestines.
When possible, a *kaishakunin*
performed a beheading after the cut
was made to shorten the agony.

shima

The zone of death.

shinobi

Ninja. The *yama-metsuke* work
undercover, unlike the *dai-metsuke*
in Edo.

Sun Tzu

The great 500 B.C. chinese military
strategist, author of the classic *Sun
Tzu Bingfa* ("The Art of War").

Tōkaidō

The most important of the Edo-era
travel routes, connecting Edo with the
"*kamigata*" region of Kyōto and Ōsaka.
Now traversed by freeways and high-
speed "bullet" trains.

Tokugawa

The Tokugawa clan, the warlord family
that unified Japan following its victory
at the battle of Sekigahara in 1600,
and ruled until 1867 from its castle
in the city of Edo. The period is
commonly known as the Edo period.
The shogun was both the head of the
Tokugawa clan and the head of the
Tokugawa *bakufu* — the shogunate
government — that ran national
policy and kept the often unruly *han*
at heel.

tono

Lord, *daimyō*. Sometimes used as a
form of address, as in *tono-sama*.

toseinin

Literally, "rootless one," one who
travels the world. A euphemism for a
wandering *yakuza*.

KAZUO KOIKE

Though widely respected as a powerful writer of graphic fiction, Kazuo Koike has spent a lifetime reaching beyond the bounds of the comics medium. Aside from co-creating and writing the successful *Lone Wolf and Cub* and *Crying Freeman* manga, Koike has hosted television programs; founded a golf magazine; produced movies; written popular fiction, poetry, and screenplays; and mentored some of Japan's best manga talent.

Lone Wolf and Cub was first serialized in Japan in 1970 (under the title *Kozure Okami*) in *Manga Action* magazine and continued its hugely popular run for many years, being collected as the stories were published, and reprinted worldwide. Koike collected numerous awards for his work on the series throughout the next decade. Starting in 1972, Koike adapted the popular manga into a series of six films, the *Baby Cart Assassin* saga, garnering widespread commercial success and critical acclaim for his screenwriting.

This wasn't Koike's only foray into film and video. In 1996, Crying Freeman, the manga Koike created with artist Ryoichi Ikegami, was produced in Hollywood and released to commercial success in Europe and is currently awaiting release in America.

And to give something back to the medium that gave him so much, Koike started the *Gekiga Sonjuku*, a college course aimed at helping talented writers and artists — such as *Ranma 1/2* creator Rumiko Takahashi — break into the comics field.

The driving focus of Koike's narrative is character development, and his commitment to character is clear: "Comics are carried by characters. If a character is well created, the comic becomes a hit." Kazuo Koike's continued success in comics and literature has proven this philosophy true.

GOSEKI KOJIMA

Goseki Kojima was born on November 3, 1928, the very same day as the godfather of Japanese comics, Osamu Tezuka. While just out of junior high school, the self-taught Kojima began painting advertising posters for movie theaters to pay his bills.

In 1950, Kojima moved to Tokyo, where the postwar devastation had given rise to special manga forms for audiences too poor to buy the new manga magazines. Kojima created art for *kami-shibai*, or "paper-play" narrators, who would use manga story sheets to present narrated street plays. Kojima moved on to creating works for the *kashi-bon* market, bookstores that rented out books, magazines, and manga to mostly low-income readers. He soon became highly popular among *kashi-bon* readers.

In 1967, Kojima broke into the magazine market with his series *Dojinki*. As the manga magazine market grew and diversified, he turned out a steady stream of popular series.

In 1970, in collaboration with Kazuo Koike, Kojima began the work that would seal his reputation, *Kozure Okami* (*Lone Wolf and Cub*). Before long the story had become a gigantic hit, eventually spinning off a television series, six motion pictures, and even theme song records. Koike and Kojima were soon dubbed the "golden duo" and produced success after success on their way to the pinnacle of the manga world.

When *Manga Japan* magazine was launched in 1994, Kojima was asked to serve as consultant, and he helped train the next generation of manga artists.

In his final years, Kojima turned to creating original graphic novels based on the movies of his favorite director, Akira Kurosawa. Kojima passed away on January 5, 2000 at the age of 71.

THE RONIN REPORT

by Tim Ervin-Gore

As with most occasions of men taking up arms, the reason for the evolution of the samurai warrior was simple: to protect the people of an organized society, to control a population in that society, and to go forth and conquer new lands. From the time Japan was first occupied it was besieged with violence. Waves of immigrating peoples washed across the shores of the Japanese island chain. From the North came a Caucasian race from what is now southern Russia, and from the South came what would be later known as Korean peoples, carrying Chinese customs and religions. Naturally, the societies clashed and elbowed for room on the islands. This struggle for land and survival fueled the structures of a society in need of protection from outside influences, and as we see in society today, in order to defend one's people from another's it is necessary to raise arms and join together in force. Thus samurai warriors naturally evolved in what would become Japan.

Legend, however, tells the story differently, involving elemental gods forming Japan through divine influence and bestowing weapons with supernatural powers upon mortal warriors. One of these warriors was Prince Yamato. In his book *Samurai: The Story of a Warrior Tradition*, Harry Cook asserts that Prince Yamato was "in many ways a role model for (future) samurai." Yamato was fearless, cunning, and highly skilled in martial arts. Legend says that he was given the divine sword "Cloud Cluster" (or "Sword of the Village of the Clustering Clouds") in order to help him quell the barbarian Ainu people, a largely Caucasian people who defied bureaucratic order and competed for land. In an interesting aside, Cook writes in his book that Prince Yamato's father, Emperor Keiko, was by legend the first to apply the title "shogun" to one of his generals, and the term "shogun" literally translates to "barbarian-subduing general."

When the first shogun was named such, the imperial court was strong in influence but short on military prowess. Imperial forces sent to subdue the barbarians were often defeated miserably, and, in order to defend their claims, many land owners began training and keeping armed retainers (or knights). These retainers form the basic root of what we know as samurai. As the overlords became more powerful and claimed imperial descent, they began to clash amongst one another for control of land and vassals. Samurai warriors acted as pawns in power struggles, and those who were the most cunning, skilled, and powerful succeeded in claiming more land and influence for their lords. Constant wars and intermarrying between powerful clans led to consolidation of power, and eventually a small number of clans were fighting large-scale, bloody wars. These wars continued for hundreds of years, relying on generation after generation of familial revenge and hunger for land and power. These civil wars, as well as wars against invading forces such as Kublai Khan's massive Mongolian onslaught in the late 12th century, brought refinement to samurai warrior tactics and changed the focus of weaponry from the bow and arrow to the sword.

(to be continued)

MANGA! M... COLLECTIONS!

APPLE
Masamu
BOOK O
ISBN: 1-
BOOK T
ISBN: 1-56971-071-6 $14.95
BOOK THREE
ISBN: 1-56971-072-4 $14.95
BOOK FOUR
ISBN: 1-56971-074-0 $14.95
DATABOOK
ISBN: 1-56971-103-8 $12.95

BLADE OF THE IMMORTAL
Hiroaki Samura
BLOOD OF A THOUSAND
ISBN: 1-56971-239-5 $14.95
CRY OF THE WORM
ISBN: 1-56971-300-6 $14.95
DREAMSONG
ISBN: 1-56971-357-X $12.95
ON SILENT WINGS
ISBN: 1-56971-412-6 $14.95
ON SILENT WINGS II
ISBN: 1-56971-444-4 $14.95

THE DIRTY PAIR
Adam Warren • Toren Smith
BIOHAZARDS
ISBN: 1-56971-339-1 $12.95
DANGEROUS ACQUAINTANCES
ISBN: 1-56971-227-1 $12.95
A PLAGUE OF ANGELS
ISBN: 1-56971-029-5 $12.95
SIM HELL
ISBN: 1-56971-159-3 $13.95
FATAL BUT NOT SERIOUS
ISBN: 1-56971-172-0 $14.95

DOMINION
Masamune Shirow
DOMINION
ISBN: 1-56971-488-6 $16.95

DOMU: A CHILD'S DREAM
Katsuhiro Otomo
ISBN: 1-56971-140-2 $17.95

GHOST IN THE SHELL
Masamune Shirow
ISBN: 1-56971-081-3 $24.95

GUNSMITH CATS
Kenichi Sonoda
BONNIE AND CLYDE
ISBN: 1-56971-215-8 $13.95
MISFIRE
ISBN: 1-56971-253-0 $14.95

ISBN: 1-56971-442-8 $13.95
BEAN BANDIT
ISBN: 1-56971-453-3 $16.95

INTRON DEPOT
Masamune Shirow
INTRON DEPOT 1
ISBN: 1-56971-085-6 $39.95
INTRON DEPOT 2: BLADES
ISBN: 1-56971-382-0 $39.95

LONE WOLF AND CUB
New volumes released monthly! Collect the complete 28 volume series!
VOLUME 1–THE ASSASSIN'S ROAD
ISBN: 1-56971-502-5 $9.95
VOLUME 2–THE GATELESS BARRIER
ISBN: 1-56971-503-3 $9.95
VOLUME 3–THE FLUTE OF THE FALLEN TIGER
ISBN: 1-56971-504-1 $9.95
VOLUME 4–THE BELL WARDEN
ISBN: 1-56971-505-X $9.95
VOLUME 5 – BLACK WIND
ISBN: 1-5671-506-8 $9.95
Available January 2001
VOLUME 6 – LANTERNS FOR THE DEAD
ISBN: 1-56971-507-6 $9.95
Available February 2001
VOLUME 7 – DRAGON CLOUD, TIGER WIND
ISBN: 1-56971-508-4 $9.95
Available March 2001
VOLUME 8 – THREAD OF TEARS
ISBN: 1-56971-509-2 $9.95
Available April 2001

OH MY GODDESS!
Kosuke Fujishima
1-555-GODDESS
ISBN: 1-56971-207-7 $14.95
LOVE POTION NO. 9
ISBN: 1-56971-252-2 $14.95
SYMPATHY FOR THE DEVIL
ISBN: 1-56971-329-4 $13.95
TERRIBLE MASTER URD
ISBN: 1-56971-36
THE QUEEN OF V
ISBN: 1-56971-43
MARA STRIKES B
ISBN: 1-56971-44

...RS MANGA
...PE
...s • Hisao Tamaki
ISBN: 1-56971-362-6 $9.95
VOLUME 2
ISBN: 1-56971-363-4 $9.95
VOLUME 3
ISBN: 1-56971-364-2 $9.95
VOLUME 4
ISBN: 1-56971-365-0 $9.95
THE EMPIRE STRIKES BACK
George Lucas • Toshiko Kudo
VOLUME 1
ISBN: 1-56971-390-1 $9.95
VOLUME 2
ISBN: 1-56971-391-X $9.95
VOLUME 3
ISBN: 1-56971-392-8 $9.95
VOLUME 4
ISBN: 1-56971-393-6 $9.95
RETURN OF THE JEDI
George Lucas • Shin-ichi Hiromoto
VOLUME 1
ISBN: 1-56971-394-4 $9.95
VOLUME 2
ISBN: 1-56971-395-2 $9.95
VOLUME 3
ISBN: 1-56971-396-0 $9.95
VOLUME 4
ISBN: 1-56971-397-9 $9.95
EPISODE 1—THE PHANTOM ME
George Lucas • Kia Asimiya
VOLUME 1
ISBN: 1-56971-483-5 $9.95
VOLUME 2
ISBN: 1-56971-484-3 $9.95

3x3 EYES
Yuzo Takada
HOUSE OF DEMONS
ISBN: 1-56971-059-7 $12.95
CURSE OF THE GESU
ISBN: 1-56971-175-5 $12.95

WHAT'S MICHAEL?
Makoto Kobayashi
OFF THE DEEP END
ISBN: 1-56971-249-2 $5.95
MICHAEL'S MAMBO
ISBN: 1-56971-250-6 $5.95

Available from your local co

To find a comics shop in your area, call 1-888-266-... ...t:
•On the web: www.darkhorse.com •E...
•Phone: 1-800-862-0052 or (503) 652-970...
*Prices and availability subjec...

Dark Horse Comics: **Mike Richardson** *publisher* • **Neil Hankerso**... ...*ide of finance* • **Randy Stradley** *vice president of publishing* • **Chris**... ...*ent marketing* • **Anita Nelson** *vice president of sales & licensing* ... ...*em* **Cindy Marks** *director of production & design* • **Mark Cox** *art direct*... ...*olc* • **Kim Haines** *director of human resources* • **Darlene Voge**... ...*un*